FLOODED PASTS

FLOODED PASTS

UNESCO, NUBIA, AND THE
RECOLONIZATION OF ARCHAEOLOGY

WILLIAM CARRUTHERS

CORNELL UNIVERSITY PRESS
Ithaca and London

Copyright © 2022 by William Carruthers

All rights reserved. Except for brief quotations in a review, this book, or parts thereof, must not be reproduced in any form without permission in writing from the publisher. For information, address Cornell University Press, Sage House, 512 East State Street, Ithaca, New York 14850. Visit our website at cornellpress.cornell.edu.

First published 2022 by Cornell University Press

Library of Congress Cataloging-in-Publication Data

Names: Carruthers, William, 1982– author.
Title: Flooded pasts : UNESCO, Nubia, and the recolonization of archaeology / William Carruthers.
Description: Ithaca, New York : Cornell University Press, 2022. | Includes bibliographical references and index.
Identifiers: LCCN 2022001211 (print) | LCCN 2022001212 (ebook) | ISBN 9781501766442 (hardcover) | ISBN 9781501766459 (epub) | ISBN 9781501766466 (pdf)
Subjects: LCSH: International Campaign to Save the Monuments of Nubia—Influence. | Archaeology—Social aspects—Nubia. | Nubia—Colonial influence.
Classification: LCC DT159.6.N83 C37 2022 (print) | LCC DT159.6.N83 (ebook) | DDC 930.10939/78—dc23/eng/20220422
LC record available at https://lccn.loc.gov/2022001211
LC ebook record available at https://lccn.loc.gov/2022001212
ISBN 979-1-5017-8675-4 (pbk.)

To Ruchama, Simon, and our families

Contents

Acknowledgments ix
List of Abbreviations xi
A Note on Transliteration xiii

Introduction: Flooding Nubia	1
1. The View from the Boat	25
2. Documenting Nubia	64
3. Valuing Egyptian Nubia	96
4. Making Sudan Archaeological	129
5. Peopling Nubia	170
6. Nubia in the (Non-Aligned) World	206
7. Traces of Nubia	237
Conclusion: Repeopling Nubia	274

Bibliography 285
Index 311

Acknowledgments

Writing this book has involved the help of countless institutions and individuals. Foremost among them are Christina Riggs and Jim Secord, who not only read everything I sent them but have also provided truly wonderful support for over a decade. Without their help, *Flooded Pasts* would not be the same book. The same is true of Bethany Wasik, editor extraordinaire, who has gone above and beyond in getting this manuscript to print. Thank you, all of you. All mistakes, as they say, remain my own.

Funding from the Gerda Henkel and Max Weber Stiftungs, and stints as a Visiting Guest Fellow at the German Historical Institute London and as a Fellow of the M. S. Merian–R. Tagore International Centre of Advanced Studies in the Humanities and Social Sciences in Delhi allowed me to undertake research and writing. An Honorary Lectureship at the UCL Institute of Archaeology was also invaluable, in addition to, latterly, my time as a Leverhulme Early Career Fellow at the University of East Anglia's Department of Art History and World Art Studies. To all my colleagues: thank you.

Many other people played an integral part in this project. A book about archaeology requires experience of archaeology to write. Nearly twenty years ago now—and far away from Nubia—I thank Chantal Conneller, Chris Evans, Amy Gray Jones, Nicky Milner, Barry Taylor, and Thomas Yarrow for teaching me how to dig (and how to think about digging). Elsewhere, for (among other things) their support and supervision during various degrees and fellowships, I thank Walter Armbrust, Richard Bellamy, Khaled Fahmy, Andreas Gestrich, Sue Hamilton, David Jeffreys, Eleanor Robson, Tim Schadla-Hall, Simon Schaffer, Indra Sengupta, Ann Thomson, Stéphane Van Damme, and David Wengrow. As an undergraduate, the late Norah Maloney helped me more than I knew, as did Judy Medrington and Audrey Reed.

Whether through advice, conversation, friendship, or reading drafts, numerous other people have been similarly supportive. I therefore thank the late Bill Adams, Menna Agha, Sahar Bazzaz, Carol Bell, Charlotte Bigg, Mirjam Brusius, Beverley Butler, Elliott Colla, Raph Cormack, Ayman A. El Desouky, Mohieldin Gamal, Sudeshna Guha, Rodney Harrison, Vivian Ibrahim, Madonna

Kalousian, Morag Kersel, Chihab El Khachab, the late Henrika Kuklick, Jim Lance, Peter Mandler, N. A. Mansour, Jane Murphy, Eva-Maria Muschik, Shatha al-Mutawa, Claudia Näser, Hussein Omar, Stephen Quirke, Donald Reid, Nancy Reynolds, Yorke Rowan, Omnia El Shakry, Nora Shalaby, Heather Sharkey, Daniel J. Sherman, Costanza de Simone, Alice Stevenson, Amara Thornton, Willeke Wendrich, and Sonia Zakrzewski.

Many years ago in Cairo, Mariam Attia and Saeed Al Wakil gave me the strongest possible start in Arabic (although I am also thankful that Christopher S. Rose checked my transliteration in this book). Andrew Bednarski and Tom Hardwick both provided homes in the city. Michael Jones, Fatma Keshk, and Sarah Marei all provided advice and conversation, as did Menha el-Batrawi, Faiza Haikal, the late Tohfa Handoussa, and Salima Ikram. At the then Ministry of State for Antiquities, I thank Sara Kayser and Hisham el-Leithy. At the Egyptian Museum, I thank Marwa Abdel Razek and the Registrar's Office. At the AUC Rare Books and Special Collections Library, Ola Seif's expertise was invaluable, as was that of the staffs of Dar al-Kutub and Dar al-Watha'iq. At the German Archaeological Institute, Daniela Rosenow and Mustafa Tupev were unfailingly helpful. At the Nubia Fund, Mahrous Said offered invaluable support. At the Nubia Museum in Aswan, the advice, conversation, and interest of Rageh Mohamed has been crucial.

Elsewhere, I owe thanks to the staff of various archives. At UNESCO, the help of Adele Torrance, Alexandre Coutelle, Phan Sang, Eng Sengsavang, and Jens Boel was invaluable. At the Egypt Exploration Society, Steph Boonstra, Carl Graves, Chris Naunton, and Patricia Spencer all provided essential assistance over the years. At the British Museum, Neal Spencer and Julie Anderson were similarly helpful, as were Alex Pezzati and Eric Schnittke at the University of Pennsylvania Museum, and Maureen DaRos White at Yale's Peabody Museum. At the University of Chicago's Oriental Institute, my thanks go to Anne S. Flannery, John Larson, and Susan Allison. I also thank Tad Bennicoff and Heidi Stover at the Smithsonian Institution Archives.

In the United States, countless friends provided homes, conversation, and meals during research trips. To Harold Gabel, Arnau Gallard, Melanie Hopkins and Jake Spicer, Lisa Kovack and Leon Morse, Meredith Larson, Alexis Larsson, Callie Maidhof, Bobi Morris, Jordan Reiter and Marylyle McCue, Miriam Steinberg-Egeth and Marc Egeth: thank you, one and all. In Delhi, nothing would have been possible without Tina and Anup Rawla throwing open their doors to a homeless researcher.

Last, but certainly not least, I thank Ruchama, Simon, and our families. Without you, this book simply wouldn't exist.

List of Abbreviations

ASI	Archaeological Survey of India
CEDAE	Centre d'étude et de documentation sur l'Ancienne Égypte
CPAS	Centre of Planning and Architectural Studies (Markaz al-Dirasat al-Takhtitiyya wa-l-Miʿmariyya), Cairo
CPE	Combined Prehistoric Expedition
DAIK	Deutsches Archäologisches Institut Kairo
DGFAA	Director-General of Financial and Administrative Affairs, Egyptian Ministry of Culture
EAO	Egyptian Antiquities Organization
EES	Egypt Exploration Society, London
HADETU	Al-Haraka al-Dimuqratiyya li-l-Tahrir al-Watani (Democratic Movement for National Liberation, Egypt)
IBRD	International Bank for Reconstruction and Development
ICOMOS	International Council on Monuments and Sites
IMF	International Monetary Fund
MSRCA	Ministry of Scientific Research and Cultural Affairs, India
NAM	Non-Aligned Movement
NMEC	National Museum for Egyptian Civilization, Cairo
OI	Oriental Institute, University of Chicago
OIMA	Museum Archives at the Oriental Institute of the University of Chicago
SPMAE	Society for the Preservation of the Monuments of Ancient Egypt
TVA	Tennessee Valley Authority
UAR	United Arab Republic
UN	United Nations
UNCTAD	United Nations Conference on Trade and Development
UNESCO	United Nations Educational, Scientific and Cultural Organization
VBB	Vattenbyggnadsbyrån, Sweden

A Note on Transliteration

Given the myriad ways in which Arabic-language names of archaeological sites—and the names of Egyptian and Sudanese archaeologists themselves—have been rendered in the discipline's non-Arabic scholarship, English transliteration can be difficult. In this book, if an English-language spelling of a particular site name has become accepted, I use it. Likewise, I have spelled the names of Egyptian and Sudanese archaeologists and officials in accordance with their own preferred spellings. For other Arabic transliteration, I have used the system set forward by the *International Journal of Middle East Studies*.

FLOODED PASTS

Introduction
Flooding Nubia

In April 2020, the online magazine *Cairo Scene* posted a photograph of Egyptian archaeologist Wafaa Refaat on its Facebook page (figure I.1). *Cairo Scene*'s remit is the publication of articles about the city's fashion, hospitality, and social events, together with other news about Egypt of interest to its readership. Published in English, the website's audience is primarily Cairo's young, well-to-do, and expensively educated: the sort of people—graduates of the city's American University, for instance—who can afford to go to the nightclubs and five-star hotels that the platform's articles promote, alongside those who aspire to that life and the diaspora communities and expats who sometimes take part in it. Alongside the hashtag "#SceneThrowback," the website's editors labeled the photo of the archaeologist along these monied and aspirational lines. "This vintage #girlboss is Egyptian archaeologist Wafaa Refaat in June of 1966," the caption says. "Exuding both grace and hustle, she's seen here on site at the Abu Simbel Temple where she took an active role in rescuing and relocating the monument after it was threatened by flooding from the Aswan High Dam."[1] *Cairo Scene*'s reading

---

1. For the caption, see "#Scene Throwback," *Cairo Scene*, April 24, 2020, accessed January 15, 2021, https://m.facebook.com/CairoScene/photos/a.720706911293350/3141070329256984/?type=3&source=57&__tn__=EH-R. For many of the people mentioned throughout this book (but not Wafaa Refaat, who has proven impossible to locate), see Morris L. Bierbrier, ed., *Who Was Who in Egyptology?*, 4th ed. (London: Egypt Exploration Society, 2012).

FIGURE I.1. Wafaa Refaat at Abu Simbel. Courtesy of ullstein bild/Granger, item #0640792.

meant that a photograph taken at the height of the "revolutionary," anticolonial presidency of Gamal Abdel Nasser—and at the height of state socialism in Egypt—had suddenly become emblematic of a particular type of neoliberal feminism: "lean-in" for the Egyptian archaeology crowd.[2]

---

2. On "lean-in"-style feminism, see Dawn Foster, *Lean Out* (London: Repeater, 2016).

What *Cairo Scene* did not acknowledge, however, is why this image exists in the first place or the many thousands of people whose displacement made the presence of Wafaa Refaat and other specialists at Abu Simbel possible. Refaat could work at the site because the population of its surrounding region was no longer able to live there. In 1898, British officials in the "veiled protectorate" of Egypt had ordered construction of the Khazan Aswan, or Aswan Dam. Several times, flooding associated with that structure and its subsequent heightening submerged Nile-side settlements in the region of Nubia, located to the dam's south. The Nubian population had consequently been forced to move to higher ground and, increasingly, to travel to Cairo and Alexandria in search of work. In 1954, however, the Nasser government's decision to bolster the earlier barrage's impact and build the larger Aswan High Dam (al-Sadd al-'Ali) meant that this process of irrigation intervention took on an even more destructive intensity.

Under construction from 1960 to 1970, the High Dam (whose reservoir was filled by 1976) has become emblematic of many things, not least the vagaries of Cold War geopolitics. After Britain, the United States, and the World Bank reversed a combined offer to underwrite the structure in 1956, Soviet financial and technical assistance enabled the building of the dam just south of Aswan and the Nile's First Cataract, one of six such rapids on the river.[3] Consequently, the High Dam became connected to Nasserist policies of nonalignment and anticolonialism: when Nasser nationalized the Suez Canal in July 1956, his intention was not only to assert Egyptian sovereignty over Britain's last interest in the country, but also to use the waterway's revenues to help finance the new dam's construction. Ironically, however, the High Dam also signaled how the impact of colonial engineering projects continued into the era of formal decolonization. Unlike the earlier Aswan Dam, the High Dam's flooding spread beyond what had become the Egyptian side of the Nubian border (see map 1 for Nubia and sites mentioned throughout this volume). Now, the deluge also stretched southward into Sudanese Nubia, and in a way that officials in recently independent Egypt and Sudan deemed final. In the face of this flooding, ancient temples and archaeological sites in Nubia would be recorded and "salvaged" in a campaign mediated by UNESCO (the United Nations Educational, Scientific and Cultural Organization). Nubia's population, however, found itself helpless. By 1965, at least ninety-thousand Nubians—and likely many more—had been forced to move within both Egypt and Sudan, their homes and former lives abandoned to floodwater.[4] As *Cairo*

---

3. On the High Dam's construction, see Ahmad Shokr, "Hydropolitics, Economy, and the Aswan High Dam in Mid-Century Egypt," *The Arab Studies Journal* 17, no. 1 (2009): 9–31.
4. No accurate number of the displaced exists.

Scene's occlusion of this displacement might suggest, the trauma caused by that event has never been resolved.

In this context, the photo of Wafaa Refaat constitutes what Lucie Ryzova has termed an "orphan image."[5] Such images have become "alienated from the analogue referent, medium, provenance and social context in which they previously circulated" as Egyptians distribute them on platforms like Facebook.[6] Social media users attach new meanings to the photos, often in a bid "to prove visible truths: the culture, civilization and modernity, or authenticity, cleanness and simplicity Egyptians once possessed."[7] In the portrait of the well-styled, modern, and independent woman promoted by *Cairo Scene* it is difficult not to see this practice put into action for an elite (or aspiring elite) readership engaged with the creation of a cosmopolitan and "global" Egyptian future.[8] Equally, it is hard to miss that the act of mourning Egypt's "lost" and "secular" mid-twentieth-century modernity itself constitutes part of that process, especially with the short-lived presidency of Muslim Brotherhood member Mohamed Morsi having occurred within (for some Egyptians, far too) recent memory.[9] This "orphan image" has become metonymic "clickbait" of a country, its place in the world, the future that (at least) some of its population aspire to, and the future that some of them argue Egypt once had.[10]

Futures, however, are always built on visions of the past, in addition to the unintended detritus of those representations. In this book, I address how such visions have occluded Nubian displacement entirely, enabled by archaeological and preservation work. By the mid-1970s, it seemed that Nubia—and Nubians—had disappeared for good. In their stead were representations of the places like the one where Wafaa Refaat stood. In the *Cairo Scene* photograph, Refaat is pictured at an Abu Simbel storage area in front of a dismembered head of the pharaoh Ramses II. At the site, just north of the Egypt-Sudan border, two colossal rock-hewn temples dedicated to Ramses and his "Great Royal Wife" Nefertari had been cut into pieces by an international engineering consortium. That act, starting in 1964, enabled the temples' movement

---

5. Lucie Ryzova, "Unstable Icons, Contested Histories: Vintage Photographs and Neoliberal Memory in Contemporary Egypt," *Middle East Journal of Culture and Communication* 8 (2015): 46–47.

6. Ryzova, "Unstable," 47.

7. Ryzova, "Unstable," 48.

8. On that readership, see Anouk de Koning, *Global Dreams: Class, Gender, and Public Space in Cosmopolitan Cairo* (Cairo: American University in Cairo Press, 2009).

9. On this mid-twentieth century nostalgia, see Ryzova, "Unstable," 63. On the 2011 Egyptian revolution that helped bring Morsi to power, see Walter Armbrust, *Martyrs and Tricksters: An Ethnography of the Egyptian Revolution* (Princeton, NJ: Princeton University Press, 2019).

10. For such "clickbait" outside of Egypt, see Amy Malek, "Clickbait Orientalism and Vintage Iranian Snapshots," *International Journal of Cultural Studies* 24, no. 2 (2021): 266–89.

away from, and their reconstruction above, the flooding caused by the High Dam. In the process, the structures became materially and visually emblematic of a developing, globalized form of monumental heritage. Abu Simbel became the centerpiece of the sort of monumental past that Egypt under Nasser sought to preserve.[11] The site also became a centerpiece of UNESCO's burgeoning interest in what would later become "world heritage."

Running from 1960 until 1980 (and funded in large part by the US government), UNESCO's International Campaign to Save the Monuments of Nubia aimed, in Arabic, to ensure the *inqādh* ("salvage" or "rescue") of numerous ancient structures and archaeological sites from the High Dam's floodwaters. Alongside the temples at Abu Simbel, the famous Graeco-Roman temple complex on the island of Philae, just south of Aswan, was also threatened, hastening calls for the campaign's success.[12] A vision of Nubia's ancient remains drawing on years of earlier archaeological and preservation work in the region consequently took on great importance. Entangled with long-standing representations of ancient Egypt and Sudan, that vision highlighted sites like Abu Simbel and Philae and experts like Wafaa Refaat. Yet it also elided many thousands of other people: those who carried out the bulk of the project's work, and those who were forcibly displaced due to the High Dam's construction.

Concentrating on UNESCO's campaign, its genealogies, and its aftermath, I show how Nubia became Nubia, why a certain, de-peopled vision of the region's past became so important, and what happened (and continues to happen) to that past, that people, and to the "world" heritage resulting from this imagery. I discuss both the literal flooding of a region and the other metaphorical floods and visions that the High Dam's deluge enabled. Most importantly, I show why earlier British occupation and colonial rule in Egypt and the Anglo-Egyptian Sudan meant that Nubians and the remains and structures that they lived among have been treated in questionable—and racist—ways: not least the forced displacement of the entire Nubian population that the High Dam put into motion, and which earlier archaeological work in Nubia created the conditions for.[13] Coupled with a consideration of the policies and practices of the two independent nation-states that emerged in Egypt and Sudan in the mid-1950s, this treatment raises questions about the end(s) of colonialism itself,

---

11. On that vision, see William Carruthers, "Visualizing a Monumental Past: Archeology, Nasser's Egypt, and the Early Cold War," *History of Science* 55, no. 3 (2017): 273–301.

12. The Nubian campaign's official history is Torgny Säve-Söderbergh, *Temples and Tombs of Ancient Nubia: The International Rescue Campaign at Abu Simbel, Philae and Other Sites* (London and Paris: Thames and Hudson and UNESCO, 1987).

13. On the displacement, see Nicholas S. Hopkins and Sohair R. Mehanna, eds., *Nubian Encounters: The Story of the Nubian Ethnological Survey, 1961–1964* (Cairo: American University in Cairo Press, 2010).

and about the status of archaeology as a "postcolonial" discipline. Like archaeological excavation, floods constitute a destructive force, but one that contains constructive presences. Likewise, time moves on, yet it often holds traces of other moments within itself. As *Cairo Scene* reinvented Wafaa Refaat for Egypt's 2020s, so the image of the archaeologist, however much of a "#girlboss" she was, also recalled other eras and their consequences for Nubia and its population. I show what the results of such temporal elasticity have been. "Nubia" gained shape as an object—and an image—of colonial archaeology. During UNESCO's Nubian campaign, archaeology in the region continued to shape and perpetuate that vision, in a sense becoming "recolonized." That process had local and global consequences that are still relevant today.

The High Dam, Nubia, and Archaeology

The Aswan High Dam was only the latest piece of irrigation technology to be built on, and manipulate the course of, the Nile, the unpredictable strength of whose annual inundation—dependent on seasonal rainfall in Ethiopia—has been central to discourses about Egypt's development.[14] The post-1805 rule of Mehmed Ali and his family had been pivotal to promoting such technology in the then nominally Ottoman possession of Egypt, as had Britain's 1882 occupation of the territory and the 1899 formation of the Anglo-Egyptian Sudan. The destructive consequences of the High Dam would perhaps be greater than any other Nile irrigation project, however, even those schemes in Nubia, which had become no stranger to such impacts. In 1959, Egypt and Sudan signed the newest iteration of the Nile Waters Agreement, which regulated the proportion of the river's flood allocated to each country as it flowed through the proposed High Dam. After years of controversy, the agreement greenlit building of the structure: the key, among other outcomes, to controlling the Nile's inundation and enabling countrywide perennial irrigation in Egypt. Consequently, Nubia, the region located to the south of (and behind) the new barrage, would be permanently flooded to 180 meters above sea level, a significant increase over flooding caused by previous irrigation work. Over the next sixteen years, this deluge created a reservoir known as Lake Nasser

---

14. On Nile irrigation and Egyptian development, see, e.g., Jennifer L. Derr, *The Lived Nile: Environment, Disease, and Material Colonial Economy in Egypt* (Stanford, CA: Stanford University Press, 2019); Timothy Mitchell, *Rule of Experts: Egypt, Techno-Politics, Modernity* (Berkeley: University of California Press, 2002); Terje Tvedt, *The River Nile in the Age of the British: Political Ecology and the Quest for Economic Power* (London: Bloomsbury Academic, 2004; Cairo: American University in Cairo Press, 2006). Citations in this book refer to the Cairo edition.

(in Egypt) and Lake Nubia (in Sudan) and submerged most structures not only on the Egyptian side of the Nubian border, but also as far away as Sudan's Dal Cataract, 170 kilometers to the border's south. The building of the High Dam presaged destruction through irrigation at an unprecedented scale.[15]

That this was renewed destruction is pivotal. Nubia had already experienced large-scale intervention in the quest for Egyptian perennial irrigation, which ultimately became constitutive of what would transpire even under independent postcolonial government. The High Dam's predecessor, the Aswan Dam, was located about ten kilometers to its north, and had gone some, but not all the way toward achieving the perennial irrigation goal. Built under the oversight of British engineers between 1898 and 1902, the dam was heightened twice over the following decades. The first heightening took place from 1907 until 1912, two years before Britain declared a formal protectorate over Egypt at the onset of the First World War. The second—partly funded by Egyptian businessman Muhammad 'Abbud Pasha—happened from 1929 to 1933, following a popular revolution in 1919 and a highly qualified British declaration of Egyptian "independence" in 1922. This construction heralded flooding of ancient remains and Nubian settlements. Yet that destruction, limited to the Egyptian side of the Nubian border, never seemed as final as that accompanying the High Dam. During the work, many flooded Nubian villages were moved to higher ground, and visible ancient structures in the region were only partially submerged.[16]

The High Dam presented a different equation. Despite plans for the structure emerging in the 1940s, the High Dam became emblematic of the rise of Nasser, who, together with the other "Free Officers" (al-ḍubāṭ al-aḥrār), seized power over Egypt in July 1952 in "a military coup ... with unfocused goals" that would nevertheless become an anticolonial *thawra*, or "revolution."[17] The High Dam was so large, meanwhile, that its reservoir would destroy the entirety—as perceived by archaeologists—of the (ancient) remains located in the region. The flood would also demolish Nubia's Nile-side settlements, including a major center at Wadi Halfa in the very north of Sudan. With no obvious prospect left of moving these settlements to higher ground, the building of the High Dam necessitated the forced migration of the entire Nubian population.

That move compelled the region's people to relocate to two new settlements located many hundreds of miles apart from each other: al-Nuba al-Jadida

---

15. On elements of this transformation, see Nancy Y. Reynolds, "Building the Past: Rockscapes and the Aswan High Dam in Egypt," in *Water on Sand: Environmental Histories of the Middle East and North Africa*, ed. Alan Mikhail (New York: Oxford University Press, 2013), 181–205.

16. On the Aswan Dam and its political contexts, see Derr, *The Lived Nile*.

17. Joel Gordon, *Nasser's Blessed Movement: Egypt's Free Officers and the July Revolution* (New York: Oxford University Press, 1992), 4. On the genealogies of the High Dam, see Shokr, "Hydropolitics."

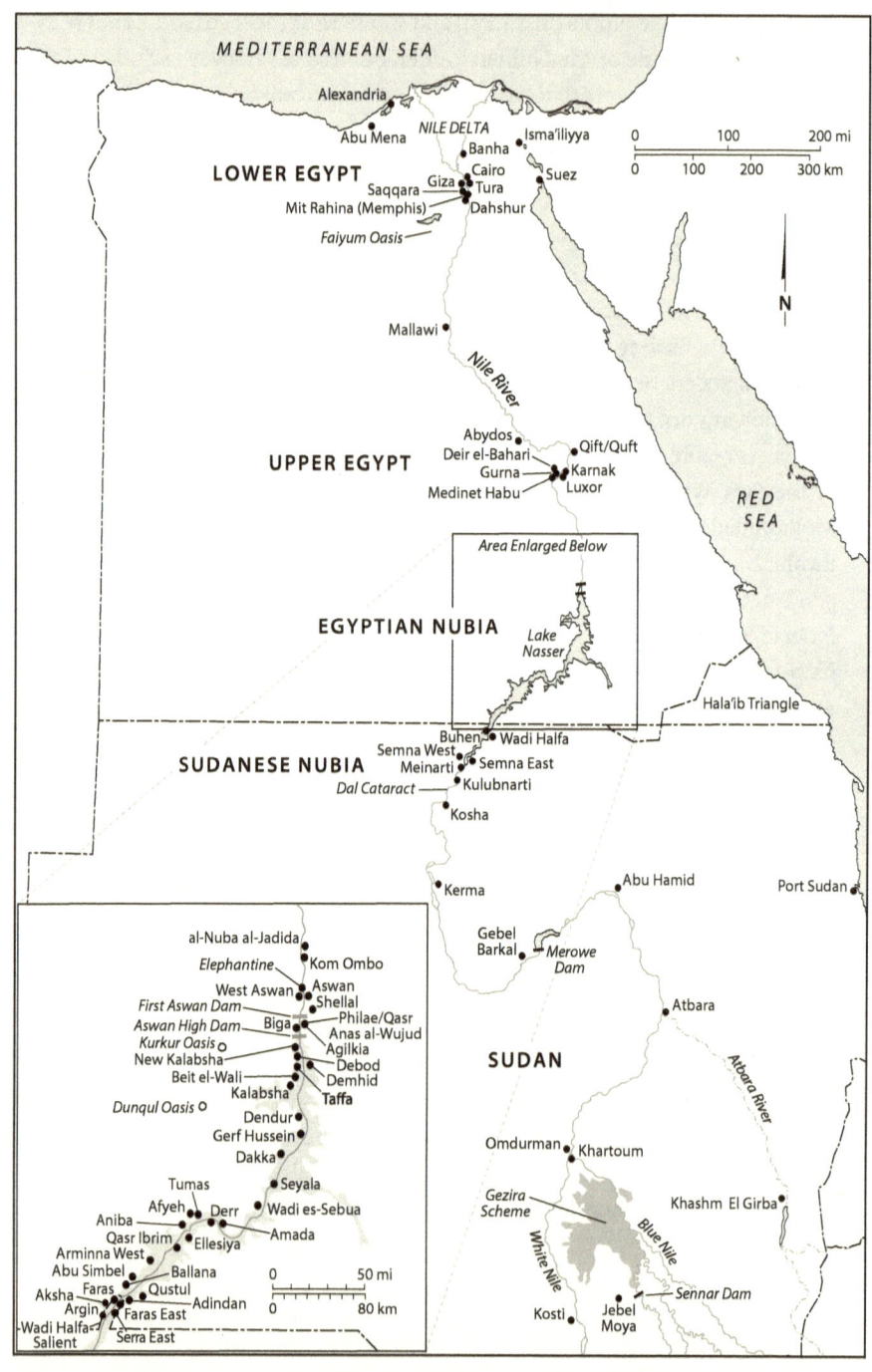

MAP 1. Nubia in context, including sites mentioned throughout the book. Map drawn by Bill Nelson.

(New Nubia) in Egypt and Khashm El Girba in Sudan. These settlements wrought a further form of destruction by helping to solidify the (second-class) place of Nubians within developmentalist national imaginaries. The 1952 abdication of Egypt's King Faruq, the 1953 cessation of the Egyptian monarchy, the 1954 negotiation of British withdrawal from the country, and the conflict over Suez (the Tripartite Aggression) in 1956 made these events possible, as did the February 1953 agreement between Britain and Egypt that paved the way for Sudanese independence in January 1956.[18] Consequently, as they became modernized Egyptian and Sudanese Nubians, Nubia's population could no longer enjoy the cross-border mobility that they had previously experienced. The High Dam became constitutive of new national realities tied to massive destructive power, foreshadowing the social and physical destruction of other large dam schemes elsewhere.[19] As Cornelia Kleinitz notes, recent archaeological work connected to the building of Sudan's Merowe Dam (located on the Nile's Fourth Cataract) led to archaeologists being asked to leave the area by the local Manasir community: a clear consequence of distrust related to the destruction caused by the High Dam and other large dam projects and one reason why investigation of the older project remains so urgent.[20]

Attempts to counter the High Dam's destruction were several. The Ford Foundation (in Egypt) and the Sudan Antiquities Service sponsored anthropological surveys of Egyptian and Sudanese Nubians.[21] In Egypt, the Ministry of Culture and National Guidance, founded in 1958, also sponsored an artist's campaign to document Nubian life, initiated by Minister of Culture Tharwat Okasha. Okasha, who served in that role from 1958 to 1962 and again from 1966 to 1970, has been deemed instrumental to the other major project that now took place in Nubia: one that built on archaeological surveys of the Egyptian part of the region conducted during the two phases of heightening the Aswan Dam.[22] At the formal request of the Egyptian and Sudanese

---

18. On these events, see Gordon, *Nasser's Blessed Movement*. On the Nubian migration, see Hopkins and Mehanna, *Nubian Encounters*.

19. For a Turkish dam project with similar impacts, see Laurent Dissard, "Learning by Doing: Archaeological Excavations as 'Communities of Practice,'" *Bulletin of the History of Archaeology* 29, no. 1, article 5 (2019): 1–8.

20. Cornelia Kleinitz, "Between Valorisation and Devaluation: Making and Unmaking (World) Heritage in Sudan," *Archaeologies: Journal of the World Archaeological Congress* 9, no. 3 (2013): 441–42. In contrast, a recent dam project in Turkish Kurdistan with similar consequences to the High Dam proceeded despite local (and some archaeological) opposition: see Maggie Ronayne, "Archaeology against Cultural Destruction: The Case of the Ilısu Dam in the Kurdish Region of Turkey," *Public Archaeology* 5, no. 4 (2006): 223–36.

21. Hopkins and Mehanna, *Nubian Encounters*.

22. In between, the institution, whose name was changed to the Ministry of Culture in 1965, was led by Muhammad 'Abd al-Qadir Hatem. For Okasha, see his autobiography, *Mudhakkirati fi al-Siyyasa*

governments (in April and October 1959, respectively), UNESCO launched its Nubian campaign at the newly opened UNESCO House in Paris. In March 1960, that launch (which included a speech by French Minister of Culture André Malraux) urged archaeologists and Egyptologists the world over to excavate, survey, and record in the region.[23] Archaeological and engineering teams from across the world proceeded to descend on Nubia, dominated by countries like Britain, France, Italy, and the United States, but also including participants from Egypt, Sudan, India, and Scandinavia.[24] As these teams navigated the region by boat and, at times, worked in searing heat, the scale of their effort was aided by the skill of several thousand local laborers. Though undetectable in the *Cairo Scene* photo, Wafaa Refaat stands defined by these pivotal events and arguments, beckoning forward the past that UNESCO's project was calculated to reveal and occluding the destruction that action enfolded.

By the time UNESCO's campaign came to its official end in 1980, Nubia's ancient structures had been taken apart and reassembled within Egypt and Sudan. Nubian temples had also appeared in New York, Turin, Leiden, and Madrid after Egypt "donated" them as gifts to the campaign's major national donors.[25] So, too—although I do not discuss them here for lack of space—had various exhibitions of objects from Tutankhamun's tomb designed to generate interest in and (sometimes) raise funds for the Nubian work taken place across North America, Europe, Japan, and the USSR.[26] The first citations, meanwhile, had been added to UNESCO's World Heritage List, made possible by the organization's 1972 Convention Concerning the Protection of the World Cultural and Natural Heritage. Among other events, the initiation of the World Heritage Convention has often been connected to the high profile and international media spectacle of the Nubian campaign itself (even as heritage in the UNESCO sense was not a term used by many of the project's ar-

---

wa-l-Thaqafa [My reminiscences in politics and culture] (Cairo: Madbuli, 1988; Cairo: Dar al-Shuruq, 2000). Page references are to the 2000 reprint.

23. For an overview of this moment, see Säve-Söderbergh, *Temples*.

24. Beyond Egyptian and Sudanese institutions, various archaeological and epigraphic teams came to Egypt from institutions in Austria, Britain, Canada, Czechoslovakia, France, the Federal Republic of Germany, Hungary, India, Italy, the Netherlands, Poland, Spain, Switzerland, the United States, the USSR, and Yugoslavia. In Sudan, teams arrived from Argentina, Belgium, Britain, Denmark, Finland, France, the German Democratic Republic, Ghana, Norway, Poland, Spain, Sweden, the United States, and Yugoslavia. For a list, see Säve-Söderbergh, *Temples*, 223–26.

25. The Temple of Dendur is on display at New York's Metropolitan Museum, The Speos of Ellesiya is at the Museo Egizio in Turin, the Temple of Taffa is at the Rijksmuseum van Oudheden in Leiden, and the Temple of Debod stands in a park in Madrid, for which see Säve-Söderbergh, *Temples*, 138–44.

26. On the Tutankhamun exhibitions, see Christina Riggs, *Photographing Tutankhamun: Archaeology, Ancient Egypt, and the Archive* (London: Bloomsbury, 2019), 207–32.

chaeological participants).[27] Uncovering and creating Nubian antiquity not only helped make national pasts, but also helped to constitute a global treaty dedicated to preserving pieces of them, and whose citations, from 1979, included Nubian sites.[28] That Nubians no longer lived around those sites was unimportant. As the Nubian campaign's genealogy shows, it was archaeology's colonial basis that made that act of deletion possible.

Archaeology, Colonialism, Decolonization?

By the time UNESCO's Nubian Campaign started, the archaeological surveys carried out during the two heightenings of the Aswan Dam had become a foundational narrative for the project. The surveys—conducted from 1907 until 1911 and 1929 to 1934—constituted the first two events in the history of "salvage archaeology" set out in 1961 by John Otis Brew, the director of Harvard's Peabody Museum of Archaeology and Ethnology and a member of UNESCO's International Committee for Monuments, Historic Sites, and Archaeological Excavations. In his history, Brew defined salvage archaeology as the rescue of "the remnants of our past" from the threat caused by industrial and technological development.[29] Brew wrote that definition to bolster that practice not only in the United States, where salvage work had been taking place since the interwar foundation of the Tennessee Valley Authority development scheme (TVA), but also in relation to UNESCO's project, which he played a part in initiating.[30] His discussion, however, elides the connection of the earlier Nubian work to the colonial irrigation project of the Aswan Dam. Brew did not discuss how British officials in Egypt actively supported the first survey, or how the country's French-directed Antiquities Service (since 1929 part of Egypt's Ministry of Education) had overseen the second.[31] Laced through with coloniality as it was, for Brew, the history of archaeology in Nubia was something to elide.

---

27. UNESCO itself promotes this connection, for which see UNESCO, "Abu Simbel: The Campaign That Revolutionized the International Approach to Safeguarding Heritage," n.d., accessed January 18, 2021, https://en.unesco.org/70years/abu_simbel_safeguarding_heritage.

28. "The Nubian Monuments from Abu Simbel to Philae" were inscribed on the World Heritage List in 1979, for which see UNESCO, "World Heritage List," n.d., accessed October 15, 2020, http://whc.unesco.org/en/list/&order=year.

29. John Otis Brew, "Emergency Archaeology: Salvage in Advance of Technological Progress," *Proceedings of the American Philosophical Society* 105, no. 1 (1961): 2.

30. On that role, see Lucia Allais, "The Design of the Nubian Desert: Monuments, Mobility, and the Space of Global Culture," in *Governing by Design: Architecture, Economy, and Politics in the Twentieth Century*, ed. Aggregate Architectural History Collaborative (Pittsburgh: University of Pittsburgh Press, 2012), 185–86.

31. Brew, "Emergency Archaeology," 2–3.

In the same article, however, Brew noted that "for the most part . . . the salvage consists of study and excavation" and "actually lies in the publication of the report of the archaeological research."[32] Aside from the physical act of excavation, Brew suggested that salvage archaeology took place after the fact, in the embodied practices of reflection and study that led to the appearance of archaeological reports and monographs: archiving, indexing, photographing, and reading, for instance.[33] Noting this reliance on the consultation and careful integration of older records and publications, Brew provided an ancestry for the Nubian project that implied how archaeology's colonial roots would be hard to elide. Likewise, he noted that UNESCO's campaign heralded a newly generous system of Egyptian *partage*: the means by which excavated objects were divided between finder and regulating state.[34] Yet that system had a genealogy whose colonial underpinnings were hard to ignore in both Egypt and Sudan.[35] Even during the peak of global decolonization, archaeological practice in Nubia—not to mention more widely—assuredly drew on its colonial roots as UNESCO's campaign began.

If the Nubian campaign and archaeology rested on this genealogy, however, how does Wafaa Refaat's photo reflect this condition? How, also, might contemporary archaeological practice be filtered through its own coloniality? For good reason, archaeology and the institutions tied to the discipline's development have increasingly become the target of "decolonization" efforts. Simultaneously, museums, universities, and other archaeological bodies have co-opted these demands, capturing them within diversity and equality initiatives whose frequent short-term nature often gives the lie to any substantive action.[36] If there is any hope of ever "decolonizing" archaeology, it is necessary to understand how and if the discipline changed in the period in which formal, global "decolonization" occurred, in addition to how many of the archaeological institutions and practices in place today took on new force through events like UNESCO's Nubian campaign. As Walter Mignolo and Rolando Vazquez state, the key issue is one of empire and its end(s): how to address "the continuing hidden process of expropriation, exploitation, pollution, and

---

32. Brew, "Emergency Archaeology," 2.
33. Riggs, *Photographing*, is particularly strong on these practices.
34. Brew, "Emergency Archaeology," 8.
35. On which see Alice Stevenson, *Scattered Finds: Archaeology, Egyptology and Museums* (London: UCL Press, 2019).
36. On this situation, see William Carruthers, "Heritage, Preservation, and Decolonization: Entanglements, Consequences, Action?," *Future Anterior: Journal of Historic Preservation History, Theory, and Criticism* 16, no. 2 (2019): ii–xxiv.

corruption that underlies the narrative of modernity" and that constitutes, too, the coloniality of archaeology.[37]

Such work is difficult, not least because "decolonization" is a historically contingent term.[38] As Stuart Ward notes, "'decolonization' was made in Europe, as part of a major realignment of metropolitan assumptions and expectations with an ever-encroaching post-imperial world."[39] First deployed in French in 1836, the term was not coherently used until the second half of the twentieth century.[40] As Todd Shepard has discussed, even in the 1950s, as the number of newly independent nation-states in the world increased, "European and American scholars and politicians hesitantly applied it to describe specific shifts of sovereignty in particular territories."[41] That hesitance ultimately points to the word's widespread emergence only in the early 1960s, when the political need for Europeans to "manage" the end of empire became much more urgent.[42] As Brew claimed that "prehistory transcends nationalism and that archaeology belongs to us all," then, he in fact made a rhetorical move promoting the sort of Enlightenment universalism that many Europeans hoped would make former colonies manageable (a style of thought to which UNESCO in particular seemed to subscribe).[43]

Despite the historical contingency of decolonization as a geopolitical event, however, Elisabeth Leake has noted that "as a scholar whose work is rooted in histories of decolonization . . . I am struck by the fact that decolonization as a historical phenomenon is [currently] conspicuously absent." Leake emphasizes that "there is little discussion or reflection on the processes of empire and its ending, even though these are historical forces that have been absolutely crucial to the world we live in today."[44] By addressing the Nubian

---

37. Walter Mignolo and Rolando Vazquez, 2013, "Decolonial Aesthesis: Colonial Wounds/Decolonial Healings," *Social Text Online*, accessed July 13, 2020, https://socialtextjournal.org/periscope_article/decolonial-aesthesis-colonial-woundsdecolonial-healings/. On coloniality and Egyptology, cf. Christian Langer, 2017, "Informal Colonialism of Egyptology: The French Expedition to the Security State," *E-International Relations*, accessed June 16, 2021, https://www.e-ir.info/2017/06/16/informal-colonialism-of-egyptology-the-french-expedition-to-the-security-state/.

38. The next two paragraphs reproduce parts of Carruthers, "Heritage," vii, viii, ix.

39. Stuart Ward, "The European Provenance of Decolonization," *Past and Present* 230 (2016): 231.

40. Ward, "The European Provenance," 231.

41. Todd Shepard, *The Invention of Decolonization: The Algerian War and the Remaking of France* (Ithaca, NY: Cornell University Press, 2006), 5.

42. Ward, "The European Provenance," 255–56.

43. Brew, "Emergency Archaeology," 9. On that universalism, see Shepard, *The Invention*, 6. On UNESCO's liberal universalism, see Lucia Allais, *Designs of Destruction: The Making of Monuments in the Twentieth Century* (Chicago: University of Chicago Press, 2018).

44. Elisabeth Leake in Amanda Behm et al., "Decolonizing History: Enquiry and Practice," *History Workshop Journal* 89 (2020): 170–71.

campaign, its colonial genealogies, and its (post?) colonial aftermaths, this book contributes to the small and insufficient amount of scholarly work on the histories of archaeology and heritage that does reflect on this historical moment and its consequences.[45] I argue that this reflection can be made most effective by understanding the small-scale work of excavation and "salvage" that Brew set out and that the Nubian campaign's vast effort multiplied at scale. Understanding that work, the temporal elasticity, coloniality, and racially constituted actions of archaeology become most obvious.

Importantly, my book is not the only one to address these issues in relation to Egypt: Alice Stevenson's *Scattered Finds* and Christina Riggs's *Photographing Tutankhamun* have concentrated on similar, "bottom-up" themes.[46] Here, though, I concentrate on the period when archaeology moved from a colonial—and often explicitly racial—science, to a "post-" colonial—and allegedly race-free—one, enabling me to question this historical narrative. Furthermore, my engagement with Arabic sources moves this study away from a Euro-American framework that has perpetuated an uncritical understanding of decolonization and constituted how histories of archaeology, heritage, and their connection to UNESCO's "race statements" of the 1950s have been written.[47] Even as Arabic was not spoken by all Nubians (most of the population spoke—and still speak—either Kenzi or Fadija), this linguistic shift presents an opportunity to reframe archaeology and heritage as constituted from within different arenas.[48] Those arenas include the newly independent nation-states whose position within the postwar multilateral system had not necessarily been a given, but which were rendered concrete entities through actions like UNESCO's Nubian campaign itself.[49] Nubia's past was filtered through a coloniality entangled with other forms of power.

---

45. See, e.g., Allais, *Designs*; Marieke Bloembergen and Martijn Eickhoff, *The Politics of Heritage in Indonesia: A Cultural History* (Cambridge: Cambridge University Press, 2020); Michael Falser, *Angkor Wat: A Transcultural History of Heritage*, 2 vols. (Berlin: De Gruyter, 2020); Marie Huber, *Developing Heritage—Developing Countries: Ethiopian Nation-Building and the Origins of UNESCO World Heritage, 1960–1980* (Berlin and Boston: De Gruyter, 2021); Christina Luke, *A Pearl in Peril: Heritage and Diplomacy in Turkey* (New York: Oxford University Press, 2019); Lynn Meskell, *A Future in Ruins: UNESCO, World Heritage, and the Dream of Peace* (New York: Oxford University Press, 2018).

46. Riggs, *Photographing*, and Stevenson, *Scattered*.

47. On UNESCO's "race statements," see Perrin Selcer, "Beyond the Cephalic Index: Negotiating Politics to Produce UNESCO's Scientific Statements on Race," *Current Anthropology* 53, supplement 5 (2012): 173–84.

48. In "The Nubian Ethnological Survey: History and Methods," in *Nubian Encounters*, 10, Hopkins and Mehanna discuss how "Nubians spoke three different languages—Kenzi (Matoki) in the north, Arabic in a small pocket in the centre, and Fadija (Mahas) in the south. The name 'Nubian' is sometimes used to refer only to the last of these groups, at other times to all together."

49. On the geopolitical contingency of newly independent nation-states, see, e.g., Frederick Cooper, "Possibility and Constraint: African Independence in Historical Perspective," *Journal of African*

On the Archive

"The archive" is as integral to my project as irrigation interventions have been to Nubia and its past. Accessing Egyptian archives has long been subject to stringent security clearance, and material held (or meant to be held) within some of those repositories has either been filtered or simply never archived at all.[50] Likewise, during most of the time I was researching and writing this book, Sudan was designated a State Sponsor of Terrorism by the United States, only being removed from that list at the end of 2020. This situation made it impossible for me to investigate archival material there, and also indicates how the understanding of archaeological and heritage histories is contingent on (geo-) political conditions, fundamentally shaping the (Egypt-centric) content of this volume. That said, I do not seek to read archival material as empirically objective, not least because work in the last several decades has clarified the limits of that approach. Rather, I seek to read a variety of sources, Arabic-language or otherwise, both against and "along the archival grain."[51]

As Ann Laura Stoler discusses, such a reading helps make the colonial practices at hand "transient, provisional objects of historical enquiry that themselves need to be analyzed, if not explained."[52] That reading makes the apparent familiarity of UNESCO's Nubian project null and void at the same time as rendering the Nubian campaign's spectacle unspectacular by allowing concentration on the archaeological and other disciplinary practices that constituted the campaign's day-to-day action. That the campaign *was* spectacular (and how it became so on a monumental architectural level) has been discussed in some detail by Lucia Allais.[53] The point, however, is that mundane archaeological work helped to constitute that situation, and often in conversation with the practices of other disciplines such as Egyptology, whose dwindling

---

History 49, no. 2 (2008): 167–96; Adom Getachew, *Worldmaking after Empire: The Rise and Fall of Self-Determination* (Princeton, NJ: Princeton University Press, 2019); Gary Wilder, *Freedom Time: Negritude, Decolonization, and the Future of the World* (Durham, NC: Duke University Press, 2015).

50. On security, danger, and the Egyptian archive, see Aya Nassar, "Where the Dust Settles: Fieldwork, Subjectivity and Materiality in Cairo," *Contemporary Social Science: Journal of the Academy of Social Sciences* 13, nos. 3–4 (2018): 412–28. On the history of Egypt's state archives, see Yoav Di-Capua, *Gatekeepers of the Arab Past: Historians and History-Writing in Twentieth-Century Egypt* (Berkeley: University of California Press, 2009).

51. Ann Laura Stoler, *Along the Archival Grain: Epistemic Anxieties and Colonial Common Sense* (Oxford: Princeton University Press, 2009). The scholarship on archives is voluminous. For a thoughtful discussion of the possible archives of decolonization, see Omnia El Shakry, "'History without Documents': The Vexed Archives of Decolonization in the Middle East," *American Historical Review* 120, no. 3 (2015): 920–34.

52. Stoler, *Along*, 50.

53. Lucia Allais, "Integrities: The Salvage of Abu Simbel," *Grey Room* 50 (2013): 6–45.

postwar—and postcolonial—popularity UNESCO's project helped to revive.[54] Egyptology's basis in philology and epigraphy possessed a historically vexed relationship with archaeology whose consequences became clear throughout the campaign.[55] The colonial practices of Egyptian and Sudanese archaeology also became entangled with changing practices in prehistory, anthropology, and geology in ways that shaped the project's archaeological work. As Nadia Abu el-Haj suggested, archaeology has long constituted "facts on the ground."[56] Despite their connection to the racial imaginings of colonial anthropology, UNESCO used the facts that had developed during earlier archaeological work in Nubia to the campaign's advantage: the region was somewhere that people should want to come and dig. Yet during the campaign, those facts helped to build new associations between disciplines. Colonial facts on the ground helped to constitute the conduct of archaeology in UNESCO's Nubia, at the same time as that conduct became entangled within shifting disciplinary associations. More importantly still, evidence of this work was vested in the archives and other forms of paperwork that constitute the stuff of archaeological study and authority, and thus provide an analytical opportunity here.

As Christina Riggs has noted, "archival and photographic practices were inseparable in archaeology and . . . ongoing care of the resulting archive underpins the discipline's epistemological and professional structures."[57] As John Otis Brew implied, meanwhile, such archives are similarly the ones on which archaeological "salvage" was (and is) based.[58] Consequently, this book examines what is visible of the colonial—and colonial-style—treatment of Nubia and its population within such archives, not to mention the racial underpinnings of that act: its coloniality, in other words.[59] Despite the "ongoing care" associated with archiving, it is clear that archaeological and related archives—and the Euro-American museum storerooms that often hold Nubian objects—are subject to the sort of (re-) organization, winnowing, and downright disaster often (unfairly) associated with such repositories in Egypt,

---

54. On Egyptology's changing fortunes in this period, see Riggs, *Photographing*, and Stevenson, *Scattered*.

55. In late-Victorian Britain, "practical" field archaeology was often contrasted with the "aesthetic" pursuit of Egyptology: see David Gange, "Unholy Water: Archaeology, the Bible, and the First Aswan Dam," in *From Plunder to Preservation: Britain and the Heritage of Empire c. 1800–1940*, Proceedings of the British Academy 187, ed. Astrid Swenson and Peter Mandler (Oxford: Oxford University Press, 2013), 108. The distinction often continued to stick.

56. Nadia Abu el-Haj, *Facts on the Ground: Archaeological Practice and Territorial Self-Fashioning in Israeli Society* (Chicago: University of Chicago Press, 2001).

57. Riggs, *Photographing*, 38.

58. Brew, "Emergency Archaeology," 2.

59. On "coloniality," see Mignolo and Vazquez, "Decolonial Aesthesis."

Sudan, and elsewhere in the "global South."⁶⁰ Researching at UNESCO House, some of the records related to the Nubian campaign turned to ashes in my hands, a result of a fire there in the 1980s.⁶¹ Yet most Nubian records are likely not consulted at all: the unprecedented amount of work that UNESCO's project generated produced a mountain of archival material that is often, quite literally, covered in dust.⁶²

Deeper discussion of the colonial vestiges at stake within such material matters. When the High Dam's reservoir was finally full, a dual-language, Arabic-English supplement entitled *The High Dam and Its Effects* came attached to the Egyptian newspaper *al-Ahram al-Iqtisadi*. The supplement was a report by Egypt's National Council for Production and Economic Affairs: one spurred into existence by Anwar al-Sadat's May 1971 "Corrective Revolution" (*Thawrat al-Taṣḥīḥ*), an event that purged Nasserist officials and altered state policies while simultaneously styling itself as a continuation of the earlier revolutionary project.⁶³ Following the same strategy of giving with one hand while taking with the other, the report admitted to several unintended consequences of the High Dam's construction, even as it sought to reassure readers that those consequences were under control.⁶⁴ In this respect, the supplement's title in Arabic—*al-Sadd al-ʿAli wa-Atharihi*—is perhaps more meaningful than in English. The word *āthār* has multiple meanings: in this case "effects," but also "vestiges," "traces," or "antiquities." In the context of the Nubian campaign and its archives, it is a significant, if unintentional, pun. Just as the building of the High Dam had (side-) effects or left its own traces, so the campaign's work with—and in the definition of—antiquities and Nubia's past contained traces from other times. Thinking through the campaign's archive, those traces become visible.

On UNESCO and Its Discontents

Investigating the archive also clarifies the Nubian campaign's—and archaeology's—place within UNESCO's wider (world) heritage project. As

---

60. On museum storerooms, see Mirjam Brusius and Kavita Singh, eds., *Museum Storage and Meaning: Tales from the Crypt* (London and New York: Routledge, 2018).

61. On that fire (and related accusations of arson), see Paul Lewis, "Fire at UNESCO in Paris Is Called Arson," *The New York Times*, March 23, 1984.

62. Cf. Carolyn Steedman, "Something She Called a Fever: Michelet, Derrida, and Dust," *American Historical Review* 106, no. 4 (2001): 1159–80.

63. National Council for Production and Economic Affairs, *al-Sadd al-ʿAli wa-Atharihi / The High Dam and Its Effects* (Cairo: Al-Ahram, 1976), 2.

64. *Al-Sadd al-ʿAli wa-Atharihi*, 25–26.

Tim Winter states, discussions of the institution "commonly take UNESCO as a metonym of global governance, reading it as a monolithic or monologic body that imposes Eurocentric world views upon localised environments and institutions."[65] That analysis has "tended to overlook the structural context within which . . . [UNESCO] operates, the ways in which its operations have reflected shifting world orders, and the consequences this has had." Consequently, "critique of UNESCO has often revolved around claims of unprecedented levels of power or, by contrast, its ineptness or impotence as an intergovernmental organisation."[66] The institution's Nubian project only buttresses Winter's words. As one of few UNESCO schemes to engage with archaeological research, the Nubian campaign became a vehicle for archaeologists to criticize what they saw—and were sometimes justified in seeing—as UNESCO's growing preference for monument preservation.[67]

Most archaeologists did not engage with "heritage" during day-to-day fieldwork in Nubia. Rather, discussions relating to the term's development as a global—and implicitly liberalizing—concept often seemed to happen in a different sphere entirely, revolving around UNESCO General Conferences and official meetings in places like the White House.[68] Archaeologists could become embroiled in the nascent heritage conversation by becoming officials and committee members. For example, both John Otis Brew and the Egyptian prehistorian-geographer Mustafa Amer—the former (and, in 1953, first Egyptian) director-general of Egypt's renamed Department of Antiquities—were members of UNESCO's Committee on Monuments, Artistic and Historical Sites and Archaeological Investigations. In 1961, the pair gave an interview to UNESCO Radio where they discussed not only that committee's purpose, but also the International Monuments Campaign that the organization was promoting.[69] The pair were far removed, however, from events taking place in—and in relation to—the Nubian "field."[70]

UNESCO, founded in 1945, has always been in the eye of the beholder, even as a particular postwar style of liberal internationalism obviously sits at the

---

65. Tim Winter, "Heritage Diplomacy," *International Journal of Heritage Studies* 21, no. 10 (2015): 998–99.
66. Winter, "Heritage Diplomacy," 999.
67. Meskell, *A Future*, 30.
68. The term "world heritage" was used at the 1965 White House Conference on International Cooperation, for which see Allais, "Integrities," 7.
69. UNESCO Radio, "World Heritage: A Conversation between Dr. Brew, Dr. Amer and Rex Keating on the Purpose of the Committee on Monuments, Artistic and Historical Sites and Archaeological Investigations," produced by Rex Keating, Paris, 1961.
70. On the blurriness of where "the field" actually is, see, e.g., James Clifford, "Notes on (Field) notes," in *Fieldnotes: The Makings of Anthropology*, ed. Roger Sanjek (Ithaca, NY: Cornell University Press, 1990), 64.

heart of its mission.⁷¹ Not only are the organization's interests beyond heritage often forgotten—initial finance for Nubian archaeology in Sudan came attached to requests for funding in libraries and education—but so, too, are the limits of what a multilateral institution can do. In the following chapters, I show how the organization's claimed success as mediator of the Nubian campaign was often misleading given the multiple instances—of countries, excavating institutions, and individuals—acting during the project in any way that they pleased. In one notorious instance in 1968, UNESCO's name was omitted from the Arabic-English plaque commemorating the relocation work at Abu Simbel, which suggested (before hasty correction) that only Nasser himself had been responsible for the project.⁷² Yet the attribution of agency to UNESCO has continued to be inconsistent in relation to the campaign: over fifty years later, *Cairo Scene*'s caption describing Wafaa Refaat's work at the site did not mention UNESCO either. The organization has continued to stand for whatever people have made of it. In Nubia, UNESCO might well have "opened a new space for cultural action."⁷³ The organization's lack of agency during the project, however, meant that traces of past practices remained. From its beginning, UNESCO's hands-off approach baked colonial traces into the Nubian campaign. Understanding those traces constitutes my point of departure.

The Nubian Campaign: A Brief History

Writing a comprehensive history of the Nubian campaign or of archaeological work in Nubia would be a monumental and pointless exercise, especially given the contingencies of the project's archives. To attempt that job would inevitably lead to reproduction of the very categories that the campaign's practices constituted and which I seek to question. Therefore, the campaign's chronologies need to be addressed as just that: *chronologies* (multiple) whose colonial traces, material or otherwise, became entangled with the project in various ways. Nevertheless, it is possible to relate the straightforward narrative of the Nubian campaign favored by UNESCO while simultaneously outlining the contexts of work on the High Dam and postwar geopolitics connected to the project. Here, then, I not only emphasize how impervious UNESCO's narrative has become, but also situate the book's discussions within it.⁷⁴

---

71. See, e.g., Allais, *Designs*, 212.
72. Christiane Desroches Noblecourt, *La grande Nubiade, ou, le parcours d'une Égyptologue* (Paris: Stock/Pernoud, 1992), 330. Repeated in Meskell, *A Future*, 32–33.
73. Allais, "The Design," 208.
74. Much of this narrative derives from Säve-Söderbergh, *Temples*, particularly the timeline on pages 228–31.

INTRODUCTION

After the building of the Aswan Dam and the archaeological surveys that accompanied its heightening, the threat to Nubia posed by plans for the High Dam began to crystallize. Chapter 1 discusses these earlier surveys and how they created an idyllic image of Nubia that influenced UNESCO's Nubian project. Chapter 2 then discusses how the creation of this representation overlapped with discussions about perceived threats and opportunities related to Egyptian antiquities. Addressing a proposal presented by former (French) officials of Egypt's Antiquities Service, UNESCO partnered with Egypt's new Department of Antiquities to institute the Centre d'étude et de documentation sur l'Ancienne Égypte (or CEDAE) in Cairo. CEDAE sought to create a massive photographic and documentary archive relating to tombs located in Luxor, Upper Egypt. As plans for the High Dam reached fruition, however, CEDAE's resources were diverted to Egyptian Nubia, where the institution's staff—delayed by the Tripartite Aggression of 1956—was sent to work on the region's temples. That work, coupled with a 1955 Department of Antiquities report on Nubia, laid the foundation for discussions about the Nubian campaign itself.

In 1959, several events set the campaign in motion: requests from both the Egyptian and Sudanese governments for UNESCO assistance; the meeting of an international expert delegation in Cairo and Nubia that October; and the signing of the Nile Waters Agreement on November 8. Work on the first phase of the High Dam started on January 9, 1960, and the inauguration of UNESCO's campaign followed swiftly on March 8. In theory, the project itself was governed by committee. To aid with the organization of the campaign, UNESCO, whose Museums and Monuments Division initially oversaw the project, formed an Action Committee (later replaced by an Executive Committee) and a Committee of Patrons. Later, in 1961, the Executive Committee voted to initiate a Service for the Monuments of Nubia to relieve the Museums and Monuments Division from the campaign's burden. For their part, moreover, beyond the roles played by Egypt's Department of Antiquities (which in 1971 became the EAO, or Egyptian Antiquities Organization) and the Sudan Antiquities Service, at the start of the project the Egyptian government formed a Consultative Committee (constituted of a mix of foreign and Egyptian archaeologists and UNESCO officials), and the Sudanese government followed suit with its own international Panel of Experts. Egypt also inaugurated the Hay'at Sunduq Inqadh Athar al-Nuba, or Organization for the Preservation of Nubian Monuments (Nubia Office), which was overseen by the archaeologist Shehata Adam under the aegis of Egypt's Ministry of Culture.[75] Enmeshed within "the [postwar] bureaucratization of world politics" as

---

75. On the Nubian campaign's many committees, see Säve-Söderbergh, *Temples*, 91–97.

UNESCO and the Nubian campaign were, however, events "on the ground" did not always follow suit.[76] Chapters 3 and 4 thus examine the guiding practices and sometime differences of the survey and excavation segments of the campaign: chapter 3 treating Egypt and Egyptology, and chapter 4 relating how work in Sudan helped to constitute Nubian archaeology as a cross-border phenomenon.

As the campaign took place, the Egyptian and Sudanese governments simultaneously made plans for the resettlement of Nubians, who were forced to migrate from 1963 until 1965.[77] At the same time, thousands of Egyptian and Sudanese laborers became involved with archaeological survey, excavation, and preservation work in both countries. Chapter 5 relates this human aspect of the Nubian campaign, placing it in conversation with the Nubian resettlement. Elsewhere, for a select few, global mobility was a fact that UNESCO's project enabled, as much of the Nubian campaign was carried out under the aegis of Euro-American missions. Yet so, too, did the project involve teams from countries who were members of the Warsaw Pact and the Non-Aligned Movement, as chapter 6 discusses, in addition to a small mission from the Soviet Union. The campaign, which also saw excavations run by Egypt and Sudan, was never wholly of the Cold War. Indeed, as the same chapter relates, pan-Arab considerations also played their part. A pivotal position in the "Arab world" had become increasingly important to Nasser's presidency and, in 1958, the short-lived United Arab Republic (UAR) of Egypt and Syria had come into being. Syria left in 1961 even as Egypt was known as the UAR for another decade, yet that did not stop Egyptian relations with other Arab countries from influencing the Nubian campaign's development.[78]

Everyone involved with the project billed the work as a race against time. Nancy Reynolds argues that the High Dam—and Nasser's statement that the structure constituted "a pyramid for the living"—encapsulated the revolutionary Egyptian "state's effort to restore time to the nation through [the massive] geological manipulation" associated with its construction.[79] Building the dam thus represented a "geology of national development," one that embodied piecemeal—yet progressive—progress.[80] Accordingly, in a May 1964 commemorative issue of the newspaper *al-Ahram*, an article asserting a "step-by-step" (*khuṭwa khuṭwa*) chronology set out key events in the dam's construction from

---

76. On UNESCO's "bureaucratization," see Allais, "The Design," 208.
77. See Hopkins and Mehanna, *Nubian Encounters*.
78. On the UAR, see James Jankowski, *Nasser's Egypt, Arab Nationalism, and the United Arab Republic* (Boulder, CO, and London: Lynne Rienner, 2002).
79. Reynolds, "Building," 199.
80. Reynolds, "Building," 182.

September 1952 onward, anchoring the structure in what had become revolutionary time itself.[81] And on May 14, 1964, Nasser, Soviet premier Nikita Khrushchev, and Abdullah al-Sallal, president of the Egypt-allied Yemen Arab Republic, initiated an explosion that diverted the Nile and inaugurated the second stage of building the High Dam (misplaced explosions and other industrial accidents killed countless workers during the barrage's construction).[82] Slowly, the waters behind the dam started to rise, meaning that archaeological work in Egyptian Nubia ended in 1965. In Sudan—where floodwaters took longer to reach their full height—excavation and survey continued until 1969, the same year that Ja'far Numayri ascended to the country's presidency and a new Sudanese "revolution" began. Previously, that work had been no less embedded in narratives of national development than work connected to the High Dam in Egypt: in the early years of its independence, Sudan was committed to developmentalist policy under the prime ministerships of (in 1956) Isma'il al-Azhari, (from 1956 to 1958) 'Abdallah Khalil, and (from 1958 until 1964) the combined prime ministership and presidency of General Ibrahim 'Abbud, who came to power following a military coup.[83]

As all these events took place, the relocation of Nubian temples progressed amid fierce arguments. At the heart of these disagreements was money, since UNESCO was dependent upon donations from member-states to run the Nubian campaign. What type of preservation the campaign's often precarious financing made possible, and whose interests that money promoted, therefore became key concerns.[84] In 1959, as project planning commenced, a report drawn up by Italian architect Piero Gazzola had suggested that any Egyptian Nubian temples that could be removed to nearby higher ground should be.[85] Members of the October 1959 expert delegation in Cairo went further and insisted that a definition of "integrity" that kept particular structures in their original setting was paramount: transferring monuments was possible only "under conditions which ensured the preservation of the monument's surrounding environment."[86] The initial proposal to protect the temples at Abu

---

81. "Ajinda al-Sadd" ["Diary of the Dam"], in *Al-Sadd al-'Ali: 'Adad Khas Yasduruh al-Ahram* [The High Dam: Special Number Issued by al-Ahram], ed. al-Ahram (Cairo: al-Ahram, May 15, 1964), 8.

82. For deaths at the High Dam, see, e.g., Elizabeth Bishop, "Control Room: Visible and Concealed Spaces of the Aswan High Dam," in *Landscapes of Development: The Impact of Modernization Discourses on the Physical Environment of the Eastern Mediterranean*, ed. Panayiota Pyla (Cambridge, MA: Harvard University Press, 2013), 80; Alia Mossallam, "'We Are the Ones Who Made This Dam "High"!' A Builders' History of the Aswan High Dam," *Water History* 6, no. 4 (2014): 304.

83. On Sudan's developmentalist state, see Alden Young, *Transforming Sudan: Decolonization, Development, and State Formation* (Cambridge: Cambridge University Press, 2017).

84. Allais, "The Design," 204.

85. Säve-Söderbergh, *Temples*, 71.

86. Säve-Söderbergh, *Temples*, 100.

Simbel therefore involved surrounding them with a dam, despite Gazzola's warnings of the continued risks of floodwater intrusion.[87] At Philae, too, the first proposed project involved a dam encircling the island.[88] Ultimately, the campaign's financing needs became clear in how temple relocation progressed. Some structures would be moved near to their original sites. Many, however, would be relocated—and, if UNESCO member-states were financially forthcoming, they would be relocated abroad.[89]

Money spoke. At Abu Simbel, for instance, money constituted Abu Simbel's "integrity," as Lucia Allais has discussed. Rather than being protected by a dam (or numerous other plans promoted during the first few years of the campaign), the two temples at the site were cut into pieces and moved to higher ground because the US money that paid for the Abu Simbel work—twelve of a total forty million US dollars, about eighteen-and-a-half of which came from Egypt—paid for that solution.[90] At the start of the Nubian campaign, President John F. Kennedy had pledged support for Abu Simbel, Philae, and other work in Egypt and Sudan. Participating US institutions thus benefited substantially through grants administered by the Smithsonian Institution and the National Science Foundation. By 1964, however—and after wrangling about the site had frayed nerves at UNESCO's 1962 General Conference—Congress only agreed to pay for the US part in the Abu Simbel operation when it became clear that Egyptian pounds garnered through the sale of surplus American wheat to Egypt as part of the US "Food for Peace" program could be used for UNESCO's project.[91] That work, undertaken by an international consortium and countless Egyptian laborers—and which also required a large Kuwaiti loan, discussed in chapter 6—took place from April 1964 until September 1968. From 1960 until 1967, meanwhile, a mixture of Egyptian and international missions dismantled and dispersed the other Egyptian Nubian temples: whether to locations abroad or to be rearranged in groups at "New Kalabsha" (just south of the Aswan Dam), Wadi es-Sebua (110 kilometers to the south), or Amada (a further forty-five kilometers upstream). In Sudan, where all the Nubian temples were moved to the garden of Khartoum's new National Museum, relocation took place from 1963 until 1967; the museum itself opened in 1971, as chapter 7 discusses.

Planning for Philae, meanwhile, waited until all this work had finished and only took place after Egypt had a new president. Nasser died in 1970, both

---

87. Säve-Söderbergh, *Temples*, 101.
88. Säve-Söderbergh, *Temples*, 71.
89. Allais, "The Design," 204–205.
90. Säve-Söderbergh, *Temples*, 104.
91. Allais, "Integrities," 21–22.

hero—millions attended his funeral—and anti-hero due to the *naksa* ("setback") of the 1967 Six Day War, after which he momentarily resigned from office. Reacting to these events, his successor, Anwar al-Sadat, expelled the Soviet advisers working on the High Dam and other Egyptian projects. Later, after the 1973 Arab-Israeli War (in which Egypt regained a foothold on the east bank of the Suez Canal), Sadat would start to realign Egypt toward the Western bloc, including through 1974's *infitāḥ* (or "open-door") economic policies. That process ultimately concluded with 1978's Camp David Accords between Egypt and Israel. As Sadat's 1981 assassination demonstrated, these were not necessarily popular moves. Amid these events, however, work on Philae took place.

Located between the old Aswan Dam and the site of the new High Dam, Philae had become temporarily located in a subsidiary reservoir whose height was maintained at a constant level to drive electricity turbines connected to the older structure. Ultimately—after adoption of another "less-expensive, realistic project" to which Egypt's contribution roughly matched international donations of just over fifteen million US dollars—the temple complex was taken apart and moved to the nearby island of Agilkia between 1972 and 1980, when the Nubian campaign ended on March 10.[92] As chapter 7 relates, the end of that work (and the listing of Egyptian Nubian sites on the nascent World Heritage List in 1979) nevertheless presaged the start of another project. UNESCO's International Campaign for Egyptian Museums, which began in 1982, led to the 1997 opening of Aswan's Nubia Museum, designed to display Nubia's ancient and more recent history. That project, meanwhile, has not dampened calls for a Nubian "right-to-return," which have become increasingly vociferous in the twenty-first century. In the conclusion, I outline possibilities for addressing those calls using the archives of the Nubian campaign itself. One vision of Nubia exists on paper. That material, however, offers the opportunity of creating another view entirely.

---

92. Säve-Söderbergh, *Temples*, 169.

CHAPTER 1

The View from the Boat

The entanglement of monument preservation, archaeological survey, and dam building on the Nile did not constitute the innovation that publicity for UNESCO's Nubian campaign claimed. Nor did those practices come together in the serendipitous way that images of the work suggested. Throughout the 1960s, as the Aswan High Dam took shape, representations of the structure's progress saturated global media alongside representations of work on UNESCO's project. Images of workers moving sand and constructing the High Dam (figure 1.1) seem remarkably close to images of laborers extracting objects from the desert and clambering around on scaffolding while dismantling ancient structures (figure 1.2). When viewed relative to previous hydrological and archaeological work in Nubia, the mirrored nature of these representations was predictable. Regulating the Nile as it flowed through Nubia had always meant regulating the region's remains, a process that shaped the Nubian past constituted by UNESCO's campaign.

In the decades preceding UNESCO's project, the construction of dams and the undertaking of archaeological work in the region came to be inseparable. The actions of officials, engineers, and archaeologists meant that particular Nubian pasts and presents coalesced, impacting the work done during the Nubian campaign from its beginning. Central to this outcome were three things: the result of the power assumed by one Egyptian dynasty; the expansion of the British colonial presence in Egypt, Sudan, and sub-Saharan Africa; and the

FIGURE 1.1. Workers at the High Dam site. *Al-Musawwar* 1944, January 12, 1962, 27.

way that hydro-political thinking connected these events. One curious aspect of discussions of UNESCO's campaign is the extent to which they occlude the work's roots in such *longue durée* histories. The project seems to have become too big to discuss in terms other than those referencing the campaign—or UNESCO's role in it—itself. To persevere with this historical separation, however, is to obscure the Nubian campaign's connections with the histories that enabled both its birth and its undertaking. Discussing the campaign in response to the Soviet backing of the High Dam, Lucia Allais suggests that "as soon as

FIGURE 1.2. Waiting for a crane at the temple of Kalabsha, the village of Kalabsha in the rear. Deutsches Archäologisches Institut Kairo Photo Archives neg. no. 8964, photograph by George Roy Haslam Wright, ©DAI Cairo.

the dam became a bargaining chip in Nasser's international policies, the fate of temples became dissociated from the project."[1] Yet the long, interconnected histories of Nile irrigation, colonial archaeology, and the observation and preservation of Nubia's ancient remains meant that it was impossible for such dissociation to take place.

The High Dam project, the earlier irrigation and archaeological work that informed it, and the politics and practice of water administration helped to shape UNESCO's Nubia even before the organization's campaign started. On an administrative level, the Nubian campaign operated separately from the project to build the High Dam. But such separation does not tally with how colonial genealogies of irrigation informed the new barrage's construction and

---

1. Allais, "The Design," 184.

helped to constitute the sort of Nubia that UNESCO's campaign generated. Because of these genealogies and their links to archaeology, the campaign took a specific form. The project's historical connection to the entangled concerns of irrigation and archaeology prioritized certain remains and obscured others, often in relation to preconceived ideas about race. The Nubian past investigated during UNESCO's campaign was not simply waiting to be unearthed. Instead, for decades prior to that event, it had been made according to the whims of a select group of people, and with reference to the engineering and survey work that made such investigation possible.

Dams and the Nubian Past

Intervention in Nubia's remains required governmental interest, which ultimately meant the attribution of value to them along the lines that officials accustomed to viewing Egypt from the deck of a boat or a river terrace deemed desirable.[2] Consequently, "the Nubian past" came into being not only due to the actions of the ruling family who had assumed control of Egypt in the early nineteenth century, but also due to the British imperial intervention in Egypt and Sudan that followed and the way in which these actions intersected with the development of irrigation and survey projects on—and the experience of sailing down—the river Nile. Over 150 years, the national and transnational politics of water constituted what the Nubian past could be through the work of the officials charged with making decisions about the ways in which Nile water might flow.

The early-nineteenth-century creation of an autonomous Ottoman khedivate of Egypt under the rule of the family of Mehmed Ali Pasha led to expansive modernization work: the developing territory materialized through the expansion of its infrastructure.[3] This work included changes to irrigation systems that enabled the Pasha's introduction of cotton as a cash crop for sale to global markets.[4] It also involved the construction of the Suez Canal, which

---

2. On the role of representations generated by river travel in this process, see Derek Gregory, "Colonial Nostalgia and Cultures of Travel: Spaces of Constructed Visibility in Egypt," in *Consuming Tradition, Manufacturing Heritage: Global Norms and Urban Forms in the Age of Tourism*, ed. Nezar Al-Sayyad (London: E. and F. Spon and Routledge, 2001), 111–51.

3. For Mehmed Ali, see Khaled Fahmy, *All the Pasha's Men: Mehmed Ali, His Army and the Making of Modern Egypt* (Cambridge: Cambridge University Press, 1997).

4. On irrigation and the Egyptian Nile, see Derr, *The Lived Nile*, particularly 16–23. For earlier, Ottoman-era irrigation interventions, see Alan Mikhail, "From the Bottom Up: The Nile, Silt, and Humans in Ottoman Egypt," in *Environmental Imaginaries of the Middle East and North Africa*, eds. Diana K. Davis and Edmund Burke III (Athens: Ohio University Press, 2011), 113–35.

opened in 1869, creating new shipping routes between Europe, South Asia, and beyond.[5] These projects, however, left Egypt greatly indebted to European creditors. When the price of cotton collapsed after the end of the US Civil War in 1865, Khedive Isma'il, Mehmed Ali's grandson, was unable even to cover the interest on the loans he had allowed Egypt to take out to finance such projects, the canal included.

Britain and France consequently seized joint control of Egypt's finances in 1876. They also intervened in other areas of governance, forcing Isma'il from power in 1879 in favor of his son, Tawfiq.[6] In 1882, during an uprising against khedival rule and British and French financial interference led by the colonel Ahmad 'Urabi, Britain occupied Egypt. British officials justified this act by stating that occupation would help to ensure stability of the country and its stretched finances. They also knew that this move would allow imperial control over the Suez Canal and the route the waterway provided to India. This action led to Britain retaining some form of presence in Egypt until 1956, when the Tripartite Aggression (or Suez Crisis) finally led to the expulsion of the remaining British troops stationed in the country. In 1914, at the beginning of World War I, the occupied khedivate became a British protectorate—one that would then be rocked by a 1919 revolution. When, in 1922, Britain unilaterally declared Egypt's independence, the nominal nature of that declaration meant that the British government, through its representative in Cairo, could continue to interfere in the country's new constitutional monarchy and parliament. Accordingly, the Egyptian constitution was promulgated in 1923, replaced by a different document in 1930, and reverted to the original 1923 document in 1935 as Egypt and Britain struggled over the future of the country. For British diplomatic agents in Cairo, controlling access to the corridor provided by the Suez Canal justified such interventions.[7]

Suez was of paramount importance to Britain, as control of the Canal's water meant control of the Nile's water, too. Continuing the Mehmed Ali dynasty's irrigation policies, Evelyn Baring (Lord Cromer), Britain's agent and consul-general in Egypt from 1883 to 1907, viewed the Nile as central to

---

5. On the Suez Canal and its afterlives, see Gilles Gauthier, Nala Aloudat, and Agnès Carayon, eds., *L'épopée du canal de Suez* (Marseille and Paris: Musée d'Histoire de Marseille, Gallimard, and Institut du monde arabe, 2018).

6. On the institution that controlled these finances, the Caisse de la Dette Publique (Public Debt Commission), see Derr, *The Lived Nile*, 25–26.

7. On Britain's "Veiled Protectorate" in Egypt, see Robert L. Tignor, *Modernization and British Colonial Rule in Egypt, 1882–1914* (Princeton, NJ: Princeton University Press, 1966). On the era of Egypt's constitutional monarchy, see Arthur Goldschmidt, Amy J. Johnson, and Barak A. Salmoni, eds., *Re-Envisioning Egypt, 1919–1952* (Cairo: American University in Cairo Press, 2005).

Egyptian financial and political stability.[8] British officials, whose knowledge of Nile irrigation was often based on their work in India and not on well-developed local practices, agreed: viewing control and development of the river's waters as essential to Britain's position in Egypt.[9] Every year at the end of summer came the Nile's annual inundation, whose unpredictable height set the basis for the rest of the agricultural year. The development of the river to enable controlled perennial irrigation would, however, produce a stronger cotton crop, not only helping to pay down Egyptian debt, but also (they presumed) enhancing Britain's ability to mollify Egyptian protests about control of the Suez Canal. More widely, this perception of the shared importance of river and canal helped constitute what Terje Tvedt has characterized as the "British Nile imperial system," the work of actors throughout the country's empire whose activities helped to turn the Nile and its tributaries into a "political and hydrological planning unit" geared toward British imperial interests.[10]

As Tvedt notes, from 1882 until 1956, "a strong and close alliance between [British] water engineers and Nile strategists . . . financed large and small waterworks" the length of the river, from the Egyptian Delta to Lake Victoria.[11] That system included the Anglo-Egyptian Sudan, established through a power-sharing ("condominium") agreement in 1899. Britain hoarded most of the power in the country, helping to mesh its territory within the realm of British imperial hydro-politics. The agreement also, however, built on older notions that control over Sudan constituted an Egyptian national priority, notions whose resonances continued to manifest themselves at the time of UNESCO's Nubian campaign. Ottoman-Egyptian rule (the so-called *Turkiyya*) had first been instituted in Sudan in 1821 under Mehmed Ali, ostensibly creating a territory united with Cairo-controlled Nubia, situated to Sudan's north (the regions of Lower and Upper Nubia, as they became known, respectively straddling a porous Egyptian-Sudanese border at Wadi Halfa). It would only be later in the century that Egypt managed to extend effective administrative authority over Lower Nubia.[12] But in the meantime (and into the twentieth century), Egyptians conflated the predominantly black populations of Nubia and Sudan not only as one, but also as natural objects of their rule. Whether Nubian or Sudanese, people from these regions constituted *"al-barbari,* or the Nubian, whose

---

8. On Cromer, see Roger Owen, *Lord Cromer: Victorian Imperialist, Edwardian Proconsul* (Oxford: Oxford University Press, 2004).

9. For the relationship between British and Egyptian irrigation practices, see Derr, *The Lived Nile,* 15–43.

10. Tvedt, *The River,* 7.

11. Tvedt, *The River,* 11.

12. Eve Troutt Powell, *A Different Shade of Colonialism: Egypt, Great Britain, and the Mastery of the Sudan* (Berkeley: University of California Press, 2003), 69.

color, customs, and accent Egyptian writers sketched out in numerous essays, dialogues, and stories."[13] These often disparaging representations presaged not only the ease with which the Egyptian government's archaeological surveys began to record and define the Nubian past in the first half of the twentieth century, but also the way in which UNESCO's Nubian campaign would itself often seem to be an Egypto-centric affair. The identity of a distinct Nubian region would develop due to such survey work, but the intervention that produced that development was made considerably simpler by Egypt's pejorative relationship with the areas to, and sometimes within, its south.[14]

Sometimes, however, those areas struck back. In 1881, a revolt against the *Turkiyya* led to the establishment of what became known as the *Mahdiyya* over much of Sudan. During the uprising, the mystic *shaykh* Muhammad Ahmad Ibn ʿAbd Allah (the Mahdi) and his followers used the momentary power vacuum that the revolt established to foment a political-religious uprising and establish a revolutionary state. Initially, attempts to overcome the *Mahdiyya* were unsuccessful: in the process of one such venture, the Mahdi's followers killed the British general Charles Gordon in Khartoum in 1885. From 1896 to 1899, however, British and Egyptian troops led by Kitchener undertook a military campaign that hastened the *Mahdiyya*'s end. Consequently, Egypt and Britain established the 1899 condominium agreement that gave both countries sovereignty over Sudan's territory. Britain now felt free to undertake projects like the construction of the Sennar Dam and the development of the Gezira Scheme, a massive irrigation project.[15] But this "triangulated conquest," as Eve Troutt Powell has characterized it, meant that, as plans for the High Dam developed, Egypt's relationship with Sudan often seemed much like the one that Britain had established with it.[16]

In Egypt, many of the British engineers and strategists whose irrigation work preceded this development found themselves concentrated in the Ministry of Public Works. Lord Cromer's interest in their projects ensured that—even as some of those officials expressed ambivalence toward him—the institution enjoyed exceptional power.[17] For example, ministerial officers enjoyed control over many of the ancient Nile-side remains in the country: Egypt's (French-run but often British-staffed) Antiquities Service was in the

---

13. Powell, *A Different*, 70.
14. Nubia was not the only place where the Egyptian state struggled for authority. Inhabitants of Upper Egypt had long rebelled against local political structures, as related in Zeinab Abul-Magd, *Imagined Empires: A History of Revolt in Egypt* (Berkeley: University of California Press, 2013).
15. Tvedt, *The River*, 90–113.
16. Powell, *A Different*, 5.
17. Jennifer L. Derr, "Drafting a Map of Colonial Egypt: The 1902 Aswan Dam, Historical Imagination, and the Production of Agricultural Geography," in Davis and Burke III, *Environmental Imaginaries of the Middle East and North Africa*, 140.

ministry's portfolio until 1929, when it joined the Ministry of Education.[18] As their hydrological plans developed, so these officials grappled with ruins dispersed throughout the country: including in Nubia, whose pharaonic and Graeco-Roman temples—many of which had later been converted for Christian use—enjoyed significant fame.

To enable partial perennial irrigation of Egyptian land, the ministry began building the Aswan Dam. The dam's construction led to partial submersion of the area to its south where the structure's reservoir formed. (Egyptian) Nubia flooded, an event that not only began to threaten ancient remains in the region in an unprecedented manner, but also led to the forced resettlement of the population living there. As Nicholas Hopkins and Sohair Mehanna note, "the Nubians living in the valley were forced to adjust to this variation either by moving farther up the sides of the valley or to a new location altogether": often Cairo, where many took up work in domestic service.[19]

Water made Nubia—and Nubians—contingent, subjects of circumstance. It also made them and the region in which they lived more visible. This situation ultimately resulted in a series of government-sponsored archaeological surveys and preservationist interventions as construction of the various stages of the Aswan Dam progressed, and even as official treatment of the Nubians themselves was considerably less magnanimous. The constitution of Nubia as an object of archaeological enquiry did not occur immediately, however. Nubia became contingent due to water, but water itself only ever constituted a circumstantial threat to ancient ruins. Overcoming such contingency shaped the values attributed to those remains and the people who lived among them.

Making Water Threatening

Despite the flooding caused by the Aswan Dam's construction, the threat that water posed to ancient remains was never viewed as self-evident. Instead, the fact and nature of that threat had to be constituted through officialdom. As David Gange notes, certain archaeologists reacted to initial plans for the dam in an "astonishingly subdued" manner. "Progress," Britain's Egypt Exploration Fund suggested, "must come first." As Gange argues, this lack of opposition to the plans was not altogether surprising. "The Fund had an engineer [Sir John

---

18. On the history of the Antiquities Service, see Donald Malcolm Reid, *Whose Pharaohs? Archaeology, Museums, and Egyptian National Identity from Napoleon to World War I* (Berkeley: University of California Press, 2002), and Reid, *Contesting Antiquity in Egypt: Archaeologies, Museums, and the Struggle for Identities from World War I to Nasser* (Cairo: American University in Cairo Press, 2015).

19. Hopkins and Mehanna, "The Nubian Ethnological Survey," 5.

Fowler of Forth Railway Bridge fame] as its president," and "British Egyptologists themselves ... had spent so much of the last decade attempting to define themselves as men of science ... that they were much more inclined to see the perspective of the dam builders." A rival organization, London's Society for the Preservation of the Monuments of Ancient Egypt (SPMAE), expressed a certain amount of hostility to the proposed dam. British Egyptologists, however, would not "commit themselves to the aesthetic terms on which artists ... expressed the SPMAE's opposition."[20] Archaeology has long been embroiled in preservationism, but this preservationist impulse has always been selective, a function of the interests and representations of the past at play.[21]

Ultimately, the French reaction to the potential flooding of the temple complex on the island of Philae (located just south of the proposed new dam) propelled preservationist tendencies forward. There was significant French opposition to the potential submersion of the famous "pearl of Egypt," meaning that "the capacity of the [initial design of the] dam was ... reduced by more than 50 per cent."[22] As the engineer (and under-secretary of state in the Ministry of Public Works) William Garstin noted, however, the reduction still meant that "some parts of the structures must unavoidably be flooded for a short period of each year."[23] Thus, despite the protests of concerned parties, floodwater was not automatically classed as an archaeological threat, even at Philae (figure 1.3) or by the officials who had the power to define it that way. Those officials promised that the temple complex on the island would at least be consolidated before the new dam's forthcoming deluge, but that deluge would still flood part of those ruins.[24]

In the face of such flooding, the ability to decide which remains were of value and which were not existed firmly in the hands of ministerial officials. Moreover, the reduction in scale of the initial plan for the Aswan Dam meant that those officials had to make such decisions again much sooner than they had intended. The alteration to the structure as originally planned meant that "the reservoir could ... meet only 25 per cent of what were believed to be Egypt's future needs," an outcome that not only started to make "upstream [extra-Egyptian] water imperialism a rational option," but also meant that work on heightening the structure began almost immediately after its completion.[25]

---

20. Gange, "Unholy," 108.
21. Mirjam Brusius, "Towards a History of Preservation Practices: Archaeology, Heritage, and the History of Science," *International Journal of Middle East Studies* 47, no. 3 (2015): 574–79.
22. Tvedt, *The River*, 25.
23. William Garstin, "Introductory Note" to *A Report on the Island and Temples of Philae*, by Henry George Lyons (London: Waterlow and Sons, 1896), 5.
24. Garstin, "Introductory Note," 5.
25. Tvedt, *The River*, 25.

FIGURE 1.3. Philae flooded, c. 1906. Amédée Baillot de Guerville, *New Egypt* (New York: E. P. Dutton and Company, 1906), 230a.

It was with reference to this heightening that colleagues of the British irrigation engineers in the Ministry of Public Works now argued for the necessity of launching what would become known as the Archaeological Survey of Nubia. During December 1904 and January 1905, Gaston Maspero, director-general of the Antiquities Service, made a visit to Nubia. During the Nile's annual inundation, which hit its peak in Egypt each October, there had always been a risk of flooding in Nubia. Now, Maspero argued that floodwaters and neglect constituted so much of a threat to the region's ancient remains that recording them had become a necessity.[26] Using the literary technology of "virtual witnessing" to bolster his case, he sent his Inspector-General of Antiquities, Arthur Weigall, to conduct a survey of the remains. When published in 1907, that survey helped to produce in its readership the necessary alarm just as the heightening process was about to begin, although Maspero did not forbid his employer from going ahead with work at the dam.[27] Maspero did,

---

26. Gaston Maspero, *Les temples immergés de la Nubie: rapports relatifs à la consolidation des temples*, vol. 1 (Cairo: Service des antiquités de l'Égypte, 1911), 1–2.

27. Arthur Weigall, *A Report on the Antiquities of Lower Nubia (the First Cataract to the Sudan Frontier) and Their Condition in 1906–7* (Oxford: Oxford University Press, 1907). For Weigall himself, see Julie Hankey, *A Passion for Egypt: A Biography of Arthur Weigall* (London and New York: I. B. Tauris, 2001). For virtual witnessing, "the production in a *reader's* mind of such an image . . . as obviates the necessity for . . . direct witness" of a phenomenon, see Steven Shapin and Simon Schaffer, *Leviathan and the Air-Pump: Hobbes, Boyle, and the Experimental Life*, 2011 reissue (Princeton, NJ: Princeton University Press, 2011 [1985]), 60.

however, suggest that the government would have to license archaeological intervention in Nubia before doing so.

Emphasizing that such intervention was never preordained, Maspero continued trying to make the work attractive to ministerial officials for the next several years. In a report on the Nubian temples published in 1911, he suggested that water could be used as a reason for material intervention into, and increased control over, ancient remains by a ministry that already desired to regulate such things.[28] As he remarked, earlier military administration of the region had frustrated official attempts to carry out such actions in Nubia.[29] Now there was a chance for officials to reverse this wrongdoing. Perhaps just as, if not more, crucially, Maspero also made a populational argument. He reasoned that the risk to ancient remains constituted by the Aswan Dam's floodwaters could be used as a reason for increased control over the lives of the people who lived near both the remains and the river that ministerial officials argued needed controlling.

Doing so, Maspero made a rhetorical move familiar from arguments about ancient remains in other parts of Egypt, which served to emphasize the scientific reason of Europeans in the same way that his ministry's engineers asserted their own expertise in relation to Egyptian irrigation knowledge.[30] Accusing Nubian villagers of superstitious treasure hunting and removal of decayed mud-brick from ancient structures for use as *sebakh* (or fertilizer), Maspero singled them out for causing structural damage to ancient buildings in Nubia even before the Aswan Dam's flooding had commenced.[31] At the Graeco-Roman temple of Dakka, for instance, he stated that "the inhabitants of the neighboring village . . . searched under the temple for the treasures which tradition says exists there; not finding them, they exploited the bricks as a *sebakh* quarry."[32] Exasperated, Maspero claimed that not even "severe police measures" would permanently stop such activity, since such actions always fell by the wayside.[33] An implicit invitation to carry such measures out was now in place, however. Water could be used to regulate lives as well as ancient remains.

---

28. On the nexus between ancient remains and colonial control of Egypt, see Elliott Colla, *Conflicted Antiquities: Egyptology, Egyptomania, Egyptian Modernity* (Durham, NC: Duke University Press, 2007).
29. Maspero, *Les temples*, 12.
30. Derr, *The Lived Nile*, 33–35.
31. For similar (and earlier) accusations of irrational treasure hunting, see Colla, *Conflicted*, 100–103.
32. Maspero, *Les temples*, 12–13.
33. Maspero, *Les temples*, 23.

Picturesque Ruination at Philae

Officials were keen for such populational regulation to go ahead. Maspero's archaeological suggestions reflected the broader imperatives of the Ministry of Public Works, which now agreed to the Archaeological Survey of Nubia's necessity not least because, in ministerial minds, the parts of the Nile where intervention seemed imperative were free of people. In Egypt or elsewhere, it was irrigation projects and a Nilotic environment of picturesque ruination that mattered, not the populations whose lives were entangled with the river. Garstin, whose wider ministerial duties meant that he was also involved with the construction of Cairo's Egyptian Museum (opened in 1902), wrote several reports on Upper Nile irrigation projects in the late nineteenth and early twentieth centuries.[34] As Tvedt notes, "only one of the three Garstin reports had a paragraph devoted to the people of the Upper Nile." The documents implied that "the growing importance of the Nile plan made the local people on the [Sudanese] plains ever more marginal." Yet "Garstin's uninhabited region, where only mosquitoes could thrive, was the home of perhaps millions of people and cattle, and it certainly meant something to the local inhabitants," among them the Nuer, Shilluk, and Dinka.[35]

For Ministry of Public Works officials, the Nile constituted a picturesque engineering project with a population problem. In Nubia, this situation had been evident since plans for the Aswan Dam placed ancient structures located on the island of Philae at risk. Reacting to this issue, the ministry had commissioned the geologist Captain Henry Lyons of the Royal Engineers (later the director of London's Science Museum) to write a report on the island's temple complex, its archaeology, and its structural stability. In his report, Lyons noted that "the whole island has . . . been inhabited more or less . . . up to the early part of this century."[36] Even while his investigation there was ongoing, he noted that "the earth . . . which was thrown on to the river bank [during excavation] was cleared away by the inhabitants of the villages near, to put on their fields as a manure."[37] Rather than an integral part of Philae's existence, however, Lyons and his colleagues believed that local inhabitants and their ways of life constituted a threat to the remains that stood there—the polluting present impeding on the pristine past that he now sought to constitute.

---

34. *Oxford Dictionary of National Biography*, s.v. "Garstin, Sir William Edmund, (1849–1925)."

35. Tvedt, *The River*, 76. For similar thoughts on Egypt, see Derr, "Drafting," 145.

36. Henry George Lyons, *A Report on the Island and Temples of Philae* (London: Waterlow and Sons, 1896), 10.

37. Lyons, *A Report*, 12.

During his 1895–96 mission to Philae, Lyons and his workers cleared away any evidence of recent life on the island. This obfuscation occurred not least through the publication of *A Report on the Island and Temples of Philae*, which neglected to mention the island's local name.[38] For many years, Philae had been known as Qasr Anas al-Wujud (the Palace of Anas al-Wujud). The name hailed from one of the tales collected in *A Thousand and One Nights*: in *The Story of Anas al-Wujud*, the eponymous hero of the tale was said to have been buried in a temple on the island. Accordingly, when the Swiss traveler Johann Ludwig Burckhardt visited it in 1813, he noted that Qasr Anas al-Wujud was the locale's name.[39] The 1892 edition of Karl Baedeker's *Egypt* also made mention of the island being known this way "to the natives," giving a detailed description of the story at hand.[40] Moreover, the island's Arabic name continued in use after Lyons's work ended. A 1949 Arabic-language guide to Aswan noted that the island was called Qasr Anas al-Wujud; it also gave a lengthy explanation as to why.[41] So, too, did Muhammad Shahin Hamza relate the tale in his 1954 *Rihla ila al-Sudan (Journey to Sudan)*.[42] Even UNESCO repeated the story in a celebratory volume which backhandedly stated that "fortunately, the Great Temple was spared great structural damage during . . . [the] years of change" after its ancient florescence, and whose title (*Philae Resurrected*) made very clear that the point of the Nubian campaign had been the renaissance of the island's Graeco-Roman remains.[43] Qasr Anas al-Wujud retained local resonance in the second half of the twentieth century. By negating that identity, Lyons's work also created the conditions in which such a renaissance seemed necessary and plausible.

Furthermore, Lyons's work illustrated the power of material destruction. A "Coptic village" was built above many of the earlier structures on Philae. As Garstin discussed in his "Introductory Note" to the work's report, Lyons made sure that a plan was made of the village to record its proportions. It was likely, though, that the settlement would now "inevitably disappear." Still, the loss did not seem that important: "there are many people who consider that the general aspect of the island will be improved by the removal of this mass

---

38. Lyons, *A Report*.

39. *The Story of Anas al-Wujūd: Nineteenth-Century Verse Recensions of an "Arabian Nights" Tale in Egyptian Colloquial Arabic*, introduced and ed. Mark Muehlhaeusler (Oxford, OH: Faenum, 2015), xv.

40. Karl Baedeker, ed., *Egypt: Handbook for Travellers*, vol. 2, *Upper Egypt with Nubia as Far as the Second Cataract and the Western Oases* (Leipzig: Karl Baedeker, 1892), 281–82.

41. *Aswan li-l-Ma'rid al-Zira'i al-Sina'i al-Sadis 'Ashar* [Aswan on the occasion of the sixteenth agricultural and manufacturing exhibit] (Cairo: Matba'at al-Ittihad, 1949), 14.

42. Muhammad Shahin Hamza, *Rihla ila al-Sudan* [Journey to Sudan] (Cairo?, 1954), 19–20.

43. UNESCO, *Philae Resurrected* (Paris: UNESCO, 1980), 7.

of small mud buildings, which hides in a great measure the outlines of the temples."[44] For the Ministry of Public Works, ensuring that the temples of Nubia enjoyed a particular sort of visibility in the face of the floodwaters that would (partially) submerge them mattered. Yet the people who had made—and continued to make—their lives around the location of those structures were of significantly less concern. As Jennifer L. Derr notes, in Egypt, "colonial officials did not recognize the importance of localized agricultural relationships associated with specific plots of land."[45] Life on Philae suffered as a result.

Nubian Temple Tourism

The lack of concern exhibited at Philae was coupled with the actions of the burgeoning (and imperially enabled) Egyptian tourist industry. By the time the Aswan Dam had been heightened for a second time, Nubia's temples were well on their way to becoming picturesque, de-peopled ruins; "the pearl of Egypt" was simply the most notable of the set. The floodwaters that seasonally rose around the structures constituted an attraction to the Euro-American tourists who visited Upper Egypt and Nubia on river tours operated by Thomas Cook and other companies.[46] Floodwater was never neutral: it had become a threat in a way that not only compelled Egypt's Antiquities Service to intervene in Nubia, but also meant that that water's presence was integral to the region's developing tourist industry. Floodwater had become entangled with Nubian tourism as its deluge had initiated a process of ruination and population engineering that constituted a positive touristic selling point.

Of course, this process was only logical given that officials in the Ministry of Public Works experienced Egypt primarily as river tourists and aimed to transform the country in that image. As Tvedt notes, ministerial officials embraced a "hydraulically oriented" perspective. "When the British administrators met . . . in the Gezira Sporting Club on the Gezira [island] in the middle of the river at Cairo," their perception of the importance of that river "was constantly nourished by the Nile flowing slowly and mightily past them." Indeed, "everybody knew that the Nile had sustained the life of the country for thousands of years," and "most, if not all, of the administrators had been to

---

44. Garstin, "Introductory Note," 7. Ironically, Rex Keating wrote that "the loss of the unrecorded town-site was a catastrophe for Egyptology" in his *Nubian Rescue* (London, Robert Hale, 1975), 30.

45. Derr, "Drafting," 150.

46. On the relationship between Thomas Cook and imperial expansion, including British military intervention in Sudan, see Gregory, "Colonial Nostalgia," 128–29.

see the [ruined Nile-side] temples at Luxor and to Aswan . . . where the river marvellously enters Egypt under the permanently blue sky."[47] To use Timothy Mitchell's now well-worn formulation, fueled by imaginaries of both the biblical and the ancient Egyptian past, it was as if British administrators encountered Egypt "as an exhibit" that they had only previously witnessed in the universal expositions of the nineteenth and early twentieth centuries. Once these same officials established themselves in the country, however, that exhibit did not behave like one, appearing to them "orderless and without meaning."[48] Irrigation officials thus gave Egypt—and other countries on the Nile—the order that they thought was necessary by transforming the way that irrigation in those places worked. As Derr notes, "the effect of this reading of the Egyptian landscape was to renaturalize [it] . . . despite the existence of complex historical practices tied to irrigation and cultivation."[49] Ironically, this process also transformed the ancient ruins—like Philae—located on the Nile's Nubian banks; hydraulic development caused not only picturesque, but also *accelerated* ruination.

Such acceleration created dynamic ruins whose "relative art-value" was keenly debated, placing them firmly within "the modern cult of monuments" defined by Alois Riegl a few years after Lyons's intervention—and only a year after the opening of the Aswan Dam in 1902.[50] The imbrication of irrigation engineering and tourism moved ever closer, hastening the accompanying process of Nubian depopulation. True to Riegl's formulation, not everyone welcomed such ruination: sometimes even those responsible for guiding overseas visitors. Baedeker's 1929 edition of *Egypt and the Sûdân* noted that Philae "formerly ranked as one of the most beautiful points in Egypt." Yet the island had "lost much of its charm since the construction of the Nile Dam [sic], whereby its rich vegetation has been destroyed."[51] Floodwater was, however, turned into an integral part of the Nubian tourist experience. One Egyptian State Tourist Administration guidebook opined that "beneath the waters of the reservoir, sometimes almost submerged, sometimes entirely visible is the Island of Philae with its beautiful temple."[52]

---

47. Tvedt, *The River*, 74; cf. Derr, "Drafting," 142.

48. Timothy Mitchell, *Colonising Egypt* (Berkeley: University of California Press, 1988), xiv–xv. On biblical and ancient Egyptian imaginaries, see, e.g., Derr, "Drafting," 142; Gange, "Unholy."

49. Derr, "Drafting," 144.

50. Alois Riegl, "The Modern Cult of Monuments: Its Character and Its Origin," trans. Kurt W. Forster and Diane Ghirardo, *Oppositions* 25 (1982; originally published in German in 1903): 21–51.

51. Karl Baedeker, *Egypt and the Sûdân: Handbook for Travellers*, 8th rev. ed. (1929; repr., Newton Abbot: David & Charles, 1974), 390.

52. Egyptian State Tourist Administration and the Tourist Development Association of Egypt, *Egypt Tourist Guide: General Information on Travelling* (Cairo: E. and R. Schindler, ca. 1940s), 248.

Another guidebook, published in 1930, noted that "Phylae towards the end of the season is entirely submerged after the second heightening of the Dam." But the volume also stated that "there is no reason to any grievance, if we take in consideration the benefits of the enormous quantity of water."[53] Meanwhile, the cover (figure 1.4) of the 1949 guide to Aswan discussed previously juxtaposed an image of Philae's well-known Kiosk of Trajan with the Aswan Dam, emphasizing the promotional benefits of this link between modernity and the past. Indeed, the guide mobilized that link in a way that helped to prompt Egyptian claims to oversight of the island's preservation. In response to "the many foreigners who have expressed their willingness to assist in the expense of moving it," and to the fact that "this talk has started again," the guide noted the explicit concern of Egypt's King Faruq—his portrait featured as frontispiece—with "the fate of the island" (bi-maṣīr al-jazīra).[54]

Discussing Nubia south of Philae, meanwhile, the 1930 guidebook noted that "the tourist who . . . visits Nubia . . . on board Messrs Ths. Cook & Son's luxurious tourist steamer 'Thebes,' or sailing on by Dahabieh (Houseboat) is delighted by this charming country."[55] That tourist, according to the guidebook, "wonders at the sight of temples and palaces partly out of the water."[56] Elsewhere, Baedeker took care to note that "all the ruined sites of Nubia are free from floods in summer and autumn" (the Nile's inundation usually having progressed to Aswan and Upper Egypt in late July or early August).[57] Still, "travellers who desire to inspect the ruined sites of Nubia more closely will avail themselves of Messrs. Thos. Cook & Son's tourist steamer *Thebes*." That steamer "plies during the season," December to March.[58] (Egyptian) Nubia was becoming a picturesque land of ruinous—and often semi-submerged—desolation. The same guidebooks dutifully noted the settlements dotting the Nubian landscape, but never in as much detail as the temples there, and often only to inform readers of the presence of post and telegraph offices.[59] In Nubia, people seemed to be missing, their lives subordinated to, and purposefully disconnected from, the flooded remains that dotted the riverbanks and among which they made their lives. It is unsurprising that, as they worked, the officials in charge of the Archaeological Survey of Nubia had hastened this process. Picturesque riverside ruins became archaeologically

---

53. P. Condopoulo, *An Illustrated Guide Book on Egypt and Nubia* (Cairo: E. Menikidis, 1930), 164–65.
54. *Aswan li-l-Ma'rid*, 17.
55. Condopoulo, *An Illustrated*, 200.
56. Condopoulo, *An Illustrated*, 201.
57. Baedeker, *Egypt and the Sûdân*, 409.
58. Baedeker, *Egypt and the Sûdân*, 410.
59. Baedeker, *Egypt and the Sûdân*, 424, lists such offices at the village of Seyala, for instance.

FIGURE 1.4. Front cover of *Aswan li-l-Ma'rid al-Zira'i al-Sana'i al-Sadis 'Ashr* [Aswan on the occasion of the sixteenth agricultural and manufacturing exhibit] (Cairo: Matba'at al-Ittihad, 1949).

important, but only ever in relation to the negation of the people who lived among them.

The First Archaeological Survey of Nubia, 1907–1911

The first Archaeological Survey of Nubia, carried out in preparation for the Aswan Dam's initial heightening, set out to record specific material. Overseen by US archaeologist George Andrew Reisner, assisted by the Australian-British anatomist Grafton Elliot Smith, and with leadership later taken over by British archaeologist Cecil Mallaby Firth, the values attributed to material recorded by the survey were constituted not only by that material's relationship to water, but also by its fit within a set of anthropological principles whose racial grounding ensured a disregard of local populations.[60] Written simply, the Archaeological Survey recorded material whose value was constituted by the wider contexts in which that project had come into being—contexts, moreover, that the survey now helped to reproduce.

During the work, the survey's laborers moved southward up the Nile, following the route taken by Messrs. Thomas Cook & Son's vessels. Traveling from Shellal, just south of Aswan, to Dakka, about halfway to the Egyptian-Sudanese border, the laborers excavated sites up to the future (113 meters above sea level) limit of the dam's floodwaters.[61] Water—in addition to Nile navigation—was of paramount importance, determining not only the extent of the survey, but also how the gangs of workers carried out and experienced their labor.[62] As Timothy Mitchell notes, "the topographic image of the river, the desert surrounding it, and the population jammed within its banks" has come to define international development reports about Egypt.[63] That image, though, had to be naturalized, and archaeology was as responsible as other fields of knowledge for naturalizing it.

---

60. Reisner has long been denoted a "founding-father" of scientific archaeology. For more nuanced discussions of him, see David Gange, *Dialogues with the Dead: Egyptology in British Culture and Religion, 1822–1922* (Oxford: Oxford University Press, 2013); Reid, *Contesting*; Stevenson, *Scattered*. Grafton Elliot Smith, meanwhile, has become notorious among archaeologists for his "hyper-diffusionism," for which see Bruce G. Trigger, *A History of Archaeological Thought* (Cambridge: Cambridge University Press, 1989), 152–54.

61. Keating, *Nubian Rescue*, 31 notes that "the result [of this flood-defined border] was calamitous," increasing looting south of the point where Reisner's survey stopped.

62. On bodies and Nile irrigation, cf. Jennifer L. Derr, "Labor-Time: Ecological Bodies and Agricultural Labor in 19th and Early 20th-Century Egypt," *International Journal of Middle East Studies* 50, no. 2 (2018): 195–212.

63. Mitchell, *Rule*, 210.

For example, the workforce of the survey's "exploratory gang" in October 1907 "was divided into two gangs moving parallel to each other, one along the lower face of the cliff and the other along the top." These gangs "went as far as Demhid, and reported a number of sites on both sides of the river."[64] Walking (not floating), and exerting a considerable amount of effort in doing so, the bodily experience of the Archaeological Survey's workers emphasized their hierarchical separation from leaders ensconced on a boat sailing gracefully down the Nile. This bodily hierarchy also constituted the sort of material that the survey might investigate, as the leadership kept the workers' course firmly in sight. If any material was located outside the riverine zone, it was not to be investigated. Nubia's past, much like its present, was defined by its relationship to the Nile.

Returning to notions of the destiny of Egypt's control of Sudan, this riverine archaeological practice itself reflected sloganeering regarding "the unity of the Nile Valley" that coalesced in Egypt throughout the nineteenth and early twentieth centuries. As the territory's relationships with the areas to its south had developed and Egyptian rulers and nationalists sought to define the boundaries of a dominant "Egypt," this process also defined understandings of ancient northern dominance.[65] In his 1869 *Manahij al-Albab al-Misriyya fi Mabahij al-Adab al-'Asriyya* (The paths of Egyptian hearts in the joys of the contemporary arts), the reformer and polymath Rifa'a Rafi' al-Tahtawi valorized Egypt's control of Sudan on the basis that "it was . . . an affirmation of Egypt's ancient identity and borders."[66] Hydro-politics was particularly important to this vision. As Eve Troutt Powell notes, al-Tahtawi

> narrated the history of [Mehmed Ali's] irrigation reform from the north of Egypt to the south, city by city, area by area. The utilization of the Nile was thus an important means by which to unify Egypt, and from which the ruler could chart his own country.[67]

Simultaneously, al-Tahtawi praised Mehmed Ali's sponsorship of the 1839–42 expeditions to (and annexation of) lands in the region of the White Nile led

---

64. George Andrew Reisner, "The Archaeological Survey of Nubia: Progress of Survey," in *The Archaeological Survey of Nubia: Bulletin No. 2, Dealing with the Work from December 1, 1907, to March 31, 1908*, ed. Ministry of Finance, Egypt; Survey Department (Cairo: National Printing Department, 1908), 3.

65. Powell, *A Different*, 7, 69–70. The interpretation of ancient Egyptian power over Sudan was so widespread that the major synthetic volume to emerge from UNESCO's campaign largely constituted an argument against it, for which see William Y. Adams, *Nubia: Corridor to Africa* (London: Allen Lane, 1977).

66. Powell, *A Different*, 53. For the original, see Rifa'a Rafi' al-Tahtawi, *Manahij al-Albab al-Misriyya fi Mabahij al-Adab al-'Asriyya* [The paths of Egyptian hearts in the joys of the contemporary arts] (Bulaq: al-Matba'a al-Kubra al-Amiriyya, 1869).

67. Powell, *A Different*, 53.

by the "Turkish-speaking naval officer" Selim Qapudan.[68] Crucially, as Powell notes, those expeditions had multiple interlinked geographies. Elements of Selim Qapudan's diary from the third expedition "were published in French in 1842, and the expedition was heralded by M. [Edme-François] Jomard, the head of the French Geographic Society, as one of the greatest moments in Egyptian history."[69] Consequently, "for European geographers and scientists interested in the Nile Valley, it was a knowledge-seeking campaign," albeit one that—like the earlier Napoleonic expedition to Egypt—depended on imperial power. Yet for Mehmed Ali, "the real author of the expedition, it was a gesture that would dignify Egyptian control of the Nile Valley with European ideals about the values and uses of such scientific information."[70]

Now, the creation of such information was controlled by Europeans themselves, with predictable results. Beyond the practice of riverine recording, the Archaeological Survey of Nubia deployed anthropological practices not only geared toward "establishing the regional distribution and physical characteristics of various prehistoric ethnic groups," but also embedded in thinking about "gradual racial differentiation" promoted by Grafton Elliot Smith.[71] Such racial—and racist—thinking led to the predominance of cemeteries in terms of sites excavated so that the human remains found within them could be, as Elliot Smith put it, studied "with a view to the classification of their distinctive features and the determination of their racial characteristics."[72] Plates of "typed" skulls in the survey's official reports constituted one upshot of this practice, depicting groups organized within categories like "foreigner," "typical archaic Egyptian," or "negro."[73] Another upshot of this racial work was the assumption that "Nubia failed to keep pace with Egypt," which meant that neighboring, soon-to-be-flooded Nubian settlements merited little attention from the survey's leadership. For the staff of the Archaeological Survey of Nubia, the ways in which local populations interacted with the Nile mattered very little, meaning that those populations became almost invisible.

---

68. Powell, *A Different*, 42.
69. Powell, *A Different*, 43.
70. Powell, *A Different*, 47.
71. Gange, "Unholy," 112. For Elliot Smith and British anthropology, see Henrika Kuklick, *The Savage Within: The Social History of British Anthropology, 1885–1945* (Cambridge: Cambridge University Press, 1991).
72. Grafton Elliot Smith, "The Anatomical Report," in *The Archaeological Survey of Nubia: Bulletin No. 1, Dealing with the Work up to November 30, 1907*, ed. Ministry of Finance, Egypt; Survey Department (Cairo: National Printing Department, 1908), 25.
73. Smith, "The Anatomical Report," pl. XIX.

FIGURE 1.5. View of the "cemetery" and settlement at El Biga. George Andrew Reisner, "The Archaeological Survey of Nubia," in *The Archaeological Survey of Nubia: Bulletin No. 1, Dealing with the Work up to November 30, 1907*, ed. Ministry of Finance, Egypt; Survey Department (Cairo: National Printing Department, 1908), pl. viii.

An image at the back of the survey's first *Bulletin* emphasizes how such invisibility took shape. A plate captioned "General View of Cemetery No. 5, El Biga, looking south, before excavation" neglects to mention the contemporary houses clearly pictured in the photograph (figure 1.5). The accompanying report, written by Reisner, does mention them but only in terms of the irritation that the structures caused his mission. "The proximity of the modern village which still covers a large part of the cemetery, and the obvious disturbance of part of the cemetery by excavations for fertilizing material may have robbed us of the objects accidentally left on the surface [in the past] on festival days."[74] Nubians, it seems, obstructed not only modern irrigation programs, but also the modern science of archaeology. This view—and the values accompanying it—would continue as the second survey of Nubia got under way in 1929.

---

74. George Andrew Reisner, "The Archaeological Survey of Nubia," in *The Archaeological Survey of Nubia: Bulletin No. 1, Dealing with the Work up to November 30, 1907*, ed. Ministry of Finance, Egypt; Survey Department (Cairo: National Printing Department, 1908), 15–16.

The Second Archaeological Survey of Nubia, 1929–1934

> Our reception as we progressed south varied very much in different villages, but we were never very popular, for the inhabitants naturally looked upon us as the precursors of the destruction of their homes by the [Aswan Dam's] new water-level.
>
> —Walter Bryan Emery *Nubian Treasure*

Bryan Emery, the British archaeologist who directed the second Archaeological Survey of Nubia (and who would become a central figure in UNESCO's Nubian campaign), was clear about the nature of the region, in addition to the characteristics of Nubians. There was, he said, "something very attractive about the clean, orderly Nubian villages in comparison with their rather untidy counterparts in Egypt. This feature," however, "is largely due to Egyptian influence, for most of the Nubian menfolk spend the greater part of their lives as servants in the large towns of Egypt." There, he argued, those same Nubians—forced to become economic migrants due to the building of the Aswan Dam—were "undoubtedly influenced by ideas of orderliness and cleanliness."[75]

In its shape-shifting (il)logic and backhanded valorization of a region about to disappear, Emery's description was characteristic of much colonial thought.[76] His viewpoint also reflected both the colonial Cairene milieu within which he moved and more widespread pejorative views about Egypt's southerners.[77] No wonder the renewed Archaeological Survey lacked a positive reception. As the project progressed, Nubians in fact lobbied Egypt's Ministry of Public Works for several things: compensation money related to their submerged property, membership on the committee that decided the value of that compensation, and the provision of new land free of charge.[78] Through lobbying, Nubians made their voices heard and their presence felt. As Derr notes, a consequence of this action was that Nubians started "to imagine themselves as a community in national terms."[79] For Emery, though, Nubia was not even a land that its inhabitants seemed capable of excavating. Emery described Nubians as:

---

75. Walter Bryan Emery, *Nubian Treasure* (London: Methuen, 1948), 7.
76. Exuding something of the anxious "epistemic uncertainties" discussed in Stoler, *Along*, 1.
77. As Powell, *A Different*, 6, notes, in Egyptian "popular and print culture the Sudanese were often portrayed as no more than an empire of domestics." For Nubians (whose separation from the Sudanese in this imaginary was not always clear), this domestic identity was a lived reality.
78. "Mutalib al-Nubiyyin" ["Nubian demands"], *al-Ahram*, February 7, 1932.
79. Derr, *The Lived Nile*, 71.

racially distinct from the Egyptians, being inferior in almost every quality, particularly when it comes to a matter of work. On two or three occasions we attempted to employ them as labourers on the excavations, but their complaints of the heat, the dust and the speed of the work soon compelled us to relinquish the attempt. It was partly for this reason and the lack of man-power that we employed only Egyptian workmen, brought from Upper Egypt, throughout the five years that we worked in Nubia.[80]

For Emery, Nubia itself was interesting but its population inconsequential. In the late-nineteenth and early-twentieth centuries, the differentiated expansion of perennial irrigation in Egypt had shaped bodily experiences of agricultural labor.[81] Now, Emery's racial judgment shaped bodily experiences of part of what had become the Egyptian past. Nubian complaints about bodily discomfort were not taken seriously. This decision led to the physical separation of the Nubian population from the remains among which they lived, both perpetuating a practice started during earlier work and making its later continuation more likely.

Sailing along the river, the second survey maintained earlier practices in other ways, too. Moving southward on two boats chartered from Thomas Cook, the survey's means of movement emphasized the extent to which the company's tours shaped Nubia's past. The "view from the boat"—including one banally named the "Thames"—was paramount, as Menna Agha has also noted.[82] "When once a site was discovered a preliminary excavation was undertaken to ascertain its value and period," wrote Emery. Only "when these tests proved satisfactory" were "the boats . . . stopped, the workmen's camp erected, and the systematic clearance commenced."[83] Without a site's value and period deemed important enough, the survey's boats kept on sailing, the party on board keeping time like a river boat keeping to a timetable.[84]

Such values came preordained. Emery—assisted during the project by Laurence P. Kirwan, later director and secretary of the Royal Geographical Society—adhered to detailed instructions given to him by former survey director Cecil

80. Emery, *Nubian Treasure*, 14.
81. Derr, "Labor-Time."
82. Emery, *Nubian Treasure*, 2. Citing Gregory, "Colonial Nostalgia," Menna Agha, "Nubia Still Exists: On the Utility of the Nostalgic Space," *Humanities* 8, no. 1 (2019), 3, discusses how this sort of work generated a colonial image of Nubia that academics "saw from a boat in the Nile."
83. Emery, *Nubian Treasure*, 4.
84. Cf. On Barak, *On Time: Technology and Temporality in Modern Egypt* (Berkeley: University of California Press, 2013), for other ways in which timetables shaped Egyptian life in this period.

Firth.⁸⁵ The renewed project thus conducted excavations by finding exactly what its directors expected. The survey also continued to ignore contemporary Nubian settlements. As Emery noted, "until the last raising of the Aswan Dam, [the village of] Ed Derr represented what little there is of Western civilisation in Nubia—a police station and a school."⁸⁶ The view from the boat meant that nothing contemporary appeared worth saving from the coming flood; how could it if the marker of what made civilization had been set elsewhere? The maps used in the work's final report locating excavated sites had been adapted from those used by the governmental Survey of Egypt and noted the location of the Nile-side Nubian villages that the project's boat passed.⁸⁷ Appearing on such maps, Nubia took on a substance that the Egyptian conflation of the region with Sudan had otherwise denied it, even as it now became cartographically incorporated into Egypt itself. Mapped acknowledgment of Nubian settlements did not mean that the project's leadership considered such villages to be of value.

The second survey therefore recorded sites with reference to norms set down during the first one. Circular as that practice was, such sites were what Emery and his associates expected to find. The survey team again prioritized cemeteries by reexamining the penultimate cemetery (number 150) that the first survey investigated and continuing with the sequential numbering system for those burial grounds that the earlier work introduced.⁸⁸ The survey's laborers also excavated the occasional settlement. Yet in startling contrast to the number of "plundered" graves recorded during the work, the connection of these settlements to later interference also seems to have negated any interest in them.⁸⁹ For example, a "small town . . . situated about half a kilome-

---

85. These instructions were contained in 1929–32 correspondence between the two men, detailed in Geoffrey Thorndike Martin, "The Early Dynastic Necropolis at North Saqqara: The Unpublished Excavations of W. B. Emery and C. M. Firth," in *The Archaeology and Art of Ancient Egypt: Essays in Honour of David B. O'Connor*, Supplément aux Annales du Service des antiquités de l'Égypte 36, vol. 1, ed. Zahi A. Hawass and Janet Richards (Cairo: Supreme Council of Antiquities, 2007), 121–26. On Kirwan, see *Oxford Dictionary of National Biography*, s.v. "Kirwan, Sir (Archibald) Laurence Patrick [Larry], 1907–1999."

86. Emery, *Nubian Treasure*, 11.

87. See, e.g., Walter Bryan Emery and Laurence P. Kirwan, *The Excavations and Survey between Wadi es-Sebua and Adindan, 1929–1931*, vol. 2, *Plates*, Mission archéologique de Nubie, 1929–1934 (Bulaq: Government Press, 1935), pl. 61.

88. Walter Bryan Emery and Laurence P. Kirwan, *The Excavations and Survey between Wadi es-Sebua and Adindan, 1929–1931*, vol. 1, *Text*, Mission archéologique de Nubie, 1929–1934 (Bulaq: Government Press, 1935), 70–102. For Cemetery 150, see Cecil Mallaby Firth, *The Archaeological Survey of Nubia: Bulletin No. 7; Dealing with the Work from November 1, 1910 to February 28, 1911* (Cairo: National Printing Department, 1911), 15–16.

89. In Emery and Kirwan, *The Excavations*, vol. 1, *Text*, 413–16, for instance, all twenty-one graves excavated in Cemetery 210 were "plundered."

tre to the north of Cemetery 215" had "brick walls . . . largely destroyed by the digging of natives." Thus, "owing to the denuded character of the site it was decided that it would not repay excavation."[90]

The survey's publications again addressed excavated material in terms of race. The publications discussed presumed moments of racial florescence and degeneration using the human remains excavated during the work, in addition to pieces of ancient pottery connected to them. Emery and Kirwan's comments on Nubia in the period of the early pharaonic Egyptian dynasties are instructive here, emphasizing the extent to which the survey's leaders subscribed to concepts of scientific racism, and demonstrating the way in which such ideas allowed the casting of Nubia's past and present as liminal at best:

> Until the time of the third dynasty, the civilisation and physical type in Nubia was primarily Egyptian though the occurrence of a peculiarly fine variety of Nubian painted pottery shows a certain degree of native culture. By the end of the second dynasty Nubia had relapsed once more into poverty: whether due to hostile attacks or to an exodus of a large part of the inhabitants attracted by the richness and prosperity of contemporary Egypt it is hard to say. The graves of the B-group period (third to sixth dynasty) show a continuation of the early dynastic culture in a greatly degenerated form, and it is apparent that Nubia took no part in the artistic and economic revival which came in Egypt with the pyramid builders. Many of the B-group skulls show strong traces of negroid blood and it may have been that this . . . mixture with a more backward race lead to a subsequent degeneration.[91]

Work carried out during the later Nubian campaign would undermine the idea that the "B-group" had existed at all (even as racial thought continued to course throughout UNESCO's project).[92] Yet as in the original survey, racial thought was embedded within the second Archaeological Survey of Nubia's practices. Emery and Kirwan's opinions, however, faced dissent from their own teammates. For some, such a view from the boat had become difficult to support.

---

90. Emery and Kirwan, *The Excavations*, vol. 1, 417.
91. Emery and Kirwan, *The Excavations*, vol. 1, 1.
92. Harry S. Smith, "The Nubian B-Group," *Kush: Journal of the Sudan Antiquities Service* 14 (1966): 69–124.

Racial and Religious Contentions

Beyond the work's laborers, numerous Egyptian staff were employed as part of the team that undertook the second Archaeological Survey of Nubia.[93] This assistance did not come without controversy, however. Reflecting the broader concerns of Egypt's "new *effendiyya*" social grouping with who exactly modern Egyptian society should benefit, at least one member of the survey's Egyptian staff would question their leadership's judgment.[94] However carefully couched, that staff member questioned his management's attitude to race and, moreover, the earlier work of Elliot Smith from which that attitude arose.

Ahmed El Batrawi worked both as the second survey's anatomist and as its physician. Later a professor of anatomy at Cairo University, he had graduated from the institution's Medical Faculty in 1926 and, in 1940, earned his PhD in anthropology in London. El Batrawi was an accomplished, authoritative figure, who would later publish an Arabic translation of *Gray's Anatomy* and whose work enjoyed increasing recognition.[95] His authority had not always been so obvious, however. El Batrawi's official report on the second Archaeological Survey, published in 1935, had been cautious, indicating only that "owing to . . . the fortunate discoveries of the C-group period, more light has been thrown on the different problems of Nubian anthropology."[96] As William Y. Adams noted, El Batrawi in effect seemed "reluctant to challenge . . . [earlier] historical theories even while he disputed their empirical foundation."[97]

By 1946, however, he published the second part of his article on "The Racial History of Egypt and Nubia" in *The Journal of the Royal Anthropological Institute of Great Britain and Ireland* and seemed to have gained confidence. In the article, El Batrawi's words countered previous racial claims made by the Archaeological Survey's staff. Thus, he cautioned at the article's beginning that "the literature dealing with the racial history of Egypt provides an outstanding example of

---

93. Emery and Kirwan, *The Excavations*, vol. 1, vii, states that Abdel Baki Yusef Effendi and Rizkallah Macramallah Effendi conducted a large part of the field work, Mohammed Hosni Effendi was surveyor, and Ahmed Abdel Monem Effendi oversaw photography.

94. On the "new *effendiyya*," see Lucie Ryzova, *The Age of the Efendiyya: Passages to Modernity in National-Colonial Egypt* (Oxford: Oxford University Press, 2018) and Ryzova, "Egyptianizing Modernity through the 'New Effendiya': Social and Cultural Constructions of the Middle Class in Egypt under the Monarchy," in Goldschmidt, Johnson, and Salmoni, *Re-Envisioning Egypt*, 150.

95. Bierbrier, *Who*, 46. During UNESCO's Nubian campaign, El Batrawi would develop links with Czechoslovak Egyptologists, for which see Eugen Strouhal, "In Memory of Professor Ahmed Mahmoud el-Batrawi," *Anthropologie* 4, no. 3 (1966): 93–94.

96. Ahmed M. El Batrawi, *Report on the Human Remains*, Mission archéologique de Nubie, 1929–1934 (Bulaq: Government Press, 1935), 160.

97. Adams, *Nubia*, 92.

the danger of assessing biological relationships from cultural evidence."[98] He also emphasized that the narratives of racial florescence and degeneration that the Nubian surveys had promoted had no basis in evidence, noting that "the Nubian series [of populations] offer a good example of the persistence, with little modification, of a type over a long period."[99]

Carefully written, El Batrawi's words were nonetheless damning to previous interpretations of the material excavated during the two Nubian surveys, in addition to the scientific racism that had bolstered that earlier work. As Adams emphasized, "this long-overdue admonition, appearing in a journal little consulted by historians, went almost entirely unheeded."[100] There is more, however, to the anatomist's lack of impact even than the publication in which he placed his argument. In his 1946 article, El Batrawi noted the difficulty of carrying out his study in reference to Christian and Islamic periods, due to "the lack of an adequate amount of relevant material."[101] Implicitly addressing the Archaeological Survey of Nubia's lack of attention to contemporary—or even post-"ancient"—remains, El Batrawi directed attention to earlier judgments about what counted as worthwhile evidence at the same time as suggesting the impact of those decisions on his own scientific authority.

In the period during which the second Archaeological Survey took place, the Antiquities Service (assisted by the Ufficio delle Missione Scientifiche in Levante of the Italian Ministry of Foreign Affairs) had in fact paid the Milanese archaeologist and architectural historian Ugo Monneret de Villard to survey "all the Christian monuments between the first and second cataracts" of the Nile.[102] Yet this conceptual separation of expertise reflected a temporal division of Egyptian remains into "ancient" (i.e., pharaonic), "Graeco-Roman," "Coptic [Christian]," and "Islamic" increasingly institutionalized in the country's museums (and elsewhere).[103] This practice of periodization created significant issues, not least when it came to examining evidence outside the bounds of specific forms of expertise. Monneret de Villard had long been involved in the study of Christian and Islamic art in Egypt.[104] His employment

---

98. Ahmed M. El Batrawi, "The Racial History of Egypt and Nubia, Part II: The Racial Relationships of the Ancient and Modern Populations of Egypt and Nubia," *The Journal of the Royal Anthropological Institute of Great Britain and Ireland* 76, no. 2 (1946): 131.

99. El Batrawi, "The Racial History," 154.

100. Adams, *Nubia*, 92.

101. El Batrawi, "The Racial History," 155.

102. Ugo Monneret de Villard, *La Nubia Medioevale*, vol. 1, *Inventario dei Monumenti*, Mission archéologique de Nubie, 1929–1934 (Cairo: Institut français d'archéologie orientale, 1935), xii.

103. For which see Reid, *Contesting*.

104. Silvia Armando, "Ugo Monneret de Villard (1881–1954) and the Establishment of Islamic Art Studies in Italy," *Muqarnas* 30 (2013): 35–71.

to conduct a specialized survey of Christian monuments, however, not only served to highlight how tenaciously a racialized and temporally discrete vision of ancient Egypt had taken hold, but also how that vision—together with the foregrounding of the Nile as an arterial unit of analysis—now impacted excavations in Nubia and the possibility, however slight, of constructing alternative histories from them. Monneret de Villard's work in Nubia was as free from reference to the local population as the second Archaeological Survey itself, at the same time as the structures he worked on themselves suffered from a relative lack of importance: in representations of Egypt, it was the pharaonic period that had taken on paramount value.[105] As he and the directors of that survey all took a particular sort of view from the boat, so El Batrawi struggled to promote an alternative.

Emery's own actions in relation to Nubia's non-"ancient" antiquities themselves emphasize how particular forms of expertise in Egyptian archaeology had started to rigidify. During his time directing the Archaeological Survey, the mission excavated a group of large "royal" burial mounds dating from around the fourth to the sixth centuries AD, whose contents included silver crowns and horse burials. Located just south of Abu Simbel at the sites of Ballana and Qustul, the announcement of the excavation caused predictable (if limited) excitement. "Important Discoveries in Nubia: Old Abyssinian Tombs," reported *The Egyptian Gazette* on January 12, 1932.[106] And on February 6, the same newspaper's correspondent in Aswan noted that the tombs constituted "the chief topic of conversation here at the moment," not least because "mention is made of eight golden horses."[107] That the tombs only solidified the view from the boat almost goes without saying, the same article reporting that:

> a large party of archaeologists from Luxor will leave for this new Mecca of ancient glory, by the next sailing of Messrs T. Cook's s.s. Thebes, in order to pave the way for the large number of tourists anxious to take an early opportunity of visiting the latest discoveries of ancient Egypt.[108]

The entanglement of the view from the boat with specific forms of expertise also conditioned Emery's report on the excavation, which showed how that entanglement had begun to constitute what could be said about Nubia and who could say it. In the report's preface, Emery wrote that:

---

105. Reid, *Contesting*.
106. "Important Discoveries in Nubia: Old Abyssinian Tombs," *The Egyptian Gazette*, January 12, 1932.
107. "Great Excitement at Assuan: New Discoveries Near Abu Simbel; Archaeologist's Enthusiastic Report; Eight Golden Horses," *The Egyptian Gazette*, February 6, 1932.
108. "Great Excitement at Assuan," *The Egyptian Gazette*, February 6, 1932.

I . . . feel that, as so many of the objects belong to a period and culture beyond the bounds of my Egyptological experience, this detail work may be safely left in the hands of experts in Byzantine and Early Christian antiquities. I have therefore endeavoured to give a detailed account of the history of the discovery, description of the tombs, and a catalogue of all the objects found, and I trust that it will be sufficient foundation for the work of the specialist.[109]

By the time the second survey had concluded, the region to which that work was dedicated had taken on certain characteristics. Reflecting the irrigation work and tourist experience to which the survey and its predecessor were linked, Nubia had become defined by its relationship to the Nile. The sort of riverside sites investigated during the survey's first iteration now became the sites that the second survey's director would moor its boats to excavate; the sites themselves were not so far from the Nile-side temples that the boats of Messrs. Thomas Cook & Son's touristic concern enabled tourists to gaze at in their picturesque ruination. The view from the boat mattered, as did the way in which that view coincided with a racialized attitude that not only gave short shrift to local populations, but also embedded such judgment in dubious historical theorizing itself linked to the perceived value of excavated locales.

In this context, opinions like those of Ahmed El Batrawi went unheeded and under- or unvalued. Relative to such adjudication of knowledge, moreover, it is notable that it was the Arabic—and not English—press who made efforts to discourage the spread of sensationalism related to the work that the view from the boat engendered. On February 11, 1932, Egypt's leading Arabic-language newspaper, *al-Ahram*, reported on a story published in an English-language newspaper in Egypt, *The Egyptian Mail*. A couple of days earlier, the paper had reported (unspecified) news about the second survey's recent discoveries (presumably at Ballana and Qustul); news apparently then repeated in some Arabic newspapers. *Al-Ahram* clarified that "the strongest sources" (*awathiq al-maṣādir*) had rejected the news as untrue or, literally, "devoid of health" (*ʿār al-ṣiḥa*).[110] The damage, however, had already been done. As the view from the boat predominated, so it continued to constitute not only the Nubian, but also the Egyptian past. Moreover, as it became increasingly clear that the Aswan High Dam would be built, this combination formed a heady brew. By itself becoming linked to irrigation, Egypt's past guaranteed that the Nubian past would be connected to it, too.

---

109. Walter Bryan Emery, *The Royal Tombs of Ballana and Qustul*, vol. 1, *Text*, Mission archéologique de Nubie, 1929–1934 (Bulaq: Government Press, 1938), v.

110. "Hawla al-Athar al-Mustakshifa" ["About the antiquities discovered"], *al-Ahram*, February 11, 1932.

Revolutionizing Archaeology

After the 1952 Free Officers' coup and the end, in 1953, of the country's monarchy, the development of irrigable land continued to be an urgent priority in Egypt. So, too, did the intersection of that process with archaeological work. A policy of land reform and redistribution, announced soon after the officers came to power, aided this process. But equally important were other modernization and land reclamation schemes promoted by the officers that aimed to manage and better the lives of Egypt's rural poor. The theoretical basis of these schemes articulated with similar projects that had been in progress across the world for some time, not least America's TVA. The undertaking of such work was also accelerated by the rise of what Odd Arne Westad has termed the "global Cold War" and the proliferation of modernization projects made possible by US investment in development aid as a means of curbing Soviet influence.[111] In Egypt under the Free Officers, meanwhile, such projects intersected with the development of the revolutionary state.[112] Operating in the same milieu as these schemes, archaeology—and a repurposed and renamed Department of Antiquities now run by Egyptians—itself took on a revolutionary aspect, albeit slowly.[113] When the Aswan High Dam became the undisputed centerpiece of the country's revolutionary modernization project, the further undertaking of archaeological work linked to the development of the Nile was therefore close to inevitable.

Not all land schemes involved an archaeological component. Tahrir ("Liberation") Province, a massive land reclamation and social development scheme initiated during the mid-1950s on the edge of Egypt's Western Delta, did not

---

111. Odd Arne Westad, *The Global Cold War: Third World Interventions and the Making of Our Times* (Cambridge: Cambridge University Press, 2005). For the TVA and the global spread of experts that it presaged, see, e.g., David Ekbladh, *The Great American Mission: Modernization and the Construction of an American World Order* (Princeton, NJ: Princeton University Press, 2010); Arturo Escobar, *Encountering Development: The Making and Unmaking of the Third World* (Princeton, NJ: Princeton University Press, 1995). For the global intersection of the TVA and archaeology beyond the United States and Egypt, see Luke, *A Pearl*.

112. On modernization schemes in Egypt and post-1952 land redistribution policies see: Jon B. Alterman, *Egypt and American Foreign Assistance, 1952–1956* (Basingstoke and New York: Palgrave, 2002); Roel Meijer, *The Quest for Modernity: Secular Liberal and Left-Wing Political Thought in Egypt, 1945–1958* (London: Routledge Curzon, 2002); Omnia El Shakry, *The Great Social Laboratory: Subjects of Knowledge in Colonial and Postcolonial Egypt* (Stanford, CA: Stanford University Press, 2007).

113. For this repurposing, see William Carruthers, "The Planned Past: Policy and (Ancient) Egypt," *Egyptian and Egyptological Documents, Archives, Libraries* 4 (2015): 233, which explains in wider context how Law 22 of January 8, 1953 brought together the various bodies responsible for administration and preservation of antiquities and monuments in Egypt. The Service des antiquités de l'Égypte (or Maslahat al-Athar al-Misriyya; Department of Egyptian Antiquities), now became part of the Maslahat al-Athar, or Department of Antiquities. On the history of Egyptian antiquities law, see Antoine Khater, *Le régime juridique des fouilles et des antiquités en Égypte* (Cairo: Institut français d'archéologie orientale, 1960).

intersect with archaeological work at all.¹¹⁴ But the influence of such modernization schemes was clear as archaeological work in Egypt took place, especially in relation to foreign archaeological missions whose tenure in the country had become more reliant than ever on conforming to the wishes of Egyptian officials (however implicitly). In 1955 and 1956, for instance, the University Museum of the University of Pennsylvania undertook collaborative excavation work with the Department of Antiquities at the site of Mit Rahina (ancient Memphis), located just south of Cairo. The project was rhetorically (although not officially) connected to the technocratic rhetoric of overseas aid set forward by the US government since the inauguration of its "Point Four" development program under President Harry S. Truman: ostensibly designed to advance the needs of Egypt at the same time as developing American interests in the country, experts from the University Museum would train Egyptians in the practices of archaeological fieldwork. Beyond that Cold War–inspired goal, when the work had been negotiated, the University Museum's Egyptological representative, the German émigré Rudolf Anthes, had agreed that the excavation should take place at Mit Rahina because work at the site could support land reform and reclamation schemes. "I should like to stress that . . . the Egyptian government is immediately interested in its [Mit Rahina's] clearance," Anthes wrote. "The question is how far this area should be reserved to the Antiquities Department and the rest be given free to the peasants, for cultivation." Rather gently (and coupled with a firm belief in international scientific cooperation), the geographer and prehistorian Mustafa Amer, the department's first Egyptian director-general (and former rector of the University of Alexandria), had played Anthes's hand. Anthes now believed that archaeology, mobilized as a technocratic tool, could play a vital role in the future development both of Egypt's irrigable land resources and its people.¹¹⁵

The Mit Rahina excavations ended abruptly, a consequence not only of the 1956 Suez conflict, but also of general disinterest in the site.¹¹⁶ Post-Suez, however, with the revolutionary possibilities of archaeology made manifest, the necessity of excavating other, similar areas of Egypt's land began to be promoted under a changing departmental leadership. The 1957 Cultural Cooperation Agreement between Egypt and Poland led, among other things, to a Polish archaeological mission starting excavations at the site of Tell Atrib, located near the town of Banha in the Nile Delta. The site, as an article in *Egypt Travel Magazine* emphasized, had significant potential, because so few ancient

---

114. Alterman, *Egypt*, 78–80; El Shakry, *The Great*, 212.
115. For this episode, see Carruthers, "Visualizing," 278. For Amer, see El Shakry, *The Great*, 68.
116. Carruthers, "Visualizing."

settlements in Egypt had been excavated (the Mit Rahina excavations having ended almost as soon as they had begun). Ironically, the article noted that the building of the Aswan Dam had led to a rise in the level of groundwater both at Tell Atrib and elsewhere in Egypt, something with which the archaeologists digging at the site now had to contend. Nevertheless, the piece stated that "the attention of archaeologists should be turned to town sites," not least because "on cultivated lands the mounds [comprising sites like Tell Atrib] are a nuisance and are steadily cut into." Moreover, "for long ages the peasants have known that the decayed organic matter from town or cemetery makes an invaluable fertilizer."[117] Where once Reisner had been irritated by Egyptians digging archaeological sites for *sebakh*, now government policy seemed to permit such digging if sites had been in some way investigated. The development of irrigable land mattered, especially if "peasants" could be ordered in ways conducive to that process, and especially, too, if archaeologists could be persuaded to excavate it.

That development did not sit well with everyone, particularly since the Polish mission had proven itself only too pleased to undertake such work. The *Newsletter* of the American Research Center in Egypt noted that the Polish excavations had happened "as part of the cultural exchange between Egypt and Communist countries" and that "the [Egyptian] government is extending to them many courtesies and privileges," including "a share of the finds it has made."[118] The Cold War tension was implicit, but ever present. Deaccessioning was taking place in some US museums, and there was dwindling interest in sponsoring the British work that had helped to build US Egyptian collections. Yet how should American institutions apparently still eager for ancient Egyptian objects react to Poland's amenity to Egypt's fieldwork wishes?[119] Helen Wall (later Helen Jacquet-Gordon), an Egyptologist who had worked at Mit Rahina, told Anthes that

> it is essential for all the European countries not involved in the recent [Suez] debacle and of course for the U.S. too, to try to fill that cultural vacuum. There should be people here who can work together with the

---

117. Rowland Ellis, "Poland Digs in Egypt," *Egypt Travel Magazine* 37 (September 1957), 14.

118. Edward Wente, "Letters from Egypt," *American Research Center in Egypt, Incorporated: Newsletter* 26 (1957): 4. Alongside the Polish-Egyptian Cultural Cooperation Agreement, there was also a 1957 Cultural Agreement between Egypt and Czechoslovakia, which paved the way for the establishment of a Czechoslovak Institute of Egyptology in Cairo, and for which see Adéla Jůnová Macková, "Journey of Czechoslovak Cultural Delegation to Egypt in 1956: 'Cultural Agreement' between Egypt and the Czechoslovak Republic," *Acta Fakulty filozofické Západočeské univerzity v Pizni* 3 (2011): 101–110.

119. Stevenson, *Scattered*, 188–90, discusses this postwar reversal of American interest. In this instance (and during UNESCO's Nubian campaign), low-level Cold War tensions occasionally seem to have inflamed older object passions.

Egyptians, who can give advice without seeming to do it, who can by the example of their own work show tactfully how work should be done. If we do not do it, the Egyptians will be forced to take people from the Russian zone who are only too willing and eager to come here.[120]

At times, the revolutionary development of archaeology as part and parcel of Egyptian land reform and reclamation only served to heighten Cold War tensions, underlining the importance of following official wishes relating to it. Archaeological sites became constant backdrops for Nasser and other Free Officers guiding foreign leaders around Egypt. For instance, in January 1960, just before UNESCO's Nubian campaign began, Muhammad V, King of Morocco, visited Egypt and toured the Nile-side archaeological sites of Luxor. *Al-Ahram* ran a story headlined "The King and the President Amid Our Immortal [khālida] Antiquities," in which images of Nasser, Muhammad V, and Tharwat Okasha touring the temples of Karnak and Deir el-Bahari provided a powerful affirmation of the Egyptian president's apparent commitment to mobilizing the ancient past of the Nile Valley as part of Egypt's future.[121] Coupled with the geopolitical maneuvering evident in accompanying the leader of a recently independent (in 1956) and soon to be non-aligned (1961) country like Morocco around such places, the revolutionary symbolism attached to the Nile Valley's archaeological sites was obvious.

Even among Egyptians, tensions surrounding archaeology were high, as Abbas Bayoumi (then director-general of the Department of Antiquities) at one point had to deflect questions posed by a disgruntled *al-Ahram* journalist. The Polish excavations at Tell Atrib had reportedly uncovered a royal tomb. Noting that the work had been conducted with "permission from the Egyptian authorities" (*idhan sulutāt misriyya*), the reporter wanted to know when the mission would publish a communiqué on the results.[122] But tension, too, was coupled with excitement. In February 1960, just before the official launch of the Nubian campaign, the same newspaper ran an article headlined "The Greatest Archaeological Discovery [*azam kashf āthari*] in the History of Nubia" in relation to excavations already being run by the University of Cairo's Abdel Moneim Abu Bakr at the site of Aniba. "400 ancient tombs" had been found there, according to the article, pointing to the future archaeological possibilities not only of areas

---

120. Helen Wall to Rudolf Anthes, May 4, 1957. "Excavation Records: Egypt; Mitrahineh; Correspondence—Anthes, 1957–1958," Box 38, Folder 9, University of Pennsylvania Museum of Archaeology and Anthropology Archives, Philadelphia, PA (hereafter University Museum Archives).

121. "Al-Malik wa-l-Ra'is bayna Atharna al-Khalida [The king and the president amid our immortal antiquities]," *al-Ahram*, January 13, 1960.

122. "Athar Talaqi Adwa' 'ala Tarikh Misr" ["Antiquities shed light on the history of Egypt"], *al-Ahram*, April 14, 1957.

around the Nile, but also of Nubia itself.[123] As plans for the High Dam took shape, the role of archaeological work in them started to coalesce. The river and the land connected to it continued to play a crucial role in Egypt's archaeological future. Now, though, the necessity of attending to Egyptian wishes had started to clarify as Cold War tensions relating to archaeological work in Egypt heightened. To ease those tensions, someone, somewhere, would have to pay attention to the coming flood. The transformation of nature ultimately meant the transformation of culture, too.

The View from the Boat, Again

This somewhat forced process of entanglement began in the mid-1950s. While the Greek-Egyptian engineer Adrian Daninos had formulated plans for the High Dam as early as 1947, it was only in 1954, after Egypt's Permanent Council for the Development of National Production published a report on the matter, that the Free Officers decided to go ahead with construction and seek the necessary international funding.[124] Ahmad Shokr emphasizes that the initiation of the High Dam project "was enmeshed in broader transnational linkages that had histories predating the revolution, and reflected new kinds of global knowledge in multi-purpose development and national accounting." Contesting much of the commentary on the project, Shokr makes clear that the High Dam was not simply the result of a nebulous "authoritarian exceptionalism" attributed to the revolutionary Egyptian state by many of its detractors.[125] Rather—continuing the entanglement of large-scale irrigation projects with notions about the country's development—the analysis of the proposed structure using novel forms of statistical analysis linked to the appearance of "the economy" as a global sphere of governance meant that the High Dam became perceived by the Free Officers as "an inclusive solution appropriate for the exigencies of [Egyptian] agriculture and industry in the long-term future."[126]

Preliminary archaeological work connected to the High Dam reflected these conditions. Despite continued uncertainty surrounding funding for the project, Egypt's Department of Antiquities reacted to the likelihood of the dam's construction with concern for Nubian remains, manifesting a renewal of the sort of work carried out during the earlier Nubian archaeological surveys.

---

123. "Azam Kashf Athari fi Tarikh al-Nuba" ["Greatest archaeological discovery in the history of Nubia"], *al-Ahram*, February 25, 1960. For Abu Bakr, see Reid, *Contesting*.
124. Shokr, "Hydropolitics," 12.
125. Shokr, "Hydropolitics," 26.
126. Shokr, "Hydropolitics," 22–24.

Pre-Suez, at least, departmental officials couched that renewal in the language of international collegiality, connecting such work to the development discourse that circulated around projects like the one at Mit Rahina. Despite the Cold War policies buttressing such projects, officials from the Department of Antiquities seemed to have some belief in that work's value, launching a preliminary new Nubian survey that paid heed to global development rhetoric. The massive environmental transformation to be wrought by the High Dam would go ahead, but international archaeological assistance would be sought.[127]

Given these conditions, this new survey predictably remobilized colonial archaeological priorities. Once again, Nubia's salvageable past was circumscribed by the view from the boat. In December 1954 and January 1955, a committee appointed by Egypt's Higher Council of Antiquities sailed the (Egyptian) Nubian Nile on the Ministry of Public Works' boat Indiana to ascertain the danger posed by the High Dam's floodwaters to monuments and archaeological sites in the region.[128] Rather than colonial officials, the new committee comprised Egyptian experts trained during the colonial period, among them Sub-Director of the Department of Antiquities Selim Hassan, Professor of Ancient History of Egypt at Cairo University Ahmed Fakhry, and Chief Inspector of Antiquities for Upper Egypt Labib Habachi.[129] The committee reordered the colonial hierarchies of the previous Nubian surveys, publishing the report with recommendations not only in English and French, but also in Arabic, a language whose addition emphasized that reordering. Many of the committee's survey practices, however, remained familiar.

Traveling south up the Nile from Aswan, the committee visited the various monuments and sites located in proximity to the river without making physical interventions. Despite the priority given to such areas in earlier surveys, the committee's report continued to highlight how important these locations were. At Ballana, for instance, the report stated that

> the zone that lies on the banks of the Nile badly needs investigation, and the Committee feels that it is incumbent upon it to stress the importance of these zones. One or more missions should carry out excavations in

---

127. For that transformation, see Reynolds, "Building."
128. Egyptian Department of Antiquities, *Report on The Monuments of Nubia Likely to be Submerged by Sudd-el-'Āli Water* (Cairo: Government Press, 1955), 2.
129. Egyptian Department of Antiquities, *Report*, 1. For Hassan and Fakhry, see Reid, *Contesting*. For Habachi, see Jill Kamil, *Labib Habachi: The Life and Legacy of an Egyptologist* (Cairo: American University in Cairo Press, 2007). The other team members were Technical Sub-Director of Buildings in the Ministry of Education Mohamed Ahmed Ibrahim, Assistant Director of Works for the Department of Antiquities Mustapha Sobhi Mohamed, and Yousif Boutros of the Inspectorate of Upper Egypt Projects of the Ministry of Public Works.

this locality, in order that no objects of value to the history of the country should be lost.[130]

Once the cause of national sensation, now the excavation of Ballana's riverside constituted an issue of national concern: a colonial practice continued as postcolonial priority. Because submersion of ancient remains by the High Dam's floodwaters would be total, meanwhile, other of the survey's recommendations repurposed earlier work in Nubia by echoing its preservationist concerns. The survey's report stated:

> as the Egyptian Government, in the previous schemes for the construction and heightening of the Aswan Dam, had focused its attention on the monuments of Nubia, and had facilitated the recording of inscriptions and the excavation of cemeteries (although then the damage was partial or limited), so now its vigilance should be doubled when the great scheme of the High Dam is put into force, lest all these priceless historical relics should be lost for ever beneath the water.[131]

Vigilance doubled meant vigilance repeated. Interestingly, though (and much as had previously been the case), such vigilance did not necessarily lead to the total protection of ancient temples and archaeological sites from floodwater. Picturesque—sometimes even total—ruination constituted a continuing possibility, a selective process made more likely because "at the time when the Committee visited Nubia . . . many of the temples were completely submerged and the Committee was unable to examine them."[132] Representative were the comments made about—and the preservationist practices suggested for—the temple of Debod, located just south of Aswan:

> Although a complete scientific publication was made of this temple, it is necessary to make a model of it. It is also desirable that cinematographic records should be made of all its architectural features, while Latex or squeeze paper impressions could be taken of its inscriptions, and the writings and paintings on the walls could be photographed.[133]

At Debod, future boats would sail over what would become underwater ruins. At Philae, meanwhile, such ruination would be less total, enabling the continuation of a more familiar picturesque experience. Taking advice from the relevant authorities, the committee noted that the construction of the High

---

130. Egyptian Department of Antiquities, *Report*, 19.
131. Egyptian Department of Antiquities, *Report*, 4.
132. Egyptian Department of Antiquities, *Report*, 8.
133. Egyptian Department of Antiquities, *Report*, 8.

Dam would lower the level of floodwater around the island, albeit to a permanent height. The island would remain a picturesque, flooded ruin, with the added possibility that that flood could be wholly abated by the construction of breakwaters around the island.[134]

Mirroring previous strategies, the new survey was selective in terms of its attitude to flooding. Even Abu Simbel, the survey committee warned, might not be salvaged from the High Dam's floodwaters: it could well be the case that Egyptians would have "to sacrifice it for the good of the country."[135] Geologists could be consulted as to the feasibility of protecting the sandstone of the two temples at the site, but even this outcome was not guaranteed due to that material's "porous nature."[136] By 1955, the Nubia that might be preserved was always already a selective space, one whose existence depended on the building of alliances between a small group of officials and experts.

The new survey's final recommendations also contained echoes from the past. The report proposed sending eight separate missions to Nubia, including ones devoted to Abu Simbel, Philae, the other temples and rock inscriptions, and archaeological excavations. The remaining four missions, meanwhile, echoed the way in which Middle Eastern archaeology more widely used multiple media to create credible documentation: a "cinematographic and photographic mission," one "for taking latex or paper impressions," one "for making models of temples and casts of some of the scenes," and one for "the preparation of the plans and designs of all the temples of Nubia."[137] Egyptians would be placed in charge of the work as a whole: "an Egyptian archaeologist is to be appointed as president-in-chief, and be assisted by an Egyptian archaeologist as deputy."[138] Meanwhile, the committee considered it "quite satisfactory that the first three missions should be presided over by a young man from the staff of the Antiquities Department." Their report, however, stated that "the other four missions should be headed by archaeologists of world-repute and vast experience, and known to have a good control over the work." In terms of more general staffing, too, "if there is any difficulty in obtaining qualified Egyptians for the purpose, foreigners may be employed, as none will be more co-operative in that great scientific work."[139] Nubia had

---

134. Egyptian Department of Antiquities, *Report*, 7.
135. Egyptian Department of Antiquities, *Report*, 16. That Abu Simbel was not worth saving was a view shared by several Egyptologists, for which see Allais, "Integrities."
136. Egyptian Department of Antiquities, *Report*, 17.
137. Egyptian Department of Antiquities, *Report*, 23–27. For the use of multiple media in archaeological recording in Iraq, see Mirjam Brusius, "The Field in the Museum: Puzzling Out Babylon in Berlin," *Osiris* 32 (2017): 278–79.
138. Egyptian Department of Antiquities, *Report*, 40.
139. Egyptian Department of Antiquities, *Report*, 40.

not yet ceased to be an international fief, foreshadowing UNESCO's involvement in the region.

Reflecting previous work, it was unclear to what extent Nubians themselves had any say in this situation. Separated from the region's past, they appear to have become objects of ethnological and museological inquiry, a startling mid-twentieth-century example of "living relics" whose extinction was close to foretold.[140] The committee's report suggested that a museum be built in Aswan not only to "house the antiquities to be transferred from Nubia," but also "the models, casts, impressions, photographs, cinematographic films, and everything relating to that zone," to ultimately become "a scientific institute for the study of Nubian antiquities and history."

Furthermore, this museum would contain "a special section . . . to illustrate the social life, customs and industries of Nubia, before they disappear from existence."[141] The committee's suggestion foreshadowed the Nubia Museum inaugurated in Aswan in 1997, as well as the ethnological campaign that would be carried out in Egyptian Nubia during the High Dam's construction. The proposal also reflected the way in which contemporary Nubian life was now viewed separately to the region's ancient remains, in addition to the way in which that separation had cast the Nubians as an object of intervention, echoing other Egyptian development schemes. The view from the boat had triumphed.

Sailing By

In February 1956, two months after Britain and the United States offered to underwrite the construction of the High Dam, the newspaper *Akhbar al-Yawm* excitedly reported that an Egyptian committee of ministers and twelve engineers and "antiquities men" (*rijāl al-athār*) had proposed a budget of six-hundred-thousand Egyptian pounds to protect Nubian antiquities (a figure presumably based on the new survey's report). More notable, however, was the process by which this decision had been made: the proposal occurred after the committee had toured Nubia by steamer (*bākhira*, pl. *bawākhir*). Salvageable Nubia had by this point solidified: bereft of any actual Nubians, the region's material remains had become circumscribed by "the temples and

---

140. On "living relics" elsewhere—and the perception of them as tied to natural, not cultural heritage—see, e.g., Paul Basu and Vinita Damodaran, "Colonial Histories of Heritage: Legislative Migrations and the Politics of Preservation," *Past and Present* Supplement 10 (2015): 243–44.

141. Egyptian Department of Antiquities, *Report*, 32.

antiquities" (*al-maʿābid wa-l-athār*) that the committee visited and the means of transport from which they viewed them.[142]

Such riverine fixity also limited potential cooperation between Egypt and Sudan, whose Nubian territory was itself due to suffer the High Dam's flooding. Arriving by boat on the Egyptian-Sudanese border at Wadi Halfa, the new Egyptian survey's prearranged meeting with members of the Sudanese authorities failed to materialize. Sudan's Commissioner for Archaeology Peter Shinnie claimed by telephone not to have been informed about the Egyptian group's presence, and his assistant, Thabit Hassan Thabit, was traveling. Unable to move beyond the border, the Egyptians turned their boat around.[143] As plans for the High Dam and preservation work in Nubia solidified, boats and the borders among which they moved conditioned the pasts that could be written.

The Egyptian Nile, and means of sailing along it, had sealed the fate of Nubia. Between the Department of Antiquities' own survey of the region and the launch of UNESCO's campaign in 1960, two further trips along the river secured the campaign's future. The first took place in January 1955, when Christiane Desroches Noblecourt, an Egyptologist and UNESCO expert working in Cairo, invited Luther Evans, UNESCO's then director-general, to fly from Cairo to Wadi Halfa and then sail north to Abu Simbel. By doing so, he could see for himself the temples that the High Dam's floodwaters would submerge, making a preservation campaign seem like a more pressing necessity.[144]

The second trip took place in 1959, when an international committee of experts assembled in Egypt to plan the Nubian campaign's work. The committee spent ten days visiting "the [Egyptian] Nubian temples and the region's most important archaeological sites" (*aham manāṭiqihā al-āthariyya*). They did so on "their own dedicated steamer" (*bākhira al-mukhaṣiṣa lahum*), a vessel named the Shaykh al-Balad, which was fondly memorialized by Tharwat Okasha.[145] Such memorialization, however, rested on other forms—and other scales—of work. In combination with the view from the boat, it was the documentation practices highlighted by the Department of Antiquities that would make "Nubia" cohere.

---

142. "600 Alf Junaih li-Himayyat al-Athar min Miyya' al-Sadd al-ʿAli" ["Six hundred thousand pounds for the protection of antiquities from the water of the High Dam"], *Akhbar al-Yawm*, February 18, 1956.
143. Egyptian Department of Antiquities, *Report*, 20.
144. Noblecourt, *La grande*, 132–36.
145. Okasha, *Mudhakkirati*, 528.

CHAPTER 2

Documenting Nubia

UNESCO's Special Representative for Nubian Affairs in Cairo, Louis Christophe, was riven with anxiety: so much so that in January 1963 he wrote a letter to headquarters explaining why his concern was so acute. From his base at Cairo's UNESCO-backed Centre d'étude et de documentation sur l'Ancienne Égypte (or CEDAE, the Centre of Documentation and Studies on Ancient Egypt, whose name was used inconsistently), Christophe wrote to Paris complaining that he had not received any number of the preliminary reports on fieldwork that archaeological teams involved in UNESCO's Nubian campaign were obliged to send to him. Christophe was concerned that "scholars the world around should be kept up to date about the work of different expeditions taking place in Egypt."[1] It seemed, however, that his expectation of making UNESCO's mission global would not be met.

UNESCO predicated its Nubian campaign on the organization's ability to generate credible acts of monumental preservation and archaeological excavation. Reflecting long-standing Egyptological practice—and furthering an epistemological slippage between the categories of "monument" and "document" that art historian Erwin Panofsky had encouraged in the mid-1930s—documentation

---

1. Louis Christophe to UNESCO's Service des Monuments de Nubie, January 7, 1963. Folder CA/120/39, 069 (62) N: 930.26: "Excavations-General," UNESCO Archives, Paris (hereafter UNESCO Archives).

and archiving constituted one way of demonstrating such credibility globally.[2] CEDAE had thus been tasked both with producing elements of this documentation and with collecting paperwork produced by other organizations during the campaign. The institution's logo was the ancient Egyptian goddess Maat, who, as one promotional booklet noted, represented *"exactitude"* and *"équilibre,"* and was responsible for *"protégeant la Documentation"*: the protection of (capitalized, no less) Documentation.[3] Yet as Christophe's letter implied, the equilibrium of CEDAE's—and the wider campaign's—work had been thrown off balance, and not simply due to this one event.

In late 1961, in the months after police carried out a massacre at a demonstration of pro-Front de libération nationale Algerians in Paris, several officials working for the French government in Cairo were arrested on espionage charges, alongside individuals accused of supplying them with information. The case was dropped by the Egyptian government in April 1962, a month after the Egypt-supported Algerian War of Independence ended. Proceedings, though, did not conclude before the trial connected to the case had begun.[4] Unfortunately, as a lengthy report in the Egyptian magazine *al-Musawwar* stated, one of the accused "French spies" (*jawāsīs Faransā*), Alexander Papadopoulo, was at the time an *"expert in archaeology"* (*khabīr al-āthār*) for CEDAE.[5] In reality, Papadopoulo had been employed by the institution to study its commercial and external services.[6] Reputational damage had, however, been done. Nonetheless, if paperwork was properly filed, at least there was a chance that CEDAE's—and, by extension, UNESCO's—reputation might be bolstered, the apparent sovereign crimes of its employee safely forgotten.

Such forgiveness was unlikely. Paper and paperwork powered the Nubian campaign at the same time as it helped channel significant tension, particularly in terms of who could claim sovereignty over the project and the knowledge it produced. UNESCO's publicity machine emphasized the campaign's

---

2. On Panofsky and this slippage, which gained ground during World War II, see Allais, *Designs*, 95–96.

3. *République Arabe Unie: Centre de documentation sur l'Égypte ancienne* (Paris: Délégation Permanente de la R.A.U. auprès de l'U.N.E.S.C.O., 1959), inside front cover.

4. "Espionage Charges Against Members of French Assets Mission," *Middle East Record* 2 (1961): 643–44.

5. Husni al-Hussaini, "Jawasis Faransa 'Amam Mahkamat 'Amn al-Dawla" ["French spies appear before the State Security Court"], *al-Musawwar*, January 19, 1962. In the same article, CEDAE is described as a *"majlis"* (council), which does not correspond to the institution's official title. Given Papadopoulo's employment history, though, the referent is clear.

6. Alexander Papadopoulo to Director-General, UNESCO (authorized by Christiane Desroches Noblecourt, March 12, 1961), "Rapport final sur des services commerciaux du Centre de Documentation d'Egyptologie." Folder CA/12/7, 069 (62) AMS (Part 13): "Documentation sur les Peintures et Inscriptions en Haute-Egypte-Programme de Participation," UNESCO Archives.

spectacular and innovative feats of engineering and recording.[7] Yet this narrative of innovation has invariably been overstated, not least because the practices of writing on, reading from, printing onto, and archiving paper played a major part in making these spectacular events happen, in addition to enabling the mundane work of archaeological survey and excavation. Documentation building on earlier norms created the possibility of the Nubian campaign's existence. At the same time, however, documentary practice helped to create the conditions for the continued undoing of the project, echoing David Edgerton's argument that the history of "technology-in-use" reveals a very different history to that of technology-as-innovation.[8]

As the campaign took place, UNESCO revealed itself as similar to other postwar intergovernmental organizations, not least by producing a mountain of administrative and procedural papers.[9] A constant stream of such material emanated from, and found its way back to, UNESCO House in Paris: letters, memos, carbon copies, telegrams, contracts, invoices, purchase orders, and reports. In Egypt and Sudan, too, archaeological and engineering missions spent their time producing various types of paper, among them correspondence, diaries, find registers, account books, photographs, and plans. The material played a sovereign role in more ways than one.

Paper made Nubia, at the same time as constituting not only who Nubia might be made by, but also to whom the region and its past belonged. As in the case of the High Dam, moreover, the position of documentation as central to the Nubian campaign became so all-encompassing that it included the self-referential recording of paperwork in action. Highlighting the material's slippage between stuff of performance and stuff of necessity, the Egyptian director Youssef Chahine's film *al-Nas wa-l-Nil* (*The People and the Nile*, a Russian-Egyptian coproduction released in 1968 but then banned in Egypt) features scenes in which Fahmi (played by 'Emad Hamdi), an Egyptian employed as a project foreman, sits at tables covered in the paper that, when handled correctly, accurately, and by the appropriate person, would enable the High Dam's construction.[10] Working in Nubia, archaeologists, Egyptologists, and other specialists produced their own documentary performances. One photo, taken during excavations conducted by the University Museum of the University of

---

7. See Allais, "Integrities."

8. David Edgerton, *The Shock of the Old: Technology and Global History since 1900* (New York: Oxford University Press, 2007), xi.

9. For the connection of this reporting practice to the UN and to a general postwar ideology of public information, see Emma Rothschild, "The Archives of Universal History," *Journal of World History* 19, no. 3 (2008): 375–401.

10. *Al-Nas wa-l-Nil* [*The People and the Nile*], dir. Youssef Chahine, 1968.

FIGURE 2.1. "Farouk and Mr. Queloz" doing paperwork at the dig house, Arminna West, Egypt. Farouk, as further records reveal, is Farouk Gomaa, an inspector of the Egyptian Department of Antiquities. Yale Peabody Museum of Natural History Archives, Division of Anthropology, Arminna West Archive, ANTAR.035515.

Pennsylvania and the Yale University Peabody Museum at the site of Arminna West in Egypt, illustrates "Farouk and Mr. Queloz" writing away inside the expedition's dig house (figure 2.1), the Egyptian not afforded an honorific even as he and Queloz did the same work.

Another image, taken for UNESCO by the (Hungary-born but Paris-resident) photojournalist Paul Almásy, shows one of CEDAE's consultants, the architect Jean Jacquet, making "an architectural survey" of the temple of Ramses II at Abu Simbel.[11] Jacquet sits working with and writing on paper and is surrounded by that material and the tools of architectural drawing. He is also accompanied

---

11. For Almásy, who did considerable work for UN organizations, see "Paul Almasy" on Deutsche Börse Photography Foundation website, n.d., accessed May 27, 2020, https://www.deutscheboersep hotographyfoundation.org/en/collect/artists/paul-almasy.php.

FIGURE 2.2. Jean Jacquet (and Helen Jacquet-Gordon?) doing paperwork at Abu Simbel. UNESCO Digital Archives PHOTO0000003311, copyright UNESCO/Paul Almásy.

by an unnamed woman (figure 2.2). Paper became entangled with Nubia in ways that often seemed to make it clear whose work counted there: presumably the woman is Jacquet's wife, Helen Jacquet-Gordon.

In this chapter, I explore CEDAE's foundation, showing how paperwork and documentation took on this central role during the Nubian campaign and emphasizing how the project's work was rooted in forms of knowledge linked to colonial practice. CEDAE arrived several years before the start of the Nubian campaign proper. Undermining the sort of cohesive temporality retrospectively attached to the project by UNESCO, discussions relating to the new "documentation center" had in fact begun as early as 1952. Starting at Abu Simbel, the institution's personnel recorded the ancient temples of Egyptian Nubia from 1955 onward. And the organization not only lent the Nubian campaign its documentary foundations, but also made clear their genealogy in older, colonial-era—and to some extent Francophone—Egyptological practices: practices that, through their concentration on the epigraphic and architectural recording of ancient temples, reflected the concentration on Nubia's picturesque ruination of earlier decades. Colonial pasts helped to propel postcolonial futures. Perhaps more than any other, meanwhile, paperwork was the medium that enabled that process. Work at the smallest scale contributed to the image of Nubia at the largest.

On Spectacle and the Archive

Paperwork was both a crutch and a curse to the Nubian campaign. Represented carefully, the often-prosaic character of CEDAE's work provided a useful means of kick-starting the global spectacle of the project: a documentary bind from which the campaign was unable to escape. In the February 1960 issue of *The UNESCO Courier* used to launch the campaign, an article about CEDAE described the scene at Abu Simbel:

> At the feet of Ramses and his queen, Nefertari, scaffolding went up. Archaeologists, philologists, photographers, draughtsmen, architects and moulders arrived on the site. Work began at dawn and often went on far into the night since the heat and blinding light prevented photographers from working in the afternoon. Invaded by cameras, searchlights and generating plants, the age-old sanctuary began to look like a film studio.[12]

Documentation made Nubia. Lending this process some innovative spectacle, UNESCO emphasized that CEDAE had employed the services of France's Institut géographique national in order to make use of

> a new science—photogrammetry—which makes it possible to determine the shape and dimensions of an object from two stereoscopic photographs and then to reconstitute it in the laboratory in the form of an exact model.[13]

This photogrammetric work would, the article claimed, overcome the issue that "photography, like drawing and even architectural plans, contains a certain element of subjectivity which can produce various degrees of distortion." Photogrammetry instead allowed "the absolute accuracy demanded by scientific recording," a process that "may even make possible the discovery of

---

12. "Under the Sign of Maat, Goddess of Precision," *The UNESCO Courier*, February 1960, 40.
13. "Under the Sign," 41.

architectural laws as yet undisclosed by Egyptologists."[14] Hyperbole unbound, UNESCO made photogrammetry the centerpiece of a Nubian spectacle focused on technological novelty, obscuring the more "everyday technologies" of documentation actually employed to do most of CEDAE's work (and promoting this marvel in an institutional magazine not yet translated into Arabic).[15] Consequently, CEDAE, like the High Dam itself, had the potential to generate floodwaters of anxiety, not least through its material perpetuation of older forms of knowledge.[16]

Such consequences were not novel. Echoing Ann Laura Stoler's suggestion to "explore the [archival] grain with care and read along it first,"[17] Christina Riggs shows how the mutability of one photographic negative held in the archives of the Egyptologist Howard Carter cautions against writing a straightforward history of photography's place in the archaeological archive, tracing instead the contradictions and anxieties that the negative has generated.[18] By doing so, Riggs echoes Stoler's caution against accepting "the notion [in colonial studies] that 'granting epistemic warrant is a covert way of distributing power'" without thinking about "how that warrant was granted, how firmly entrenched, and how much debate accompanied that process,"[19] or thinking about "the assumption that colonial statecraft was always intent on accumulating more knowledge rather than on a selective winnowing and reduction of it."[20]

What anxieties, then, did the making of the (post-) colonial archive constitute? As Todd Shepard discusses, the relationship of archival practices with the postwar foundation of newly independent nation-states was—and continues to be—contentious.[21] In the case of Egypt, Omnia El Shakry emphasizes that the historian Ibrahim ʿAbduh described the period of Nasser's presidency as possessing a "history without documents."[22] El Shakry also suggests, though, that reimagining decolonization "as an ongoing process and series of struggles,"

---

14. "Under the Sign," 43.

15. David Arnold, *Everyday Technology: Machines and the Making of India's Modernity* (Chicago: University of Chicago Press, 2013). For UNESCO's spectacle, see Allais, "Integrities."

16. For an abridged version of this analysis, see William Carruthers, "Records of Dispossession: Archival Thinking and UNESCO's Nubian Campaign in Egypt and Sudan," *International Journal of Islamic Architecture* 9, no. 2 (2020): 287–314.

17. Stoler, *Along*, 50.

18. Christina Riggs, "Photography and Antiquity in the Archive, or How Howard Carter Moved the Road to the Valley of the Kings," *History of Photography* 40, no. 3 (2016): 267–82.

19. Stoler, *Along*, 43, citing Steven Fuller, *Social Epistemology* (Bloomington: Indiana University Press, 2002), 10.

20. Stoler, *Along*, 50.

21. Todd Shepard, "'Of Sovereignty': Disputed Archives, 'Wholly Modern' Archives, and the Post-Decolonization French and Algerian Republics, 1962–2012," *American Historical Review* 120, no. 3 (2015): 869–83.

22. El Shakry, "'History,'" 922.

including figures "bypassed in or excised from traditional archives," provides one way of addressing this issue.[23] Attending to the work of Egyptologists, archaeologists, and governmental and nongovernmental officials with whom they became involved, I follow El Shakry's advice. In the last analysis, the documentation of Nubia constitutes the documentation of tension between these groups.

Egyptology and the Archive

Archiving drove this tension. The intersection of the Nubian campaign with practices common to Egyptology meant that, despite the narrative of technological innovation promoted by UNESCO, long-standing archival actions attached themselves to work carried out in Nubia and to the bureaucracy that attempted to organize what happened there. Documentation constituted the stuff around which that bureaucracy and the campaign's participants were able to gather and attempt to negotiate their various interests.

CEDAE's links to Egyptological norms are central to this story. Following Lorraine Daston's terminology, the discipline constituted not only a veritable "science of the archive," but also a science entangled with Egyptian sovereignty itself.[24] CEDAE constituted one resolution of that archival-documentary imperative. The territory of Egypt had long been the focus of writings that documented its geography and history, not least in the classical Arabic genre of the khiṭaṭ. For example, the *Kitab al-Mawaʿiz wa-l-Iʿtibar bi-Dhikr al-Khitat wa-l-Athar* of the Mamluk-era scholar al-Maqrizi (1364–1442), written between 820 and 840 h. (1417/18–36/37), documented the topography and toponymy of Cairo.[25] Centuries later, the scholar and one-time minister both of public works and education ʿAli Mubarak's *al-Khitat al-Tawfiqiyya al-Jadida*, published between 1888 and 1889, mapped Egypt's built landscape in the light of projects carried out by the Ottoman-Egyptian state.[26] As British irrigation engineers ignored the local knowledge contained in such works in favor of practices developed in colonial India, however, so too did such studies exist in contrast to those written by the Europeans—and European-trained scholars—connected to Egyptology and

---

23. El Shakry, "'History,'" 925.
24. Lorraine Daston, "The Sciences of the Archive," *Osiris* 27 (2012): 156–87.
25. Taqi al-Din Ahmad ibn ʿAli ibn ʿAbd al-Qadir ibn Muhammad al-Maqrizi, *Kitab al-Mawaʿiz wa-l-Iʿtibar bi-Dhikr al-Khitat wa-l-Athar* [Book of lessons and reflections recalling plans and monuments], 2 vols. (Bulaq: 1853).
26. Derr, *The Lived Nile*, 31–32. For the publication itself, see ʿAli Mubarak, *al-Khitat al-Tawfiqiyya al-Jadida li-Misr wa-l-Qahira wa-Muduniha wa-Biladiha al-Qadima wa-l-Shahira* [Plans of the new Tawfiqiyya for Egypt, Cairo, and its old and famous cities and lands], 3rd ed. (Cairo: Matbaʿat Dar al-Wathaʾiq wa-l-Kutub al-Qawmiyya bi-l-Qahira, 2005).

its disciplinary genealogies.²⁷ As Anne Godlewska has noted, the "map, image and text" of the Napoleonic *Description de l'Égypte* not only chronicled what Napoleon's *savants* "found" in the French-occupied territory, but also represented "a construction of Egypt designed to replace Egypt itself," one that could be "taken home and mathematically and rigorously interpreted in the silence of French libraries, laboratories and museums without the difficult complications associated with colonialism."²⁸ If, following Daston, what distinguishes the sciences of the archive is that "practices of collection, collation, and preservation [are] conceived as an intrinsically collective undertaking—and one that extends into both past and future," then CEDAE was not all that different from the *Description*, despite the institution's removal in time.²⁹ Like the *Description*, CEDAE constituted what seemed to be the material embodiment of this process: attempting to ensure Egyptology's future documentary endeavors at the same time as neutralizing previous failures from which many of the institution's practices nevertheless derived.

Such failure matters because it emphasizes how success in creating CEDAE necessitated finding not only a way to mobilize various, apparently conflicting, interests, but also doing so in a way that elided or rendered void the questions of sovereignty that such interests inevitably raised. Preserving ancient Egyptian remains through the collection and publication of documentary material did not constitute a self-evident good, despite suggestions by backers of such plans. During the 1920s, the American Egyptologist James Henry Breasted proposed the creation of a new museum and research institute for Cairo, to be backed (like his own OI—or Oriental Institute—at the University of Chicago) by John D. Rockefeller Jr. As Jeffrey Abt relates, central to Breasted's institute was to be a library "over two stories high," a place that "conformed with Breasted's scholarly priorities for Egyptology which de-emphasized excavation in favor of epigraphy, interpretation, and publication."³⁰ Alongside other projects, the institute would produce "an architectural survey of ancient Egyptian buildings, a general handbook of Egyptian archaeology 'such as we possess for Greece and Rome,' [and] a history of the development of Egyptian hieroglyphs."³¹

---

27. For British irrigation engineers and their forms of knowledge, see Derr, *The Lived Nile*, 31–35.
28. Anne Godlewska, "Map, Text and Image: The Mentality of Enlightened Conquerors; a New Look at the *Description de l'Égypte*," *Transactions of the Institute of British Geographers* 20, no. 1 (1995): 5–28, quoting article abstract.
29. Daston, "The Sciences," 162.
30. Jeffrey Abt, "Toward a Historian's Laboratory: The Breasted-Rockefeller Museum Projects in Egypt, Palestine, and America," *Journal of the American Research Center in Egypt* 33 (1996): 182–83.
31. Abt, "Toward," 183.

Breasted's proposed institute had the collection and publication of documentation at its heart. He also, however, conceived of the establishment as a place "designed to serve the needs of visiting scholars and western researchers and museums," the collective whom he presumed to have the most need of the institution.[32] Colonial habit died hard and, ultimately, this and a series of other arrogant presuppositions led to the project's failure. Breasted's plans stated that an international commission dominated by foreign Egyptologists would control the institution, since he perceived Egyptians to be lacking the know-how to run it. In interwar Egypt, when (the then Egyptian, now) Cairo University was in fact training a growing number of Egyptians in Egyptological practice—and calls for complete British withdrawal from the country started to reach fever pitch—not one of this newly trained group ever seems to have been consulted about either the institute or the museum.[33] When Breasted presented his plans to Egypt's King Fu'ad in early 1926, then, they were turned down. Ahmad Ziwar, the country's prime minister, is reported to have said that "the conditions are absolutely unacceptable, they infringe upon the sovereignty of Egypt!"[34] Breasted wanted to instantiate documentation at the center of Egypt's past, but could no longer afford to ignore Egyptian interests in the process of doing so. Sovereignty—in this instance figured through the ownership of, and ability to control, documentary information—mattered.

Despite this tension, a documentary prerogative continued to operate within Egyptology. Moreover, when mobilized in a way that satisfied the interests surrounding it, documentation started to become something of a boundary object, a "common coin which makes possible new kinds of joint endeavor" in the making of knowledge.[35] Ironically, it was the 1952 Free Officers' coup that gave added impetus to this documentary imperative, in addition to the chain of events, ending in British withdrawal from Egypt, that the coup helped to initiate. Political change promoted a knowledge practice that not only intersected with the colonial administration of Egypt, but which now used UNESCO's place within the milieu of Parisian high culture to attempt to restore Francophone dominance to the administration of the Egyptian past.

---

32. Abt, "Toward," 184.
33. Abt, "Toward," 176.
34. Abt, "Toward," 184.
35. Susan Leigh Star and James R. Griesemer, "Institutional Ecology, 'Translations' and Boundary Objects: Amateurs and Professionals in Berkeley's Museum of Vertebrate Zoology, 1907–39," *Social Studies of Science* 19 (1989): 413.

Documenting Egypt, Asserting Francophonie?

Egypt's Antiquities Service had been headed by Frenchmen since its 1858 foundation, a condition enshrined in the Anglo-French Entente Cordiale of 1904.[36] Yet the Free Officers' coup meant that the institution's then director-general, the long-embattled Canon Étienne Drioton, had been removed from his post as he summered in Europe.[37] In November that year, the Centre Culturel of the French Embassy in Egypt reported that Drioton had viewed his *"contrat résilié"* (rescinded contract). That action, though, produced other documentary results. Alongside Drioton had been Alexandre Stoppelaëre, a Belgian artist who had not only worked for the Antiquities Service restoring ancient tombs located on the West Bank of the Nile at Luxor (ancient Thebes) but had also been married to Léonie Ricou, a Parisian hostess who had welcomed the likes of Picasso, Modigliani, and Brancusi to her early twentieth-century salons on the Boulevard Raspail.[38] The cultured Egyptologists played a persuasive hand, and documentation constituted the ace up their sleeves. Jean Thomas, director of UNESCO's Department of Cultural Activities (and a man unabashedly pro-France), received a letter from the French Embassy singing the praises of the two men and enclosing a plan, originally drawn up by Stoppelaëre in 1947. Jaime Torres Bodet, soon to resign as UNESCO's director-general, had, it was claimed, apparently received this project with interest in 1949.[39] The scheme was nothing if not archival.

Stoppelaëre proposed the institution of a "Centre de Documentation Archeologique [*sic*] et Artistique." The institution's employees would make an exhaustive photographic survey of the paintings and sculptures of the Theban tombs, then make those records available to archaeologists, artists, and the public. Stoppelaëre argued that this work was necessary due to the destruction caused by atmospheric agents and poorly executed restorations. Yet "above all," he noted, documentation would counter systematic looting, hinting at (although never making explicit) a long-standing and widely circulating

---

36. Reid, *Whose*, 195–96.

37. Donald Malcolm Reid, "Indigenous Egyptology: The Decolonization of a Profession?" *Journal of the American Oriental Society* 105, no. 2 (1985): 244. On Drioton, see Michèle Juret, *Étienne Drioton: l'Égypte, une passion* (Haroué: Gérard Louis, 2013).

38. For Stoppelaëre and Ricou, see Carol Vogel, "An Unknown Brancusi Pops Up, with Its Box," *The New York Times*, March 25, 2005.

39. Philippe Ribeyrol to Jean Thomas, November 21, 1952. Folder CA/12/7, 069 (62) AMS (Part 1): "Documentation sur les Peintures et Inscriptions en Haute-Egypte-Programme de Participation," UNESCO Archives. In his *U.N.E.S.C.O.* (Paris: Gallimard, 1962), 17, Thomas asserted that "if France has exercised influence over UNESCO, it is nothing to do with a privileged regime, but instead due to the personal authority of its representatives and by the continuity and quality of its intellectual contribution."

trope that suggested that inhabitants of villages surrounding—and, in some cases, on top of—the tombs were antiquity thieves. At the heart of the proposed institution was to be a systematized *"fichier archeologique* [sic]" (an archaeological card catalogue). The cards within this catalogue were to be of a standard size, organized according to various themes, and further organized by color according to what the cards contained: photographs, plans, and copies of the texts located on tomb walls; *"notices techniques"* (presumably tomb measurements); and bibliographic details. Alongside this card catalogue would be a photography studio, a dark room, a drawing office, an office for archaeological and epigraphic study, and printing facilities.[40]

Stoppelaëre's plan made the stuff of the archive the stuff of Egypt's—and perhaps of France's—past, envisioning an institution combining card and paper with photography, epigraphy, and draughtsmanship that would lend his vision of ancient Egypt a certain sort of moral and physical sovereignty. His Centre de Documentation would be a boundary object in which, he hoped, UNESCO would take an interest, enjoying as the plan did the backing of the members of France's Académie des beaux-arts.[41] UNESCO, in turn, was enthusiastic, only professing one reservation. John W. Taylor, the organization's acting director-general, noted that Stoppelaëre's plans would *"déborde très largement"* ("far exceed") the limits of UNESCO's current budget. Concerning as this issue was, however, it did not stop the organization consulting on putting into place a more specific plan.[42] Nor did it stop Jean Thomas writing to J. K. Van der Haagen of UNESCO's Division of Museums and Monuments wondering whether, given the project's importance, *"crédit special* [sic]" could be raised to fund it.[43] Presented the right way, documentation had the ability to persuade, at least in Paris.

Almost immediately, questions were raised about what sort of archive the proposed documentation center might represent and what the institution's practices should comprise. Such rancor indicates how easily different interests circulating around Egypt's past gathered around documentary practices. As

---

40. Stoppelaëre to Jaime Torres Bodet, November 20, 1952. Folder CA/12/7, 069 (62) AMS (Part 1), UNESCO Archives. On the Luxor West Bank's inhabitants, see e.g., Timothy Mitchell, "Making the Nation: The Politics of Heritage in Egypt," in *Consuming Tradition, Manufacturing Heritage: Global Norms and Urban Forms in the Age of Tourism*, ed. Nezar AlSayyad (London: E. and F. Spon and Routledge, 2001), 212–39; Kees van der Spek, *The Modern Neighbors of Tutankhamun: History, Life, and Work in the Villages of the Theban West Bank* (New York: Oxford University Press, 2011).

41. Adolphe Boschot to Director-General of UNESCO, February 16, 1953. Folder CA/12/7, 069 (62) AMS (Part 1), UNESCO Archives.

42. Taylor to Adolphe Boschot, March 5, 1953. Folder CA/12/7, 069 (62) AMS (Part 1), UNESCO Archives.

43. Thomas to Van der Haagen, February 27, 1953. Folder CA/12/7, 069 (62) AMS (Part 1), UNESCO Archives.

soon as UNESCO took Stoppelaëre's suggestion seriously, the stuff of the archive started to take on outsize importance, particularly among the European scholars with a vested interest in creating such an institution. For instance, Henri Chevrier, a French architect, wrote a report for UNESCO stating that the project of establishing a photographic archive was urgent. He also, however, suggested that the photographs taken by the proposed center should be applied to index cards according to the method used at Luxor's temple of Karnak, where he was employed as director of works. In the Egyptological archive, the ideal form of index card was not self-evident, and neither was the identity of the person charged with their keeping. Chevrier therefore reasoned that an expert-in-charge could be engaged either from within or outside Egypt. He also suggested that *"les deux bons photographes du Caire,"* [K. S.] Diradour and "Hassia," could well be made to compete for the work. Chevrier was less enthusiastic, though, about letting the Egyptian government appoint a driver for the mission, reasoning that the institution was "incapable" of appointing a competent *"chauffeur mécanicien."*[44] Perhaps there were some ways for Europeans to reach agreement about the documentary process after all.

Elsewhere, the actions of the Griffith Institute of the Ashmolean Museum in Oxford suggested that reaching such a consensus might be difficult. Members of the institution's Committee of Management were furious that they had not been consulted about Stoppelaëre's plan. Donald B. Harden, the Roman glass specialist then acting as the group's secretary, wrote to the British National Committee for UNESCO declaring his institution's surprise that Stoppelaëre had "so astonishingly overlooked" the work that the institute had been doing on the Theban tombs, not to mention the material it had collected on them from various sources. Harden's institution constituted an Egyptological storehouse whose existence rested on a bequest of Francis Llewellyn Griffith, Oxford's first professor of Egyptology. Led by ambition, Harden therefore claimed that the Griffith's collection was so expansive "that no other body could now hope to build up anything comparable." Consequently, he suggested that this material, in addition to the editorial work of "Miss [Rosalind] Moss and Mrs. [Ethel] Burney" on his organization's connected, encyclopedic *Topographical Bibliography of Ancient Egyptian Texts, Reliefs and Paintings* meant that "the main repository for this material cannot fail to be the Griffith Institute," even as he claimed that "full liaison between Oxford and other reposi-

---

44. Henri Chevrier, "Tombes Thebaines: Archives Photographiques," undated (presumably 1953). Folder CA/12/7, 069 (62) AMS (Part 1), UNESCO Archives. Chevrier's employment at Karnak ended in 1954, for which see Bierbrier, *Who*, 120. According to Bernard V. Bothmer, *Egypt 1950: My First Visit*, ed. Emma Swan Hall (Oxford: Oxbow, 2003), 110, "Mlle. Diradour" was owner of a shop at 3 Shari'a Baehler, Cairo.

tories will always be maintained." Spotting an opportunity, Harden suggested that "the Institute would be . . . willing to collaborate with Unesco." But he also emphasized that "no part of the material it [the Griffith Institute] has collected and no part of the work it conducts can be placed under the control of any external body."[45]

As the Free Officers' coup shifted slowly toward revolution, European scholars continued to argue about which of them was best placed to study and control Egypt's ancient past, in addition to arguing about the best methods and materials with which to do so. Yet politically tone-deaf as these scholars were, they appeared to have allies in Egypt. This situation was essential because—if it approved Stoppelaëre's proposal—the procedural norms of multilateralism meant that the Egyptian government needed to make an official request to UNESCO for the documentation center project to take place. Financial concerns in keeping with those norms also weighed heavily. If the documentation center went ahead, UNESCO would initially make monetary contributions to the project for three years, as well as fund the purchase of any necessary equipment and the salaries of experts needed to consult on the organization of the work. Egypt, however, would also need to make financial contributions to the new institution, and to "allocate an annual budget for its upkeep."[46] The country's government needed to both support the project and have good reasons to do so.

Happily, Egyptological documentation seemed to constitute a credible project for governmental support. In its initial post-coup years, Egypt's renamed and reconstituted Department of Antiquities was enthusiastic about cooperation with international institutions, and Egyptologists had started to promote their work using the rhetoric of international cooperation and technical assistance. The difference now was that Egyptians could set the terms of work in ways they had been unable to previously.[47] The department and its parent organization, the Ministry of Education, were already collaborating on a volume for the "UNESCO World Art Series," which had been "launched to bring within the reach of . . . the wide art-loving public the finest quality

---

45. Donald B. Harden to British National Commission for UNESCO, December 1953. Folder CA/12/7, 069 (62) AMS (Part 1), UNESCO Archives. On Harden and the Griffith Institute, see Riggs, *Photographing*, 50, 52.

46. Raymonde Frin to Malcolm Adiseshiah, "Draft Summary of Meeting with Madame Noblecourt, Friday, 11 February 1955," February 18, 1955. Folder CA/12/7, 069 (62) AMS (Part 2): "Documentation sur les Peintures et Inscriptions en Haute-Egypte-Programme de Participation," UNESCO Archives.

47. For which see William Carruthers, "Multilateral Possibilities: Decolonization, Preservation, and the Case of Egypt," *Future Anterior* 13, no. 1 (2016): 36–48, and Carruthers, "Visualizing."

reproductions of masterpieces of art."[48] Given this precedent, Egypt's then Minister of Education Ismaʿil al-Qabbani wrote to UNESCO stating that it seemed "fitting that a joint program be studied." After all, "later on this may be developed to include other archaeological sites."[49] Egyptian and Egyptological interests joined under UNESCO's umbrella. This organizational cover, though, was not always effective at keeping such interests—and the paperwork they assembled around—in check. Documentation now started to take on a life of its own both in terms of permissible (knowledge) practices relating to it and the people who could undertake them.

Much Ado About Noting

Ironically, paperwork problems at UNESCO helped to produce a comedy of errors, meaning that not only Egypt's, but also Nubia's past fused with Egyptological archive fever to generate sovereign tensions. UNESCO's files seem organized, adhering to certain standards meant to aid their use. Affixed on their front is a "Form 292 a," the "UNESCO Central Registry Dossier," with spaces to indicate where the file has been sent to and from. Inside, meanwhile, letters, telegrams, contracts, and reports are organized according to date; officials started a new dossier when one was full or, otherwise, at the end of each year. As systematic as they seem, however, these files reveal an organization whose imprimatur was at once powerful and unwieldy. UNESCO's ability to undertake its plans was apparently authoritative but also lackadaisical, a situation with sovereign consequences for the actions its representatives proposed.

In October and November 1953, J. K. Van der Haagen spent a working holiday talking with antiquities officials across the eastern Mediterranean trying to understand how UNESCO could engage with their work. The organization saw the documentation center project as a means to a regional end and, armed with the knowledge that a limited amount of money had become available to initiate work in Egypt, Van der Haagen made certain to exploit UNESCO's position there.[50] Consequently, he seems to have been warmly welcomed by

---

48. "Editorial: A Path to Great Enjoyment," *The UNESCO Courier* 11 (1954), 3. That volume became UNESCO, *Egypt: Paintings from Tombs and Temples* (Greenwich, CT: New York Graphic Society, 1954). Not uncoincidentally, the volume mainly featured photographs of scenes from the Theban tombs taken by K. S. Diradour.

49. Al-Qabbani to John W. Taylor, June 3, 1953. Folder CA/12/7, 069 (62) AMS (Part 1), UNESCO Archives.

50. J. K. Van der Haagen, "Quelques notes d'un voyage de vacances au Proche Orient, 6 oct. 11 nov. 1953," and Van der Haagen to Mustafa Amer, October 6, 1953. Folder CA/12/7, 069 (62) AMS (Part 1), UNESCO Archives. Van der Haagen toured Egypt, Syria, Jordan, Turkey, and Lebanon.

various officials of the Department of Antiquities. Those officials included Director-General Mustafa Amer, whom Van der Haagen saw fit to describe as *"un homme de marque."* Backing the proposed new center and actively seeking UNESCO's counsel, Amer said that he wanted the advice of a foreign expert on the institution's organization.[51] Trust gained, UNESCO was keen to act.

Now, however, the mundanity of administration asserted itself. During the summer of 1954, the controller-general of the Cultural Section of Egypt's Ministry of Education Mahmoud Nahas sent a telegram to UNESCO advising who the expert Amer requested should be. Alongside asking for a *"specialiste [sic] archives"* and asserting that the organization should *"engager photographe Duradour executer [sic] photos,"* the telegram stated that Amer had proposed either the Egyptologist Christiane Desroches Noblecourt of the Louvre, Rosalind Moss of the Griffith Institute, or George Hughes, the director of Chicago House, the Luxor outpost of the OI's Epigraphic Survey.[52] Confusing matters, two weeks later Nahas wrote a letter not only suggesting Noblecourt and Moss, but also adding the Italian Egyptologist Sergio Donadoni of the University of Florence to the list.[53] Since Noblecourt appeared first in both communications, however, and since "her home is in Paris [and] we were able to have an immediate decision," UNESCO appointed her regardless.[54] Its counsel requested, the organization gladly put paperwork into action. Officials approved contracts and purchase orders for Noblecourt's mission, and US$2,070 was accordingly spent.[55] France came through again.

Lines of communication, though, could blur. After Noblecourt's appointment, W. E. Purnell of UNESCO's Cairo office cabled Paris that the Egyptian National Commission for UNESCO had suggested that any consultant needed to "be decided by mutual agreement between antiquities department and UNESCO not necessarily Noblecourt."[56] Washing his hands of the affair, Nahas had told Purnell to contact Amer, who in turn stated that he had sent the project back to

---

51. Van der Haagen, "Quelques notes."
52. Mahmoud Nahas to UNESCO, July 15, 1954. Folder CA/12/7, 069 (62) AMS (Part 1), UNESCO Archives.
53. Nahas to Director-General of UNESCO, July 28, 1954. Folder CA/12/7, 069 (62) AMS (Part 1), UNESCO Archives. When Donadoni died, one Italian newspaper ran an article entitled "Addio a Sergio Donadoni, l'archeologo che salvò Abu Simbel," *La Stampa*, October 31, 2015. It was not the first time that someone involved with the Nubian campaign had been stated as primary mover in that act—see note 59 for another instance.
54. Van der Haagen to W. E. Purnell, November 24, 1954. Folder CA/12/7, 069 (62) AMS (Part 1), UNESCO Archives.
55. UNESCO, "Request for Fee or Consultant Contract," September 14, 1954. Folder CA/12/7, 069 (62) AMS (Part 1), UNESCO Archives.
56. Purnell to Jean Thomas, November 4, 1954. Folder CA/12/7, 069 (62) AMS (Part 1), UNESCO Archives.

the Ministry of Education after giving it his approval, and had in fact suggested either George Hughes or a "Miss Davis" for the position, not Noblecourt. Attempting to clarify the situation, UNESCO's Cairo office contacted Under-Secretary Soliman Huzayyin at the Ministry of Education. Huzayyin stated that Amer had never proposed Noblecourt for the job, but had in fact proposed Moss and, once again, "Miss Davis."[57] It was, however, too late for UNESCO to change anything. Not only had Noblecourt's mission been contracted and paid for, but—as a telegram from UNESCO now informed Nahas—she was due to arrive in Cairo the following week.[58] Paperwork meant that Noblecourt had become an expert by mistake, a situation that produced sovereign tension even at the start of the twenty-first century. Then, arguments about who exactly initiated the Nubian campaign momentarily raged.[59] Still, Noblecourt had a job to do, and no one from UNESCO or the Egyptian government attempted to stop her.

Splitting Sovereignty

In late 1954, Noblecourt proceeded to consult on the formation of a documentation center in Cairo. The plan she proposed not only had archival practice at its heart, but also suggested how those archives might be used, indicating how the sovereign tensions implicit within the project were developing. Writing to Luther H. Evans, UNESCO's new director-general, Noblecourt noted how she thought it clear that Egypt did not want to be *"seulement un intermédiaire"* supplying documents to register.[60] Instead, the creation and archiving of documentation should be used to promote Egyptian interests, too. While drawing on the plans previously discussed, Noblecourt's own scheme had, she therefore claimed, one major difference.

The center would, as Stoppelaëre and others had suggested, gather material, provide a location for its consultation, and be responsible for its dissemination.[61] Noblecourt stated, however, that the new institution would also involve

---

57. Events related in Purnell to Thomas, November 4, 1954. Folder CA/12/7, 069 (62) AMS (Part 1), UNESCO Archives. "Miss Davis" was presumably the artist and copyist Nina Macpherson Davies. Together with her husband, Norman de Garis Davies, she had worked in Luxor for several decades before World War II, for which see Bierbrier, *Who*, 144–45.

58. J. K. Van der Haagen to Nahas, November 5, 1954. Folder CA/12/7, 069 (62) AMS (Part 1), UNESCO Archives.

59. Zahi Hawass, "Dig Days: Stealing His Thunder," *Al-Ahram Weekly* 885, February 21–27, 2008.

60. Noblecourt to Evans, March 9, 1955. Folder CA/12/7, 069 (62) AMS (Part 2), UNESCO Archives.

61. Noblecourt, "Création du Centre de Documentation et d'Etudes sur l'Histoire de l'Art et de la Civilisation de l'ancienne Egypte: Rapport," March 8, 1955, 4. Folder CA/12/7, 069 (62) AMS (Part 2), UNESCO Archives.

young Egyptian Egyptologists in *"travaux pratiques,"* or the work of "handling" documentation.[62] Likewise, the institution was not only to document monuments that had not been, or were only partially, published. The center's personnel were also to collect documentation on all archaeological excavations henceforth undertaken in Egypt, obtain prints of all photographs of objects held at the Egyptian Museum in Cairo, and gather documentation held in foreign Egyptological archives, whether through exchange or purchase.[63] This work would require an *"élite"* technical, scientific, and administrative personnel, both Egyptian and foreign.[64] Rather than a project devoted specifically to Theban tombs, then, the new institution would devote its resources to documenting, in great detail and with tremendous effort, the past of the Egyptian nation. Simultaneously—and however patrician Noblecourt's motives were—the center would use this project and the international resources that it made available to incorporate young Egyptians within its work. Sympathetic particularly to Amer (whom she later described as "infused with a fresh blood inspired by the most modern experiences"), Noblecourt set forward a scheme far more geared toward Egyptian national interests than initially envisaged.[65]

Despite her accidental appointment, Noblecourt's investment in the sovereign thrust of this scheme echoes UNESCO's contemporary interest in similar—and similarly tense—archival work elsewhere, a situation undoubtedly conditioned by the organization's leader.[66] Luther Evans, UNESCO's director-general from 1953 until 1958, had been director of the Historical Records Survey of the US Works Progress Administration. To take the UNESCO job, he had also resigned his appointment as librarian of Congress, a position in which he had been internationally active. Evans had been present at the foundation of UNESCO, also helping to develop the organization's 1952 Universal Copyright Convention.[67] Yet as Todd Shepard has discussed, such internationalist zeal in the (re-) constitution and development of archival practice had its tensions, not least because it found its expression

> in the era of decolonization, and the history they [archivists] focused on documenting was newly and starkly national: nation-states, which no

---

62. Noblecourt, "Création du Centre," 2.
63. Noblecourt, "Création du Centre," 14–16.
64. Noblecourt, "Création du Centre," 16.
65. Noblecourt, *La grande*, 125. That Noblecourt amplified this national message is unsurprising. As Sunil Amrith and Glenda Sluga, "New Histories of the United Nations," *Journal of World History* 19, no. 2 (2008): 270 note, "the UN was and is a body composed wholly of nation-states and committed by its resolutions to the maintenance of the sovereignty of its constituent national members."
66. For which see Rothschild, "The Archives."
67. Alfred E. Clark, "Luther H. Evans, 79; Congress Librarian and UNESCO Official," *The New York Times*, December 24, 1981.

CHAPTER 2

longer had an empire or overseers overseas. . . . [W]hile some archivists were redesigning archives, others were defining what "sovereignty" meant.[68]

For example, this process led to French archival theorist Yves Pérotin using a 1964 UNESCO report "to take advantage of the fundamental changes taking place in Algeria to define a wholly modern archivistic regime."[69] That regime was to be based on that of the United States, said to be engaged in the collection of any (written) material relating to the nation, not just documentation relating to state administration.[70] The Franco-Algerian dispute relating to this process continues, however.[71] The archives of decolonization and the making of national archival pasts constituted significant sovereign tension.

Noblecourt's words echoed such tension. Her report demonstrates how the making of national pasts collided with wider concerns about who was presumed capable of formulating what archives might contain. The new center's "technical" work would be undertaken by architects, draughts-people, photographers, and cast-makers, no specification as to the nationality of whom was made.[72] "Scientific" work, though, was to be undertaken by *"savants"* both Egyptian and foreign, employed as UNESCO experts for periods of two to three months and aided by assistants from similar backgrounds.[73] Not only did Noblecourt suggest that these scientific personnel should plan and carry out the center's documentary campaigns, but she also stated that they would classify and assemble the documentation on which the institution depended, gather information on archaeological discoveries in Egypt, and ultimately put together *"un vaste bureau"* of archaeological and Egyptological "information" (*renseignement*), "research" (*recherches*), "enquiry" (*enquêtes*), and—envisaging the center's future work—*"protection."*[74] Moreover, the institution's scientific staff was to edit and publish the documents held there, as well as organize conferences, exhibitions, and an educational service that, aided by Egyptian Egyptologists, would train tour guides for Egypt's museums and archaeological sites who could provide "exact and regular knowledge" (*"connaissances exactes et régulièrement"*).[75] Administratively, such work was to be overseen by

---

68. Shepard, "'Of Sovereignty,'" 879.
69. Shepard, "'Of Sovereignty,'" 881, citing Pérotin.
70. Shepard, "'Of Sovereignty,'" 878–79.
71. Shepard, "'Of Sovereignty,'" 878–79.
72. Noblecourt, "Création du Centre," 4.
73. Noblecourt, "Création du Centre," 16–17.
74. Noblecourt, "Création du Centre," 17–19, quotes on 19.
75. Noblecourt, "Création du Centre," 20–22, quote on 22.

three Egyptian Egyptologists, who themselves would receive advice from another UNESCO expert, again present for a period of two or three months each year (and therefore presumably non-Egyptian).[76]

Who got to define, collect, and promote the nation's past, and how those practices would be agreed upon, was open to significant international contention. Still, the architecture of the building designed to hold the new documentation center attempted to contain the rough edges of this process. The institution—initially to be housed in a former palace on the Cairo island of Zamalek—was ultimately to be placed in its own, purpose-built, five-story headquarters, including a buffet for staff members.[77] This new structure would embody not only precisely what might be recorded of Egypt's ancient past, but also what formats that information might be recorded in and how many square feet would be required to carry this process out. On the first floor were to be ten rooms of filing cabinets, each—in their respective twenty-four square meters—devoted to archiving a particular part of what was deemed to be the country's (pre-ordained) heritage, divided geographically or according to site: a *"salle Nubie,"* a *"salle Sakkarah,"* and a *"salle Tombes Gournah"* among them. On the second floor was to be a *"Conservatoire des Archives,"* whose layout provided an idealized relationship between archival infrastructure, photographs, and other forms of documentation. Two rooms would be devoted to photographic negatives, films, and microfilms, one room would be geared toward the projection of photographic positives, and another *"grande salle"* of forty-eight square meters would be devoted to storing prints. Finally, two rooms of thirty-five square meters each would store drawings, sketches, plans, and index cards.[78]

Emphasizing the sovereign tensions inherent in such a project, only the charts summarizing this plan were translated into Arabic from Noblecourt's original French. Her lengthy report on the plan did not receive the same treatment.[79] The new documentation center would constitute an institution devoted to collecting and producing forms of paper whose basics could seemingly be reduced to a few sheets of the stuff, at least in the language of the center's location. Perhaps, like the Palestinian civil service archives discussed by Ilana Feldman, the practice of archiving and "the capacity to keep filing . . . [was perceived to be] far more important than any particular content" in terms of establishing the authority of the new institution and the forms of knowledge

---

76. Noblecourt, "Création du Centre," 23.
77. Noblecourt, "Création du Centre," 26–30.
78. "Projet de Construction," enclosed in Noblecourt, "Création du Centre."
79. "Projet de Construction," enclosed in Noblecourt, "Création du Centre."

it promoted.⁸⁰ These same filing practices, however, now opened further possibilities in the production of knowledge, its geographies, and its ownership. Filing was not immutable.

Papering over Nubia

During her time in Cairo, Noblecourt sent news of her experiences with Egyptian bureaucracy back to Paris; it was lucky, she noted, that the Department of Antiquities had provided her with *"un excellent secrétaire dactylographe"* (a secretary-typist). Reporting to Luther Evans, Noblecourt described how, at one meeting of the department's Conseil Superieur des Antiquités, a new topic "seemed to impose" itself: Nubia. Given Egypt's decision to build the Aswan High Dam, Mustafa Amer had raised the necessity of saving the ancient temples located throughout the region in the presence of Free Officer Kamal al-Din Hussein, Egypt's new minister of education. Amer spoke with "a keen feeling of his responsibility toward History," suggesting that the nascent documentation center's efforts be directed toward recording the temples at Abu Simbel. Noblecourt agreed, not least because the temples were without a *"publication scientifique complete* [sic]." She also noted that the Griffith Institute's work at the Theban tombs was doing a fine job documenting them, obviating any necessity of starting the new center's efforts there.⁸¹ This opinion would come to have consequences for the constitution and ownership of Nubia itself.

Other human-paper entanglements heightened those consequences. In November 1954, Kamal al-Din Hussein sent a telegram to the geographer— and one-time colleague of Mustafa Amer at the then Fu'ad (but now Cairo) University—Muhammad 'Awad. 'Awad was Egypt's representative on UNESCO's Executive Board. As he took part in the organization's Eighth General Conference in Montevideo, the telegram noted that "government decided give priority to documentation [of] Nubian temples" and instructed him to "please contact UNESCO Director General to instruct head of documentation mission in Egypt start work immediately."⁸² Writing from Paris, Jean Thomas could only say that UNESCO would wait for Noblecourt's final report and the

---

80. Ilana Feldman, *Governing Gaza: Bureaucracy, Authority, and the Work of Rule (1917–1967)* (Durham, NC: Duke University Press, 2008), 60.

81. Noblecourt to Evans, November 25, 1954. Folder CA/12/7, 069 (62) AMS (Part 1), UNESCO Archives.

82. Hussein to "Mohamed 'Awad." Folder CA/12/7, 069 (62) AMS (Part 1), UNESCO Archives. The telegram is a copy, annotated "vers fin novembre 14." For Muhammad 'Awad (who, with Amer, was one of Egypt's two first professional geographers), see El Shakry, *The Great*, 67–69.

agreement of the Egyptian government.⁸³ Back in the city, Noblecourt held a February 1955 meeting with a number of UNESCO officials during which she reported that the Egyptian government "had strongly emphasized the necessity of giving the Nubian monuments first priority." The meeting's minutes declared that "the Centre must exist on paper in April. The Nubian project should be initiated in October."⁸⁴

Building on the earlier archaeological interventions in the region, the proposed construction of the High Dam now meant that Nubia was ripe for enfolding within the forms of national sovereignty that the proposed documentation center promoted. An April 1955 government memo written by Kamal al-Din Hussein emphasized this point. Such memos were idealized and standardized pieces of paper, their authority constituted through the succinct messages they were meant to convey.⁸⁵ By writing one, Hussein indicated not only his investment, but also the investment of his government in the project. Indeed, the Egyptian government was particularly interested in the possibilities that such work presented for constituting not only a certain type of Egyptian past, but also a certain type of consciousness about it. Hussein stated that the new institution could be "a source for equipping them [Egyptians] with the history of human civilization," noting that Egypt constituted an example of a "universal civilization" (ḥaḍāra ʿālamiyya), the sort of rhetoric promoted by UNESCO. He also, though, drew on contemporary discourse surrounding the reform of the Egyptian peasantry to stress that the institution could be "a means of educating sons of the country," a statement that at least partially nodded to rhetoric surrounding Luxor antiquity thieves. Hussein noted the concern, moreover, that "many antiquities were exported outside Egypt without registration." This concern suggests why, in Arabic, the proposed institution was called the Markaz Tasjil al-Athar al-Misriyya (the Centre for Registering (tasjīl) Egyptian Antiquities).⁸⁶ Paper begat writing practices that could fix the definition of state property.

Noblecourt's report had itself hinted at this outcome—she noted that archaeological missions working in Egypt would have to send the proposed center copies of their notes. Those missions working in Nubia specifically, though,

---

83. Thomas to Noblecourt, December 17, 1954. Folder CA/12/7, 069 (62) AMS (Part 1), UNESCO Archives.
84. Frin to Adiseshiah, "Draft Summary of Meeting."
85. Feldman, *Governing*, 41–42.
86. Memo written by Kamal al-Din Hussein, April 25, 1955, file 0081–003715, Egyptian National Archives, Cairo. Kamal al-Din Hussein wrote on similar themes in "Thaqafatuna al-Jadida" ["Our new culture"], *al-Hilal* 67, no. 1 (1959): 10–15. The Nasser regime used the Egyptian signifier "sons of the country" (awlād al-balad, sing. ibn al-balad) to stress a positive identity for the Egyptian masses. For this term's history, see Sawsan el-Messiri, *Ibn al-Balad: A Concept of Egyptian Identity* (Leiden: E. J. Brill, 1978).

would not only have to send the institution copies of any publications they produced, but also hand over their field notes as and when they were ready, a practice for which the Department of Antiquities said it would provide subventions. Moreover, those notes would have to be produced in agreement with the techniques and documentary formats used by the new center itself, additionally becoming the institution's property.[87] By agreeing to the creation of CEDAE, the Egyptian government ultimately hoped to gain control over and shape Nubia's past in Egypt's image, at least on its side of the Nubian border.

Prompted by the construction of the High Dam (and again drawing on the history of such practices in the region), this move reflected other contemporary attempts to refashion Nubia and Nubian social life as indivisible with the geographies and social norms of Egypt.[88] More specifically, it reflected official interest in regard to the ownership of the Egyptian past. The definition, ownership, and distribution of Egyptian antiquities had long been a source of controversy. Most recently, Law 215 of October 1951 had finally given Egypt's minister of education power to decide which antiquities excavating missions could export from the country.[89] In CEDAE's early years, meanwhile, the Department of Antiquities sought to control Egypt's antiquity trade further. In 1957—and in the face of opposition from Cairene antiquity dealers made plain in the magazine *Akhir Saʿa*—the department prepared legislation attempting to curb the business, which had flourished until the Suez conflict. In an interview in the magazine, the dealer Philip Mitry indicated that first Americans, then Germans, represented the trade's most enthusiastic customers.[90] The legislation, formulated in the wake of a controversy surrounding an alleged American antiquities smuggler, Charles Muses, suggested that the Department of Antiquities would itself now be responsible for selling ancient objects that came to market, establishing sovereignty over Egypt's past firmly within the state's institutional remit.[91] Establishing a documentation center constituted a different step in the same process of state ownership.

---

87. Noblecourt, "Création du Centre," 9.
88. For which see Reynolds, "Building," and Reynolds, "City of the High Dam: Aswan and the Promise of Postcolonialism in Egypt," *City and Society* 29, no. 1 (2017): 213–35.
89. Reid, *Contesting*, 352.
90. "Bi-Munasabat Qadiyat al-ʿAlim al-Amriki al-ladhi Saraqa Athar Misr" ["On the occasion of the judgment of the American scientist who stole Egyptian antiquities"], *Akhir Saʿa*, August 7, 1957: 24–25. For Mitry, see Fredrik Hagen and Kim Ryholt, *The Antiquities Trade in Egypt 1880–1930* (Copenhagen: The Royal Danish Academy of Sciences and Letters, 2016), 240.
91. Reported in Wente, "Letters from Egypt," 3–4, although it is unclear if the legislation was ever passed. Charles Muses was an "esoteric philosopher" (with a PhD in philosophy from Columbia University) who received permission to dig at the site of Dahshur, south of Cairo, and "returned to Cairo hoping to appeal in the higher courts the charge of having attempted to smuggle antiquities

This narrative of events should not efface other reasons why Amer and others had raised Nubia as an issue. This act was linked as much to their self-fashioning as dedicated national servants as to any sort of territorial interest (although clearly in practice those two concerns could elide). Amer and some of his colleagues in the Department of Antiquities enjoyed a certain amount of media attention, and their position in charge of Egypt's past constituted them not only as dedicated public servants, but also as tied to heroic imaginings of the nation itself. For instance, as the Muses case took shape, a lengthy piece in the newspaper *al-Jumhuriyya* outlined the responsibilities of the departmental Inspector for Lower Egypt, Shafiq Farid, "the responsible official" (*al-mas'ūl al-awwal*) who the American was meant to conduct excavations (*istikhrāj al-āthār*, literally "extract antiquities") in the presence of.[92] Earlier, in 1954, a more congratulatory article profiled Amer and others as members of "The Department that Researches the Glory of Egypt!"[93]

In the preface to the 1955 Department of Antiquities *Report on The Monuments of Nubia*, Amer wrote that, upon his appointment as the institution's director-general, "I naturally felt that it was my immediate duty to bring to the notice of the responsible authorities the necessity of considering the fate of the monuments of Nubia." Moreover, he highlighted that what was "pressing" in this context was "a study of the means of preserving, protecting and registering, as well as saving what can be saved of these monuments both for history and for the coming generations." To that end, "in April 1953," he had "made the necessary contacts with the Ministry of Public Works . . . steps were at once taken to form a Committee from among the staff of the Department to make a preliminary investigation."[94] Amer's concern for Nubian antiquities and investment in the cause of registering them was tied to bureaucratic best practice in the service of nation. His apparent primacy in expressing this concern again constituted an early hint of the tensions that would develop surrounding which of those parties invested in this process could claim ownership over it.

Amer's statements hinted at how the inscription of documentation relating to Nubia inevitably constituted sovereign tension, particularly in terms of

---

out of Egypt." The case was front page news, for which see "al-Qabd 'ala 'Alim Amriki" ["The seizure of the American scientist"], *al-Jumhuriyya*, June 21, 1957.

92. "Tahqiq fi Hadith Tahrib al-Athar al-Misriyya" ["Report on the incident of smuggled Egyptian antiquities"], *al-Jumhuriyya*, June 23, 1957.

93. "Maslahat al-Bahth 'an Majd Misr . . . !" ["The department that researches the glory of Egypt . . . !"], *al-Musawwar*, September 17, 1954, 30–31.

94. Egyptian Department of Antiquities, *Report*, v.

Egypt's own interest in the work. In May 1955, *al-Ahram* carried an article about the signing of the agreement between Egypt and UNESCO that made possible the foundation of CEDAE. The article depicted Kamal al-Din Hussein doing just that. Writing his signature, he was watched over by Noblecourt and various Egyptian officials. Those officials included Mustafa Amer, who, retiring from his role in the Department of Antiquities, was about to become CEDAE's first director. The article, a reminder of the intersection of paper, writing, and political power, quoted Amer as saying that the institution would, in time, document all the monuments in Egypt.[95] Who, though, enjoyed ownership of this documentation? The article elided an answer to this question through its representation of international cooperation, as did UNESCO's work in Nubia more generally. Kamal al-Din Hussein's signature, however, appeared paramount to the whole exercise. Other press reports made similarly sovereign hints. A year later, an article in the newspaper *Akhbar al-Yawm* expressed surprise that a center like CEDAE had not existed in Egypt before, especially given that Egypt "contained the greatest number of antiquities."[96] Elsewhere, a report in *La bourse égyptienne* stated that, "at the command of" Kamal al-Din Hussein, the institution's first act would be to undertake recording work in Nubia.[97] Only afterwards would CEDAE's personnel turn their attention to the rest of the Nile Valley, embedding Nubia's past within this wider Egyptian whole. Sovereign acts were framed by sovereign decisions.

Indexed Anxiety

Sovereignty, though, does not constitute a stable quantity. CEDAE gained official status through Egyptian Law 184 of 1956.[98] But that law did not speak other than in vague terms about the organization of documentation stored at the institution, stating only that what was necessary at CEDAE "was documentary testimony . . . to the widest extent possible."[99] Consequently, instituting CEDAE meant attempting to institute the ways of gathering and organizing documentation that the experts who started to consult for the center promoted, in

---

95. "Markaz al-Athar wa-l-Hadara al-Misriyya" ["The Antiquities center and Egyptian civilization"], *al-Ahram*, May 8, 1955.

96. Brief report in "Kull Shay'" ["Everything"] section, *Akhbar al-Yawm*, May 5, 1956.

97. "Le centre de documentation archeologique ouvre une ere nouvelle a l'Egyptologie," undated clipping from *La bourse égyptienne*.

98. *Markaz Tasjil al-Athar al-Misriyya* [Centre for registering Egyptian antiquities] (Cairo: Wizarat al-Thaqafa wa-l-Irshad al-Qawmi, Markaz Tasjil al-Athar al-Misriyya, n.d.), 1.

99. Hassan al-Fakahani, *al-Mawsu'a al-Tashri'iyya al-Haditha* [The contemporary legislative encyclopaedia] (Cairo: Al-Dar al-'Arabiyya li-l-Mawsu'at, 1964), 208.

addition to the forms of knowledge such practices derived from and the hierarchies of practice those forms advanced. Sovereign tensions surrounding the new center informed CEDAE's practices from the beginning. In the institution's first year, for example, expert visits were either conducted by, or planned from, not only Noblecourt herself, but also (among others) Charles Nims of the OI and Rosalind Moss of the Griffith Institute, all of whom were connected to certain, historically contingent ways of making Egyptological knowledge (Moss's visit was ultimately canceled due to the Tripartite Aggression).[100] The indexes and index cards that played a key role in pulling together the knowledge these experts were invested in therefore became conductors of sovereign tension. The registers and pieces of stiffened paper that were meant to constitute the unspoken authority of this new expert cadre instead became documents symbolizing the sovereign and knowledge anxieties surrounding CEDAE itself.

Privileging certain sorts of knowledge, at its broadest CEDAE's indexical material attempted to bring together the sort of information that had become familiar to Egyptology as the discipline had self-consciously professionalized, particularly in the period after World War I. Proper Egyptological knowledge had slowly and unevenly become anchored in the study of hieroglyphic texts and the (often monumental) architectural features connected to them, and the documentation of these things is what CEDAE's index cards materialized.[101] A mere glance at the literature explaining CEDAE's work indicates that the primary goal of the institution was, as the center's name suggested, epigraphic recording and the location of pre-Arab invasion—and post "prehistoric"—hieroglyphic inscriptions within their architectural contexts, in addition to the recording of those architectural contexts themselves. CEDAE played a documentary game closely tied to much older norms set forward by the Euro-American Egyptological institutions within which consulting experts like Nims and Moss worked, ultimately synthesizing such standards as part of Egypt's past, present, and future. Attending to the landscape of Nubian monumental ruination that had coalesced over the previous decades, the institution came perfectly equipped to make the region its primary focus of study.

A French brochure explaining CEDAE's work explained the institution's standards in detail (a similar Arabic brochure did not explain CEDAE's recording

---

100. Information on visits related by documents throughout folder CA/12/7, 069 (62) AMS (Part 4): "Documentation sur les Peintures et Inscriptions en Haute-Egypte-Programme de Participation," UNESCO Archives. Other planned/actual expert visits included those of Sergio Donadoni and Jaroslav Černý, Professor of Egyptology at Oxford, for whom see Jiřina Růžová, *The Scribe of the Place of Truth: The Life of the Egyptologist Jaroslav Černý* (Prague: Libri, 2010).

101. For this process, see Gange, *Dialogues*, 326.

practices anywhere near as carefully).¹⁰² Two registration books were created for the center, "specially designed" (*spécialement conçus*) not only to be used in, but also to weather the vicissitudes of, the field. Each measuring 0.24 by 0.17 cm, the books were covered in khaki canvas and their pages covered in a small format grid. The first book was known as the *"cahier épigraphique,"* and the second was the *"cahier archéologique."*¹⁰³ Within the *cahier épigraphique*, space was set aside to record various details of hieroglyphic inscriptions in a way that suggested not only their primacy as objects of interest, but also their assumed purity as authentic historical record: "breaks" (*cassures*) and "destructions" (*martelages*, literally "hammerings") in inscriptions were to be marked as either accidental, "incorrect" (*fautifs*), or intentional; their provenance as ancient or modern was also to be noted.¹⁰⁴ Meanwhile, the *cahier archéologique* constituted an archaeological register indicating how contingent upon Egyptology's disciplinary needs the category of archaeology was (despite the Nubian archaeological surveys of previous decades). The register almost entirely seemed to record the architectural/art-historic context of the *"scène"* being recorded, a practice that allowed either the placing of inscriptions within their architectural contexts or the recording of architectural elements themselves. The book was used to note the dimensions of the scene in question, its state of conservation, and the nature of the wall on which it was located. It was also used to note the techniques and conventions with which the scene had been carved (type of relief, for example), its composition (whether the scene had different registers, for instance), and its subject.¹⁰⁵ Combined with photographs taken by CEDAE's personnel, the information contained within these registers was then inscribed onto the institution's index cards. These cards again emphasized a notion of ancient Egyptian history centered on architectural and artistic appreciation, in addition to the recording of hieroglyphic inscriptions and, by implication, the centrality of writing itself. Alongside a photograph of the "subject" at hand, a record of the number of the photograph's negative, and an indication where on a plan that negative related to, the cards contained descriptive information about that subject: the name of the "site," the "monument" located there, its material, and its date.¹⁰⁶

CEDAE's index cards represent a certain set of Egyptological norms. Yet they also point to the inherent instability of the organization. The cards reveal how the institution's wider practices were unevenly implemented. But

---

102. The Arabic brochure is *Markaz Tasjil al-Athar al-Misriyya*. The French brochure is *République Arabe Unie: Centre de documentation*.
103. *République Arabe Unie: Centre de documentation*, 40.
104. *République Arabe Unie: Centre de documentation*, 42.
105. *République Arabe Unie: Centre de documentation*, 42–43.
106. *République Arabe Unie: Centre de documentation*, 46–49.

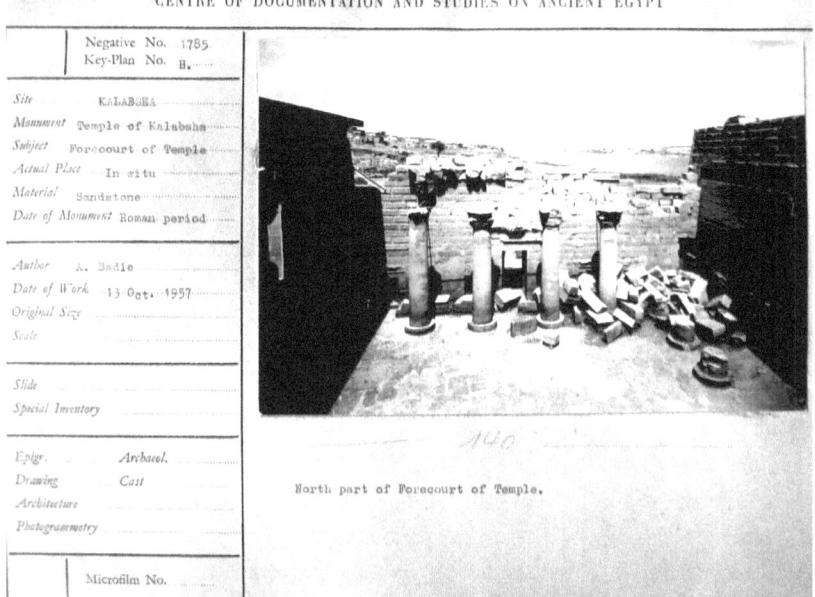

FIGURE 2.3. A Centre d'étude et de documentation sur l'Ancienne Égypte index card produced for Kalabsha (settlement of Kalabsha visible in top-left). Christiane Desroches Noblecourt Archives, 20150308/285, National Archives of France, Pierrefitte-sur-Seine.

they also reveal the extent to which this implementation became tied to who had the practical ability to make this process happen. Sovereign tension was printed onto the cards themselves. For example, we can see that a card (figure 2.3) depicting the north part of the forecourt of the Temple of Kalabsha was put together on October 13, 1957. We can also see which negative the card related to and where on the key-plan it sat.

Yet it is unclear if any other information was ever linked to the item: many of its spaces for annotation have been left blank, even though we can see that its author was "A. Badie." Presumably part of CEDAE's technical personnel (and presumably also Egyptian), this "invisible technician" put the institution's policies into practice.[107] Yet the paucity of this attribution makes it unclear to what extent, for instance, Badie selected the precise views in the photograph or authored the description typed on the card. This stiffened piece of paper constitutes a certain idea of the (ancient) Egyptian nation, yet the tensions on it are forever visible, the agency of its author unclear beyond the administrative accounting of their name.

---

107. For which see Steven Shapin, "The Invisible Technician," *American Scientist* 77, no. 6 (1989): 554–63.

Furthering such tension, Noblecourt seemed unimpressed by other attempts to create documentation. Writing privately about the Department of Antiquities' 1955 *Report on the Monuments of Nubia*, she was scathing, describing the volume as "the laughing stock" (*la risée*) of "all Egyptologists dignified by the name around the world." Noblecourt claimed that Mustafa Amer had been obliged to publish the report. She also noted that neither he, Osman Rostom (the one-time chief architect of the Antiquities Service), nor the now chief architect of the department, Muhammed Mahdi, had been involved with the mission, and claimed that "they completely agreed with our [i.e., my?] opinion" (*partagent complètement notre opinion*) as to the publication's quality.[108] Whether or not this last claim was true—and in fact indicates that domestic Egyptian tensions related to the recording of the Nubian past also existed—Noblecourt's words emphasize how CEDAE's documentation had started to channel sovereign anxiety.

Ironically, despite the 1955 *Report* reflecting the landscape of picturesque Nubian ruination that CEDAE now set out to record, Noblecourt noted with some concern that, when the departmental committee that wrote the document had visited Nubia, three-quarters of the temples there had been submerged by the Nile's inundation. Moreover, she stated that "despite the presence of architects," no plans were made in the field. Consequently, all the plans printed in the eventual report were copies of those previously published, including, she emphasized, those from Baedeker tourist guides. Implicitly, then—and despite reflecting the way in which "Nubia" was already entangled with touristic visions of the region—these plans were inaccurate, unlike those to be used or made by CEDAE. Indeed, when Muhammed Mahdi arrived at Abu Simbel to help start CEDAE's work there, Noblecourt claimed that he had been forced to find "*un plan fidèle*" of the temples and the site.[109] Defining accuracy in documentation produced significant tension as CEDAE came into being and as the task of deciding who would be allowed to record Nubia took shape.

Not unrelated, Noblecourt's criticisms connected to long-standing controversy surrounding Selim Hassan, the leader of the committee that had worked in Nubia. Hassan had often been at the center of colonial-era contention surrounding the place of foreign Egyptologists in the Antiquities Service. He was an unpopular figure among many of their number, and Drioton had ultimately

---

108. "Programme des travaux pour le premier secteur de Nubie," 25–26. Folder CA/12/7, 069 (62) AMS (Part 5): "Documentation sur les Peintures et Inscriptions en Haute-Egypte-Programme de Participation," UNESCO Archives. This "programme" is unsigned but contained within Noblecourt's annual report. For Rostom and Mahdi, see Noblecourt, *La grande*, 135, 144.

109. "Programme des travaux," 25.

acted to force his retirement from the institution in 1939. Noblecourt's complaint that one of the two members of the Nubian committee who she deemed "disreputable" (*"peu recommandables"*) had been "abruptly removed of their functions" just before the war thus indicates that she was discussing the Egyptian, reviving this long-standing intrigue both to her advantage and to that of the allies she seemed to have made in Amer, Rustom, and Mahdi.[110] The past was a limited and historically contingent resource, one that Noblecourt—and perhaps others—were willing to start a documentary conflict over. It was also one whose sovereign anxieties, international or domestic, occasionally boiled over as a result.

Ironically, there was clearly little to differentiate much of the work set forward by CEDAE and the recommendations for work in Nubia proposed in the departmental *Report*. Noblecourt, though, was direct in her views about what was appropriate. "It was preferable," she deemed, "that UNESCO intervene" in Nubia, "since it was the only organization equipped to deal with it."[111] Besides, did the Egyptian Department of Antiquities "possess the scientific personnel necessary to carry out quick and delicate work"? "At the time of writing," Noblecourt derided this possibility as *"pas possible."*[112] If preservation work took place in Nubia, UNESCO would have to take charge, and CEDAE was perfectly placed to help the organization master that role and promote the right sort of recording practice both in Egyptian Nubia and in Egypt more widely. Such an act—albeit with a little added spectacle—is almost entirely what occurred as the Nubian campaign began. The channels formed by this documentary process would produce tension in the same way that the forms of water management produced by the High Dam's construction did.

Bibliographies of the Past

During the first three months of 1960, at the very moment that UNESCO was launching the Nubian campaign, Rosalind Moss of the Griffith Institute finally visited CEDAE as an expert "Consultant in Egyptian Bibliography," a posting that perhaps emphasized how Egyptology—and the Griffith Institute itself—often delegated such "clerical" work to women.[113] Moss spent her time "examining [the institution's] . . . work and methods," in addition to "visiting Abu Simbel in order to see the actual recording of sites in process." This effort

---

110. "Programme des travaux," 25. For Selim Hassan, see Reid, *Contesting*, esp. 290.
111. "Programme des travaux," 36.
112. "Programme des travaux," 30.
113. On such "clerical" work at the Griffith Institute, see Riggs, *Photographing*, 62.

CHAPTER 2

resulted in Moss judging that "while the arrangement and registration-system of the recording of the Nubian temples was admirable, there was not sufficient provision for dealing with other material already in the possession of the Centre, or expected in the future." Consequently, it was "necessary to enlarge the scope of the present system to meet future developments."[114] The Griffith Institute had finally gained a foothold in CEDAE as the Nubian campaign began, doing little to disarm the sovereign tension that surrounded the institution's documentary practices.

Adding to that tension, Moss increased the reams of archival paper needed to carry out CEDAE's work, advising on "supplementary registers to cover the additional material." "[P]rovision was [also] . . . made for dealing with photographs and plans expected from the forthcoming excavations in Nubia." Perhaps more notable than these actions, though, was that Moss thought it "desirable to increase the number of card-indexes already made by a general geographical index to cover every site represented, with cross-references for subsidiary localities, and to prepare card-indexes of museums, subjects, etc. for future use." All of this work would prove "specially useful when the Centre's activities are developed to cover an even wider field."[115] Meanwhile, Moss made these arrangements in a way logical to an employee of the institution where she worked. For example, she organized subsidiary indexes along the lines of the indexical categories used in volumes of the Griffith Institute's *Topographical Bibliography* itself. The index to a 1964 edition of one of the *Bibliography*'s volumes, devoted to the *Royal Tombs and Smaller Cemeteries* of Thebes, was arranged according to categories such as "Kings," "Private Names," "Divinities," "Geographical," "Objects in Museums," and "Excavators."[116] At CEDAE, Moss added subsidiary registers devoted to "Excavations" and "Museums." She also seems to have added subsidiary registers titled "Religious," "Titles" (i.e., personal titles), and "Geographical" within the institution's "Philological" register.[117] Moss's own institutional background was stamped upon her organizational work at CEDAE, even if the categories she used seemed straightforward, if not banal.

That banality is pivotal. Moss's consultancy at CEDAE was neither ill-intentioned nor much other than pedestrian in its process. Asked to consider the organizational capabilities of the institution in relation to a particular way

---

114. Rosalind Moss, "Report on Work in Cairo as Consultant in Egyptian Bibliography," May 17, 1960. Folder CA/12/7, 069 (62) AMS (Part 12): "Documentation sur les Peintures et Inscriptions en Haute-Egypte-Programme de Participation," UNESCO Archives.

115. Moss, "Report on Work in Cairo."

116. Bertha Porter and Rosalind L. B. Moss (with the assistance of Ethel W. Burney), *Topographical Bibliography of Ancient Egyptian Hieroglyphic Texts, Reliefs, and Paintings*, vol. 1, *The Theban Necropolis*, part 2, *Royal Tombs and Smaller Cemeteries*, 2nd ed. (Oxford: Clarendon Press, 1964), ix.

117. Moss, "Report on Work in Cairo."

of making knowledge, she did so. And in its workaday style, Moss's consultancy bore a similarity to the process of CEDAE's foundation, which was not dissimilar to the wider contemporary work of constituting archives in newly independent nation-states elsewhere. As CEDAE's institution generated tense categories of knowledge that both reinforced Egyptological norms and helped to channel a specific vision of (ancient) Egypt and Nubia, there was little motive for anyone involved with the work to question such practices. The workaday character of the institution belied the tensions embodied by it, as Louis Christophe's own anxieties demonstrated.

Yet taking the High Dam's floodwaters as a useful metaphor, the tensions embodied by CEDAE also had the potential to burst their banks. Noblecourt's criticisms of Selim Hassan illustrate this point, as do the later tensions surrounding Alexander Papadopoulo. CEDAE generated sovereign tensions without resolving them. And much like the gigantic drain built to channel Nile water into the reservoir that started to form behind the High Dam, once opened, the institution provided an easy outlet for such anxieties to flood through. Making possible the continuation of historically contentious practices, despite UNESCO's rhetoric, the Nubian campaign never operated smoothly.

Chapter 3

Valuing Egyptian Nubia

Tensions surrounding knowledge created during the Nubian campaign were occasionally bureaucratized into irrelevance. Arguments about, and instrumental problems related to, recording Nubia's past became occluded through paperwork, much as they had been during CEDAE's creation. At the start of the campaign proper, Christiane Desroches Noblecourt, continuing to oversee CEDAE, requested that the Field Equipment Division of IBM produce an "Executive Electric Typewriter" whose keys could produce transliterated hieroglyphs. Her description of those keys, however, was too vague to help IBM produce them. At the end of March 1960, the corporation's divisional head, Gerda Friedmann, wrote to UNESCO to ask the organization "to consult Mrs. Noblecourt regarding this matter" and "if necessary to obtain the required clarifications and an actual printed sample of these symbols."[1] A purchase order stamped "PAID" indicates that UNESCO reimbursed IBM for its work that May.[2] Two months later, however, Friedmann wrote back to the organization requesting payment "to cover the cost of a sixth special type matrix" in addition to the five that IBM had already produced. Again, a purchase order was stamped and a further forty dollars sent

---

1. Friedmann to Giorgio Rosi, March 30, 1960. Folder CA/12/7, 069 (62) AMS (Part 12), UNESCO Archives.

2. Gerda Friedmann to Taghi Nasr, May 11, 1960. Folder CA/12/7, 069 (62) AMS (Part 12), UNESCO Archives.

to the company.³ Hieroglyphs could now be typed at CEDAE to Noblecourt's satisfaction. It had, though, taken several months, and large amounts of paper, to ensure that outcome. Monumental hieroglyphs could be preserved one key at a time. Yet it had required persistence to create the conditions in which this form of "data" might be prioritized.⁴

Not every difficulty connected to Nubia inspired such effort. Tensions about knowledge practices coursed through the Nubian campaign, constituting multiple, overlapping visions of Nubia's past at the expense of both the project's coherence and UNESCO's credibility as organizer. Emerging from complex genealogies of work on ancient Egypt and Sudan, these tensions in turn helped to solidify, but never fully concretize, the border between the two newly independent countries. At stake was how the preservation of Nubia's past should happen once UNESCO's campaign began: what remains should be recorded and where, how that recording might happen, and which instruments should be deployed during that process. As in all preservation work, at stake also was which remains might be ignored and destroyed by the High Dam's flooding.⁵ Beyond the Nubian settlements already damned to destruction, not everything could be salvaged with a typewriter key. Notwithstanding CEDAE's norm-setting activities, for instance, there was no guarantee that any of the organization's recommendations would be followed, even by UNESCO's own experts. Given that the institution's management of the Nubian campaign in fact lent organizations involved in the project considerable autonomy once they were on the ground, standardized norms of recording were often conspicuous by their absence. On that ground (and working on publications in the years afterward), institutions and practitioners made "the field" in which they worked, sometimes ranging across two countries in the process, but sometimes, too, drawing a firm boundary between them.⁶

---

3. Gerda Friedmann to Taghi Nasr, July 13, 1960. Folder CA/12/7, 069 (62) AMS (Part 12), UNESCO Archives.

4. If "data" was a term used during the Nubian campaign, its incorporation as part of the project was mixed, but the category is a useful heuristic for understanding how knowledge of Nubia's ancient past came into being if, following Elena Aronova, Christine von Oertzen, and David Sepkoski, "Introduction: Historicizing Big Data," *Osiris* 32 (2017): 13, we "adopt the principle that data is what its makers and users have considered it to be."

5. On preservation, see Mirjam Brusius, "Introduction—What Is Preservation?," *Review of Middle East Studies* 51, no. 2 (2017): 177–82. For a discussion of the ethics of who makes such choices, see William Carruthers, "Rule of Objects: On the De-Peopling of Safe Havens," *Review of Middle East Studies* 51, no. 2 (2017): 228–33.

6. There was nothing exceptional in this process of field-making, as much literature in anthropology and the history of science relates. As Clifford, "Notes," 64, discusses, the field and "fieldnotes are enmeshed in writing and reading that extends before, after, and outside the experience of empirical

CHAPTER 3

For all the consultative committees instituted by UNESCO, the Nubian campaign constituted an assortment of methods that had often emerged in earlier eras and settings and that were shot through with boundary work and competing notions of distinction: about what the recordable past should be and which disciplines should record it, about what preservation implied, and about who, anyway, was best placed to carry out the job.[7] As the campaign progressed, these circumstances and their material traces became more pronounced. Complicating this situation was the difference between the campaign in Egypt and Sudan, where archaeological fieldwork had enjoyed a much less prominent history and had long been seen through the lens of the country to the north. In Sudan, archaeologists often represented the campaign as dealing with unknown terrain. This move—epistemological, material, and territorial—began to raise serious questions for archaeologists and Egyptologists working north of the Sudanese border. Likewise, it complicated the notions of territorial and nation-state integrity that multilateral organizations like UNESCO were conditioned upon and that newly independent countries like Egypt and Sudan had started to embody.[8]

Before turning to Sudan, here I outline how differences regarding the Nubian campaign in Egypt developed, explaining how UNESCO's devolution of responsibility for the project constituted the conditions in which spaces opened for differing interests to emerge. Coursing through documentation connected to the campaign, this situation began to constitute competing visions of the Egyptian Nubian past, even as those visions were inescapably connected to earlier work in the region. I follow this process as it took place, considering the constitution of Egyptian Nubian pasts through fieldwork that generated links between documentation, instruments, and the things those tools were used to find, record, and manipulate. Sudan might have been promoted as constituting previously unexplored terrain. Yet events in Egyptian Nubia demonstrate how, left alone to do as they pleased, fieldworkers in Egypt could just as easily conjure a blank slate.

---

research." Likewise, Brusius, "'The Field,'" 274, emphasizes the "blurring [of] the lines between field and museum science."

7. Rehearsed ever since, this disciplinary unease was so obvious that it was (diplomatically) discussed even in the campaign's official account: Säve-Söderbergh, *Temples*, 187–205.

8. As Jankowski, *Nasser's Egypt*, 8, notes, despite the brief existence of the UAR, the Nasser regime's "initiatives and involvement in Arab nationalism were developed within a primarily Egyptian frame of reference and often pursued with hesitance." Elsewhere, recent scholarship emphasizes how the rise of the newly independent nation-state within the postwar international system was far from inevitable, for which see: Cooper, "Possibility"; Getachew, *Worldmaking*; Wilder, *Freedom*.

Tinkering Accuracy

Given its centrality to the instigation of the Nubian campaign, CEDAE constitutes a vital starting point in understanding how such blank slates developed. The institution had been riven by tensions at its planning stages, but Noblecourt's vision for the center did not always coalesce on the ground either. The unequalled accuracy in the copying of texts and reliefs that CEDAE promoted seemed not only to be in the eye of the beholder, but also constituted through the tinkering (or field *bricolage*) necessary to render those copies tangible, loosening the institution's grip over fieldwork. As the Nubian campaign progressed, "a political logic ultimately seemed to take precedence over any coherent preservation theory": national and international political imperatives, for example, rendering it possible to cut apart and reassemble the Abu Simbel temples while concurrently claiming their integrity as monuments (objections from technical experts be damned).[9] Yet a similar, low-level political logic also begat significant amounts of tinkering as individuals on the ground not only worked with the—sometimes wanting—tools and instruments placed at their disposal, but also made use of the campaign's imprimatur to promote their own methodological objectives. CEDAE's record of the Egyptian Nubian past resulted from this tinkered practice. The Nubian campaign was an undoubted result of high geopolitics. On the ground, however, the project and its development were often the result of the politics not only of make do and mend, but also of cynical opportunism.[10]

This situation developed from the birth of CEDAE in 1956, just after its creation (and before events at Suez temporarily halted its work). CEDAE tasked

---

9. Allais, "Integrities," 19.

10. "Tinkering" (or *bricolage*), with its connotations of improvisation, constitutes a useful frame of analysis here. Equally, one might use other similar terms developed in the history and sociology of science, not least because CEDAE's fieldwork involved the use of the *Hathor*, a specially altered "bateau-laboratoire," as Noblecourt, *La grande*, 138, puts it. Discussing attempts to move the laboratory into "the field," Robert Kohler, *Landscapes and Labscapes: Exploring the Lab-Field Border in Biology* (Chicago: University of Chicago Press, 2002), coined the phrase "border practice." Elsewhere, Simon Werrett, *Thrifty Science: Making the Most of Materials in the History of Experiment* (Chicago: University of Chicago Press, 2019) has demonstrated how scientific practice in early modern England made use of, and reused, materials readily available in the home, a process of make do and mend not dissimilar to the one discussed here. Werrett also discusses how, in the postwar age of "Big Science . . . thrifty science has not disappeared, though it has certainly been obscured" (*Thrifty Science*, 194). It is tempting to suggest that the Nubian campaign constitutes evidence of this phenomenon. With its sometimes-tinkered approach, the project demonstrated some (but not all) characteristics of what Aronova, von Oertzen, and Sepkoski, "Introduction," 2, characterize as a "shift toward enormous scientific undertakings that were incredibly costly, involved hundreds or even thousands of investigators, adopted a corporate-style management structure, and tended to monopolize support from public and private sources."

CHAPTER 3

University of Chicago Egyptologist Charles Nims to photograph the sculptural and hieroglyphic reliefs in the temple of Ramses II at Abu Simbel. Nims was otherwise employed by the OI; his photographic work for Chicago House, the field headquarters of the OI's Epigraphic Survey in Luxor, meant that his expertise was in demand as CEDAE searched for expert advisers. In a report summarizing his time at Abu Simbel, however, Nims revealed how he had been forced to tinker his skills to fit the work's circumstances. He complained, for instance, that he had experienced trouble because "many of the pieces of equipment ordered by UNESCO for the work had not arrived." Noblecourt had "obtained substitutes . . . but they presumably were not as good as those ordered." Thus "there were no ladders tall enough to reach the top of the scenes in the large hall of the temple, [and] not enough planks to adequately cover the scaffold." Those ladders, though, were the least of Nims's worries. Beyond equipment shortages, he also complained that "during the first week the flood lights and dark room were utilized most of the time by the group making photogrammetric records."[11] Nims's photographic efforts were forced into competition for scant resources with a team whose work constituted the spectacle that UNESCO's publicity demanded.

Scant resources consequently called for a tinkered response. Discussing the photography of relief work in the temple, Nims noted that "in the upper register the lighting is somewhat uneven due to the fact that the lights could not be elevated above about 3–3 ½ meters." He also admitted that "there is some variation in scale," although "this latter can be corrected, if necessary, on an enlarger." Nims produced photographs through which, due to the way he had been forced to adapt himself to conditions on the ground, he suggested that it would only be possible to generate a certain type of accuracy. Even then, however, there were no guarantees. "Due apparently to a misunderstanding," he wrote, "bromide (enlarging) paper was sent instead of cloro-bromide [sic] (contact printing) paper." Forced to make do with this unsuitable material, Nims admitted that "one print of each negative brought from Cairo was made on this paper, though they are not quite satisfactory."[12] The prints were imperfect, at least in Nims's eyes, but there seemed to be no choice other than to tinker with them in order to produce acceptable representations.

Ironically, his superiors may not have been as concerned by this issue as Nims himself was. At Abu Simbel, accuracy really was in the eye of the beholder, especially for those concerned with the site's aesthetic characteristics.

---

11. Report by Charles Nims, February 1956. "Work Done in Abu Simbel, Egypt, for the Centre de Documentation . . . de l'Egypte Ancienne." Folder CA/12/7, 069 (62) AMS (Part 6): "Documentation sur les Peintures et Inscriptions en Haute-Egypte-Programme de Participation," UNESCO Archives.

12. Report by Charles Nims, February 1956.

The quality of the sculpture there was a source of some contention among Egyptologists, many of whom did not consider the temples worth saving from the forthcoming deluge.[13] And this issue itself seemed to be of some concern to Christiane Desroches Noblecourt as she attempted to drum up support for work at the site. Viewing the statues of the Ramses II temple up close, she noted that "the faces were broad, the features rude and thick, the expression hard, frozen." The statues, in other words, had been sculpted to be viewed from a distance, the whole greater than the relative crudity of its parts. "Seen from the ground," Noblecourt realized, "the result was a masterpiece in comparison with [what would be produced by] photogrammetric analysis," even if "the measurements taken were going to be of unfailing accuracy."[14] Facing this problem, perhaps Nims's tinkered precision would do a better job persuading viewers of the temple's beauty than he had imagined. Ironically, too, this situation was perhaps not one that necessitated concern. In the history of monument preservation, this sort of doubled aesthetics—one in which people might perceive beauty and crudity to coexist in a single location—had once been considered innovative. Preservation work at Athens's Parthenon in the 1930s had produced a monument that purposefully existed in two complementary states: one restored and "complete," and the other designed to be indicative of the long years of destruction that the structure had in fact undergone.[15] Yet even this history did not stop concerns about preservation at Abu Simbel.

Emphasizing CEDAE's transposition of colonial norms, however, the racial logic of the institution's work provided one way of dulling such issues. Any "fault" in the photographs produced under the aegis of CEDAE's experts— and perhaps any fault in the work at the site as a whole—could be ascribed to other people, because the tinkered accuracy of those images was tied to the racial hierarchies suffusing technical assistance projects at large. CEDAE incorporated not only "Western 'know-how' . . . [but also] its hands-on counterpart, 'show-how.'"[16] Accordingly, Nims had been given Egyptian assistants to train, and he linked his judgments surrounding accuracy to them rather than to the equipment they had been forced to use. "In seeking to obtain accuracy, there must be careful positioning of the camera and exactness in levels," Nims began, and "both the photographers were instructed in this need of exactness, and shown the use of mirrors and reflectors." A photographer from Luxor, "Abdel Latif Hassan [even] took several photographs without assistance

---

13. Allais, "Integrities," 33.
14. Noblecourt, *La grande*, 152.
15. Allais, *Designs*, 67–68.
16. David Webster, "Development Advisers in a Time of Cold War and Decolonization: The United Nations Technical Assistance Administration, 1950–59," *Journal of Global History* 6, no. 2 (2011): 251.

from me." Yet despite the acknowledged skill of his assistants, Nims damned them with faint praise: "Hassan Eff. Zaki is already an accomplished photographer, but his interest is more in artistic photographs." Worse still, "either can, with proper supervision, continue the work . . . [but] Hassan Zaki may not have the necessary patience."[17] As it turned out, the adjudication of accuracy in architectural field photography was never anything but social—which meant that it was racial, too. As the Nubian campaign proper began, that act would continue to privilege some more than others.

The Chicago House Method

UNESCO's project saw multiple teams working simultaneously in the field. Given that situation, the social basis of accuracy allowed for various—and often quite particular—definitions of precision to take root. In these conditions, making do could transform into making hay, at least for some. Nims and his OI counterparts were heirs to a very specific practice of copying ancient Egyptian reliefs and inscriptions. As the Nubian campaign began in earnest, so too did that method continue to flourish as the institution itself undertook work in the region, despite the ways in which it conflicted with the practices promoted by UNESCO's own experts.

The "Chicago House Method" was instituted in 1927 by the founder of the OI, James Henry Breasted, together with Harold H. Nelson, the institution's Luxor field director; the practice's name was a self-referential nod to their organization's headquarters in the town.[18] The technique constitutes a complex set of activities: a combination of photography, line drawing, "collation" of the two forms of visualization by two Egyptologist-epigraphers, and final "checking" of the work by the field director. Pulled together, these practices—at least according to the institution—are meant to create "documentation so precise it could stand alone as a replacement in the absence of the original monument," thus providing further evidence of Egyptology eliding material objects with the documentary means of their recording across multiple media.[19] Through use of this method, texts, reliefs, and their copying took cen-

---

17. Report by Charles Nims, February 1956.
18. Jeffrey Abt, *American Egyptologist: The Life of James Henry Breasted and the Creation of His Oriental Institute* (Chicago: University of Chicago Press, 2011), 78–80.
19. Compare Brusius, "The Field," 278–79 on the use of multiple types of documentary media to enable credible field recording in archaeology in Iraq. For the OI's take on the Chicago House Method, see "The 'Chicago House Method,'" accessed July 9, 2020, https://oi.uchicago.edu/research/projects/epi/chicago-house-method. For further details of how Breasted and Nelson developed the process, see Abt, *American Egyptologist*, 292–95.

ter stage in a way familiar from, but not entirely similar to, other iterations of Egyptological practice. Breasted's time in Berlin spent working with European colleagues on Adolf Erman's exhaustive *Wörterbuch der äegyptischen Sprache* project influenced the midwesterner's work, for example, adding a "German" influence to the proceedings.[20] Consequently, the Chicago House approach to precision was one that its partisans might have favored, but not one that everyone involved in epigraphy in Egyptian Nubia agreed with. The process, for instance, was decidedly slow, "more like an ongoing research seminar than a sleek copying machine": appropriate for the seminar rooms of Berlin's then Friedrich Wilhelm University, maybe, but hardly auspicious in the face of the time constraints that the Nubian campaign faced.[21] The denizens of Chicago House, however, now used the relative isolation offered by their work in Nubia to promote their technique. Removed from CEDAE's oversight, the Chicago House Method could prosper.

Despite CEDAE's best efforts, precision recording of Nubian remains continued to be adjudicated by reference to the cast of people involved at particular sites rather than with respect to any standardized system. Chicago-style judgments as to what constituted accuracy continued to have valence as the Nubian campaign began, legitimating practices from Egypt's interwar years as appropriate for the post-Suez era. In October 1960, George R. Hughes, Chicago House's then director, was busy preparing to lead a group from the institution away from its customary work in and around Luxor. Moving temporarily to Egyptian Nubia, this team, among them Charles Nims, would copy hieroglyphic inscriptions at the temple of Beit el-Wali at the same time as colleagues from Cairo's Schweizerisches Institut für Ägyptisches Bauforschung und Altertumskunde investigated the history of the structure's architecture. The temple was built during the reign of Ramses II, and many hundreds of years later converted into a church.[22] It had also been documented once before: the German Egyptologist Günther Roeder carried out work in 1907 and 1909 as a result of Gaston Maspero's intervention in the preservation of the region's ancient remains.[23] Ever ready to promote the work of Chicago House, Hughes would describe Roeder's volume on the temple as "the most nearly

---

20. Abt, *American Egyptologist*, 78–82. On Erman and the *Wörterbuch*, see Thomas L. Gertzen, *École de Berlin und "Goldenes Zeitalter" (1882–1914) der Ägyptologie als Wissenschaft: Das Lehrer-Schüler-Verhältnis von Ebers, Erman und Sethe* (Berlin: De Gruyter, 2013).

21. Abt, *American Egyptologist*, 295.

22. Herbert Ricke, "The Architecture and Construction of the Temple," in *The Beit el-Wali Temple of Ramesses II*, by Herbert Ricke, George R. Hughes, and Edward Wente. The University of Chicago Oriental Institute Nubian Expedition 1 (Chicago: University of Chicago Press, 1967), 5.

23. Günther Roeder, *Der Felsentempel von Bet el-Wali* (Cairo: Institut français d'archéologie orientale, 1938).

CHAPTER 3

adequate of the publications of temples in the ... series."[24] Yet it was a letter written by Hughes to his Chicago colleague Keith Seele that indicated what he really thought of other epigraphic methods.

Writing to Seele after seeking assistance from CEDAE staff members, Hughes was blunt. "After being around the Centre of Documentation being indoctrinated about how we should copy the temple," he wrote, "I did not feel I had gotten much of anywhere." The problems with CEDAE were manifold. "First off, we use the wrong size film for them and I am not on the verge of using their notebooks to handcopy all texts and write descriptions of all scenes." Method, however, was not Hughes's only source of concern. "Next day at lunch at Groppi's" (a restaurant and café in downtown Cairo that had been a hub of the colonial city's social whirl), Hughes and Labib Habachi (now acting as consultant to the OI's Nubian Expedition) bumped into Louis Christophe, who had begun work at CEDAE earlier that year. Christophe "told me to come to the center to see the photogrammetry workings and that he had bibliography cards on the Beit el-Wali temple for me." That meeting, though, turned out to be impossible: "he would not be in his office that day and I left that night." Worse still, "he also told me that he had prints of the aerial photos [of Egyptian Nubia, commissioned by CEDAE from France's Institut géographique national in 1959], but only one set and he could not give me that."[25] Chicago House, perhaps to Hughes's relief, would have to do things its own way.

Yet the results of that work (published relatively speedily in 1967) indicate how even the Chicago House Method could be altered to fit its circumstances, not to mention the perceived value of the monument to be recorded.[26] Again, accuracy rested in the eye of the beholder, an outcome that became especially possible if conditions, as at Beit el-Wali, allowed a limited and relatively isolated group of people to decide if such alterations did not hinder the "precision" desired. Avowedly an expedition formed of true believers in the OI's methods, no one questioned the group's decisions as they approached a

---

24. George R. Hughes, "The Epigraphic Record," in *The Beit el-Wali Temple of Ramesses II*, by Herbert Ricke, George R. Hughes, and Edward Wente. The University of Chicago Oriental Institute Nubian Expedition 1 (Chicago: University of Chicago Press, 1967), 7.

25. Hughes to Seele, October 17, 1960. "George R. Hughes Correspondence with Keith Seele" file, Museum Archives at the Oriental Institute of the University of Chicago (hereafter Oriental Institute Museum Archives, or OIMA). For an account that details (and occasionally amplifies) the colonial-era lore of Groppi's, see Artemis Cooper, *Cairo in the War, 1939–1945* (London: Penguin, 1989), 120–21. For an alternative view (on the setting alight of sugar and flour from Groppi's during the Cairo fire of January 1952), see Nancy Y. Reynolds, *A City Consumed: Urban Commerce, the Cairo Fire, and the Politics of Decolonization in Egypt* (Stanford, CA: Stanford University Press, 2012), 186.

26. For comparison, the OI has been working at, and publishing on, the temple of Medinet Habu on Luxor's West Bank since 1924—and with no end in sight, for which see "Chicago House Projects," accessed July 9, 2020, https://oi.uchicago.edu/research/projects/epi/chicago-house-projects.

temple that they decided was not worthy of the sort of work they carried out elsewhere.

Only in a few instances have we attempted to show, as has been done consistently in other Oriental Institute epigraphic publications, painted lines or the margins of different colors painted on the carved reliefs. No color survives in the Entrance Hall, but in the interior of the temple it is still preserved in very large part. To have indicated color lines and margins carefully throughout would have almost doubled the work of the artists and the time required for the task of recording, and the results would not have been wholly satisfactory in any case. Although we photographed extensively whole scenes and details wherever significant color could be captured on film, the value of including numerous color photographs has seemed scarcely commensurate with the cost of printing them and we have limited ourselves to presenting only five of the best.[27]

Even the most "precise" practice of documentation could be altered if agreement among colleagues occurred. Those colleagues, too, were to remain a small group, ever limiting the number of people who might be able to judge them and once again constituting that limit through the mobilization of race. Writing to Hughes the week prior to his trip to CEDAE, Keith Seele noted that John Wilson, the OI's acting director, "has had his reply from the Rockefeller Foundation."[28] The OI had been created in 1919 with the help of a donation from John D. Rockefeller Jr., although funding from the family had long since dried up.[29] Yet Wilson—previously (from 1939 to 1946) an OI director, and also heavily involved in the national and international committee structures of the Nubian campaign—now saw an opportunity.[30] Hoping that the massive undertaking in Nubia would unlock further financing, he approached the Rockefeller Foundation for support, visiting Dean Rusk, president of the board, in New York in June 1960.[31] The foundation's response was mixed, even as Rusk was mere months from becoming John F. Kennedy's secretary of state (a situation that might well have played into the later adoption

---

27. Hughes, "The Epigraphic Record," 7.
28. Seele to Hughes, October 12, 1960, "George R. Hughes Correspondence with Keith Seele" file, OIMA.
29. See Abt, *American Egyptologist*.
30. For John Wilson, see his autobiography, *Thousands of Years: An Archaeologist's Search for Ancient Egypt* (New York: Charles Scribner's Sons, 1972).
31. According to John Wilson, "Nubian Program: Rockefeller Foundation–June 28, 1960," "Nubia: Rockefeller Foundation" file, Records of the Nubia Excavation (Box 048), OIMA, he also tried to get meetings with the Carnegie, Bollingen, and Commonwealth Foundations, to no avail. Wilson would also have an unsuccessful meeting with Henry Heald, president of the Ford Foundation, on July 6.

of Nubia as something of a presidential *cause célèbre*).³² As Seele wrote to Hughes, "they refused to give us a penny, yet suggested that they would provide assistance for six or eight students to be trained as archaeologists, Sudanese, Egyptians, or even Americans, if we would undertake to train them." This scheme was well within the purview of the sort of technical assistance work that CEDAE had been instituted to undertake and that the Kennedy administration would itself promote: Kennedy would launch the UN's "Decade of Development" that very year. Seele, however, was unenthusiastic, writing that "the trainees would get some kind of a stipendium, and we would use our personnel to make them into archaeologists *at our own expense* [emphasis Seele's own]. A bit magnanimous, what?"³³ The itself-racialized logic of technical assistance did not seem to apply to Chicago Egyptology, or so Seele thought. For some, making documentation precise meant keeping that documentation not only privileged, but also racially exclusive.

Composites of the Past

In contrast, CEDAE's documentation was far less attuned to the overt practice of racial distinction than that of the OI, or at least it attempted to be. In 1981, just after the Nubian campaign had ended, CEDAE released a catalogue of its publications emphasizing the strategy that had been used to attempt to counter such issues: popularization. The catalogue listed several *"brochures culturelles (destinées à un large public* [sic])," all of which were translated into English, French, and Arabic. In a bid not only to educate, but also to make a public for the center's work, the temples at Philae, Abu Simbel, Kalabsha, and Gerf Hussein all had brochures devoted to them, and in a way that attempted to include a "local," Arabic-reading crowd (which, needless to say, did not include non-Arabic-speaking Nubians).³⁴ Yet despite such attempts to reach this audience, notions and practices of distinction themselves coursed through CEDAE's work in ways that fashioned the temples and inscriptions of Egyptian Nubia as exclusive to a small readership.

Given the history of survey work in the region, the collective in question is the limited group of people who had helped to conjure the images of an-

---

32. On the role of the Kennedys in Nubia, see Luke, *A Pearl*, 114–15.
33. Seele to Hughes, October 12, 1960. On the "Decade of Development," see Ekbladh, *The Great*, 190.
34. CEDAE, *Publications du Centre d'études et de documentation sur l'Ancienne Égypte* (Cairo: Centre d'études et de documentation sur l'Ancienne Égypte, 1981), 1, 15–16.

cient Nubia found in tour guides and encountered by passengers on Nile steamers. CEDAE focused its actions on the temples those passengers had long sailed past, helping to further the impression that they were timeless ancient monuments even though later structural accretions—and the meanings related to them—had in fact been widespread at the sites. Yet successfully reading CEDAE's published records about these places involved another link to social distinction: the ability to comprehend the scholarly norms that had previously been applied to the structures. Egyptologists had long published the temples in scholarly monographs, summarizing such work for the guidebooks they had been intimately involved in writing.[35] It was the reproduction of that scholarship as a publicly visible, but still often exclusive, form of knowledge that was now at stake as CEDAE's experts created records and trained Egyptians.

Beyond CEDAE's own offices and certain libraries in Cairo and Alexandria, the repositories that purchased the institution's publications seem, in the main, to have been a small number of European and American museums and universities.[36] Only a very small and distinct readership, increased slightly in number by the trainees taken under CEDAE's wing, would enjoy the ability to understand and work with these reports. CEDAE's publications were available for sale in Cairo. Only a limited number of institutions, though, would order them, and only a small number of people had access to those places and the training required to understand the forms of knowledge they promoted. CEDAE may have constituted a technical assistance project, but it also promoted assistance in a form of distinction shot through with colonial norms of racial superiority. Egypt, so Clio told, had once possessed the world's greatest library. But that library, so the same histories remembered, had burned.[37] Knowledge about the country was still perceived to be in safer hands elsewhere, whatever Christiane Desroches Noblecourt claimed.

The similarities between CEDAE's publications and the OI's volume on *The Beit el-Wali Temple of Ramesses II* emphasize the force of this racially tinged practice. The Chicago publication in fact constituted several items collected within one hardbound case: several large folio-sized plates and an accompanying booklet that could only realistically be accessed in select research libraries

---

35. As Reid, *Whose*, 72, notes, the Egyptologist Auguste "Mariette wrote a guide [to Egypt] for guests at the Suez Canal festivities, and [Wallis] Budge [of the British Museum] wrote for Cook.... Baedeker obtained chapters from ... [among others] Capt. H. G. Lyons ... and Egyptologists Samuel Birch, Georg Ebers, and George Steindorff."

36. At least judging by searches on worldcat.org.

37. A memory whose consequences played out during the UNESCO-sponsored building of the Bibliotheca Alexandrina in the late 1990s, for which see Beverley Butler, *Return to Alexandria: An Ethnography of Cultural Heritage, Revivalism, and Museum Memory* (Walnut Creek, CA: Left Coast Press, 2007).

due to its size. Consequently, the volume anticipated the ability to partake of such access for its contents to be properly comprehended; there was simply no way to use the booklet and the plates together other than to spread them all out on an appropriately sized desk or table (not unlike those in the OI's own library).[38] Such necessity was not unusual for volumes based on Egypt (or in archaeology more generally). As Andrew Bednarski has noted, the Napoleonic *Description de l'Égypte* constituted a similar problem: "the sheer [folio] size of the corpus' plates meant that it had to be set down to read," and "the size, cost, and format [of the work] . . . detracted from its sale in Britain."[39] CEDAE's "Collection Scientifique" (as the institution denoted its publications of Egyptian Nubia's temples) did little to alter this situation. UNESCO's organ of technical assistance thus further materialized the notion that the monumental structures at hand might equally well constitute composite collections of paper that only initiates could enjoy.

CEDAE's publications dispensed with the book format entirely, presenting collections of unbound card pages within either sturdy hardbound portfolios or rather less sturdy card folders. The collections did not constitute easy—or easy to handle—reads. Take for example the 1968 publication of *Le Speos d'El-Lessiya*. Nominally formed of two volumes (*Cahier I: Description Archéologique; Planches* and *Cahier II: Plans d'Architecture; Dessins-Index*), the collection's pages are held in either side of its folder, the ability to mix and match its parts central to its existence; the publication acts as if the reader were simply placing together selections from CEDAE's filing cabinets in front of them (figure 3.1). The institution's 1981 catalogue noted of the Collection Scientifique that initial volumes in the series would "be completed by the very diverse group of elements permitting their diffusion as working documents: geographical maps, plans, sections, key-plans, descriptions and architectural notices, indexes, tables etc."[40] It was access to these "very diverse" other elements that meant that potential readers had to lay out the parts of CEDAE's publications on tables in specific research libraries in order to gain any real understanding of their coherence.

Spreading them out in this way, the publications allowed readers quite literally to hold the elements of ancient Nubia in their hands, assembling a

---

38. For a (celebratory) history of the OI's library (now called the "Research Archives"), see Foy Scalf, "A Kind of Paradise: The Research Archives of the OI," in *Discovering New Pasts: The OI at 100*, ed. Theo van den Hout (Chicago: The Oriental Institute, 2019), 134–56.

39. Andrew Bednarski, *Holding Egypt: Tracing the Reception of the 'Description de l'Égypte' in Nineteenth-Century Great Britain* (London: Golden House, 2005), 40. The *Description* constituted nine folio volumes of text, eleven folio volumes of plates, and a three-volume atlas, as Bednarski, *Holding Egypt*, p. 3 details.

40. CEDAE, *Publications*, 1.

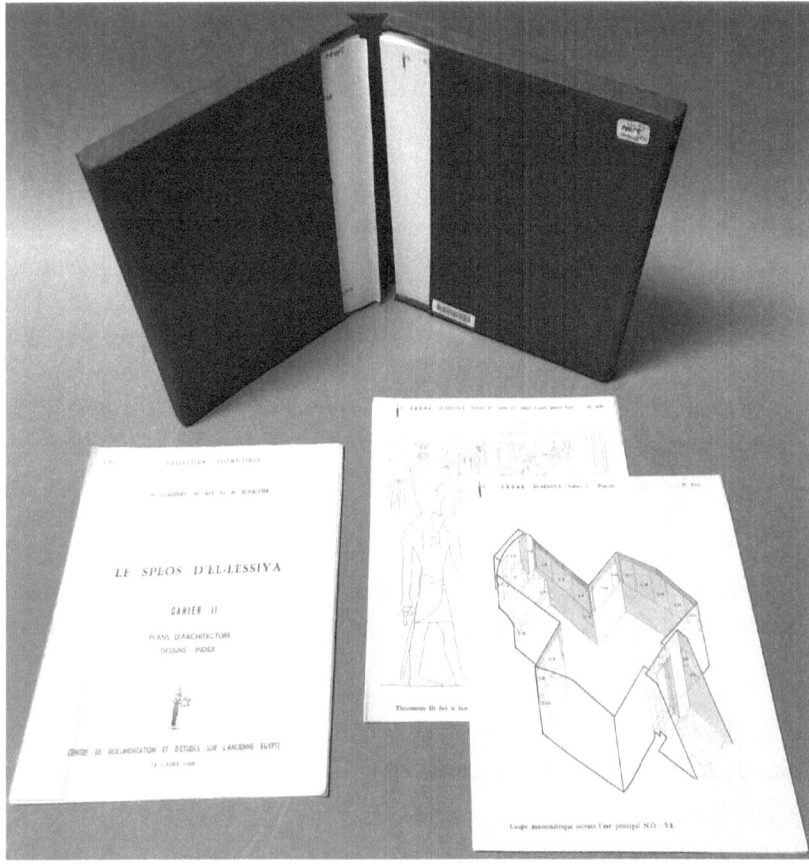

FIGURE 3.1. The Centre d'étude et de documentation sur l'Ancienne Égypte's publication *Le Speos d'El-Lessiya*. Christiane Desroches Noblecourt, Gamal Moukhtar, Sergio Donadoni, Michel Dewachter, Hassan el-Achiery, and M. Aly, *Le Speos d'El-Lessiya*, 2 vols (Cairo: Centre de documentation et d'études sur l'Ancienne Égypte, 1968). Image: Carl Graves.

composite—and exclusive—set of images reflecting chapter 1's "view from the boat." Through the act of constructing such composites, Egyptological and other readers found the images of Nubian temples they had helped to constitute reflected back at them in an almost infinitely combinable number of ways. A mirror of this group's power, this process was at the same time limited to the small readership who enjoyed access to the spaces where that work could occur.

That readership nevertheless took issue with the way in which CEDAE's work happened, reflecting the way in which forms of Egyptological distinction continued to be entwined with that process. In a 1973 review of several of CEDAE's publications (including the volume on *Le Speos d'El-Lessiya*), Cyril

Spaull, the reviews editor of *The Journal of Egyptian Archaeology*, noted that "all in all the 'Collection scientifique,' so far as it has at present progressed with the publication of the Nubian remains, offers an adequate archaeological record of the structure, decoration, and inscriptions of the sites included."[41] Damning CEDAE's work with faint praise, Spaull at least provided warmer congratulations than another reviewer. Discussing the OI's Beit el-Wali volume, the Egyptologist Hans Goedicke of Johns Hopkins University (who had in fact spent some time working for CEDAE in both Cairo and Abu Simbel during the late 1950s) noted that "if all monuments which were in Nubia had been recorded in the same fashion as Beit el-Wali, their loss, regrettable as it remains, might be less tragic."[42]

Goedicke, of course, might not have been directing his criticism at CEDAE. Yet he was not alone in making such claims: a 1962 letter written by Keith Seele carped that George Hughes had been "told . . . that the Documentation Center in Cairo had made such a mess of Abu Simbel that the authorities now wished to request the Oriental Institute to copy" the temples.[43] Goedicke's own comments on CEDAE in a 1958 report to UNESCO suggest that he indeed harbored doubts about the new institution, meanwhile. His time at CEDAE had, he said, "culminated in the removal of the chief of this [photographic] section on my request after it became clear that he not only was unable to direct this section but intentionally sabotaged the needed collaboration" with the organization's scientific department. Gatekeeping apparently as standard, Goedicke also went on to display significant racial prejudice, discussing the need "for constant guidance of the local personnel."[44] Racialized distinction seemed to constitute CEDAE's guiding value, even in an institution at one glance designed to counter such thinking.

Mopping Up Egyptian Nubia

If the temples of Egyptian Nubia became a racialized fulcrum in a contest of methodological distinction and Egyptological boundary work, then there was quite purposefully no distinction whatsoever placed in archaeological work in

---

41. Cyril H. S. Spaull, "Centre de Documentation et d'Études sur l'Ancienne Égypte: Collection Scientifique," *The Journal of Egyptian Archaeology* 59 (1973): 251.

42. Hans Goedicke, "The Beit el-Wali Temple of Ramesses II by Herbert Ricke, George R. Hughes, Edward G. Wente," *Journal of the American Research Center in Egypt* 7 (1968): 138.

43. Seele to William R. Boyd, May 22, 1962. "Nubia: Boyd, William R" file, Records of the Nubia Excavation (Box 048), OIMA.

44. Goedicke to UNESCO Director-General, February 16, 1958. Folder CA/12/7, 069 (62) AMS (Part 12), UNESCO archives.

the region: excavating Egyptian Nubia constituted the pits (pun intended). As we have seen, both CEDAE and the Department of Antiquities' 1955 *Report on the Monuments of Nubia* had anticipated archaeological survey and excavation as necessary. Such work, though, was characterized as a "mopping-up" exercise: completing the work of previous surveys by excavating any previously unsubmerged remains. The 1955 *Report* clearly stated this limit: "a special mission, similar to the one operating in 1929–1934, is to excavate the remaining parts of the cemeteries, and inspect the whole zone to the limits of the Egyptian territory in the south." The volume's authors did not expect this work to be hugely productive, either, at least in comparison to the sort of excavation that might be carried out in the Sudanese part of Nubia. "Before discussing the formation of this mission, or estimating the sum needed for its expenses," they declared that

> we must stress the fact that the whole zone lying between Adindan [the Egyptian-Sudanese border town] and Kerma [further south in Sudan] . . . which will be submerged, has been partly excavated. But in it are important ancient areas which greatly need excavation, as important ancient towns lie under their mounds, as well as temples and cemeteries of the flourishing ages in the history of the country. These zones will later be a subject of study, and the Committee will determine, with the collaboration of the archaeologists of the Sudan Government, what arrangement should be made regarding these sites.[45]

This contrast between Egyptian and Sudanese Nubia—and the perception of Egyptian Nubia as almost entirely excavated before the Nubian campaign began—played a key role as planning for the project gathered pace. Constituted over decades by the "view from the boat," the widespread nature of this representation meant that institutions presumed to be interested in such work displayed little to no interest in Egyptian excavation. Despite UNESCO's public pronouncements, barely anyone was interested in digging through what seemed like archaeological—and artifactual—slim pickings. The "golden age" of Euro-American museums taking what they wanted from the field might well have been over.[46] Its attitudes, however, often seemed to continue. Certain objects mattered more than others. Consequently, many Egyptologists and archaeologists felt that excavation in Egyptian Nubia was not worth their time.

In July 1957, post-Suez (and with political momentum seemingly in its favor), the Egyptian Department of Antiquities sent a form letter to institutions engaged in excavation and survey in the country, inviting them to dig in

---

45. Egyptian Department of Antiquities, *Report*, 25.
46. On changing attitudes to the collection of Egyptian objects, see Stevenson, *Scattered*.

Nubia in accordance with the most recent Egyptian antiquities law (Law 215 of 1951). Attaching a list of possible sites for excavation, the letter was as polite as possible, a strategy that evinced little success.[47] As a result, that October, a half-hearted request by the University of Pennsylvania's University Museum to renew its excavation concession at the site of Mit Rahina was put on hold by the Egyptian authorities in expectation that the institution would move its work to the south (the Department of Antiquities attached the same list of sites to its reply).[48] Civility gave way to conditionality: the official delimitation of where excavations might now take place. Despite such actions, however, still no one seemed interested in what Nubia offered. Froelich Rainey, the University Museum's director, wrote to Department of Antiquities Director-General Moharram Kamal, saying: "I do not know just what we can do, or who we have available, but in the event we can arrange such an excavation I will certainly advise you."[49] In January 1958, meanwhile, CEDAE's archaeologist-architect Jean Jacquet wrote a letter to University Museum Egyptologist Rudolf Anthes noting that "noone [sic] has shown any interest in digging in Nubia and I think they have more or less given up the idea of trying to force people down there."[50] Some institutions did decide to go to the region: the newly opened branch of the [West] German Archaeological Institute in Cairo obtained a concession to work at the site of Amada in October 1958.[51] Others, though, remained cautious.

Importantly, this caution was not due to Egypt's antiquities law, as much as that legislation itself generated a certain amount of disquiet. Law 215 of 1951 was the newest—and least permissive—of Egypt's pre-republican antiquities laws. Created in the dying days of Britain's influence in the country (and in the aftermath of the struggle to curtail the export of excavated objects that had been raging since the discovery of the tomb of Tutankhamun in 1922), the law in fact enabled limited export of antiquities from Egypt. Permission for export, however, had to be given by the minister of education, a situation primed to cause (geopolitical) upset.[52] For example, to the apparent conster-

---

47. Abbas Bayoumi [presumably?] to "Messieurs," July 16, 1957. Expedition Records, Egypt, Box 46, File 1: "Egyptian Research, Correspondence, 1956–1957," University Museum Archives.

48. Moharram Kamal to Froelich Rainey, October 31, 1957. "Egyptian Research, Correspondence, 1956–1957," University Museum Archives.

49. Rainey to Kamal, November 14, 1957. Expedition Records, Egypt, Box 38, File 9: "Mitrahineh—Correspondence, Anthes, 1957–1958," University Museum Archives.

50. Jacquet to Anthes, January 18, 1958. "Mitrahineh—Correspondence, Anthes, 1957–1958," University Museum Archives.

51. Susanne Voss, *Die Geschichte der Abteilung Kairo des DAI im Spannungsfeld deutscher politischer Interessen*, vol. 2, *1929–1966* (Rahden, Germany: Marie Leidorf, 2017), 179.

52. Reid, *Contesting*, 352–53. See throughout Reid's volume for the struggle to change antiquities law in nominally independent Egypt.

nation of one employee of the American Research Center in Egypt, the Polish archaeologists at Tell Atrib discussed earlier in this book had been "(rather exceptionally) granted a share of finds" in 1957. Yet even the possibility of such artifactual favoritism and Warsaw Pact advantage did not make Nubia a promising venue for excavation. According to the same commentator, in early 1958 "the Department of Antiquities was [now] endeavouring to persuade them to transfer their activities to the region south of Assuan."[53] The contingency in that statement indicates the extent to which that transfer was not a foregone conclusion. Nubia simply did not constitute a promising locale for excavation, at least to archaeologists who thought they had seen it all.

The minutes of a March 1958 meeting of Britain's Egypt Exploration Society (EES) perhaps put it best (the society had previously been the Egypt Exploration Fund). Consulting the list attached to the Department of Antiquities' form letter, Bryan Emery (now the Society's field director), noted "no promising site among those listed. It was doubtful whether any foreign excavators would be able to continue work [in Egypt] at present."[54] Nubia, so the predominant view went, had been excavated. Any "Nubian treasure," as Emery once put it, was long gone.[55] Edward Wente, the director of the American Research Center, concurred: "while one can sympathise with the aim of the Department of Antiquities to preserve a record of the monuments which will ultimately be submerged," the center's *Newsletter* paraphrased him as saying, "one can not help wishing that excavations in areas of Egypt proper, which seem more promising of results, were not at present an impossibility." Wente's words implied that the potential ancient—and presumably pharaonic—remains to be excavated might help repay the capital outlay of that work: "quite aside from anything else, the great cost of Nubia excavation [sic] can well act as a deterrent to foreign institutions wishing to work in the Nile Valley."[56] Nubian archaeological survey and excavation was seen to be of negligible (artifactual) value in relation to the cost of working in the region, especially regarding the periods from which any excavated objects might derive.

To many Egyptologists and archaeologists, pharaonic Egypt continued to trump all, especially if it could be excavated: while digging north of Nubia had been forbidden, as Wente pointed out, "there has been no limitation placed by the Department of Antiquities on epigraphic work undertaken in Egypt

---

53. Anon., Untitled, *American Research Center in Egypt, Incorporated: Newsletter* 27 (1958): 1.
54. Minutes of the Executive Committee of the EES, March 27, 1958; *Egypt Exploration Society Committee Minutes, 1956–1963*. Egypt Exploration Society Archives, London (hereafter EES Archives).
55. Emery, *Nubian Treasure*.
56. Anon., Untitled, 2.

CHAPTER 3

by foreign institutions."[57] Indeed, it was only when "areas of Egypt proper" came into play that attitudes to Nubian excavation would change. In October 1959, Emery reported to the EES's committee on his involvement in the international conference of experts, called by the Egyptian government and UNESCO, that set the Nubian campaign in train. The meeting's minutes noted that, as had previously been the case, "Professor Emery was of opinion that as far as Pharaonic Egypt was concerned, Nubia had already been fully explored." At the same time, "he considered that a survey should be made of prehistoric sites, e.g. palaeolithic sites which have not yet been touched."[58] Perhaps some parts of Nubia might still be interesting after all.

What caused this change of heart? Emery's about-face was not due to an announcement that the Egyptian government "would be prepared to give to excavators not less than half the finds [from Nubia] with the additional reservation that items which are needed to complete the collections of the Museums of the United Arab Republic" would be kept in the country.[59] Egyptian Nubia was likely to be archaeologically (and artifactually) worthless, even if Paleolithic objects remained in the ground. Instead, what was now valuable was the accompanying—and itself newly promoted—opportunity to excavate in the north of the country after any Nubian excavations had ended, and under the exact same set of rules regarding object division. "Egypt proper"—a clear allusion to the Nile-side tombs and temples that had long drawn Egyptologists—had come back into play. As the EES Committee noted, in the case that "the Foreign Office could provide the funds the Society could take over the survey of prehistoric sites and thus ensure the return [of the institution] to Saqqara," a site in the pharaonic burial grounds just south of Cairo where Emery had excavated during the interwar years and, briefly, after the Second World War. Indeed, "the Minister of Culture and National Guidance, Dr. S[arwat]. Okacha [sic], had asked Professor Emery to write him a personal letter on the subject."[60] This compromise over future excavation concessions was never fulfilled in as straightforward a manner as initially implied. Froelich Rainey's constant requests for a concession to dig at the pyramid site of Dahshur, for instance, were ultimately rebuffed, even as Emery returned to Saqqara in 1964.[61] Yet encour-

---

57. Anon., Untitled, 2.
58. Minutes of the Committee of the EES, October 14, 1959; *Egypt Exploration Society Committee Minutes, 1956–1963*. EES Archives.
59. Minutes of the Committee of the EES, October 14, 1959.
60. Minutes of the Committee of the EES, October 14, 1959.
61. As Rainey to Lucius D. Battle, September 26, 1966, "Rainey-Egypt; Yale-Penn Expedition; Correspondence 1966–1967," University Museum Archives, notes, "our request for a site at the pyramids did not meet with an entirely favorable reception." Battle was a US ambassador to Egypt and had earlier (prior to that appointment) been fundamental in securing funding—and the support of the Kennedys—

age a small-scale "scramble for Nubia" by archaeologists the promise of work in "Egypt proper" did.

Long Division

Simultaneously, the process of artifact division itself reverted to the colonial rules of "Egypt proper" once it had been adjusted for the campaign. Lucia Allais argues that the Nubian campaign enacted "an elaborate legal and bureaucratic procedure that completely transformed the terms of colonial archaeology, replacing it with a new international regimen for cultural exchange among nations" that allowed, as we shall see, for the distribution of (some) excavated objects abroad with the permission of the Egyptian government.[62] Yet it is important to remember that the situation in Egypt was much more sutured to the colonial era than this explanation allows.[63] Adapting the limited export provisions of 1951's Law 215, UNESCO's campaign did so with reference to earlier thinking about object exchange. The colonial genealogy of that thinking—coupled with the similar genealogy of the archaeological concessions through which excavation areas in Nubia were distributed—meant that "the terms of colonial archaeology" were not exactly transformed by the Nubian campaign. More accurately, they were tinkered with.[64]

Concessions—regulated through fixed coordinates on a survey map—had long constituted the vehicles through which archaeological excavation and survey work in Egypt had taken place. So, too, had concessionary contracts provided the legislative basis on which distributions of excavated objects occurred: such agreements to excavate fixed areas provided the (asymmetric) means through which any objects removed from the ground might be divided between the Egyptian government and their excavator. As it attempted to entice

---

for the salvage project at Abu Simbel, for which see Luke, *A Pearl*, 113–40. Rainey's correspondence reveals him to have been vigorously involved with that process, and presumably he thought that Battle might come through again. As Luke, *A Pearl*, 140 notes, however, Battle, once ambassador, was never again quite as supportive of archaeology (140).

62. Allais, "The Design," 192.

63. The Nubian campaign's "regimen for cultural exchange" in fact turned out to be rather exceptional given the development of other, more restrictive, export laws in this period, not least UNESCO's own 1970 Convention on the Means of Prohibiting and Preventing the Illicit Import, Export and Transfer of Ownership of Cultural Property, which Egypt accepted in 1973, and for which see Ana Filipa Vrdoljak, *International Law, Museums and the Return of Cultural Objects* (Cambridge: Cambridge University Press, 2006).

64. For a history of concessions written from the perspective of business history, see Cyrus Veeser, "A Forgotten Instrument of Global Capitalism? International Concessions, 1870–1930," *International History Review* 35, no. 5 (2013): 1136–55.

institutions to excavate in Nubia by offering such concessions according to the advice of its Consultative Committee, however, so the Department of Antiquities attempted to subvert concessionary power to its advantage. In this way, Egypt followed the example of countries like Iran, who now "asserted [or, notoriously, attempted to assert] their right to control their [concessional] resources by relying on the principle of permanent sovereignty over natural resources" like oil.[65] Yet not only does the crude division between natural and cultural in legislation like UNESCO's 1972 World Heritage Convention occlude the evident and entwined postwar development of both words in that opposition as "resource" adjectives.[66] It also obscures the fact that countries like Iran and Egypt "had played [little] to no role in the formulation of international law, which originated in Europe," and whose expansion had been enabled by colonialism and in the sorts of agreements that governed concessions themselves.[67] Instead of subverting colonial practice by distributing antiquities, the implementation of a new "regimen for cultural exchange" during the Nubian campaign—and its adaptation of Law 215 to that effect—in fact asserted a set of practices around the division of antiquities that had been developed as Egypt attempted to negotiate the withdrawal of British forces in the 1930s. Rather than an event that "transformed the terms of colonial archaeology," by allowing for the export of some excavated objects from concessionary areas, the campaign ironically allowed for the continued implementation of a system designed to favor colonial powers.

As Antoine Khater noted in 1960, Egypt's legal regime for antiquities conformed to prevailing international norms.[68] Central to the implementation of those norms in Egypt was the Anglo-Egyptian Treaty of 1936. The treaty required Britain to withdraw most of its troops from Egypt (those stationed in the Suez Canal region being permitted to stay, at least for the time being). It also paved the way for Egyptian membership, in 1937, of the League of Nations. That institution, while giving voice to its member states, had itself been designed in an attempt to uphold the global imperial system.[69] And that same

---

65. Katayoun Shafiee, "Technopolitics of a Concessionary Contract: How International Law Was Transformed by Its Encounter with Anglo-Iranian Oil," *International Journal of Middle East Studies* 50 (2018): 636.

66. Cf. Allais, *Designs*, 27–28.

67. Shafiee, "Technopolitics," 637; cf. Veeser, "A Forgotten Instrument," 1142. For a critical perspective on the historiography of Egyptian law (and an argument for the existence of a legal profession before the British invasion of 1882), see Omar Youssef Cheta, "A Prehistory of the Modern Legal Profession in Egypt, 1840s–1870s," *International Journal of Middle East Studies* 50 (2018): 649–68.

68. Khater, *Le régime*, 257.

69. On the Anglo-Egyptian Treaty, see Israel Gershoni and James P. Jankowski, *Redefining the Egyptian Nation, 1930–1945* (Cambridge: Cambridge University Press, 1995), 155–56. For the League of Na-

year, the International Museum Office of the League's International Institute of Intellectual Cooperation, one of UNESCO's predecessor bodies, held an International Conference on Excavations in Cairo. Given its genealogy in the League, that conference (and the *Manual on the Technique of Archaeological Excavations* that resulted from it) was an unsurprisingly asymmetric affair, shot through not only with assumptions about "archaeological science and the history of world civilisation," but also about who might best be placed to investigate that civilizational history: Europeans, in the main, and along the lines of many of the documentary practices embodied in institutions like CEDAE.[70]

The conference's Final Act, meanwhile, "reflected the ascendancy of the notion of the common right of all humankind to archaeological sites and cultural objects," doing so "in much the same way as the [League of Nations] mandate system guaranteed the free trade [of] and equal access to these cultural resources."[71] The document thus suggested that "the [national] government department concerned may hand over to the excavator some of the objects which he has discovered, with a view to promoting—outside the country—archaeological studies."[72] And even as that same document stated that "ownership of movable objects found in the course of the excavations shall be determined by the internal legislation of the country,"[73] the position of a set of possible, if limited, conditions for export was the one that Egypt's 1951 antiquities law, forged in the context of such late-colonial recommendations, took. Likewise, divisions made as a result of excavations during the Nubian campaign were limited to objects unnecessary to "complete the collections of the Museums of the United Arab Republic," therefore reflecting the *Manual's* suggestion that "duplicates" should be sent to smaller museums within countries.[74] That process also drew on an older, nineteenth-century practice of distributing "duplicate" natural history specimens that had found its way into

---

tions, see Susan Pedersen, *The Guardians: The League of Nations and the Crisis of Empire* (Oxford: Oxford University Press, 2015).

70. International Museums Office, *Manual on the Technique of Archaeological Excavations* (Paris, International Institute of Intellectual Cooperation, 1940), 12. The overwhelmingly Western European editorial committee is listed on p. 8. The list of participants on pp. 227–28 is little better, although it does include attendees from Egypt, Syria, Iraq, and Turkey. The *Manual* and its conference have been subject to more attention recently, for which see: Sarah Griswold, "High-Tech Heritage: Planes, Photography, and the Ancient Past in the French Mandate for Syria and Lebanon," *Future Anterior: Journal of Historic Preservation, History, Theory, and Criticism* 16, no. 2 (2019): 1–15; Lynn Meskell, "Imperialism, Internationalism, and Archaeology in the Un/Making of the Middle East," *American Anthropologist* 122, no. 3 (2020): 554–67, and Meskell, *A Future*, 7–8.

71. Vrdoljak, *International Law*, 116.
72. International Museums Office, *Manual*, 210.
73. International Museums Office, *Manual*, 219.
74. International Museums Office, *Manual*, 208.

museum collecting actions more widely, not least those of colonial anthropology: nature and culture again entangled.[75] The Nubian campaign's division of excavated antiquities wore its colonial logic on its sleeve. Tellingly, Egypt revised its law to forbid export of antiquities in 1983, shortly after the Nubian campaign officially ended.[76] Yet before that, artifact division in Egyptian Nubia was free to happen, however muted enthusiasm for it.

Fungible Archaeology: Profit, Loss, and Paper

Archaeological teams working in Egyptian Nubia translated their equivocation over the objects that might be found there into the language of profit and loss, in addition to the sort of legal- and bureaucratese that might protect their financial interests. Given the government money that often funded their work—in addition to the forms of official accountability that such funding engendered—that translation should be unsurprising. Combing through government-level reports on Nubia, one striking theme is the interweaving of words and numbers that made financing the work possible: the translation of qualitative arguments and legal contracts into a quantitative language of governance that not only justified international donations to the campaign on the basis of country- (Egypt- or Sudan-) level geopolitical strategies, but also echoed the way in which multilateral development and national administration came together in newly independent countries more widely.[77] If the "Nubia" that UNESCO's campaign was concerned with ever constituted a coherent space, it was one bisected by the nation-states that comprised its two parts and by the multilateral (and national) development policies that encouraged that division. This practice of documented accountability, meanwhile, echoed the workings of archaeology—and especially archaeological survey—to a degree that enabled that work to seem like it had always already been geared to the rise of technical assistance funding.[78] Archaeological missions

---

75. For the translation of collecting practices from natural history to anthropology, see Catherine A. Nichols, "Exchanging Anthropological Duplicates at the Smithsonian Institution," *Museum Anthropology* 29, no. 2 (2016): 130–46. For this phenomenon within Egyptian archaeology, see Stevenson, *Scattered*, 33–34, 47–48, 185–87.

76. Stevenson, *Scattered*, 260.

77. For this argument in relation to Sudan, see Young, *Transforming*. In Egypt, the Central Agency for Public Mobilisation and Statistics was founded in 1964, for which see United Nations Statistics Division, "Country Profile of Egypt," accessed July 27, 2020, https://unstats.un.org/unsd/dnss/docViewer.aspx?docID=506#start.

78. Discussing the Nubian campaign's work at Abu Simbel, Allais, "Integrities," 21, has described the processes under question as denoting *"calculability* . . . the potential of an architectural project to be incorporated into a project of economic development." It is the inscription of words and numbers

that had once been the domain of state-led, colonial-era public works projects now entered, with little to no friction, the postwar domain of state-led, multilaterally funded development practice. Those same missions, meanwhile, used the language of such practice to mask their disdain for the work at hand.

The archaeological survey of Egyptian Nubia now led by the EES (seen as vital to persuading anyone to work in the region) embodied this translation most directly. During two separate survey seasons in 1961, the institution undertook work similar to—but not quite the same as—that which Emery had suggested it might. An EES team under the charge, in the field, of Harry S. Smith of the University of Cambridge set out to perform the following, quite specific task:

> to explore, map, and record all sites of archaeological importance for the history of Nubia from the beginning of the ancient Egyptian dynasties onwards, that were to be found in those areas of Egyptian Nubia below River Level 180 [sic], which had not been previously surveyed and had not yet been conceded to other expeditions contributing to the campaign to save the monuments of Nubia. Prehistoric sites, inscriptions, and rock-drawings were to be the province of a Survey or Surveys undertaken by some other body: but the Egypt Exploration Society party agreed to note on their behalf such inscriptions or prehistoric sites as it came across.[79]

As expected with Emery's overall directorship of this work, the new survey—while simultaneously being used to advertise sites that might still be conceded to interested parties—constituted an exercise in "completing" the previous surveys in the region. Indeed, the project was carried out according to much the same standards, "with the following modifications in view of the size of the area involved and the extreme urgency." Thus:

> (i) where the aerial photographic survey, provided through the Government's Centre of Documentation and Studies on Ancient Egypt, showed beyond reasonable doubt that an area was barren of ancient monuments, that area need not be traversed on foot; (ii) sites were to be investigated by the sondage method to ascertain their character, extent, date, and state of preservation, rather than by full-scale excavation; (iii) Reisner's

---

on paper that interests me here, however. For similar reflections, see Mitchell, *Rule*, 89 (discussing the survey of Egypt under Henry Lyons).

79. Harry S. Smith, *Preliminary Reports of the Egypt Exploration Society's Nubian Survey*, United Arab Republic, Ministry of Culture and National Guidance, Antiquities Department of Egypt: UNESCO's International Campaign to Save the Monuments of Nubia (Cairo: General Organisation for Government Printing Offices, 1962), 2.

recording procedures might be slightly modified, particularly in respect of site-mapping and photography.[80]

It is the legalistic denotation of points and clauses in these words—not to mention the hedging of bets made possible by the deployment of the phrase "reasonable doubt"—that is telling in terms of what "completion" in the Egyptian Nubian case meant. The new survey would sort through what Emery perceived as the archaeological dregs while simultaneously protecting itself from accusations of neglect through legalese and the precedent of aerial survey.[81] International investment in the bare bones of Nubian survey work would be protected by contractual agreement.[82] The survey's field notebooks, meanwhile, dropped the legalese entirely, making do with the language of pure financial balance. Alongside descriptions of work carried out and remains excavated as the survey team moved along the Nile, notes about which sites would be "unprofitable," which "would not repay further exploration," and which were "probably not worthy of further work" were all listed throughout the first of the society's "Day Book[s]."[83] Occasionally, prospects for profitable excavation were discussed: the next volume noted that "practical and economical" excavation "on a very small scale" might be carried out at the site of Afyeh.[84] Yet those recommendations never came accompanied by great enthusiasm.

Unsurprisingly, Harry Smith did not seem to find much profit in keeping the artifacts excavated during the work. At the end of both seasons of the survey, he deposited the objects collected at Aswan's Museum. And at the end of the first season of work, he explicitly noted the "EES's desire not to claim division this year."[85] Yet even this magnanimous act only encompassed certain items. During the work, the survey team encountered any number of pottery sherds, using them to date and "type" sites according to the norms of archaeological work last used in the region by Emery: the sherds becoming a material metonym for the type (and quality) of site that might be excavated in their

---

80. Smith, *Preliminary Reports*, 2.

81. As Allais, *Designs*, 128–35, notes, aerial survey had been one of the technologies used to guide allied bombing raids around historical structures during World War II. That practice enabled the potential destruction of monuments to be reduced to a form of accountability linked to probability. The Nubian campaign drew on that precedent.

82. Given the Nubian campaign's use of excavation concessions, bilateral contracts between excavating institution and concessional country in fact governed much of the project.

83. "Egypt Exploration Society Sondage Survey, Season 1961: Day Book," January 26 and February 11 and 15, 1961. EES Archives (folder NUB.001).

84. "Egypt Exploration Society Nubian Survey, 1960–1961: Day Book 2," March 14, 1961. EES Archives (folder NUB.001).

85. "Egypt Exploration Society Nubian Survey, 1960–1961: Day Book 2," March 30, 1961.

find-spots. If considered worthwhile, however, these same sherds could be drawn and then dumped: the 159 items deposited with the Aswan Museum at the end of the first survey season, and the eighteen objects deposited after the second, clearly do not correspond to the number of sherds encountered during the work.[86]

Once again, paperwork played a key role in Nubia: documentation could be as valued as material. Making the wholesale dumping of a certain type of excavated object possible, the paper on which the survey team drew pots and their pieces made those objects fungible in a way that Nubia's monuments had proven not to be.[87] The doubled spectacle of monument disassembly and reconstruction had proven an essential part of the Nubian campaign's promotion: among other forms of media, UNESCO produced publicity films concentrating on that work. Paper could not take the place of monuments, despite CEDAE's best efforts (and even as mechanical reproduction on film almost did).[88] Yet the interchangeability of paper with the sort of commodity represented by the fragment of a pottery vessel was deemed acceptable in the eyes of archaeologists on the ground. Documentation of excavated objects was as important as the objects themselves, if not more so.

Value, Documentation, and National Completion

The interchangeability of paper and potsherd was not without its issues, however, not only due to who decided on the attribution of value to such objects in the first place, but also in terms of how that process played fast and loose with the material remains of a sovereign country. The *Manual on the Technique of Archaeological Excavations* made heavy use of documentary metaphors when discussing excavated items, likening excavation to "assembling corroborative documents."[89] And the Final Act of the 1937 Cairo Conference, published at the end of the volume, noted that such "documents, in so far as they replace the original records destroyed by the excavations, constitute a common scientific heritage and consequently, are the property of the concessionary State."[90]

---

86. "Egypt Exploration Society Nubian Survey, 1960–1961: Day Book 2," March 30, 1961, and "Day Book: Egypt Exploration Society Nubian Survey, October–November 1961 (Second Season)," November 9, 1961. EES Archives (folder NUB.001). See throughout the EES day books for the practice of typing. For prewar instances of finds being entirely "unrecorded on site," see Stevenson, *Scattered*, 156.

87. As Stevenson, *Scattered*, 14, notes, documentation relating to artifacts could delineate "the fungible from the inimitable."

88. Allais, "Integrities," 28–29.

89. International Museums Office, *Manual*, 12.

90. International Museums Office, *Manual*, 210.

This documentary metaphor took on literal materiality in the drawings made by archaeological teams in Egypt, and also in the other paper records that those teams assembled: Harry Smith, we know, handed over some sort of "object register" to Egypt's Department of Antiquities at the end of his survey.[91] That many of these documents seemed to find their way into foreign institutional archives, however, constituted a significant consequence of the Nubian campaign: one that CEDAE tried in vain to address.

After the Second World War, the Cairo Conference and its recommendations had become the basis of a set of International Principles Governing Archaeological Excavations ratified at UNESCO's General Conference in New Delhi in 1956. Those recommendations, however, were nonbinding.[92] Given that situation, it is notable that, very often, the way in which documentation was removed from Egypt led to the loss of information about—and the loss of epistemological control over—objects that were themselves meant to be sovereign (even as the Egyptian officials overseeing such work were themselves engaged in a process of sovereign management). Beyond the EES, a joint expedition of the University Museum of the University of Pennsylvania and the Yale Peabody Museum used paper records in a variety of ways as it set about documenting Egyptian Nubian sites, itself removing those records from the country. And the Yale-Penn team too devoted that documentation to creating fungible objects. The expedition created an indexical list that allowed not only the possibility of accounting that the institutions involved had carried out their job both to completion and with accuracy, but also the possibility of discarding objects deemed to be "similar" to a type already registered during the dig, mobilizing the discourse of "duplicates" discussed earlier to its own—and not the state of Egypt's—benefit. The list of discarded pottery compiled for the site of Arminna West conveyed with some detail where such pieces had been found and how many of them had been thrown away. It also indicated the reason for such acts of discard, the list bearing the title: "types of pottery similar to a registered pot, to an EK [Emery and Kirwan] type, or in an arbitrary description."[93] The Yale-

---

91. "Day Book: Egypt Exploration Society Nubian Survey, October–November 1961 (Second Season)," November 9, 1961.

92. For the background to the principles, see UNESCO, "International Principles Governing Archaeological Excavations: Preliminary Report Compiled in Accordance with the Provisions of Article 10.1 of the Rules of Procedure Concerning Recommendations to Member States and International Conventions Covered by the Terms of Article IV, Paragraph 4, of the Constitution," UNESCO/CUA/68, Paris, August 9, 1955. For the principles themselves, see UNESCO, "Records of the General Conference, Ninth Session, New Delhi, 1956: Resolutions," Paris, 1957, 40–44.

93. "Index of types" from the Yale-Penn excavation at the site of Arminna West, Egypt. Yale Peabody Museum of Natural History Archives, Division of Anthropology, Arminna West Archive, "Arminna West Cemetery B (AWB) Pottery Discarded" file, ANTAR.037151.

Penn team played fast and loose with what was meant to be sovereign Egyptian material, glossing over the fact that the Emery and Kirwan types had been developed during a mission one of whose organizing principles was that pottery style could be directly linked to people. Yet as that link was itself connected to notions of racial florescence and degradation, so the Yale-Penn pot sherds became "facts on the ground." Reconstituted artifacts of colonial racial thinking, those sherds played into international arguments about (ancient) Egypt's populational history that would rage for decades afterward, as chapter 7 discusses.[94]

On the one hand, the Yale-Penn expedition's discard of objects similar to other, previously excavated items did the Egyptian government's job of judging what was necessary to "complete" national collections for it. On the other, judging such similarity was meant to be left to Egyptian officials. Moreover, by following the tacit norms of archaeological routine and judging object similarity in the field, the expedition ensured that it was not forced to accept items that it did not want to retain.[95] Whether through the behest of a conference in interwar Cairo or through the urging of Erwin Panofsky, the drawing of an equivalence between an object and its paper record seemed to negate any possible criticism that archaeologists had not completed their work in a fit and proper manner. Indeed, the primacy of documentation in archaeology seemed largely to anticipate that this criticism might arise, a colonial-era get-out clause conditioning what had become "postcolonial" field practice.[96]

It was not, though, as if foreign excavating missions were the only ones to rid themselves of objects excavated in Egypt. As chapter 6 reveals, the Egyptian Department of Antiquities itself ceded all the items excavated at the site of Afyeh to the Archaeological Survey of India. Perhaps this move simply constituted a generous act to a non-aligned partner. It also indicated, however, that Egypt was not overly keen on retaining Nubian finds, particularly the potsherds that much of the material excavated at Afyeh constituted (and which

---

94. For the connection between "facts on the ground" and archaeological pottery analysis, see Abu el-'Haj, *Facts*.

95. My use of "tacit" does not discount the possibility that the vagaries of object discard were also explicitly discussed (and, in fact, had to be, given the sometimes systematic practice of making lists of discarded items). Explaining the formation of academic "schools," Kathryn M. Olesko, "Tacit Knowledge and School Formation," *Osiris* 8 (1993): 28, notes that "overemphasizing the role of tacit knowledge in school formation has entailed ignoring a key factor in school formation: learning by explicit precept." It is hard to believe that there was no explicit discussion of what the practice of object discard in the field might mean in terms of artifact division between Egypt and the excavating institution.

96. This situation explains why the legal consultant to Egypt's then Supreme Council of Antiquities Ashraf al-'Ashmawi authored a book called *Sariqat Mashru'a* [Legal robberies] (Cairo: Al-Dar al-Misriyya al-Lubnaniyya, 2012). Discussing historical artifact division, al-'Ashmawi notes on p. 71 that "unfortunately those were the letters and words set down on paper," calling into question the very circumstances in which that paper gained its force.

CHAPTER 3

the Yale-Penn mission had so casually discarded). This disregard for objects excavated in Nubia was not always apparent: the 1947–1970 volume of the *Journal d'Entrée* of the Egyptian Museum in Cairo—one of the museum's accession registers—records objects and object groups from the Nubian campaign under 740 different registration numbers.[97] And as the Egyptologist and art historian Edward Terrace of the Boston Museum of Fine Arts did when writing to Yale Egyptologist William Kelly Simpson in May 1964, it was still possible to discuss who "made, I hear, a very good division" as a result of the Nubian campaign.[98] Yet love of their excavated objects was not always clear among field teams involved in the Nubian campaign.

Items were still valuable, though, on an institution-by-institution basis. The OI made clear to its supporters exactly the worth that work in Nubia held for the organization. In letters addressed to "Friends of the Oriental Institute" (alternately known as the institution's "Archaeological Newsletter"), Keith Seele, who had been placed in overall charge of the OI's Nubian campaign, boasted of his institution's artifactual success. Discussing the OI's work at Qustul in early 1963, Seele wrote that:

> In a cemetery considered exhausted after the excavations of two previous expeditions, we entered into our catalogue of finds in the first ten days a total number of objects equal to the total of last year's entire season at Serra East in the Sudan. At the present writing, this number has increased to more than 950, and the season is only half gone.[99]

Seele's was an entitled tone, candid about the aim of the excavations and expectant that the rules of division would now work in favor of his institution, which ultimately shipped forty-five boxes of antiquities back to Chicago.[100] In a later missive ("issued confidentially to members and friends"), Seele wrote of excavating a burial shaft where "we realised that we might well have hit the jackpot."[101] He was not a subtle man. In an official report on the OI's earlier work at Beit el-Wali, Seele wrote that "I should hope that the totality

---

97. *Journal d'Entrée, 1947–1970*, Egyptian Museum, Cairo.
98. Terrace to Simpson, May 19, 1964. Yale Peabody Museum of Natural History Archives, Division of Anthropology, "1964, William K. Simpson Other Correspondence" file, ANTAR.037199.
99. Seele to "Friends of the Oriental Institute," February 26, 1963. "Nubia: Chicago, University of; Oriental Institute Archaeological Newsletters" file (1047.8, Box 048), Records of the Nubia Excavation (Box 048), OIMA.
100. Seele to OI, July 10, 1963. Untitled file of interim reports, Records of the Nubia Excavation (Box 033), OIMA.
101. The OI *Archaeological Newsletter*, April 23, 1963. "Nubia: Chicago, University of; Oriental Institute Archaeological Newsletters" file, Records of the Nubia Excavation (Box 048), OIMA.

of the finds for our expedition might be offered" to the institution. "Then it would be possible to select from the comparative rubbish which comprises the aggregate a few items worth the cost of packing and transport to Chicago."[102] That Seele's report would be seen by officials of the Department of Antiquities only underlined the cynicism of his strategy: persuading those officials of the *lack* of value of certain excavated objects had long been a strategy used to remove them from Egypt.[103] In contrast, when Seele organized the import into the United States of objects excavated at Qustul in 1963, he made clear to carefully enumerate the contents of the boxes and to fill out a customs form emphasizing their (duty-free) future use for unspecified "educational purposes."[104] Valuing artifacts, Seele managed to have it both ways.

It was Froelich Rainey, constantly trying to organize an excavation for his museum in Lower Egypt, who made the importance of such equations of value most obvious, however. In March 1962, discussing what to do with the money that had been appropriated by the American government for the Egyptian Nubian work (and at a time when discussions surrounding what to do at Abu Simbel had become more heated), he noted that he agreed with a strategy set forward by the Cultural Attaché at the US Embassy in Cairo.

> Now I agree with John Slocum that a million dollars from the million and a half appropriated for excavations should be turned over to the monuments project <u>with the assumption that the Egyptian government now considers the archaeological work in Nubia completed and that American institutions should proceed to work in Lower Egypt</u>. . . . I am not inclined to push for another appropriation for Abu Simbel if [Tharwat Okasha] does not come through with his agreement [to offer a site in Lower Egypt].[105]

Rainey, moreover, was clear about why his irritation had grown: "Okasha must know by this point as well as I do that excavations in Nubia these days are for

---

102. "Oriental Institute Egyptian Assuan High Dam Program: Joint Expedition with the Schweizerisches Institut, Report of Season of 1960–1961 by Keith C. Seele, Director," 8. Untitled file of interim reports, Records of the Nubia Excavation (Box 033), OIMA.

103. Most famously in the case of the bust of Nefertiti now at Berlin's Neues Museum, for which see Reid, *Contesting*, 88. Cf. Alice Stevenson, "Artefacts of Excavation: The British Collection and Distribution of Egyptian Finds to Museums, 1880–1915," *Journal of the History of Collections* 26, no. 1 (2014): 89–102.

104. "Declaration for Free Entry of Works of Art, Artistic Antiquities, Oriental Paintings, Statuary, Etc.," signed by Seele, undated but presumably July 1963. Untitled file of interim reports, Records of the Nubia Excavation (Box 033), OIMA.

105. Rainey to John Otis Brew and John Wilson, March 14, 1962 (underlining Rainey's own). "Yale-Penn Expedition Corresp. 1962 (1 of 2)," Box 43, University Museum Archives.

the birds."[106] Objects were time, time was money and—to some people, anyway—objects from Egyptian Nubia were not that valuable.

Boats, Faltering

Assumptions of value like Rainey's, however, stood close to those made by the Egyptian government itself. During the Nubian campaign, Egypt propelled the (temple-centric) view from the boat with some alacrity. Officials devoted considerable effort to ensuring the availability of vessels that could promote an Egypt whose monumental ancient glories stood revivified in tandem with the High Dam's ascension. In 1963, for example, the Ministry of Culture and National Guidance commissioned the construction of two houseboats for the campaign, naming the vessels after the owner and architect of Saqqara's Step Pyramid: Zoser and Imhotep, respectively. Conforming to Nasser-era policies of import substitution, this project was also cast as wholly Egyptian. The ministry's Engineer's Office declared that furnishings at "the lowest price" (*aqal al-āsʿār*) should be procured from recently nationalized department stores in Cairo: Sednaoui and Omar Effendi.[107]

By 1966, Egypt's Nubia Office administered twenty-six boats plying the rapidly flooding region, floating manifestations of the vision of Nubia that had become predominant over the previous decades. Many of them named after the temples that the Nubian campaign had partially been launched to preserve, the steady movement of the boats encompassed the past within the nation's present. Al-Dakka, Beit al-Wali, Qasr Ibrim, Dendur: all of these were vessels involved in the work, and all of them (like Zoser and Imhotep) were emblematic of a nation attempting to revive the glories of an ancient—and implicitly pharaonic—past.[108] As they sailed past the slowly reconstituted Nubian landscape, those same vessels proffered a view of the region that was idyllic and timeless, but also very much of its time.

Nancy Reynolds has discussed how, as the construction of the High Dam progressed, Egypt invested in other building initiatives as part of the country's revolutionary project. "The promise of a renewed Aswan," the center of operations for the High Dam's construction, formed part of this work. Among

---

106. Rainey to Brew and Wilson, March 14, 1962.
107. Agreement dated December 28 and 29, 1963. File 2A-a2, "al-A'imatayn Zūser wa-Imhutab" ["The two boats Zoser and Imhotep"], Nubia Museum Documentation Center (hereafter Nubia Museum). Egypt's department stores were nationalized in 1961, for which see Reynolds, *A City*, 211.
108. Report dated August 30, 1966. File 2A-a8, "Muʿaddalāt al-Istihlāla li-l-Waḥdāt al-Māʾiyya, 1963/1964" ["Initial rates for water units, 1963/1964"], Nubia Museum.

FIGURE 3.2. Temple blocks on Elephantine Island, Aswan. Deutsches Archäologisches Institut Kairo Photo Archives neg. no. 8964, photography by George Roy Haslam Wright, ©DAI Cairo.

other developments (and the programmed destruction that accompanied them), a new, Nile-side corniche "appeared 'almost overnight,' using 'an army of workers and equipment' in order to impress Nikita Khrushchev and other visitors" when the first phase of the dam was completed in 1964.[109] The corniche "became a choice location for many new hotels and shops, and made space for local Egyptian leisure in the old colonial-administrative core of the city."[110] The development of this infrastructure, meanwhile, meant that national and international tourists might be exposed to riverside pleasures anew.

Beyond the vessels plying the Nile as part of the Nubian campaign's day-to-day work, Egypt contracted an Italian company to provide a hydrofoil service from Aswan to Abu Simbel, allowing tourists staying in the redeveloped city to travel up the Nile and take in the state of the riverside temples.[111] When those structures had been taken apart, so, too, were many of their pieces stored next to the Aswan Museum on Elephantine Island, which was located on the Nile in the heart of the city: the view from the boat transposed to the town where tourists took those vessels from (figure 3.2).

---

109. Reynolds, "City," 223, citing Henry Tanner, "Mood of the Old Egypt Lingers Amid Changes in New Aswan," *New York Times*, March 24, 1975.

110. Reynolds, "City," 224.

111. Sarwat [Tharwat] Okasha, "Ramses Recrowned: The International Campaign to Preserve the Monuments of Nubia, 1959–1968," in *Offerings to the Discerning Eye: An Egyptological Medley in Honor of Jack A. Josephson*, ed. Sue H. D'Auria (Leiden and Boston, MA: Brill, 2010), 234.

It is little wonder that participants in the Nubian campaign continued to draw on this perspective. Not everyone involved with the project, however, aligned themselves with this view. Primed for a return to "Egypt proper"—and buoyed by an Egypt representing itself as just that—many Egyptologists worked toward that vision. Yet other modes of fieldwork existed, not least in Sudan. There, some practices familiar from Egypt stayed relevant. Borders, however, could (be made to) speak.

CHAPTER 4

Making Sudan Archaeological

CEDAE's index cards were not the only documentary objects related to the Nubian campaign. In Sudan, another "documentation center" came into being, although less well-resourced than the one in Cairo. This new center's existence helped to shape notions of value connected to the Sudanese Nubian past, in addition to that of Nubia more generally. In Sudanese Nubia, it became possible—and encouraged—to represent the past as a blank slate in a way impossible in Egypt, and as an archaeological *tabula rasa* in particular. Consequently, work during the Nubian campaign helped to destabilize the boundary between newly independent Egypt and Sudan even as it made part of that border more concrete.

Notwithstanding wider geopolitical ruptures, the specifics of that boundary had long been liminal, foreshadowing how what seemed like a firm frontier in fact remained ambiguous.[1] The January 1899 Anglo-Egyptian Condominium Agreement had established the border between Egypt and Sudan "at the parallel of 22° North." On March 26 that year, however, the transfer of a sliver "of land along the Nile from Egypt to the Sudan" took place, creating what became known as the Wadi Halfa Salient.[2] This transfer took place so that the station

---

1. A situation whose consequences Agha, "Nubia," outlines.
2. The Geographer, Department of State, *International Boundary Study No. 18—July 27, 1962: Sudan-Egypt (United Arab Republic) Boundary (Country Codes: SU-EG)* (Washington, D.C.: United States

furthest from Khartoum on the Sudan railway could be built just north of Wadi Halfa at the border settlement of Faras, then "the upstream limit of river navigation in Egypt and a transhipment point for goods."[3] Sixty years later, with the construction of the Aswan High Dam, the Salient would be submerged almost in its entirety, leaving at most thirty to forty square kilometers of uninhabited land free from water. Yet that flood would not stop geopolitical dispute.

In February 1958—over a year-and-a-half before Egypt and Sudan signed the Nile Waters Agreement—the Egyptian government requested "the return of all territory north of the 22nd parallel to Egyptian administration."[4] This request related to the plebiscite on the creation of the UAR taking place later that month and in which Nubia's population—beneficiaries of what had become a relatively porous border—were meant to vote. In response, the Sudanese government noted that Nubians had not been asked to participate in Egypt's last plebiscite (a 1956 referendum on Egypt's new constitution and Nasser's presidency); it also noted that the Wadi Halfa Salient had effectively been administered by Sudan for half a century.[5] Egypt did not counter these arguments, and has never raised the issue of the Wadi Halfa Salient again, even as other border disputes with Sudan continue to simmer, not least over the Hala'ib Triangle on the Red Sea coast.[6] Legally speaking, however, the geopolitical status of the Salient remains unconfirmed, emphasizing the way in which Nubia itself remains a liminal space, the migratory trauma inflicted there echoed by an uncertain border sitting flooded and difficult to perceive.

UNESCO's Nubian campaign only increased that uncertainty, helping to fix the Egyptian-Sudanese boundary at the same time as calling that border into question. Teasing out the relationship between large-scale geopolitical actions and the small-scale politics of documentary material, I discuss in this chapter the ways in which index cards and other pieces of paper helped to materialize archaeological claims about Nubia at the same time as that paper held the Egyptian and Sudanese portions of the region apart. Those claims, centering on the relative inattention paid to archaeology during the Nubian campaign, have often been considered self-evident.[7] To some extent, too, they hold firm: as I have detailed, UNESCO treated archaeological survey in

---

of America Department of State, Office of the Geographer, Bureau of Intelligence and Research, 1962), 2.

    3. The Geographer, Department of State, *International Boundary Study*, 4.

    4. The Geographer, Department of State, *International Boundary Study*, 5.

    5. The Geographer, Department of State, *International Boundary Study*, 5.

    6. See Ahmed H. Adam, "What Is Going on between Egypt and Sudan?", *Aljazeera.com*, January 12, 2018, https://www.aljazeera.com/indepth/opinion/egypt-sudan-crisis-180110134022602.html.

    7. See, e.g., Allais, "The Design," 193; Meskell, *A Future*, 40.

Nubia as being of secondary importance to the preservation of monuments, particularly Egyptian ones. Yet as work in Sudan took place, and as archaeologists started to form connections across the Egyptian-Sudanese border, this process gave way to complaints about the secondary importance of archaeology that doubled as strategies for disciplinary advancement. At UNESCO, it is true that "archaeological research would be relegated to the wings" after fieldwork in Nubia ended and the World Heritage project developed.[8] Fieldnotes, correspondence, and other records, however, suggest that most archaeologists working in Nubia had little interest in UNESCO's schemes as long as those projects appeared to have little relevance to their own work: it is notable how little the term "heritage" is mentioned by such archaeologists even as they criticized the organization.[9] Likewise, the dis-attachment of archaeologists from UNESCO's later work did not hinder their continued use of Nubia to promote their own interests.

Here, I demonstrate how the constitution of Sudan as an archaeological *terra incognita*—and as an independent nation-state—enabled these disciplinary and professional strategies to prosper. I show how these strategies involved the work of British colonial administrators, the development-minded officials of a newly independent Sudanese government, and American archaeologists who mobilized their own experiences dealing with archaeology, anthropology, and modernization in the United States. My discussion complements Alden Young's contention that postcolonial "Sudanese officials were not struggling to imagine new development schemes as much as they were trying to select which [schemes] to expend the state's limited resources pursuing."[10] Young's words relate to economic plans set forward by departing British administrators in the strictest bureaucratic sense of what they understood "the economy" to encompass.[11] Yet archaeology inhabited the same bureaucratic domain, and its promotion by the independent Sudanese government was as much a result of these circumstances as the promotion of irrigation schemes designed to bolster

---

8. Meskell, *A Future*, 58.
9. William Y. Adams, "Organizational Problems in International Salvage Archaeology," *Anthropological Quarterly* 41 (1968): 110–21, is at least even-handed, taking both UNESCO and archaeologists themselves to task. Torgny Säve-Söderbergh, "International Salvage Archaeology: Some Organizational and Technical Aspects of the Nubian Campaign," *Annales Academiae Regiae Scientiarum Upsaliensis* 15–16 (1971–72): 116–40, criticizes the organization more directly.
10. Young, *Transforming*, 95.
11. On "the economy," see most famously Mitchell, *Rule*. Cf. Timothy Mitchell, *Carbon Democracy: Political Power in the Age of Oil* (London and New York: Verso, 2013), 136–42. For nuanced discussion of Mitchell's work and the economy, see Aaron Jakes, *Egypt's Occupation: Colonial Economism and the Crises of Capitalism* (Stanford, CA: Stanford University Press, 2020).

national economic productivity. This point is not to suggest that British officials were solely responsible for post-independence Sudanese archaeology. It is, however, to emphasize that the circumstances through which archaeology collided with an independent Sudanese officialdom helped to promote ways of thinking about the discipline that had clear colonial resonances even as their connection to "New World" archaeology was emphasized. It was in the mid-1950s that this collision between archaeology and governmental bureaucracy began.

Witnessing Sudan's Archaeological Unknown

As construction of the Aswan High Dam became imminent, Sudanese authorities mobilized a rhetoric of the threat posed to ancient remains familiar from Egypt. Despite the lack of contact between members of the 1954 Egyptian Department of Antiquities mission to Nubia and their Sudanese counterparts, the Sudan Antiquities Service had started to gear up for the coming inundation, its officials using what Steven Shapin and Simon Schaffer have denoted "literary technology" to help make its case.[12] Work to promote the High Dam as both a threat and an opportunity had been under way since the mid-1950s. The pages of Sudanese government publications constituted the venue in which that doubled case—itself dependent on colonial groundwork—was made.

Independence from Britain and the end of the Anglo-Egyptian Condominium had arrived in January 1956 after a 1953 referendum had seen a majority in Sudan vote for self-rule. And in 1954, between referendum and formal independence, came self-government and the increased "Sudanization" of government posts. In early 1955, however, Peter Shinnie, Sudan's Oxford-educated commissioner for archaeology, "was succeeded by the distinguished French Egyptologist Jean Vercoutter on the grounds that a Frenchman, being 'neutral' in the political issues then facing the Sudan, was acceptable."[13] Shinnie would later head the Department of Archaeology at the University College of Ghana and would lead a Ghanaian expedition back to Sudan during the Nubian campaign. Vercoutter, meanwhile, had been trained in Egyptology, taking a diploma in the subject at Paris' École pratique des hautes études in 1939. Yet he was also experienced in archaeological excavation *qua* excavation. Having dug in Egypt after the Second World War, Vercoutter had overseen the

---

12. Shapin and Schaffer, *Leviathan*, 25.
13. Peter L. Shinnie, "A Personal Memoir," in *A History of African Archaeology*, ed. Peter Robertshaw (London and Portsmouth: James Currey and Heinemann Educational, 1990), 227–29.

French archaeological mission in Sudan since 1953. Vercoutter put that experience to work, using the print venues at his disposal to become a virtual witness to the fact—previously highlighted by Shinnie—that Sudanese Nubia constituted an archaeological *terra incognita*.[14] Whereas Egyptian Nubia had been considered almost entirely excavated before the Nubian campaign began, in Sudan and Sudanese Nubia it now became vital to claim the opposite.

Almost immediately upon his appointment as director of the Sudan Antiquities Service, Vercoutter used a variety of publications to highlight that the country would repay urgent archaeological excavation. Those publications included his department's relatively new journal, *Kush*, first published in 1954, and the older *Sudan Notes and Records*, which had been established by the British administration in 1918 as a means of creating "an 'encyclopedia' of scientific information on the country and its people." That "encyclopedia" was thought necessary to ease Sudan's governance as an entity separate from Egypt, whose 1919 revolution—and forthcoming (nominal) independence—had made that outcome necessary.[15] As Bushra Hamad notes, within the journal "the British resorted to the diffusion of knowledge about the Sudan, especially from archaeological sources," in order to counteract Egyptian claims over the country.[16] The pages of *Sudan Notes and Records* therefore made the importance of increased archaeological survey in the country clear, a point emphasized by the appointment of the Oxford-educated archaeologist and administrator Anthony Arkell as Sudan's first commissioner for archaeology and anthropology in 1938.[17] As the likelihood of Sudanese independence grew, editorial policy changed to balance anthropological and archaeological articles alongside pieces relating to the natural and social sciences: such articles were thought to provide a basis for the enactment of modernization policies that the possibility of self-rule seemed to foreshadow.[18] Archaeology and anthropology, however, continued to appear in the journal's pages. That *Sudan Notes and Records* had an unstable readership—many of whom lived outside the country—seemed to matter little: "it was essential to show the Sudanese how their predecessors had once been a world power." Ultimately, it was thought that a national museum

---

14. Jean Vercoutter, "Sudanese Nubia: 'Terra Incognita' of Archaeologists," *The UNESCO Courier* (May 1960): 46–49.

15. Bushra Hamad, "*Sudan Notes and Records* and Sudanese Nationalism, 1918–1956," *History in Africa* 22 (1995): 266.

16. Hamad, "*Sudan Notes*," 261. Ironically, Sudan's first Prime Minister, Isma'il al-Azhari, had long promoted "the unity of the Nile Valley," for which see Robert O. Collins, *A History of Modern Sudan* (Cambridge: Cambridge University Press, 2008), 51.

17. Hamad, "*Sudan Notes*," 254.

18. Hamad, "*Sudan Notes*," 264.

would be the vehicle "that could possibly diffuse such knowledge on a large scale."[19] But field archaeology in print played a role in this process, too.

Despite being appointed as a "neutral" administrator, Vercoutter built on this printed argument. In his "Editorial Notes" in *Kush*'s second volume, Shinnie had suggested that "the problems [involved with understanding Sudan's past] are as immense as the area involved. Only the most accessible parts of the country have yet been examined by the trained archaeologist and even in these areas the examination has been, in most cases, superficial."[20] Vercoutter echoed this argument. In his own "Editorial Notes" to *Kush*'s fourth, 1956 volume, Vercoutter argued that "the best way we can show him [Shinnie] our gratitude is to carry on his work." This effort would involve "the help of all those scholars who take an interest in the archaeology of the Sudan, which is so complex and yet so little known."[21] In the next year's volume of *Sudan Notes and Records*, meanwhile, Vercoutter suggested that the portion of Nubia on the Sudanese side of the region's border "is always difficult of access, sometimes even impossible except on foot, and consequently it is little known archaeologically. It is probable, therefore, that the real number of sites is greater than those noted on the map."[22] To a cohort of English-language readers, Vercoutter became a virtual witness that Sudan—and Sudanese Nubia—constituted potentially productive archaeological ground.

Sudan's *terra incognita* now became a matter of fact among British practitioners interested in the development of archaeological methodology for whom access to the country continued to be relatively simple. Those archaeologists themselves published their judgments about Sudan in key journals. In 1954 (and not for the first time), the British archaeologist O. G. S. Crawford, editor of the influential journal *Antiquity*, used the inauguration of *Kush* to describe undertaking fieldwork in Sudan aimed at demonstrating "that the methods of field-archaeology employed in Britain could be applied with equally good results in another and very different geographical environment."[23] Reviewing this contribution in 1955's *Sudan Notes and Records*, Crawford's archae-

---

19. Hamad, "Sudan Notes," 262.
20. Peter Shinnie, "Editorial Notes," *Kush: Journal of the Sudan Antiquities Service* 2 (1954): 3.
21. Jean Vercoutter, "Editorial Notes," *Kush: Journal of the Sudan Antiquities Service* 4 (1956): 3.
22. Jean Vercoutter, "Archaeological Survey in the Sudan, 1955–57," *Sudan Notes and Records* 38 (1957): 111.
23. O. G. S. Crawford, "Field Archaeology of the Middle Nile Region," *Kush: Journal of the Sudan Antiquities Service* 1 (1954): 2. Crawford made similar claims as early as 1948 in his "People Without a History," *Antiquity* 22 (1948): 8–12. More recently, David Edwards, *The Nubian Past: An Archaeology of the Sudan* (London and New York: Routledge, 2004), 8, has taken such claims to be an argument for "a more broad-ranging archaeology." For Crawford himself, see Kitty Hauser, *Shadow Sites: Photography, Archaeology, and the British Landscape, 1927–1955* (Oxford: Oxford University Press, 2007).

ological compatriot Oliver H. Myers (who had excavated in Egypt) suggested that "there seems to be nothing particularly confined to British Archaeology about these methods." Still, "it is not now the large spectacular Near Eastern excavation of the old type that is required, but careful survey and small scale carefully selected excavation of stratified sites." This point was especially true because "Sudan is a fruitful field for the adventurous archaeologist."[24] Readers of these journals thus witnessed—and virtually verified the pertinence of—a debate about the vast untapped archaeological resource of a country whose north would soon be flooded by the High Dam. They also confirmed how Sudan might become experimental archaeological ground, a status that grew in importance as specifically archaeological documentation came into being there during the Nubian campaign.[25] That they did these things, meanwhile, only aided the steps now taken by Sudan's government in the face of the new dam's construction.

Developing Sudan

Like a colonial-era resource concession, Sudan's archaeological riches seemed to be up for grabs; as chapter 3 argued, it was no coincidence that archaeological excavations themselves constituted concessional agreements. That reality, meanwhile, allowed the Sudanese government to claim development assistance from relevant international bodies. After a military coup in 1958, the government's leadership switched: no longer under a parliamentary system and Prime Minister 'Abdallah Khalil, Sudan was now led by General Ibrahim 'Abbud and the Supreme Council of the Armed Forces. As in other areas of governance in Sudan, that change in leadership did little to alter archaeological policy.[26] Yet strategies for dealing with Nubia started playing a role consonant with development schemes taking place in the country. In the early years of independence, Sudanese officials "concerned with balancing their budget" had realized that "the enormous contribution of cotton to Sudan's national revenue . . . meant that according to the logic of accounting, the Gezira Scheme," a massive British-era irrigation project located southeast of Khartoum, "and a few other

---

24. Oliver H. Myers, "Review of 'Kush: Journal of the Sudan Antiquities Service, Annual, 1953,'" *Sudan Notes and Records* 36, no. 2 (1955): 196–97.

25. For other forms of knowledge experimentation in the dying days of empire, see Lyn Schumaker, *Africanizing Anthropology: Fieldwork, Networks, and the Making of Cultural Knowledge in Central Africa* (Durham, NC, and London: Duke University Press, 2001) and Helen Tilley, *Africa as a Living Laboratory: Empire, Development, and the Problem of Scientific Knowledge, 1870–1950* (Chicago: University of Chicago Press, 2011).

26. For wider Sudanese policy in this period, see Young, *Transforming*, 110–11.

prominent irrigated schemes could credibly stand in for the territorial economy as a whole." That move also "rationalized the decision of officials in Khartoum to ignore vast areas of the country."[27] Archaeological work in Sudanese Nubia was palpably not the same as such schemes, even as its undertaking constituted the result of an irrigation project started in Egypt. Archaeology did, though, play a similar role *vis-à-vis* the relationship between newly independent Sudan's regional and national priorities.

Submitting its annual request for funding under UNESCO's "Participation Programme" in January 1959, the Sudanese government made use of the image of Sudanese Nubia as an untapped archaeological territory, while also characterizing the existence of that territory—contrary to Egyptian claims—as explicitly Sudanese, intimating that Nubia had the potential to contribute to national aims. Writing on behalf of Sudan's commissioner for development, Hilary N. Paul of the Development Branch of the Ministry of Finance and Economics enclosed a request for funding for three different projects under the headings "Museums and Monuments," "Extension of Library Services," and "Promotion of education and enlightenment among the workers." The Museums and Monuments project was top priority, incorporating not only a request for "a chemist specialized in object cleaning," but also "an expert in Photogrammetry" who was simultaneously "an expert in air photographs." Paul requested this expert because the government, as in Egypt, had "undertaken a complete aerial survey of an important archaeological area lying between Faras and Kosha": Sudanese Nubia, in other words.[28] What that survey revealed was telling in terms of how Sudan's government now understood its developmental priorities.

Prefiguring—and attempting to ease—the coming forced migration of the Nubian population, the report described the area as having been "very much more inhabited than it is to-day." Indeed, "ancient settlements with formerly cultivated areas have been spotted. Existence of former cultivations has been checked by excavations." Paul therefore requested an expert in air photographs not only because they were needed to "spot the ancient archaeological sites," but also to "determine the extent of formerly cultivated land." Sudanese Nubia was not simply of local interest. Instead, it was of national—and perhaps even international—concern. Archaeological work in the region was connected not only "with the preservation of cultural heritage" (including "the

27. Young, *Transforming*, 87–88.
28. Paul to Luther H. Evans, January 10, 1959. Folder 069 (62) N: 930.26 (624) (Part 1): "Museums-Egypt-Nubia-Excavations-Sudan," UNESCO Archives.

establishment of a national museum"), but also, as Paul noted, with "the Arid Zone Research," itself sponsored by UNESCO, taking place in Sudan.[29] British officials in Egypt had perceived the building of the first Aswan Dam and the possible destruction of ancient monuments by its floodwaters as collateral damage in the resurrection of pharaonic-era engineering schemes and a once-great civilization.[30] In a post-independence echo of such thought, Sudan's request for international expertise now linked the coming destruction of ancient remains and Nubian homes to the development of national preservation infrastructure. It also linked that process to UNESCO's Arid Zone Program, itself developed with the collaboration of former colonial officials.[31] Sudan's request would develop both the country's agricultural productivity and make Sudan a crucial node in the "international battle against deserts" that the Arid Zone Program constituted.[32]

The development of archaeology in Sudanese Nubia could stand in for the development of Sudan more generally. Simultaneously, the country and its officials could stake out a role in an international effort centered on the "climatological" Middle East: a "desiccated" area stretching from Morocco to India which not uncoincidentally incorporated countries involved in the nascent Non-Aligned Movement with whom UNESCO wanted to curry favor.[33] The UNESCO Major Project on Scientific Research on Arid Lands had been launched in 1952, becoming a "Major [cross-departmental] Project" in 1956 after several years of preparatory work aimed at countering the threat of global "desertification": the idea (and "scientific fiction") that "because soils, vegetation, and climate were interdependent, human-induced deforestation and soil erosion could desiccate the environment, turning forests into savannahs and prairies into dust bowls."[34] At the same time, the project promised—as in the case of Sudanese Nubia—future agricultural development, which would enable

---

29. Paul to Evans, January 10, 1959.
30. Gange, "Unholy," 105.
31. A 1962 UNESCO "Report on Arid Zone Research in the Sudan" (Unesco/NS/AZ/657) was authored by Frank Dixey, formerly head of the British Directorate of Colonial Geological Surveys, and Georges Aubert, formerly of France's Institut de recherches agronomiques, who had worked in French Algeria. For Dixey, see Kingsley Dunham, "Frank Dixey: 7 April 1892–1 November 1982," *Biographical Memoirs of Fellows of the Royal Society* 29 (1983): 158–76. For Aubert, see Stephen Nortcliff (adapted from the French by Georges Pedro), "In Memoriam—Georges Aubert (1913–2006)," *International Union of Soil Sciences* website, accessed September 5, 2019, https://www.iuss.org/about-the-iuss/iuss-history/obituaries-to-great-soil-scientists/g-aubert-1913-2006/.
32. Perrin Selcer, *The Postwar Origins of the Global Environment: How the United Nations Built Spaceship Earth* (New York: Columbia University Press, 2018), 98.
33. Selcer, *The Postwar Origins*, 106.
34. Selcer, *The Postwar Origins*, 98, 110.

UNESCO to establish its "competency over the great underdeveloped regions of the world."[35] The scaling up of that competency, though, also allowed the newly independent countries involved in the work to assert their own priorities.

As Perrin Selcer notes, "elites from developing countries needed to cultivate productive, loyal citizens."[36] In Egypt, for instance, the geographer Muhammad ʿAwad had noted that "the prominence given to local tribal solidarity has often been a handicap in the development of a national spirit and outlook." Consequently, it was "not enough from the point of view of the country's welfare merely to settle the nomads—they must also be socially integrated."[37] As in Egypt, Sudanese officials now made the bet that Nubians, too, could best be socialized elsewhere in the nation-state. At the same time, the region that had once been their land might be used to power the High Dam, helping to develop the nation through the division of floodwater and other benefits specified in the 1959 Nile Waters Agreement. Despite its forthcoming submersion, that Sudanese Nubia might, in addition, provide a possibility of national agricultural *re*-development only strengthened this strategy.

Sudan's request for an expert in aerial photography not only played into the growing popularity of such work in archaeology, but also, therefore, represented a similar strategy to the Arid Zone Program's own methodology.[38] "Integrated surveys" developed for the scheme by the Australian Commonwealth Scientific and Industrial Research Organization's Division of Land Research and Regional Survey sought to trace "historical relationships between environmental factors rather than the separate characteristics of soils, climate, relief, and vegetation." Consequently, "instead of thematic maps of particular elements, integrated surveys began with intensive study of aerial photograph mosaics to identify 'recurring patterns' that represented 'land units.'"[39] The archaeological survey of Egyptian Nubia undertaken during the Nubian campaign used aerial photographs to bypass areas where "ancient monuments" were not apparently present.[40] In Sudanese Nubia, however, the use of, and problems associated with, such photo mosaics—coupled with bodily experience of desert terrain—lent the archaeological survey that took place there a quality closer to Arid Zone research. First, though, an expert in aerial photog-

---

35. Selcer, *The Postwar Origins*, 106.
36. Selcer, *The Postwar Origins*, 117.
37. Selcer, *The Postwar Origins*, 118, citing "Muhamad" ʿAwad, "Nomadism in the Arab Lands of the Middle East," *Arid Zone Research* 18 (1962): 325–40.
38. O. G. S. Crawford was one of the major proponents of aerial archaeology, for which see Hauser, *Shadow Sites*.
39. Selcer, *The Postwar Origins*, 104.
40. Smith, *Preliminary Reports*, 2.

raphy had to be found. That search entangled such work with further development interests.

The TVA and Accidental Expertise

The influence of the TVA on the Nubian campaign has been widely noted.[41] There has been little attention, though, as to what the precedent of this massive New Deal program of riverine, agricultural, and population development meant to the project, especially in Sudan itself.[42] That the TVA connection has gained this attention is unsurprising, however, not least because the Nubian campaign's rhetoric made it explicit. France's Minister of Cultural Affairs André Malraux helped inaugurate the project by declaring that it represented "a kind of Tennessee Valley Authority of archaeology."[43] His comparison was as canny as the politician himself, especially because Malraux's words enabled potential funders to visualize the scale and technocratic scope of what could now be perceived as a monumental development operation. This outcome, moreover, was particularly obvious in the TVA's home in an era when enthusiasm related to modernization had reached fever pitch. Like its predecessors, the Kennedy administration used American expertise to attempt to propagate US-style liberalism around the globe. It is little surprise that the "Camelot" of the Kennedy administration, which would come further under Malraux's charismatic spell in 1962 when he agreed to send the Mona Lisa to Washington, ultimately agreed to finance large parts of the Nubian work.[44]

Malraux's words, though, had made what was in fact a redundant comparison seem novel and exciting. Archaeology had not only been a part of the TVA, but also part of New Deal–era Works Progress Administration programs across the United States.[45] To speak of a "Tennessee Valley Authority of archaeology"

---

41. See, e.g., Allais, "The Design," 185–86; Chloé Maurel, "Le sauvetage des monuments de Nubie par l'Unesco (1955–1968)," Égypte/Monde arabe 10 (2013): 4; Meskell, A Future, 44–45.

42. Although now cf. Christina Luke and Lynn Meskell, "New Deals for the Past: The Cold War, American Archaeology, and UNESCO in Egypt and Syria," History and Anthropology online prepublication (2020), https://doi.org/ 10.1080/02757206.2020.1830769.

43. André Malraux, "T.V.A. of Archaeology," The UNESCO Courier (May 1960): 10.

44. On Malraux and the Mona Lisa, see Herman Lebovics, Mona Lisa's Escort: André Malraux and the Reinvention of French Culture (Ithaca, NY: Cornell University Press, 1999), 9–10. For the ways in which US development finance for archaeology fell apart due to the massive expenditure of the Nubian campaign, see Luke, A Pearl, 110–11.

45. On the development of "New Deal archaeology," see Bernard K. Means, "Introduction: 'Alphabet Soup' and American Archaeology," in Shovel Ready: Archaeology and Roosevelt's New Deal for America, ed. Bernard K. Means (Tuscaloosa: University of Alabama Press, 2013), 1–18. Cf. Erin E. Pritchard, ed., TVA Archaeology: Seventy-Five Years of Prehistoric Site Research (Knoxville: University of Tennessee Press, 2009).

was tautological. The substantive basis of Malraux's comparison therefore bears further investigation, not least because John Otis Brew made a similar (implicit) comparison of the earlier archaeological survey work in Egyptian Nubia.[46] Modernization, hydro-politics, and archaeological survey became entangled in Egypt long before the institution of the TVA in 1933. Did, then, Malraux's comparison ever have much basis in practice? It is in Sudan that we must find an answer, because it was Sudan that now seemed to offer a blank slate for something resembling a mediated version of TVA-style archaeology to come about. Not only the efforts of colonial archaeological officials and their successors, but also the specific connection of those efforts with land-use research helped this Sudanese situation materialize.

Sudan, to state the obvious, was not Egypt. Christiane Desroches Noblecourt's vision for CEDAE constituted an institution whose documentary thrust rested, broadly, on Western European Egyptology. Noblecourt drew not only on her own experiences and interests, but also on a plan for the work that was at least partially a result of disgruntled former employees of Egypt's Department of Antiquities (and her French compatriots) riding their luck with UNESCO. By 1959, when William Yewdale ("Bill") Adams, a doctoral graduate of the University of Arizona, was appointed as UNESCO's "expert in air photographs" for Sudan, times had changed. Other figures and professional networks had grown in importance as the UNESCO department that initially dealt with the Nubian campaign, the Museums and Monuments Division, had grown in stature throughout the 1950s.[47] In combination with the wishes of Sudan's archaeological administration, it was figures from these networks who called the shots and believed that the approach to archaeological survey in which Adams possessed experience would now be important as work in Nubia gathered pace. Even as events did not quite turn out as intended, it was this appointment—and Adams's (and his wife, Nettie's) growing importance as the campaign took place—that would help play a major role not only in the material prosecution of particular archaeological practices, but also to cross-border connections related to those practices and the ways in which they destabilized picturesque visions of Nubia.

Like the appointment of Noblecourt as an expert in Egypt, however, none of these outcomes were preordained, and to chalk them down to an excess of planning on UNESCO's or anyone else's part would be mistaken. Expertise in the Nubian campaign was always contingent on, and constitutive of, its social

---

46. Brew, "Emergency Archaeology," 2–3.
47. On this development at UNESCO, see Allais, *Designs*, 23–25. On William Y. Adams, see his autobiography, *The Road from Frijoles Canyon: Anthropological Adventures on Four Continents* (Albuquerque: University of New Mexico Press, 2009).

circumstances. Like Noblecourt, Adams—who ultimately stayed in Sudan until 1966—was an accidental expert, the third choice to undertake work in the country, and someone whose contract was precarious.[48] Still, something resembling but not quite constituting a TVA precedent now took shape. In April 1959, Programme Specialist Hiroshi Daifuku of the Division of Museums and Monuments wrote to Richard B. Woodbury, an archaeologist at the University of Arizona (and later of the Smithsonian Institution). In the letter, Daifuku stated that

> Jo Brew and Ralph Solecki are both in Paris right now working as consultants for UNESCO. During the course of their visits we discussed a project in the Sudan in which the Government asked for an archaeologist who has had some experience in photogrammetry to go over a series of photo mosaics to locate sites in the northern part of the Sudan, paying attention also to the existence of former traces of irrigation. I understand that you have been thinking of working in the northern sections of the Sudan, in the arid lands programme, and this would be a means of accomplishing both tasks, with UNESCO aiding the first part of the work.[49]

More than simply rhetoric, a particular vision of large-scale archaeological survey now began to structure work in Sudan in the months before the Nubian campaign coalesced. Brew had been involved in the wartime Committee on Basic Needs in American Archaeology, which sought "to define standards for archaeological research" in the face of "the paucity of professional standards and the lack of central control on the fast-moving and chaotic relief-based archaeological projects" connected not only to the TVA, but also to the US Works Progress Administration.[50] That work led Brew to publish articles on the impact of dams on prehistoric remains. It also led him to set forward recommendations on what became termed "salvage archaeology."[51] Already in May 1945, one consequence of those recommendations had been the formation of the Committee

---

48. As Säve-Söderbergh, "International Salvage Archaeology," 138, notes, "at a crucial moment," Adams' post "was taken off the [UNESCO] Regular Programme [of funding, which had paid for it] and thus ceased to exist."

49. Daifuku to Woodbury, April 6, 1959. Folder 069 (62) N: 930.26 (624) (Part 1), UNESCO Archives. On Daifuku, a signatory, on UNESCO's behalf, of the 1964 Venice Charter for the Conservation and Restoration of Monuments and Sites, see Gustavo Araoz, "In Memoriam: Hiroshi Daifuku," ICOMOS website, July 23, 2012, https://www.icomos.org/en/9-uncategorised/494-in-memoriam-hiroshi-daifuku.

50. Fred Wendorf and Raymond H. Thompson, "The Committee for the Recovery of Archaeological Remains: Three Decades of Service to the Archaeological Profession," American Antiquity 67, no. 2 (2002): 319.

51. Brew, "Emergency Archaeology"; cf. Allais, "The Design," 185–86.

for the Recovery of Archaeological Remains, which "instigated a massive federal archaeological program, the River Basin Surveys, that succeeded in recovering a significant amount of archaeological evidence threatened by" the construction of hydroelectric and other dams across the United States.[52]

Beyond the neologism—and despite the resemblance between earlier work in Egypt and that taking place in America—what was notable about the River Basin Surveys were their nationwide scope. Beyond concentrating on one fixed region, this was a program whose federated parts would come together as a synthesis into a countrywide whole: archaeology as an enterprise at both local and national scales. And in Brew's mind, there was no reason why that enterprise should not get bigger still, perhaps even become global: in 1959, as Lucia Allais has noted, he convinced UNESCO to commission "a general report on 'the consequences of large-scale engineering works as it concerns the conservation of the cultural heritage of mankind.'" Ironically, UNESCO canceled the compilation of the report due to the growing attention being paid to Nubia.[53] But it would be the intersection of this attempt at scalability with colonial norms of archaeological practice that structured and materialized the Nubian campaign in Sudan, in addition to the project's entanglement with practices familiar from UNESCO's Arid Zone Program and national policy.

As Daifuku's letter reveals, Brew transposed his thinking about salvage archaeology to his recommendations for Sudanese Nubia: colonial officials had made it seem as if the region offered a blank slate for this scalable enterprise to happen. The archaeologist Ralph Solecki of Columbia University, who was in the midst of undertaking a major prehistoric research project at the site of Shanidar Cave in Iraq, backed Brew up.[54] And their interpretation of archaeological work seemed to lend itself to the suggestion of Richard Woodbury as a possible UNESCO expert in Sudan, not least because Woodbury's work with the University of Arizona's Program of Research in the Utilization of Arid Lands seemed compatible with the "Arid Zone Research" taking place in Sudan. Ironically, that Arizona program was financed by the Rockefeller Foundation, who clearly saw more interest in the work than in the contemporary approaches of Chicago's OI. More importantly here, the Arizona project also entailed the scaling up of field survey at multiple locations, much like the River Basin Surveys: that year, the program's work "secure[d] additional details of

---

52. Wendorf and Thompson, "The Committee," 317.
53. Allais, "The Design," 186.
54. On Shanidar Cave, see Ralph S. Solecki, "Shanidar Cave, a Paleolithic Site in Northern Iraq," *Annual Report of the Board of Regents of the Smithsonian Institution 1954* (1955): 389–426.

Hohokam canals by means of cross sections at Snaketown, Gila Bend, and the Park of Four Waters in Phoenix."[55]

Rather than the sort of regimented trip down the river associated with the Nubian surveys in Egypt, then, the Arid Lands Program—like the River Basin Surveys and UNESCO's Arid Zone Program—involved visualizing an area of component parts, moving between those parts, and then synthesizing them into an interpretation of the whole. Woodbury had been a US Army Air Force weather observer during the Second World War; in the bare bones of its approach, the method was not unlike that of the integration of aerial photography and lists of monuments that occurred during that conflict. Moving between parts and wholes, that wartime work had generated different forms of monumental, post-bombing landscape across various European countries (and given rise to the so-called Monuments Men).[56] Now, a similar method was set to be globalized, and Woodbury seemed to offer a safe pair of hands with Sudan's archaeological photographs as that process took place.

The trouble was that Woodbury was unavailable. Traveling to Britain before returning to the United States, Solecki therefore asked John Spencer Purvis Bradford of the University of Oxford if he would like the job. Bradford, a renowned aerial archaeologist, had worked during the war interpreting air photographs for the Mediterranean Allied Photographic Reconnaissance Wing. The Monuments Man genealogy seemed to run strong.[57] Yet Bradford, too, turned Solecki down, citing Anglo-Sudanese "political relations" as an issue. Ironically, he then recommended Peter Shinnie, Sudan's former commissioner for archaeology, to do the job.[58] Going round in circles, Woodbury ultimately wrote to Hiroshi Daifuku recommending Bill Adams for the work. As with Noblecourt's consultancy for CEDAE, Adams had not exactly been first choice. Still, his expertise seemed to fit the bill. As Woodbury wrote:

> He will be occupied until the end of the summer . . . with the direction of the San Juan portion of the National Park Service salvage archaeology in the Glen Canyon of the Colorado River. He received his PhD [in

---

55. Richard B. Woodbury, "A Reappraisal of Hohokam Irrigation," *American Anthropologist* n.s. 63, no. 3 (1961): 551.

56. Allais, *Designs*, 128–35. On Woodbury himself, see "Obituary: Richard Woodbury, First Anthropology Chair," *University of Massachusetts Amherst* website, February 25, 2010, https://www.umass.edu/newsoffice/article/obituary-richard-woodbury-first-anthropology-chair.

57. "John Spencer Purvis Bradford (1918–1975)," *Monuments Men Foundation for the Preservation of Art* website, accessed August 13, 2020, https://www.monumentsmenfoundation.org/the-heroes/the-monuments-men/bradford-capt.-john-s.p.

58. Ralph S. Solecki to Hiroshi Daifuku, April 17, 1959. Folder 069 (62) N: 930.26 (624) (Part 1), UNESCO Archives.

anthropology] here at Arizona a couple of years ago, and in my opinion is doing a remarkably good job on the Glen Canyon program—a difficult job of reconnaissance and excavation, by boat, truck, plane, and on foot.... As far as I know he could start the work by 1 Nov.[59]

Adams, too, could move between archaeological parts and wholes. It was this method that would now structure events on the Nubian campaign, although never with as much ease as he and others desired.

Top-Down, Bottom-Up: Fielding Photographs, Pinning Down the Nation-State

Aerial photographs, it turned out, were only useful if the remains they were meant to illustrate were visible from the air. Unfortunately for Bill Adams (but fortunately for his career), the photographs of Sudanese Nubia he was sent to inspect did not enable this form of witnessing. Consequently, he had to mediate the photographic view from above with a view from below, an action that reconstituted perceptions of Nubia itself. In chapter 3, I discussed how aerial photographs of Egyptian Nubia sometimes proved to be unavailable to scholars, even as they were used to justify the lack of survey of some parts of the region. In Sudanese Nubia, however, aerial photographs proved unreliable in a different way. As Adams later admitted, he did not possess the expertise to analyze the photographs in the first place: "in New York I had looked for a book on aerial photography, hoping to give myself a crash course in my supposed specialty." He "never found one, but as it turned out I never needed it."[60] To be archaeologically useful, photographs needed to depict a particular reality.

Upon arrival in Sudan, Adams discovered that the photographs he was meant to analyze "had been taken from such a high altitude that only the most obvious forts and temples could be recognized—sites that had already been well known for years."[61] Discussing the problem with P. E. T. ("Pete") Allen, the Sudan Survey Department's aerial photographer, the two agreed that two new surveys should be conducted at lower altitudes:

> One, at a scale of 1:15,000, would cover the whole area to be flooded, and one, at a scale of 1:7,500, would cover the area most immediately threatened. The photos would be taken not in a single strip, as in the

---

59. Woodbury to Daifuku, May 21, 1959. Folder 069 (62) N: 930.26 (624) (Part 1), UNESCO Archives.
60. Adams, *The Road*, 141.
61. Adams, *The Road*, 141.

previous survey, but in a series of overlapping strips that could be used stereoscopically. The three-dimensional imaging thus created would, Pete and I hoped, make it possible to identify features not recognizable in any single photo.[62]

Undertaking these surveys during November and December 1959, Allen and the Adams' managed to construct two different photo mosaics of Sudanese Nubia.[63] As Bill Adams later related, though, even these two tools proved not to be that useful in terms of fulfilling their initial aim: "most of the sites [located in Sudanese Nubia] were simply too deeply buried under sand" (that this issue might have been one that occurred in Egypt, meanwhile, going uninvestigated as a result of "the view from the boat").[64]

The desert spoke. Rather than being used to identify potential archaeological sites, aerial photographs of Sudanese Nubia were used to mark known site positions. And those positions were marked only after those sites had been located during on-the-ground survey work that Adams—working with the archaeology graduate students G. Jan Verwers of Leiden and Hans-Åke Nordström of Uppsala—now felt obliged to undertake.[65] Arid Zone Program surveys investigated "recurring patterns."[66] Here, though, the object of investigation was reduced to one recurring pattern: the desert, the sand that constituted it, and the archaeological sites that only work in the desert could reveal. This move had several consequences for how Sudanese Nubia now came to be imagined. In a different, but related, context, On Barak has discussed how the development of the railway in Egypt simultaneously managed to produce ideas of modernity and tradition. As he notes, "Egyptian trains could not move without camels." The animals "carried railway tracks and telegraph poles, transported water (required for engine cooling and steam production) from the Nile to train stations, and moved leftover merchandise and passengers to destinations that were past the railway's reach."[67] Yet the work of these beasts of burden simultaneously led "to numerous road accidents involving camels and trains, providing fodder for the pictorial representation of the Egyptian landscape as exotic and ancient." Consequently (and much like Nile steamers), "the train was literally producing Egyptian antiquity in the collateral damage of its own modernity."[68] A similar

---

62. Adams, *The Road*, 141.
63. Adams, *The Road*, 143; cf. William Y. Adams and P. E. T. Allen, "The Aerial Survey of Sudanese Nubia," *Kush: The Journal of the Sudan Antiquities Service* 9 (1961): 11.
64. Adams, *The Road*, 143.
65. Adams, *The Road*, 144, 171.
66. Selcer, *The Postwar Origins*, 104.
67. Barak, *On Time*, 37.
68. Barak, *On Time*, 38.

process now occurred in Sudan, constituting Sudanese Nubia as a place far more geared to, and buried within, the desert than the Nile-side Nubia of the Egyptian side of the border.

Forced to look for archaeological sites on—and *in*—the ground, Adams reinforced a perception of "the featurelessness of so much of the [desert] terrain" that had not only been produced during the difficult work of attempting to stitch together photo mosaics, but also emphasized the colonial-era view of Sudan as an archaeological *terra incognita*.[69] As he noted, the desert in fact held a significant number of archaeological sites, just as colonial-era officials had suggested. Sudan's archaeological blank slate came alive even as Adams characterized its landscape as desert-like and exotic. That, moreover, seemed to be an action suiting the Sudan Antiquities Service, which became the owner of a photo mosaic of the material remnants of its own—visible but invisible—antiquity. As Adams notes,

> the mosaics became our primary instrument for recording site locations when found. We carried the individual prints with us in the field, covering whatever area we were exploring, and we made a pin hole in the photo at each location where a site was found. On the back of the photo the hole was then circled in red and the site number entered beside it. We also mounted a complete photo mosaic on the wall of our central survey office in Wadi Halfa and inserted colored pins to mark the locations of all the known sites—including those found by other archaeological expeditions. Different colored pins were used to identify sites of different culture periods.[70]

After more work than expected, the photo mosaics made a Sudanese past legible even as the High Dam's floodwaters submerged its remains: something from (what had seemed like) nothing. Simultaneously, the government of which the Antiquities Service was a part prepared to move the population that lived among those remains much further to the south, strengthening the perception that such remnants existed within an otherwise barren desert. Ironically, Adams himself would apply for, receive—but never use—a Guggenheim Fellowship to conduct ethnographic research among Sudanese Nubians.[71] Yet the perception that contemporary Nubia constituted a desert ripe only for excavation would become increasingly difficult to reverse as the Sudanese government set the Nubian migration in train.

---

69. Adams, *The Road*, 142–43.
70. Adams, *The Road*, 143.
71. Adams, *The Road*, 145–46.

In 1960, Bryan Emery published an article in *The UNESCO Courier* discussing the EES excavation at the Sudanese Nubian site of Buhen. The work there had in fact been ongoing since late 1957, well before UNESCO's campaign had begun. Perhaps that made the desolation central to the article's title still more inevitable: "In These Drear Wastes What Visionary Pasts Revive . . ."[72] As in Egypt, Sudanese antiquity was now produced "in the collateral damage of its own modernity." As Sudan's Nubians found themselves moved far to the south, so that action formed "drear wastes" still more forcefully. That population found itself as disaggregated from antiquity as Egyptian Nubians had become from the ancient remains among which they, too, had lived. Sudan—and Sudanese Nubia—would have the type of past that the military government of Ibrahim ʿAbbud demanded: one that catered to the development of a "revolutionary" (yet northern-dominated) nation and its geopolitical ambitions.

Making Sudan, through Nubia

A 1960 almanac published by Khartoum's Central Office of Information made the ʿAbbud government's strategy clear, in addition to Nubia's place within it. *Progress* enumerated the number of tourists (some 700) who had visited Sudan the previous year, while also noting that "in addition 1,714 tourists visited the Nubian Monuments." This information was used to calculate the contribution of tourism to the national economy, the almanac reckoning that all tourists together had spent in the region of "LS. 241, 400 of foreign currency." The office's tourism section had also been busy: "twenty thousand copies have been produced of a poster giving most valuable information on all monuments and antiquities areas in the Sudan, particularly those in the Northern Province which will eventually disappear beneath the waters of the High Dam."[73] Echoing other initiatives of the period, the publication of such information meant that the flooding of Nubia would not only help constitute the national economy, but also prove that the new Sudanese regime was accountable to the nation's citizenry.[74] This strategy, though, possessed resonances beyond the nation.

Through its place in Sudan, Nubia sat within the wider geopolitical circles that the newly independent country dealt with. *Progress*, for example, related

---

72. Walter Bryan Emery, "In These Drear Wastes What Visionary Pasts Revive . . . ," *The Unesco Courier* (September 1960): 30–32.

73. *Progress: 2nd Anniversary Sudan Revolution, 17th November 1960* (Khartoum: The Central Office of Information, 1960), 179.

74. Young, *Transforming*, 112, details how Sudan's "military leaders made use of new tools such as national income accounting to proclaim that their regime was accountable."

how Sudan had just become a member of the International Arab Association for Tourism. The volume also explained how, through UNESCO's sponsorship, Sudan had been involved in the first "Training Course of Arab Broadcasters," held over eight weeks in 1960 at the Omdurman Broadcasting Station. "Bringing about a common understanding, through Radio [sic], for the peace of the world" constituted the declared—and UNESCO-friendly—goal of this course. Participation, though, clearly made other pan-Arab opportunities possible. Beyond Sudan itself, the course involved representatives from Libya, Morocco, the UAR, Kuwait, Iraq, Jordan, Lebanon, Saudi Arabia, and Yemen, giving some idea of the regional circles within which Sudan's government saw itself.[75] In 1961, meanwhile, for the first time the country posted cultural attachés not only to Beirut, but also to Moscow.[76]

The Sudanese government's focus on Nubia as locus of national development was enmeshed within these wider political circles, even as discussions surrounding the region consistently referred to its place within Sudan. This assertion of Sudanese nationhood vis-à-vis Nubia seems unsurprising. Yet as Heather Sharkey has noted, "the first self-conscious use of 'Sudanese' as an epithet for national identity" had only come in 1927, when the poet and Sub-Mamur (District Official) Hamza al-Malik Tambal had "posited the existence—or possible existence—of a distinct 'Sudanese' (sūdānī) Arabic literature"; previously, the term had carried social stigma, especially among northerners, who saw themselves as "Arab."[77] By the 1960s, however, as those same northerners occupied a dominant position within the country, they saw no difficulty in using archaeology to assert not only a Sudanese national identity, but also the place of that nation within the wider world (Arab or otherwise).

In 1960, Vercoutter was replaced as director of the Sudan Antiquities Service by former Senior Inspector of Antiquities Thabit Hassan Thabit, indicating that perhaps the Frenchman was not quite such an "acceptable" choice for the job after all. And on New Year's Day, 1961, the newspaper al-Ra'i al-'Amm reported on its front page that Thabit had met with the Soviet Cultural Attaché in Khartoum. The Soviets were studying the sort of assistance they could offer toward preserving the Nubian remains. Yet the paper also made quite clear to whom those remains belonged: the headline referenced "the salvage of our antiquities" (inqādh āthārnā).[78] Tied up within the politics of the Cold

---

75. *Progress*, 170.
76. *Progress*, 99.
77. Heather J. Sharkey, "A Century in Print: Arabic Journalism and Nationalism in Sudan, 1899–1999," *International Journal of Middle East Studies* 31, no. 4 (1999): 537.
78. "Ist'idad al-Ittihad al-Sufyati li-l-Musahima fi Inqadh Atharna" ["The Soviet Union prepares to contribute to salvaging our antiquities"], *al-Ra'i al-'Amm*, January 1, 1961.

War and non-alignment, the article made a simultaneously national/territorial claim. Chances are, meanwhile, that that claim was not too far from the official line. *Al-Ra'i al-'Amm* had been founded in 1945 by Isma'il al-'Atabani, a former government official and graduate of the British-founded Gordon Memorial College (now the University of Khartoum). The country's only independent daily, funded by subscriptions from the northern Sudanese elite, the paper had previously felt free to take political sides.[79] Under 'Abbud, however, official control of the press increased: alongside banning political parties and their newspapers, the regime banned Sudan's first daily paper, *al-Nil*, "for having criticized government policy."[80] Within this restrictive environment, *al-Ra'i al-'Amm*—whose circulation had been about 4,000 copies in 1956—now provided an uncontroversial opinion.[81]

Nubian archaeology helped to constitute Sudan's global place. It also helped to constitute what could be said about Sudan and who could say it. Accordingly, during 1961, as archaeological work in the region gained impetus, Nubia provided a semiregular source of news and opinion in *al-Ra'i al-'Amm*, which generally followed a similar editorial line. In December that year, the paper published a letter from one Quranis Daud Amin of Khartoum's Technical Institute, entitling it "The Youth and Our Antiquities in Halfa." In the letter, the author noted the presence of many excavating missions and tourists in the Wadi Halfa area, wondering where this concern with excavating "our heritage" (*turāthnā*) and "our history" (*tarīkhnā*) came from. Indeed, Quranis Daud Amin noted that "we ourselves are ignorant of the value of our heritage" (*najhalu qīmat turāthnā*). Where, he asked, were "the Sudanese youth" (*al-shabāb al-sūdānī*) during this work? Likewise, why were secondary schools not organizing group trips to the archaeological sites of Nubia, and why were tourist agencies and the railway not providing more support to youth to visit these places by providing discounts for travel? After all, there was "little time" (*waqt qalīl*) remaining to do so.[82] Quranis Daud Amin's letter points to how Nubia was becoming somewhere in relation to which Sudanese negotiated an independent national identity.[83] That place, though, was not necessarily one related to Sudan alone.

---

79. Sharkey, "A Century," 542.
80. Sharkey, "A Century," 543.
81. Sharkey, "A Century," 543.
82. Quranis Daud Amin, "al-Shabab wa-Atharna fi Halfa" ["The youth and our antiquities in Halfa"], *al-Ra'i al-'Amm*, December 19, 1961.
83. For a comparison to the development of youth and national culture in Egypt, see Wilson Chacko Jacob, *Working Out Egypt: Effendi Masculinity and Subject Formation in Colonial Modernity, 1870–1940* (Durham, NC: Duke University Press, 2011).

Promoting Sudanese Nubia

Much of the Nubian reportage in *al-Raʾi al-ʿAmm* attended to specific excavations and the people directing them. The region was claimed as Sudanese, but there was also an understanding that much of the archaeological work there resulted from foreign involvement. On October 11, 1961, in its regular "Hawadith wa-Akhbar" ("Incidents and News") section, the newspaper reported that Nubian excavations were resuming that week. The accompanying piece listed the people connected to the campaign now arriving back in Sudan from abroad: not only Emery of the EES, but also Peter Shinnie, now acting as a UNESCO delegate. Notably, the paper also reported the arrival of "Egyptian workers specialized in excavation" (*al-ʿumāl al-Miṣriyyūn al-mutakhaṣiṣūn fi al-tanqīb*), presumably a reference to the "Quftis" employed in archaeological work in Egypt whose expertise seems to have enjoyed notability even among Sudanese journalists (and for whom see the following chapter).[84] Other articles, meanwhile, referenced UNESCO's universalist discourse. On December 24, 1961, the paper carried a long interview with Bryan Emery—apparently translated from English—that not only emphasized that the British government had funded his work in Nubia, but also noted that such excavations entailed the salvage of "human heritage" (*al-turāth al-basharī*).[85] Sudan was embedded within global interests, even as it ensured that the country's own officials also carried out interviews: a month earlier, a reporter from the paper, ʿAbd al-Rahman ʿAli, had spoken with Negm El-Din Mohammed Sherif, deputy director of the Antiquities Service.[86]

The excavation of spectacular frescoes from the once-prominent cathedral at the site of Faras exemplified this international tension. The images, excavated under the charge of a Polish mission, constituted perhaps the most spectacular of all remains recovered from Sudanese Nubia.[87] In that vein, then, it is notable that the discovery was advertised as being "from the Christian era in Sudan" (*min al-ʿahd al-masīḥī*).[88] This headline did not simply indicate na-

---

84. "Hafriyyat Athar al-Nuba Ist'naf Hadha al-Usbu'a" ["Nubian archaeological excavations resume this week"], *al-Raʾi al-ʿAmm*, October 11, 1961.

85. "Inqadh al-Turath al-Bashari min al-Tufan" ["The salvage of the human heritage from the flood"], *al-Raʾi al-ʿAmm*, December 24, 1961.

86. ʿAbd al-Rahman ʿAli, "al-Baʿathat al-ʿAlimiyya al-lati Tusahimu fi Inqadh Athar al-Nuba" ["The global missions participating in the salvage of Nubian antiquities"], *al-Raʾi al-ʿAmm*, November 19, 1961.

87. For Faras, see Bożena Mierzejewska, Aleksandra Sulikowska, and Tomasz Górecki, *Faras Gallery: Guidebook* (Warsaw: The National Museum in Warsaw, 2014).

88. "Iktishaf Tamathil al-Maryam al-ʿAdhraʾ wa-l-Masih wa-Rusumat al-Mikhaʿil wa-Wathaʿiq Tarikhiyya min al-ʿAhd al-Masihi bi-l-Sudan" ["Discovery of images of the Virgin Mary and Christ and

tional interest in the spread—and apparent end—of Sudanese Christianity (presumably news to the country's southern population, where Christian practice was much more widespread than in the north). Instead, it placed the discovery within the international study of Christianity itself. Similarly, grappling with the vast scale of the task ahead (and before the arrival of Thabit Hassan Thabit), in 1960 Vercoutter and Adams had authored a brochure promoting work in Sudanese Nubia that not only emphasized the region's archaeological *terra incognita*, but also placed this national territorial domain within relevant imaginaries designed to entice overseas missions. The brochure—a glossier, more concise version of the report issued by the Egyptian Department of Antiquities half a decade earlier—followed a by-now-well-established form. Comprising a map, an introduction to the topic, and a number of lists of potential sites for excavation arranged in chronological order from the paleolithic to "Christian Nubia and Later Periods," the publication was reminiscent of the tourist guides produced for countries like Egypt.[89] It was also, once again—and not uncoincidentally—similar to the lists of monuments produced for World War II bombing raids that had helped to produce "a visual and linguistic rhetoric of [monumental] fame" at the same time as territorializing different monumental schemes in various countries.[90] The brochure helped make a Sudanese past for Nubia, even as floodwaters threatened to overwhelm the region, and even as that process involved reaching out to wider circles whose interests included mapping the development of Christianity.

The map within the brochure underlined this strategy, depicting a border that claimed the Wadi Halfa Salient as Sudanese.[91] Vercoutter and Adams noted that "if, ethnically and geographically, the true border between Egypt and the Sudan lies at Aswan and not at Wadi Halfa, it is not by mere chance that the present political border has been fixed at the 22nd parallel."[92] Inscribing Sudan as both linguistic and territorial object, however, the brochure also inscribed the nation-state within other frames, foreshadowing later developments in Nubian archaeology more broadly and echoing the interests of the scholars that Vercoutter and Adams hoped to entice to the region. "This Wadi Halfa reach is one of utmost importance if," they wrote, "one wishes to understand clearly the interrelation between Egypt and the Sudan and, through

---

depictions of Michael and historical documents from the Christian era in Sudan"], *al-Ra'i al-'Amm*, October 29, 1961.

89. Jean Vercoutter and William Y. Adams, *Why Excavate in Sudanese Nubia? An Appeal of the Sudan Antiquities Service* (Gloucester: John Bellows, 1960), 16.

90. Allais, *Designs*, 99.

91. Vercoutter and Adams, *Why Excavate*, 2.

92. Vercoutter and Adams, *Why Excavate*, 3.

this, that between the classical Mediterranean World and Africa."[93] With Sudan itself seemingly a secure and stable entity, it became possible to think through the country's relationship with other geographical and intellectual imaginaries, and the brochure encouraged foreign archaeologists to do so.

Simultaneously, it became possible to divest Sudan of other geographies, an act that seemed to provide little cause for worry to northern Sudanese officials. In a guide prepared for institutions wishing to excavate in Sudanese Nubia—and as had anyway been the case under Sudan's 1952 Antiquities Ordinance—Adams made clear that each excavation "concession will provide that at least 50% of the objects found may be retained by the grantee." Now, too, "in some cases a more generous division may be made at the discretion of the Commissioner for Archaeology."[94] Some countries benefited greatly from Sudan's largesse: the "Scandinavian Joint Expedition to Sudanese Nubia" (which pooled the resources of Denmark, Finland, Norway, and Sweden) returned to Europe with a huge number of objects.[95] Beyond even this enticement, though, Adams made clear that, as under the ʽAbbud government more generally, the Sudan Antiquities Service was prepared "to ignore vast areas of the country" in the hope that concentrating on particular areas would benefit Sudan as a whole.[96] "As a further inducement to foreign expeditions," Adams noted, "ethnographic materials from the southern Sudan, which are now in the collections of the Antiquities Service, may be added to the archaeological collections which are taken from the country."[97] As Heather Sharkey has discussed, when Sudan became independent, "educated Northerners imagined a nation that took its territorial shape from the colony but its cultural shape from themselves."[98] Now, the Antiquities Service helped to constitute this geography. Nubia's past would be indexed with reference to Sudan's more generally.

---

93. Vercoutter and Adams, *Why Excavate*, 3.

94. William Y. Adams, "Living and Working Conditions for Archaeologists in Sudanese Nubia," Document CUL(60)13 (UNESCO, 1960), 12. Folder 069 (62) N: 930.26 (624) (Part 2): "Museums-Egypt-Nubia-Excavations-Sudan," UNESCO Archives. For the 1952 Antiquities Ordinance, see Jean Vercoutter, "Editorial Notes," *Kush: Journal of the Sudan Antiquities Service* 8 (1960): 6.

95. Investigating these collections—and the huge amount of archival material accompanying them—was beyond the time and budget of my project. For a summary of the Scandinavian Joint Expedition, see Torgny Säve-Söderbergh, "The Scandinavian Joint Expedition to Sudanese Nubia," *Historisk-filosofiske Meddelelser udgivet af Det Kongelige Danske Videnskabernes Selskab* 49 (1979): 1–53.

96. Young, *Transforming*, 88.

97. Adams, "Living and Working Conditions," 12.

98. Heather J. Sharkey, *Living with Colonialism: Nationalism and Culture in the Anglo-Egyptian Sudan* (Berkeley: University of California Press, 2003), 11.

Indexing Sudan, Archaeologically

Early in his Sudanese sojourn, Bill Adams had "developed a set of standard site-recording forms and procedures, drawing on models familiar to me from the" United States. Adams sought to record Sudanese Nubia following the standardizing impetus of American archaeology, as Brew and others had intended. The problem was that his procedures "didn't prove useful . . . as the enormous diversity of sites we encountered, encompassing several thousand years of prehistory and history, defied recording on any one standard form."[99] Consequently, "as the foreign expeditions left, one by one, at the end of their seasons, we got from them as much documentation as they would give us in regard to their work and entered their sites into our files along with our own."[100] This practice meant that Sudan, like Egypt, suffered from the removal of excavation records: a blow to the notion of the country's territorial integrity. Conversely, though, it also meant that the *post-hoc* standard within which Adams and his assistants lodged the remaining documentation took on an aspect whereby the specifics of Nubia became indexical of a Sudanese past more generally. Nubia's past gave shape to a Sudanese one framed through Adams's anthropologically informed archaeological background: rooted in his own North American experience and training (archaeology in the United States tended to sit within anthropology departments), such work also promoted itself in opposition to the sort of monumental recording taking place in Egypt.[101] In a 1962 newsletter, the Sudanese Embassy in Washington referred to the archaeological work in Sudanese Nubia as work in "Northern Sudan."[102] That geography figured.

Indeed, that geography figured almost literally, given not only its attachment to Adams's photo mosaic, but also to another cartographic concern. Adams's contract had been extended by UNESCO so that he could coordinate the Nubian campaign in Sudan. Considering how an archaeological survey of the region might happen, he made "a deliberate effort . . . to develop systems which would later be applicable to all parts of the country." That way, "the records from the survey of Nubia could in future years become the nucleus for a more general Archaeological Survey of the Sudan."[103] Nubia constituted

---

99. Adams, *The Road*, 143.
100. Adams, *The Road*, 157.
101. Adams, *The Road*, 149.
102. "Important Archaeological Discoveries in Northern Sudan," *Republic of the Sudan News* 2 (February 1962): 4.
103. William Y. Adams, "Archaeological Survey of Sudanese Nubia: Introduction," *Kush: Journal of the Sudan Antiquities Service* 9 (1961): 7–8.

CHAPTER 4

Sudan, and Sudan constituted Nubia, even as Adams's initial attempt to create this synecdoche failed. Luckily, his second try was more successful. Working from Sheet 35–1 ("the Wadi Halfa quadrangle") of the 1:250,000 series of maps published by the country's Survey Department, Adams created a site numbering system that took Sudanese cartography as its basis:

> For purposes of survey orientation and site documentation it was decided to divide this map into twenty-four equal sections, each covering 15 min. of longitude and latitude. These units are designated by the numbers from 1 to 24, reading in horizontal rows from left to right. Each 15-minute unit is subdivided into twenty-five squares of 3 minutes each, and these are designated by the letters from A through Y, again reading horizontally from left to right.
>
> Within each 3-minute section archaeological sites are numbered in the order of discovery, beginning with 1. For all sites the discovery number is preceded first by the number of the 15-minute section, and second by the letter of the 3-minute section. The complete site number thus always comprises three elements, as 24–E–7 and 6–B–22.[104]

Adams proceeded to document Nubian sites in ways ordered by this system and his archaeological interests, creating a field office in the one-time Wadi Halfa Museum to do so.

> Apart from the offices of the Sudan's only inspector of antiquities and his clerk, Gamal, the museum was used solely for equipment storage. We took over one of its largest rooms for our documentation center, as we liked to call it, and here we installed our site files, our aerial mosaics (mounted on the wall), and our stereographic and drafting equipment. Another room was fitted with shelves to accommodate our archaeological finds, and a third eventually became our darkroom.[105]

Ultimately, Bill and Nettie Adams returned to Khartoum in 1964 to draw and photograph finds. There, they would also start work on transferring information on those finds to catalogue cards (in Wadi Halfa, Negm el-Din Mohammed Sherif administered foreign missions in Adams's place).[106] It is worth reflecting on this new "documentation center" and the recording practices that it generated, however, not least because the differences to CEDAE's practices

---

104. Adams, "Archaeological Survey," 8.
105. Adams, *The Road*, 155.
106. Adams, *The Road*, 184, 188. Parts of this and the following section reproduce parts of Carruthers, "Records."

SITE NO.	DISTRICT	PERIOD	TYPE SITE
6-B-1	Argin	Meroitic X-Group	Cemetery

DESCRIPTION
Very large cemetery of mound tumuli with deep, end-chamber pits. Burials mostly slightly contracted, oriented south. Mostly X-Group graves with a few Meroitic.

Spanish Site SAX

EXTENT	CONDITION
About 270 graves in area c. 220 x 140 m.	Nearly all plundered

EXCAV. RECORD
Trial exc. by SAS Survey, 1956. 120 graves exc. by Spanish Exped., 1962.

MAP SHEETS	AIR PHOTOS	
Wadi Halfa	327020	(H) 624122 (28) 652158

FIELD NOTES	PHOTOS	

RECORDED BY	DATE	BIBLIO (OVER)
E. A. Wallis Budge	1907	X

FIGURE 4.1. Site register card produced for the Sudanese Nubia "documentation center." Sudan Archaeological Research Society William Y. Adams Archive ADA D007.01.

were clear. For example, the registration card (figure 4.1) for a site in the district of Argin places the locale—given the code SAX by its excavators—within the new, Sudanese registration system: SAX became 6-B-1.

Meanwhile, the card records key archaeological details like "Type Site," along with 6-B-1's "Excav.[ation] Record" and published bibliography. The card is tied to a larger "Site Register," which indexes the site alongside others in the vicinity and details of the aerial photos to which it is connected (figure 4.2). And such descriptions are themselves tied to cards recording details of objects found at sites (figure 4.3). The concentration on the site's place within a series of maps is familiar from CEDAE. But the difference in interest to the Egyptian documentation center, and the connected difference in conceptualization to what a past for Sudan might constitute, is clear. Paperwork could create different forms of knowledge, even within the same campaign.

This difference was also one that Adams did not perceive as being entirely office- or boat-bound. Adams's unease around Egyptology became clearer throughout his work in Sudan (and, later, over the border in Egypt, when he worked for the EES at the site of Qasr Ibrim). This new documentation center was not one, therefore, that afforded its inhabitants the facilities of its namesake institution in

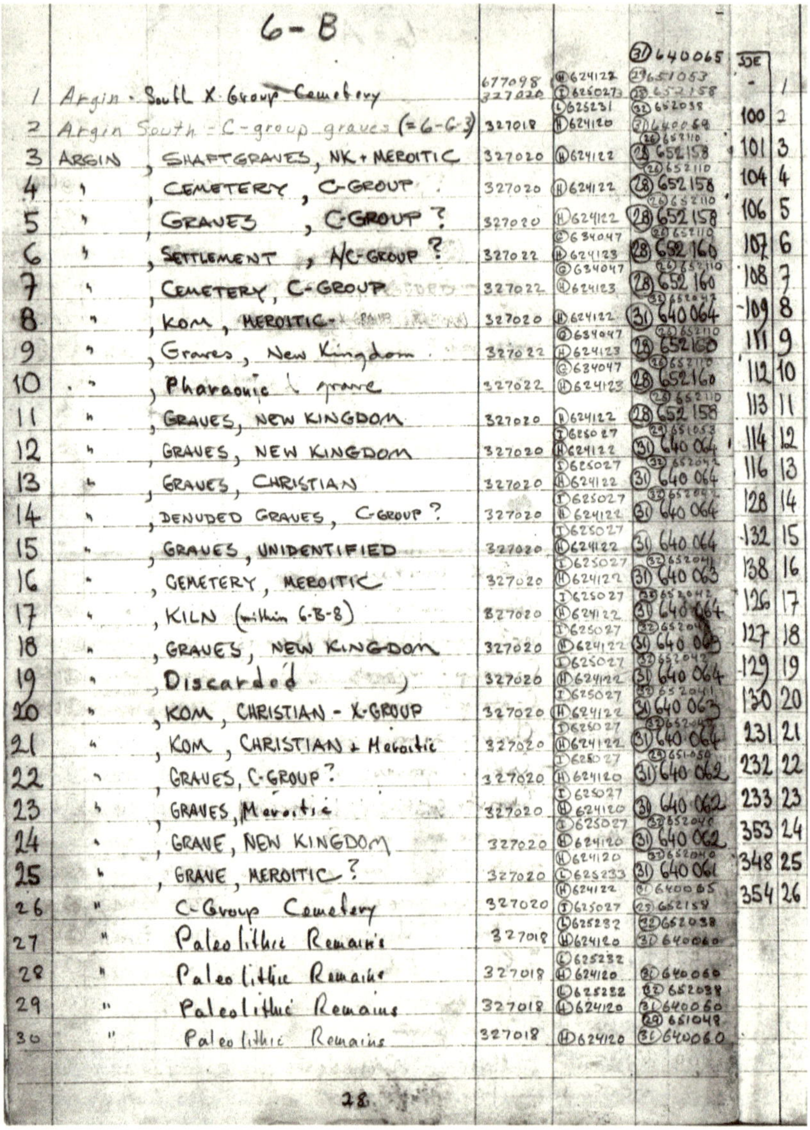

6-B

					SJE	
1	Argin - South X-Group Cemetery	677098 327020	(H)624122 (I)625027	(31)640065 (29)651053 (28)652158	-	1
2	Argin South - C-group graves (=6-G-3)	327018	(L)625231 (H)624120	(32)652038 (31)640060	100	2
3	ARGIN, SHAFTGRAVES, NK + MEROITIC	327020	(H)624122	(26)652110 (28)652158	101	3
4	″ CEMETERY, C-GROUP	327020	(H)624122	(26)652110 (28)652158	104	4
5	″ GRAVES, C-GROUP?	327020	(H)624122	(26)652110 (28)652158	106	5
6	″ SETTLEMENT, N/C-GROUP?	327022	(G)634047 (H)624123	(26)652110 (28)652160	107	6
7	″ CEMETERY, C-GROUP	327022	(G)634047 (H)624123	(26)652110 (28)652160	108	7
8	″ KOM, MEROITIC	327020	(H)624122	(32)652042 (31)640064	109	8
9	″ Graves, New Kingdom	327022	(G)634047 (H)624123	(26)652110 (28)652160	111	9
10	″ Pharaonic grave	327022	(G)634047 (H)624123	(26)652110 (28)652160	112	10
11	″ GRAVES, NEW KINGDOM	327020	(H)624122	(26)652110 (28)652158	113	11
12	″ GRAVES, NEW KINGDOM	327020	(I)625027 (H)624122	(29)651053 (31)640064	114	12
13	″ GRAVES, CHRISTIAN	327020	(I)625027 (H)624122	(32)652042 (31)640064	116	13
14	″ DENUDED GRAVES, C-GROUP?	327020	(I)625027 (H)624122	(32)652042 (31)640064	128	14
15	″ GRAVES, UNIDENTIFIED	327020	(I)625027 (H)624122	(31)640064	132	15
16	″ CEMETERY, MEROITIC	327020	(I)625027 (H)624122	(32)652041 (31)640063	138	16
17	″ KILN (within 6-B-8)	327020	(I)625027 (H)624122	(32)652042 (31)640064	126	17
18	″ GRAVES, NEW KINGDOM	327020	(I)625027 (H)624122	(32)652042 (31)640063	127	18
19	″ Discarded	327020	(I)625027 (H)624122	(32)652042 (31)640064	129	19
20	″ KOM, CHRISTIAN - X-GROUP	327020	(I)625027 (H)624122	(32)652041 (31)640063	130	20
21	″ KOM, CHRISTIAN + Meroitic	327020	(I)625027 (H)624122	(32)652042 (31)640064	231	21
22	″ GRAVES, C-GROUP?	327020	(I)625027 (H)624120	(29)651050 (31)640062	232	22
23	″ GRAVES, Meroitic	327020	(I)625027 (H)624120	(31)640062	233	23
24	″ GRAVE, NEW KINGDOM	327020	(I)625027 (H)624120	(32)652040 (31)640062	353	24
25	″ GRAVE, MEROITIC?	327020	(H)624120 (L)625233	(32)652040 (31)640061	348	25
26	″ C-Group Cemetery	327020	(H)624122 (I)625027	(31)640065 (29)652158	354	26
27	″ Paleolithic Remains	327018	(L)625232 (H)624120	(32)652038 (31)640060		
28	″ Paleolithic Remains	327018	(L)625232 (H)624120	(31)640060		
29	″ Paleolithic Remains	327018	(L)625232 (H)624120	(32)652038 (31)640060		
30	″ Paleolithic Remains	327018	(H)624120	(29)651048 (31)640060		

28

FIGURE 4.2. Site register produced for the Sudanese Nubia "documentation center." Sudan Archaeological Research Society William Y. Adams Archive ADA D001.

FIGURE 4.3. Object register cards produced for the Sudanese Nubia "documentation center." Sudan Archaeological Research Society William Y. Adams Archive ADA D007.01 (image by the author).

Cairo, or one of the Egyptian institution's four boats.[107] Instead, the American tacked between office and field: constituting the office in the field, in a sense. The Sudan Antiquities Service sanctioned this practice. That sanction came about after an argument with Thabit Hassan Thabit, who had (at least according to Adams) wanted to move the American from conducting fieldwork in Nubia to an office in Khartoum: "'we can't have a state within a state,' was the way he [Thabit] put it."[108] Whether or not this recollection is accurate, what is undeniable was the often-polemic emphasis Adams placed on what being in the field allowed him to observe and document. Allied with the interests of other archaeologists working in Nubia—the Scandinavian Joint Expedition was busy surveying the east bank of the Nile while Adams and his team surveyed the west—these claims meant that the past of the region, alongside its apparently solid border with Egypt, came to occupy a more contested position than previously.

In the Field, in the Office

For Adams and others, being in the field mattered, at least when they were not collating the results of their work. Despite characterizations of archaeological fieldwork historically promoting isolation and aggressive masculinity, however, that desire did not always mean giving up on certain of life's comforts.[109] In Nubia, Bill and Nettie Adams—who, as he emphasizes, was as much a part of the fieldwork as anyone else—lived in field houses supplied by the Sudan Antiquities Service, which "had the basic characteristics of all Nubian village houses" but that also "had servants . . . just as we did in our [Wadi Halfa] townhouse, a cook and a *saffragi* [waiter] who performed the same functions as in town. Additional servants were a water carrier, who had to make several trips a day from the river, and a toilet cleaner."[110] Still, being in the field enabled a form of archaeological witnessing that allowed Adams to claim that his methods gave him the ability to perceive information that others—particularly hidebound Egyptologists—could not. Moreover, it gave him the chance to construct what he construed as statistically controlled archaeological "data" from it, a process that the entry of information onto index cards aided.[111]

---

107. For Adams on Egyptology, see *The Road*, 214–16. For those boats, see Noblecourt, *La grande*, 139.

108. Adams, *The Road*, 170.

109. In relation to the Nubian campaign, this characterization is far clearer in Fred Wendorf's *Desert Days: My Life as a Field Archaeologist* (Dallas: Southern Methodist University Press, 2008).

110. Adams, *The Road*, 163, 182.

111. Unlike the more heuristic examples of "data" discussed in chapter 3, Adams has made clear use of the term, at least retrospectively, for which see *The Road*, 330.

Being in the field enabled Adams to claim the ability to construct temporal sequences from excavated pottery through witnessing the place of that material in stratified position. When possible (and echoing the thoughts of Oliver Myers in *Sudan Notes and Records*), it also meant the promotion of controlled stratigraphic work more generally, particularly where that work enabled the investigation of long-term settlement history. Wearing his Americanist anthropological training on his sleeve, during his time in Sudan, Adams became invested in questions of Nubian cultural change and continuity, conducting excavations at the site of Meinarti that attempted to address these themes and returning to the country in the late 1960s to conduct similar work at the site of Kulubnarti.[112] In Egypt, such work had fallen by the wayside as the constitution of a monumental and timeless Nubian landscape took precedence and the clearance of ancient (and modern) remains gathered pace. In Sudan, though, the creation of an archaeological *terra incognita* made such work possible. Colonial, national, and anthropological interests came together as one.

Ironically, the first manifestation of that work involved digging at a site that had been dug once before: one which sat directly on the Egyptian-Sudanese border created by the Wadi Halfa Salient. Faras and its "Potteries" had been excavated in 1911–12 under the *aegis* of the Egyptologist Francis Llewellyn Griffith.[113] *Being there*, though, was what really allowed the possibility of making this new work seem vital: visiting and working at the site and proceeding to publish an eyewitness account of that work in *Kush* made the excavation there appear important. Discounting Griffith's work in the same journal for which the American now began to undertake the largest portion of the editorial work,[114] Adams became a legible arbiter of proper archaeological—and certainly not Egyptological—knowledge:

> Whereas Griffith was concerned primarily with the western portion of the site, and only incidentally with the kilns, we began our investigations in and around the latter. We became aware almost at once of a quantity of material and complexity of stratification which were entirely unexpected,

---

112. For Meinarti and Kulubnarti, see *The Road*, 175–81, 201–09. Alongside his connection to more established figures like Richard Woodbury, in the early 1950s Adams had worked in Arizona for Walter Taylor, whose work sought to combine aspects of archaeology and anthropology and dealt, among other matters, with "cultural context." For that work see *The Road*, 81–84. For Taylor himself see Corey M. Hudson, "Walter Taylor and the History of American Archaeology," *Journal of Anthropological Archaeology* 27, no. 2 (2008): 192–200.

113. Francis Llewellyn Griffith, "Oxford Excavations in Nubia—Continued," *University of Liverpool Annals of Archaeology and Anthropology* 13 (1926): 63–5.

114. Adams, *The Road*, 188.

and soon found it necessary to enlarge the scope of our operations. As work progressed we were able to identify, instead of the three periods of occupation postulated by Griffith, at least six distinct stratigraphic levels.... We found also that many of the rooms shown in Griffith's plan had not been excavated to the lower floor levels. Eventually we re-excavated eight of the rooms mapped by Griffith as well as an area of about equal size lying to the east.[115]

As Adams noted, "the clear-cut stratification of both structures and refuse deposits offers an opportunity to recognize developmental sequences in the pottery."[116] Estimating that "we handled at least 50, 000 sherds, of which about half were initially saved for study," that outcome was the one that ultimately transpired after the collection from Faras had been combined with potsherds from later excavations.[117] In 1962, Adams published "An Introductory Classification of Christian Nubian Pottery" in *Kush*. Doing so, he made some disclaimers: "that the chronology as it stands is currently a relative one, and there is a distressing scarcity of datable material to which it can be tied."[118] Certain sherds used in the chronology were also not from stratigraphic contexts.[119] Yet Adams to some extent rendered—or tried to render—this concern negligible by stating not only that the classification had been "developed statistically," but also that "elimination of questionable occurrences is most easily done with the aid of frequency distribution curves for the different wares."[120] Combined with his assumed standing as a witness, statistics and strength of numbers—the constitution of archaeological data—rendered Adams authoritative.

Of course, to a great extent that data had to be developed away from the field itself. Despite Adams's protestations, archaeology was nothing without an office, and he and others knew it. In this context, the Wadi Halfa "documentation center" proved key, as did Antiquities Service facilities in Khartoum. During field seasons, either Adams, Verwers, or Nordström "would come in [to Wadi Halfa] from the field camp each Thursday afternoon." There, they would "bring in and store the finds excavated during the week . . .

---

115. William Y. Adams, "The Christian Potteries at Faras," *Kush: Journal of the Sudan Antiquities Service* 9 (1961): 30–31.
116. Adams, "The Christian Potteries," 31.
117. Adams, "The Christian Potteries," 40.
118. William Y. Adams, "An Introductory Classification of Christian Nubian Pottery," *Kush: Journal of the Sudan Antiquities Service* 10 (1962): 278.
119. Adams, "An Introductory Classification," 277.
120. Adams, "An Introductory Classification," 276.

enter the sites we had recorded into the site files and on the aerial mosaic, and . . . develop and print photos."[121] When field seasons ended, meanwhile, and it came time to produce an annual report for *Kush*, "we always went to Khartoum for part of the summer in order to make use of the Antiquities Service library. This allowed us to relate our findings to previously . . . published work."[122] The field always sat within other "landscapes of paper" that made its existence tangible, enabling the constitution of archaeological data from it.[123]

In the case of Sudan, those landscapes developed an aspect whose relationship to national sovereignty proved unstable. When it came time to leave the country in 1966, Bill and Nettie Adams "still hadn't put a line on paper in the way of our final report." They also worried that "there was no prospect that anyone else would ever write those reports, or that the Sudan would have the financial resources to publish them." Given the situation, Thabit Hassan Thabit asked Adams "to take with me all the documentation from the digs—every field note, map, photograph, site register card, and artifact card—leaving in Khartoum only the artifacts themselves." Consequently (and astonishingly), Adams took "the whole documentation center" to his "attic office in Kentucky."[124] As he noted in 2009, moreover, "only in the past year has . . . [the documentation center] been transferred to the Sudan Archaeological Research Society in the British Museum, which in the intervening years has published all the long-delayed reports."[125] The field could not exist without documentation and the offices where that documentation was compiled. Yet that paperwork proved as mobile as some of the objects found there, questioning the forms of national sovereignty upon which its existence was predicated.

Papering the Field, across Borders

It was not just relative to Sudan that such archaeological paperwork took place: the constitution of archaeological data ultimately knew no borders in other ways. In Egypt, archaeological work was as predicated on the use of various forms of paper as the work of photographing and recording monumental and other reliefs and inscriptions. And that practice of documentation was as much

---

121. Adams, *The Road*, 154.
122. Adams, *The Road*, 157.
123. See Meskell, *A Future*, 81–82, for such "landscapes" in relation to UNESCO.
124. Adams, *The Road*, 189.
125. Adams, *The Road*, 189.

162   CHAPTER 4

tied to sitting in an office (or office-like) environment as the work in Sudan. Consequently, archaeological communication across the Egyptian-Sudanese border began to take place. Not everyone agreed that archaeological work in Egyptian Nubia constituted a spent force. Paper helped to strengthen their argument.

For some people working in Egypt, paper practices, whether inside or out, materialized data in much the same way they did in Sudan. For example, the Yale-Penn excavation at the Egyptian site of Arminna West took on the polemical thrust associated with the survey undertaken under Adams at the same time as being demonstrably linked to office and field, as figure 2.1 makes clear. It is in the excavation's documentation that the data-led drive of the work at the site materializes. In the field, the excavation used an improvised card "sherd-o-meter" to sort and measure countless pieces of pottery at speed and create standardized data from them. The excavation also created any number of "Pottery Classification Form[s]," whose current presence in archive boxes belies their role as active carriers of a data standard, especially when those boxes are opened and the forms reinspected as they continue to be today.[126]

As ever, the archive mattered—and matters. The classification forms from Arminna West (figure 4.4) collated the information—"sherd type," "quality of firing," "temper"—that not only made pottery collected during fieldwork comparable after that work had ended, but also made that process possible far away from the site itself: an example of a "science of the archive" at work if ever there was one, not to mention the object mobility that such sciences promote.[127] Crucially, too, those categories allowed comparison to the classificatory scheme outlined by Bill Adams for pottery found in Sudanese Nubia. That comparison did not have to be positive: the form in figure 4.4 noted that it was possible "to rule out all Adams' classifications for this fabric."[128] The development of such comparisons, however, illustrates how paperwork, whether stored in archives or published in journals, made possible the creation of data presumed to be not only *a priori* comparable, but also comparable across borders.

Following the constitution of an archaeological *terra incognita* in Sudan, paper and its filing now made ancient material like pottery mobile in a way

---

126. When I inspected the site archive in the Peabody Museum stores in late 2016, it had recently been rearranged.

127. Daston, "The Sciences."

128. Arminna West "Pottery Classification Form" 1.0–2, "Arminna West Cemetery B (AWB) Pottery Classification Forms" file (ANTAR.037150), Yale Peabody Museum of Natural History Archives.

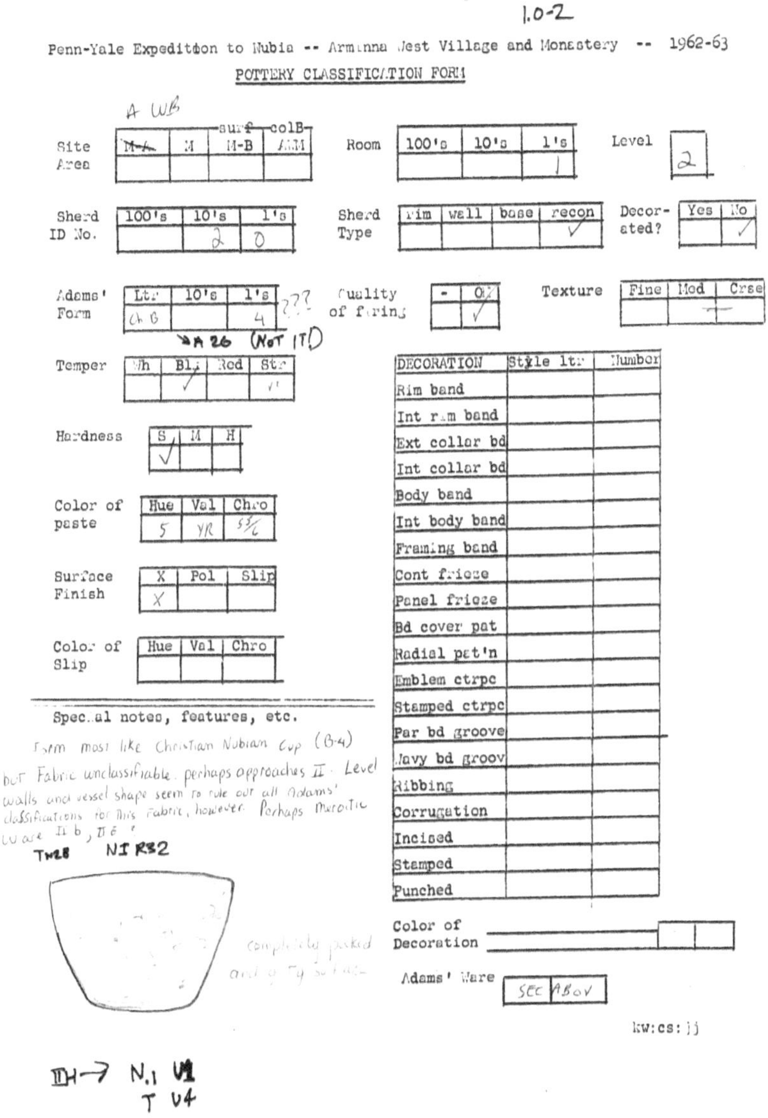

1.0-2

Penn-Yale Expedition to Nubia -- Arminna West Village and Monastery -- 1962-63

POTTERY CLASSIFICATION FORM

A WB

| Site Area | M-A | M | surf M-B | colB- AWM | Room | 100's | 10's | 1's | Level | 2 |

| Sherd ID No. | 100's | 10's 2 | 1's 0 | Sherd Type | Rim | wall | base | recon ✓ | Decorated? | Yes | No ✓ |

| Adams' Form | Ltr Ch 6 | 10's | 1's 4 | ??? →A 26 (NOT IT!) | Quality of firing | - | O✓ | | Texture | Fine | Mod ✓ | Crse |

Temper: Wh | Bl ✓ | Red | St /

Hardness: S ✓ | M | H

Color of paste: Hue 5 | Val YR | Chro 5/6

Surface Finish: X ✓ | Pol | Slip X

Color of Slip: Hue | Val | Chro

Special notes, features, etc.

Form most like Christian Nubian Cup (B-4) but Fabric unclassifiable, perhaps approaches II - Level walls and vessel shape seem to rule out all Adams' classifications for this fabric, however Perhaps Meroitic Ware II b, II e?

TW28   N1 R32

DECORATION	Style ltr	Number
Rim band		
Int rim band		
Ext collar bd		
Int collar bd		
Body band		
Int body band		
Framing band		
Cont frieze		
Panel frieze		
Bd cover pat		
Radial pat'n		
Emblem ctrpc		
Stamped ctrpc		
Par bd groove		
Wavy bd groov		
Ribbing		
Corrugation		
Incised		
Stamped		
Punched		

Color of Decoration _____

Adams' Ware   SEE ABOV

kw:cs:jj

completely pecked and a rg surface

IIH→ N,1 V1
      T   V4

FIGURE 4.4. Arminna West "Pottery Classification Form" 1.0–2, "Arminna West Cemetery B (AWB) Pottery Classification Forms" file, Yale Peabody Museum of Natural History Archives, Division of Anthropology, Arminna West Archive, ANTAR.037150, page 16.

that broke down the boundary between Egypt and its southern neighbor. That action not only hardened the perception of Nubia as a region straddling geopolitical borders. It also constituted a means of altering pottery analysis in the region from being overtly connected to the sort of scientific racism visible in the earlier—and sometimes contemporary—Egyptian Nubian surveys. Kent Weeks, chief archaeologist at Arminna West, stated in one of the site's publications that "developments in anthropology and history and, more generally, the rapid post-war rise of the social sciences gave the archaeologist a different theoretical framework and a new set of problems with which to work." Like Adams and some of his American counterparts in Nubia, Weeks had been trained in anthropology and would obtain a master's degree in the subject from the University of Washington in 1965. Thus, it was hardly surprising that he went on to argue that archaeology "was becoming an integral part of the social sciences. . . . [That] attempted to provide historical depth to the study of Man as a sociocultural being." At least rhetorically, "the decision to excavate the Classic Christian Townsite at Arminna West was prompted by the hope of finding further stratigraphic evidence for continuity and change in Nubia."[129] Weeks's words echoed the concerns of Bill Adams, in addition to those of Bruce Trigger, his companion on the dig. Trigger, then a graduate student at Yale, would soon publish a doctoral dissertation about long-term settlement patterns in Egyptian Nubia. In the dissertation, he credited the work of the Americanist archaeologist Gordon Willey on the long-term understanding of human adaptation to the environment as "a fundamental turning point in the development of archaeological theory."[130] Coupled with the process of constituting the paper-based data necessary to aid comparison across borders, Nubia as a whole now became ripe for the undertaking of such anthropologically tinged studies.

Ironically, that process continued to overlap with the interests of actors concerned with national independence, widening the in-state parameters of

---

129. Kent R. Weeks, *The Classic Christian Townsite at Arminna West*, Publications of the Pennsylvania-Yale Expedition to Egypt 3 (New Haven, CT, and Philadelphia: The Peabody Museum of Natural History of Yale University and the University Museum of the University of Pennsylvania, 1967), 2. Weeks would later edit *Egyptology and the Social Sciences: Five Studies* (Cairo: American University in Cairo Press, 1979). For Weeks himself, see "Dr. Kent R. Weeks, Director," *Theban Mapping Project* website, accessed August 25, 2020, https://web.archive.org/web/20161111093307/http://www.thebanmappingproject.com/about/staff_1.html.

130. Bruce G. Trigger, *History and Settlement in Lower Nubia*, Yale University Publications in Anthropology 69 (New Haven, CT: Department of Anthropology, Yale University, 1965), 1. As Trigger noted on pp. 1–2, Gordon Willey's *Prehistoric Settlement Patterns in the Virú Valley, Perú*, Smithsonian Institution Bureau of American Ethnology Bulletin 155 (Washington, DC: United States Government Printing Office, 1953), constituted a key influence on his work.

what such knowledge might constitute. Central to this process was Professor of Geology at Cairo University Rushdi Said, who would be appointed to Egypt's one-party (Arab Socialist Union) parliament in 1964 and become chairman of the Egyptian Geological and Mining Organization in 1968.[131] Nancy Reynolds has noted that the building of the Aswan High Dam helped to constitute "the state's effort to restore [future] time to the nation through geological manipulation."[132] Geology, though, could equally be tied to particular forms of archaeological work, and Said—a 1962 awardee of Egypt's Order of Sciences and Arts, and author of *The Geology of Egypt*, published the same year—took his opportunity to meld the two disciplines, at the same time as helping to promote a form of fieldwork whose mobilization of rough desert life as an organizing principle was clear.[133]

Said had been at Harvard with Fred Wendorf, an American prehistorian whose doctoral adviser was John Otis Brew.[134] Wendorf had also worked on the River Basin Surveys and become a member of the Committee for the Recovery of Archaeological Remains in 1954.[135] Wendorf now contacted Brew to inquire about undertaking a survey of any paleolithic material located in Nubia.[136] And when Wendorf visited Egypt to plan work there, he and Rushdi Said discussed possible collaboration after meeting, apparently by chance, at the Cairo University herbarium.[137] Consequently, in 1961, Wendorf (who had also been friends with Bill Adams for some years) wrote two grant applications.[138] Those applications reflected the idea that archaeological coverage of Nubia should not be restricted by a geopolitical border and, at the behest of Brew, were also directed toward the relevant funding sources: an application for Sudan submitted to the US "National Science Foundation for U.S. dollars, and ... one for Egypt to the State Department for Public Law 480 [i.e. 'Food for Peace'] money."[139] This action and the work that followed proceeded to knit the earlier prehistory of both countries together. Rushdi Said's centrality to this process was manifest.

---

131. For Rushdi Said's memories of these events, see his autobiography, *Science and Politics in Egypt* (Cairo: American University in Cairo Press, 2004).
132. Reynolds, "Building," 198.
133. Rushdi Said, *The Geology of Egypt* (Amsterdam and New York: Elsevier, 1962).
134. Wendorf, *Desert*, 45.
135. Wendorf, *Desert*, 53, 58.
136. Wendorf, *Desert*, 122–23.
137. Said, *Science*, 64–65.
138. Wendorf, *Desert*, 128.
139. Wendorf, *Desert*, 123.

Making Prehistory

Indicating the degree of disorganization—and also the competing forms of sovereignty—present throughout the Nubian campaign, Brew had apparently neglected to mention that other individuals had been busy in Nubia conducting similar prehistoric work. Charles Reed of Yale's Peabody Museum worked together with Phillip Smith of the University of Ontario in Egypt, while Ralph Solecki eventually did a small amount of work in Sudan.[140] None of them had found anything that they considered important, and Solecki (who wanted to return to Iraq) was prepared to bow out gracefully.[141] Reed and Smith, however, had applied to continue working in the Egyptian Nile Valley south of Kom Ombo, and heated exchanges between Wendorf and the pair followed.[142] It is hard to know whose statements about this episode to believe, but what is clear is that tension subsequently infected Wendorf's relationship with Egypt's Department of Antiquities. In Sudan, the American enjoyed a good relationship with Thabit Hassan Thabit, and was aided too by his friendship with Adams.[143] But in Egypt, his relationship with Anwar Shoukry, then director of the Department of Antiquities, was tense: Shoukry, Wendorf claimed, "bluntly told me he was disappointed I received funds to work in Egypt on prehistoric sites." Not only did Shoukry not want to reassign the concession awarded to Reed and Smith but "he'd wanted to spend that money on the salvage of Pharaonic materials."[144]

It was only through Rushdi Said and his contacts that Wendorf's difficulties would be overcome. As Wendorf acknowledged, Said made possible his eventual work on the Egyptian side of the Nubian border, acting as something more than the proverbial "go-between" by leveraging the resources of the Egyptian Geological Survey and making himself central to the work at hand.[145] This action embedded the long-running tension between Egypt's prehistory and the study and promotion of the country's later past within the institutions of the Egyptian state.[146] It also allowed a polemic insistence on a certain type of field survey standing in opposition to normative practice in Egypt and with which both Said and Wendorf made professional hay. After

---

140. Wendorf, *Desert*, 124–25.
141. Wendorf, *Desert*, 125.
142. Wendorf, *Desert*, 125.
143. Wendorf, *Desert*, 128.
144. Wendorf, *Desert*, 127. Cf. Said, *Science*, 66.
145. Wendorf, *Desert*, 128. On "go-betweens" and their role in knowledge production, see Simon Schaffer, Lissa Roberts, Kapil Raj, and James Delbourgo, eds., *The Brokered World: Go-Betweens and Global Intelligence, 1770–1820* (Sagamore Beach, MA: Watson Publishing International).
146. On the historical lack of attention paid to prehistory—and particularly to periods prior to what became known as the "Predynastic"—by Egyptologists, see Gange, *Dialogues*, 237–69, particularly 239; Cf. Stevenson, *Scattered*, 174.

discussions with Wendorf (but before Wendorf's meeting with Shoukry), Said had visited Nubia alone in 1961, "taking a train to Aswan and from there the steam boat that shuttled along the Nubian Nile from Aswan to Wadi Halfa." As he later claimed, "my first impression was that the area had a lot of potential but that its study could best be carried out from the desert side rather than the Nile side. I therefore decided to make the trip from the desert side in vehicles that I was able to get on loan from the geological survey."[147] Once again, the desert spoke: the "drear wastes" of Egyptian Nubia might lend themselves to prehistoric survey as much as the Sudanese ones.[148]

Accompanied by his former master's student Mohamed El-Bahay Issawi (now working for the Geological Survey), Said drove into the Nubian desert and searched for points of geological interest, preparing the ground for Wendorf's return to Egypt in the autumn of 1962. When Wendorf returned, the pair, accompanied by Geological Survey officials, "traveled the desert stretch along the western bank of the Nubian Nile and made a short visit to the oases of Kurkur and Dunqul, which lie on top of the cliff overlooking the Nubian plain."[149] Wendorf was impressed, collecting ancient flint implements to convince Shoukry of the relevance of the work. It was now, though, that Shoukry refused Wendorf permission to work in Nubia.[150] And it was only through Said's influence—and his insistence that the pair's work constituted a different practice to that which had otherwise taken place in the region—that the American came to conduct prehistoric survey in Egypt.

As Said claims, "I went to Dr. Shukri and was able to persuade him to grant Wendorf a concession to work in the peripheral stretches of Nubia outside the Nile valley that were beyond the reach of the other expedition, which was working from a boat docked on the river."[151] Said's position in Egypt was increasingly influential, not least because geological and other such resource discoveries were considered important for the state's future development.[152] And this ability to carry out fieldwork "by way of cars rather than by boat as had been the tradition among archaeologists and Egyptologists" now became a constant rhetorical

---

147. Said, *Science*, 65.
148. Emery, "In These Drear Wastes."
149. Said, *Science*, 66. For Issawi, who became director-general of the Geological Survey of Egypt from 1982 until 1984, and under-secretary of state for mineral wealth between 1985 and 1996 (and proceeded to sit on the Permanent Committee of Pharaonic and Prehistoric Antiquities of Egypt's Supreme Council of Antiquities), see Mamdouh M. Abdeen, "Biography of Professor M. El-Bahay Issawi," *Journal of African Earth Sciences* 136 (2017): 5–9. Like Rushdi Said, Issawi's career shows how the investigation of geology and prehistory in Egypt overlapped with political life.
150. Said, *Science*, 66.
151. Said, *Science*, 66.
152. As Said, *Science*, 66, and Reynolds, "Building the Past," discuss.

call from both men: later, Wendorf pejoratively described Reed and Smith as "houseboat archaeologists."[153] Within the year, therefore, the pair benefited from the closure of the other Egyptian prehistoric expedition and the sponsorship of the Egyptian Geological Survey, allowing them to range across (Egyptian) Nubia at will.[154] "The view from the boat" had apparently been hushed, if not entirely silenced, allowing the later formation of a Combined Prehistoric Expedition (CPE) conducting coordinated prehistoric survey across Egypt and Sudan. Wendorf and Said were not the only individuals active in this process: the initial CPE monograph lists participants from eighteen institutions.[155] What is clear, however, is that national actions constituted transnational knowledge. As Wendorf discusses, the formation of the CPE occurred during what became the one "working conference" on the archaeology of the Nubian campaign, which, sponsored by the National Science Foundation and the Society for American Archaeology, took place at Lake Como in Italy in 1964 and brought together Egyptian and Sudanese antiquities officials and various foreign missions.[156] Moreover, even as the flooding of Nubia solidified the border between Egypt and Sudan, so that same process now constituted knowledge—geological and archaeological data—that undermined that boundary, reconstituting the category of the Nile Valley that had long been used to justify unity between the two countries for another, postcolonial era.

As archaeological fieldwork in Nubia made its way into published form, so the work of the CPE used the process of print "to preserve and to record the threatened archaeological data" of an area "in both Egypt and Sudan . . . in excess of 300 miles along the Nile, at least half of it on both banks."[157] Coupled with the self-consciously archaeological work in Sudan and Egypt discussed earlier (and buttressed by the colonial and postcolonial officials who had prompted much of that work to happen), this constitution of archaeological "data" was, if anything, the way in which the Nubian campaign's links to the TVA—and to other, similar projects descended from interwar and colonial genealogies like UNESCO's Arid Zone Program—became clear. While

---

153. Wendorf, *Desert*, 125.
154. Said, *Science*, 66–67.
155. Fred Wendorf, "Preface," in *The Prehistory of Nubia*, vol. 1, ed. Fred Wendorf (Taos, NM: Fort Burgwin Research Center and Southern Methodist University Press, 1968), ix–x. Among others, Issawi and Romuald Schild of the Polish Academy of Sciences became particularly important in the CPE.
156. For the conference, which Wendorf misremembered as taking place in 1965, see Wendorf, *Desert*, 177. Cf. Albert C. Spaulding, "Conference on Prehistoric Archaeology in the Aswan Dam Area, Bellagio, Italy, August 24–28, 1964," *American Antiquity* 31, no. 2, part 1 (1965): 303–4. Given the institution's earlier disinterest in the Nubian campaign, the event ironically took place at the Rockefeller Foundation's Villa Serbelloni conference center in the lakeshore town of Bellagio.
157. Fred Wendorf, "Introduction," in Wendorf, *The Prehistory of Nubia*, vol. 1, ed. Fred Wendorf (Taos, NM: Fort Burgwin Research Center and Southern Methodist University Press, 1968), 15–16.

never methodologically coherent, such "data" ironically began to make Nubia one by assembling a new whole from manifold separate parts and from across two, apparently distinct nation-states.[158]

As Wendorf discussed,

> the basic unit of study was the individual site or settlement. A collection of artifacts was obtained from each site, or, more correctly, from each occupation horizon or distinct area of occupation within the site. These individual site, horizon, or area collections are termed 'assemblages.'[159]

Later, "most of the assemblages were grouped into several larger units that we have called 'industries.'"[160] Likewise, "because so little was known about the area, the first priorities were given to the development of a regional stratigraphic sequence."[161] Parts and wholes, stratigraphy and "the need for large, statistically significant collections":[162] familiar enough from the work of Adams and others and set down on card and paper, so these methods constituted a rough-and-ready archaeological field and its data. They also constituted Nubia as a transnational object in opposition not only to more narrowly "Egyptological" work, but also to what seemed like the wishes of the new nation-states involved in the Nubian campaign. Incorporating both a dislike of certain colonial knowledge practices and the colonial knowledge that had made such cross-border method possible, this work characterized the Nubian campaign more generally. As the next chapter shows, beyond prehistory, the same logic also governed the project's relationship to people.

---

158. As Wendorf, "Introduction," 18, notes, "because of the wide range in the training and approach represented in this group [of specialists], different opinions and interpretations naturally occurred."
159. Wendorf, "Introduction," 16.
160. Wendorf, "Introduction," 16.
161. Wendorf, "Introduction," 17.
162. Wendorf, "Introduction," 17.

Chapter 5

Peopling Nubia

If the Nubian campaign became emblematic of anything beyond the preservation and movement of ancient structures and objects, it became emblematic of the global mobility and cosmopolitan representation of people. In December 1964, just after archaeological fieldwork in Egyptian Nubia had ended and funding to move the Abu Simbel temples had been secured, *The UNESCO Courier* declared "Victory in Nubia." Inside, Director of the Service for the Monuments of Nubia Ali Vrioni wrote that UNESCO "has coordinated an unprecedented campaign of exploration, carried out by archaeological expeditions from virtually every part of the world." Pointing to his employer's cosmopolitan principles, Vrioni emphasized that UNESCO's victory was tied to the ability of people, then or in the future, to move around the globe—or at least to conceptualize monuments as universal ones. "In their new sites," Vrioni wrote, the Nubian temples "will certainly become ... focal points for the cultural interest of the world."[1]

Through the promotion of universalism during the Nubian campaign, UNESCO attempted to make tangible the cosmopolitan, internationalist values rhetorically central to the organization's foundation.[2] Unable to escape that mo-

---

1. Ali Vrioni, "Victory in Nubia," *The UNESCO Courier* (December 1964): 6.
2. As Glenda Sluga, "UNESCO and the One World of Julian Huxley," *Journal of World History* 21, no. 3 (2010): 394, notes, "late nineteenth-century conceptions of race and empire remained uneasily" connected to the "One World" values of UNESCO's first Director-General, Julian Huxley. The dif-

ment's bureaucratic underpinnings, UNESCO even found literal ways to seal people to those principles through paper. In 1961, the organization launched a philatelic drive based around the Nubian campaign, intending the global issue of stamps both to raise funds for and to promote the project. By 1964, *The UNESCO Courier* could report that "over 40 countries have issued stamps," including the Central African Republic, Gabon, Ghana, Indonesia, Laos, Lebanon, Mali, Monaco, Morocco, Nigeria, Pakistan, Togo, Tunisia, and Yugoslavia.[3] The image of people the world over—and in an expanding United Nations (UN) membership—licking these small pieces of paper is surreal. Yet it highlights how UNESCO sought to use the Nubian campaign as the gum with which to bind people around the globe together.

Such global togetherness had limits, however. Lucia Allais has noted how "UNESCO introduced Nubia to a worldwide public as a proto-international land, defined by a history of mobility" that the Nubian campaign helped to reveal. This representation proved useful, as it meant that the displacement of the Nubian population taking place simultaneously with the project could be discussed as a localized example in this mobile mold: an equal to the mobility that UNESCO promoted when discussing the influx of archaeologists to the region.[4] Such contrivance occluded not only how this migration took place, but also how the earlier Nubian displacements had helped to condition this latest example, which itself cleared the way for UNESCO's project. Likewise, UNESCO's strategic representation of its Nubian work obscured other types of mobility that made the Nubian campaign: ones that often related to colonial archaeological hierarchies and the bureaucratic means of their regulation.

Valeska Huber has discussed how the Suez Canal, opened in 1869, became a symbol of an "increasingly rapid mobility" that helped to drive processes of globalization. At the same time, though, the canal was in fact "characterised by the *channelling* [Huber's italics] of mobility . . . the differentiation, regulation and bureaucratisation of different kinds of movement."[5] I examine such bureaucratic channeling here. Nubia, quite obviously, did not take the form of a canal. The region, however, did constitute a manipulated riverine environment into and through which people (and things) could be channeled. That environment was also one where that process had occurred for quite some

---

ferential mobility discussed in this chapter points to one way in which those earlier conceptions remained firmly relevant to UNESCO's work after Huxley's departure.

3. Anon., "Stamps for Nubia," *The UNESCO Courier* (December 1964): 43.
4. Allais, "The Design," 202.
5. Valeska Huber, *Channelling Mobilities: Migration and Globalisation in the Suez Canal Region and Beyond, 1869–1914* (Cambridge: Cambridge University Press, 2013), 3.

time and where, as I have demonstrated, bureaucracy had gained a hold, whether in the undertaking of UNESCO's campaign or during the building of the High Dam. In relation to the Suez Canal, "the kaleidoscope of movement shows how, in the context of the technological innovations of the second half of the nineteenth century, mobility became a marker of Western modernity."[6] In Nubia, however, such mobility became a marker of how technological innovation could be used to promote both local modernization initiatives and UNESCO-backed cosmopolitanism. Simultaneously—and as in the case of the Suez Canal—"multiple processes of exclusion and deceleration were in fact in play."[7] I attend to these processes in this chapter, discussing the paperwork resonances connecting Nubian migration and the Nubian campaign, and showing how the documentary and archival impulses discussed throughout this book allowed for—and countered—such regulation of movement. I show how paper made possible that regulation, but also gave voice to acts that, occasionally, let slip the mask of idealized social order. Mobility could be regulated. Yet the subjects of that regulation could use the medium of paper to protest its vagaries, and that same medium could record the anxieties felt when elements of that regulatory practice seemed to go awry.

Reiterative Authority

During the Nubian campaign, paper was everywhere. At times, too, the project's participants used the material to protest the conditions under which the campaign took place. Acting as gatekeeper to, and progenitor of, mobile possibility, the campaign's bureaucracy could be used to subvert the circumstances that form filling sometimes created. Ilana Feldman notes how, in (British Mandate and pre-1967, Egyptian-controlled) Gaza, a process of "reiterative authority" in relation to filing counted "on regularity and on an expansive view of the bureaucratic domain." As Feldman shows, "files and civil servants accrued and deployed authority in part through a process that seemed to offer no alternative, no other place to go." Consequently, "bureaucracy and bureaucracy's reiterative authority shaped, constrained, and helped define possibility for all its actors."[8] Nubia was not Gaza. But the status of these two places as liminal regions under (in the case of Nubia, partial) Egyptian control renders them similar enough that this comparison of filing practices enjoys ana-

---

6. Huber, *Channelling*, 3.
7. Huber, *Channelling*, 3.
8. Feldman, *Governing*, 220.

lytical purchase. As Feldman notes, in Gaza, "the relationship among government, population, and place was not one simply of cause and effect, but rather operated in multiple directions, sometimes at the same time."[9] In Nubia too, even as their existence constrained mobility, spaces of bureaucratic documentation constituted the possibility, however slight, of attempting to direct mobility from below—or at least of ensuring that people's mobility could not be curtailed further.

For example, at the site of Wadi es-Sebua, a team from the Egyptian Department of Antiquities worked to dismantle a temple of Ramses II, and laborers used day-to-day paperwork to make a complaint (*shakwā*) about limitations placed on their contact with the mobile world around them.[10] During their work at the site (and as had become standard in the region), workers were dependent for contact with the outside world on a boat, al-Dakka, that traveled up and down the Nubian Nile. That boat did not always operate reliably. In June 1967, the workers wrote a collective letter of complaint to the Director-General of Financial and Administrative Affairs (DGFAA) and the Under-Secretary of Egypt's Ministry of Culture. In it, they complained that the Director of Works (Mudir al-A'mal) at the site had told them that they could have food and other supplies brought to them by al-Dakka rather than, as they had requested, sending "towboats" (*al-jarrārāt*) to Aswan to do the same job. Having followed the director's instructions, the workers were dismayed to discover that none of what they had requested was carried on the boat when it arrived at Wadi es-Sebua. Angered, they asked the officials: "does this please you?" (*hal hadhā yurḍīkum?*).[11] Cut off from the outside world, the workforce asserted their right to an infrastructure of mobility that not only drove the Nubian campaign but would also make their lives more bearable.

Pressing their case, the workers' vehemence was one bolstered by numbers. Signed by over thirty employees at the site, several thumbprints are impressed on the document, the signatures of illiterate individuals who would otherwise have remained unheard. Can the subaltern speak?[12] In this case, the intent at least seems to have been to operate as a vocal collective, thumbprints appearing

---

9. Feldman, *Governing*, 219.
10. For Wadi es-Sebua, see Säve-Söderbergh, *Temples*, 135–37.
11. Letter from the workers at Wadi es-Sebua to the DGFAA and the Under-Secretary of the Egyptian Ministry of Culture, (uncertain date in) June 1967. File 2A-b2, "Shakwat Hay'at al-Āthār al-Nūba" ["Complaint of the Nubian Antiquities Organization"], Nubia Museum. My thanks to Rageh Mohamed and Shatha Almutawa for their help with locating and reading this document.
12. Gayatri Chakravorty Spivak, "Can the Subaltern Speak?" reprinted (originally published 1988) in *Colonial Discourse and Post-Colonial Theory: A Reader*, ed. Patrick Williams and Laura Chrisman (Harlow: Pearson Education, 1994), 104.

among the names signed in full: Saʿid Labib ʿAbd al-Rusul and Faruq Barakat al-Dessuqi, to identify just two.[13] This was a collective statement to which, after the piece of paper had entered government files, the powers that be had no choice but to listen. In a letter written to the Resident Engineer (al-Muhandis al-Muqayyim) at Abu Simbel, the DGFAA stated that a towboat should be permanently stationed at Wadi es-Sebua "at the service of the site" (*fī khidmat al-minṭaqa*).[14] Mobility—even of this limited variety—was officially back on the table.

Not everyone thought these complaints fair. Responding to the letter, the Resident Engineer vociferously rejected the DGFAA's judgment, stating that it had no material basis and had "not been checked" (*dūn taḥaqquq*).[15] Yet embedded within the practice of reiterative authority constituted by the filing and drawing together of paperwork, this rebuttal seems to have lacked impact. On the top-left corner of the initial letter of complaint, an official wrote that the workers' "demands should be met" (*talbiyyat al-ṭalabāt*), sealing the correspondence within a mode of bureaucratic practice that gave primacy to the authoritative regularity of such inscriptions.[16] Signed, sealed, and delivered, officialdom upheld the complaint lodged by the workers of Wadi es-Sebua, enabling them to safeguard their relationship with the forms of mobility that linked them to the wider world. The constitution of that mobility, as they made clear, was not one-sided.

Paper and the High Dam

Mobility was also not a one-sided phenomenon even in the wake of the forced migrations that the High Dam constituted. In the panoply of worlds connected to the structure, the ability to put opinion to paper has long helped to puncture the pretentions around (social) mobility that its building fostered. Those pretentions, like the universalist attitudes connected to the Nubian campaign, could be close to overpowering; the paper they were printed on purifying the vast effort of building the High Dam of any negative odor. In Egypt, for instance, the structure's development dominated the press, which had been subject to increasing state control since 1954 and ultimately nationalized in 1960.

---

13. Letter from the workers at Wadi es-Sebua.
14. Letter from the DGFAA, Egyptian Ministry of Culture, to the Resident Engineer, Abu Simbel, June 12, 1967. File 2A-b2, "Shakwat Hay'at al-Āthār al-Nūba," Nubia Museum.
15. Letter from the Resident Engineer, Abu Simbel, to the DGFAA, Egyptian Ministry of Culture, June 25, 1967. File 2A-b2, "Shakwat Hay'at al-Āthār al-Nūba," Nubia Museum.
16. Letter from the workers at Wadi es-Sebua.

As Laura Bier has noted, such control, "coupled with state subsidizing of media and cultural output, resulted in more words (and because of the impact of education, a larger readership), but fewer voices."[17] Simultaneously, those voices reflected "generationally specific intellectual and political orientations."[18] Press coverage of the High Dam was thus overwhelmingly positive, echoing the perspective of the state and stressing the contribution of the project to national development. Articles memorialized the deaths that occurred as construction work took place, martyring those who had fallen victim to the dangers of tunneling and dynamiting.[19] But the sometimes grisly (and apparently uncounted) ends of many workers at the dam could also be remembered in other ways: ones where paper, although not the central material, of necessity played a supporting role.

Setting voices in print in her oral history of the experiences of High Dam workers, Alia Mossallam notes that "more often than not . . . [death] is depicted as the fault of the worker, victim to his own inexperience."[20] Perhaps because many of the Egyptians involved with the structure strove to help the project based on "their belief in . . . [a] 'revolutionary truth' and their ability and willingness to contribute to it," these personal accounts are not necessarily critical of the High Dam or the Nasser-era plans to which the project became connected.[21] By recording the thoughts of those involved with the work, Mossallam's personal histories emphasize how paper can be (and has been) used to broaden narratives surrounding the structure's social impact.[22]

Indeed, some forms of paper have constituted a space in which the High Dam's social traces have been criticized intensely. For example, the Egyptian writer Sonallah Ibrahim's 1974 novel *Najmat Aghustus* (August star) follows its journalist protagonist as he visits Aswan and the site of the project, discussing the work there with participants in the High Dam's construction.[23] Ibrahim, a one-time member of Egypt's disbanded Democratic Movement for National Liberation (al-Haraka al-Dimuqratiyya li-l-Tahrir al-Watani, or HADETU), had been a victim of state action against communists: a political

---

17. Laura Bier, *Revolutionary Womanhood: Feminisms, Modernity, and the State in Nasser's Egypt* (Cairo: American University in Cairo Press, 2011), 18.

18. Bier, *Revolutionary Womanhood*, 19.

19. See, e.g., "Shahid al-Sadd al-ʿAli" ["Martyr of the High Dam"], *al-Musawwar* 2414, January 15, 1971, 44–49.

20. Mossallam, "'We Are the Ones,'" 308.

21. Mossallam, "'We Are the Ones,'" 312.

22. For another recent oral history of the High Dam, see Yussef Fakhuri, *al-Tarikh al-Insani li-l-Sadd al-ʿAli* [The human history of the High Dam] (Cairo: Al-Haiʾa al-ʿAma li-Qusur al-Thaqafa, 2016).

23. Sonallah Ibrahim, *Najmat Aghustus* [August star] (Damascus: Ittihad al-Kitab al-ʿArab Dimashq, 1974).

prisoner from 1959 until 1964, he was released, ironically enough, on the occasion of Nikita Khruschev's visit to the country to mark the completion of the High Dam's first stage.[24] Unsurprisingly, that imprisonment did little to put an end to Ibrahim's frustrations with the Nasserist project, nor their appearance in a novel about the construction of the dam itself: *Najmat Aghustus* constituted part of an inversion of the social-realist style of writing known as *al-ādāb al-multazim* ("committed literature") undertaken by a number of writers disillusioned with the lived realities of Nasser's Egypt.[25] Céza Kassem-Draz has argued that the novel works as the "negation" of *Insan al-Sadd al-'Ali* (The man of the High Dam), a more positive 1967 reportage of work at the High Dam site written by Ibrahim, Kamal al-Qilsh, and Ra'uf Mus'ad.[26] I will not discuss this analysis in great detail. David DiMeo, however, glosses Kassem-Draz, suggesting that what is fundamentally at stake within this act of denial

> are the bedrock claims of the High Dam project: that it was first an engineering marvel that tamed nature, but also that it did so without widespread damage to the established cultural and natural environment of Upper Egypt or the workers who constructed it. Ibrahim's 1967 text supports these claims, while his 1974 novel . . . rejected them.[27]

Paper could subvert, in this case in the form of a (thinly) novelistic encounter with those involved not only with the High Dam's construction, but also with the preservation work at Abu Simbel. Banned in Egypt even when, under the presidency of Anwar al-Sadat, questioning of both Nasserism and the narrative of the High Dam had become more widespread, the first edition of *Najmat Aghustus* had to be published in Damascus, and a Cairo edition did not appear until 1976. Despite (or perhaps because of) Sadat's 1971 "Corrective Revolution," Egyptian censors could not countenance a novel that depicted personal and political alienation among the state's populace.[28] By the end of

---

24. On HADETU, see Joel Beinin, *The Dispersion of Egyptian Jewry: Culture, Politics, and the Formation of a Modern Diaspora* (Berkeley: University of California Press, 1998; Cairo: American University in Cairo Press, 2005), 143–54. Citation refers to the Cairo edition. For Ibrahim, see Paul Starkey, *Sonallah Ibrahim: Rebel with a Pen* (Edinburgh: Edinburgh University Press, 2016).
25. On "committed literature," see David F. DiMeo, *Committed to Disillusion: Activist Writers in Egypt from the 1950s to the 1980s* (Cairo: American University in Cairo Press, 2016).
26. Céza Kassem-Draz, "Opaque and Transparent Discourse: A Contrastive Analysis of the 'Star of August" and "The Man of the High Dam" by Son'Allah Ibrahim," *Alif: Journal of Comparative Poetics* 2 (1982): 35. Kassem-Draz cites Sonallah Ibrahim, Kamal al-Qilsh, and Ra'uf Mus'ad, *Insan al-Sadd al-'Ali* [The man of the High Dam] (Cairo: Dar al-Kitab al-'Arabi li-l-Tiba'a wa-l-Nashr, 1967).
27. DiMeo, *Committed*, 168.
28. On the "Corrective Revolution," see, e.g., Hamied Ansari, *Egypt: The Stalled Society* (Albany, NY: State University of New York Press, 1986), 168.

the novel, DiMeo notes that it is apparent to the protagonist that "there is genuine suffering among the laboring class that deserves to be addressed, but the writer has no confidence that he can get this message past a censoring government to reach an uncaring public."[29] It took some time for that message to be published in Egypt itself.

Other literature, mostly in Arabic and published since the late 1980s, has set forward "suppressed Nubian perspectives towards the [two Aswan] dams, perspectives which have gone unheard or unheeded by successive governments."[30] Earlier writing connected to the displacements of the first Aswan Dam also exists: Muhammad Khalil Qasim's 1968 novel *al-Shamandura* (The buoy), for instance, "metaphorically projects that experience onto the present ... highlighting the need for the Nubian people to continue to resist [the building of Nile barrages] for the sake of their rights."[31] But it is the various writers connected to the more recent movement known as *al-Sahwa al-Nubiyya* (the Nubian Awakening)—among them Yahya Mukhtar, Haggag Hassan Oddoul, and Idris ʿAli—who have, as Christine Gilmore has argued, used literature to emphasize "what [Rob] Nixon has termed the 'slow violence' of the Aswan High Dam's delayed effects on Nubian economic, social, and cultural life."[32] These authors, whose writing is "characterized by nostalgia and the deferred dream of return to Old Nubia,"[33] entertain disagreements: Haggag Hassan Oddoul has described the Nubian displacement caused by the High Dam as a *nakba*, or calamity, equivalent to the one suffered by Palestinians in 1948, while both Yahya Mukhtar and Idris ʿAli oppose this view.[34] All, however, have succeeded in riling Egypt's literary world, "leading to allegations linking [their writing] to a[n] ... agenda aimed at weakening the unity of the Egyptian state."[35] In a context—especially in the later years of Husni Mubarak's presidency—when much greater freedom of expression became possible in Egypt, literary responses to the High Dam's effects could amplify elite paranoia about the fate of the nation.

---

29. DiMeo, *Committed*, 172.
30. Christine Gilmore, "'A Minor Literature in a Major Voice': Narrating Nubian Identity in Contemporary Egypt," *Alif: Journal of Comparative Poetics* 35 (2015): 52.
31. Gilmore, "'A Minor Literature,'" 58, citing Muhammad Khalil Qasim, *al-Shamandura* [The buoy], 3rd ed. (Cairo: Al-Haiʾa al-ʿAma li-Qusur al-Thaqafa, 2011). Cf. Gilmore, "Speaking through the Silence," in *Development-Induced Displacement and Resettlement: New Perspectives on Persisting Problems*, ed. Irge Satiroglu and Narae Choi (Abingdon: Routledge, 2015), 199–211.
32. Gilmore, "'A Minor Literature,'" 52, citing Rob Nixon, *Slow Violence and the Environmentalism of the Poor* (Cambridge, MA: Harvard University Press, 2011).
33. Gilmore, "'A Minor Literature,'" 59, citing Mara Naaman, *Urban Space in Contemporary Egyptian Literature: Portraits of Cairo* (New York: Palgrave Macmillan, 2011), 115.
34. Gilmore, "'A Minor Literature,'" 57.
35. Gilmore, "'A Minor Literature,'" 57.

Those responses, though, do not encompass the totality of Nubian cultural expression. Alongside oral histories recording the experiences of workers at the High Dam, Menna Agha notes that

> there is a wealth of material in Nubian [dialects]; however, it is often orally disseminated, with very little recorded. Nubian was the main medium for the expression of Nubian women, whose isolation in old Nubia exposed them to the Arabic language significantly less than their male counterparts, who often migrated to Arabic-speaking contexts for wage work in the first half of the twentieth century. This delay made Nubian literature, printed and distributed in Arabic, a space for male authors.[36]

It has been beyond the scope of this book project to access such oral responses. Consider though, that in *Nubian Twilight* (his 1962 reportage on the Nubian campaign), the journalist Rex Keating wrote that

> an amusing indication of how Nubians feel about their forbears was provided by the Spanish Expedition from Madrid who were digging an early C-group cemetery among the scattered houses of a modern village. Each morning with unfailing regularity an old woman appeared on the dig to lay claim to the property of her 'ancestors' as she described these people who died at least 4,000 years ago. She demanded half of all the pots and human remains found, 'but you can keep the cattle horns.' She could be silenced only by the leader of the expedition, Dr Blanco Y Caro, demanding that she, in return, pay half the cost of running the expedition . . . [37]

Perhaps even to some readers at the time, Keating's words and Blanco Y Caro's actions were crass. Indeed, they are indicative of the ways in which Nubians became disaggregated from ancient remains in the region, even as writers such as Keating, echoing colonial-anthropological tropes of the racial "survival," emphasized the historical continuity of settlement in Nubia (Bill Adams and others with anthropological educations did so slightly differently).[38] Keating's words are indicative, however, of absent oral histories.[39] The considerable barriers placed on such work by the state security apparatus in Egypt—

---

36. Agha, "Nubia," 4.
37. Rex Keating, *Nubian Twilight* (London: Rupert Hart-Davis, 1962): 90–91.
38. Ibid., 45 notes that "chance has preserved in the Second Cataract many living reminders of the remote past." For the colonial (and nationalist) history of the survival in Egypt, see, e.g., El Shakry, *The Great*, 46–50. Elsewhere, Karl Georg Siegler, "Der Abbruch des Tempels," in *Kalabsha: Der grösste Tempel Nubiens und das Abenteuer seiner Rettung*, by Hanns Stock and Karl Georg Siegler (Wiesbaden: F. A. Brockhaus, 1965), 75, writes of the *"uralter orientalischer Sitte"* (or "ancient oriental custom") of Nubians living around the temple of Kalabsha.
39. Carruthers, "Records," 303–9.

and the limitations of movement imposed on researchers in Egypt and Sudan more generally—do not make recording such testimony easy.[40] Yet even during the 1960s, obstacles were placed in the way of such work, not least by the organization whose cosmopolitan principles might have suggested that it take an opposite course of action.

Accelerating the Social

As Keating's words—and recent Nubian literature—emphasize, not everyone connected to the Nubian campaign enjoyed unalloyed mobility. The constitution of a Nubian past had long been tied to the reassembly of Nubian presents and the creation of the Nubian population as a group separated from the remains among which they lived. As I have argued, the Nubian campaign itself was no different in this respect. As the transfer of ancient remains from the region occurred on an ever wider scale, so, too, did the rhetoric surrounding Nubians themselves expand: the construction of the High Dam accelerated the formation of a collective identity for the different groups comprising the Nubian population.[41] This process would also shape conceptions of Nubian mobility in distinctly national terms.

As the rise in water level caused by the High Dam meant that all settlements in Nubia would be submerged, so the Nubians remaining in the region became the subject of state-directed plans for their migration. Government officials sent members of the population from the Egyptian side of the Nubian border to newly constructed settlements near Kom Ombo, located just to the north of Aswan. Nubians in Sudan, meanwhile, were sent to the area of Khashm El Girba, many hundreds of miles to the southeast on the Atbara River (map 1). In 1959, the Sudanese government decided to construct a dam there that would both generate hydroelectricity and enable an irrigation scheme, further accelerating the newly independent country's development policies. In a contentious decision, Sudanese Nubians would ultimately be chosen to settle the region.[42] Whether in Sudan or Egypt, meanwhile, UNESCO would not

---

40. On risk and fieldwork in Egypt, see Nassar, "Where the Dust." On Egypt's "security mentality," see Khaled Fahmy, "National Security and Canned Sardines," February 9, 2013, https://khaledfahmy.org/en/2013/02/09/national-security-and-canned-sardines/.

41. Maja Janmyr, "Human Rights and Nubian Mobilisation in Egypt: Towards Recognition of Indigeneity," *Third World Quarterly* 38, no. 3 (2017): 729, footnote 3. As Janmyr notes, Nubians "comprise three culturally ethnic and linguistically distinct groups and only became collectively known as 'Nubian' after their displacement."

42. On this controversy, see Isma'il Hussein Abdalla, "The Choice of Khashm al-Girba Area for the Resettlement of the Halfawis," *Sudan Notes and Records* 51 (1970): 56–74.

seek to aid these now-separated populations. Disconnected from the campaign, not everyone could militate for their mobility.

Why did UNESCO not seek to "save" Nubians in the same way that it sought to save the monuments that earlier work had created in the region? Why did Nubian mobility take a distinctly less "global" shape than the movement enjoyed by many participants in UNESCO's campaign? The lack of attention paid to Nubians during UNESCO's project has often been noted, and implicit and explicit criticism consequently leveled at the organization.[43] As initial plans for the campaign took shape, Tharwat Okasha had even told J. K. Van der Haagen, head of UNESCO's Division of Museums and Historic Monuments, that ethnographic attention should be paid to the Nubians. There was no lack of interest from the Egyptian side, even if that interest was strictly anthropological. It was only when UNESCO's Jean Thomas objected that this suggestion was "illogical" (*illogique*) that Okasha's wish was scuppered: Thomas stated that his organization's interest in Nubia related to monuments and not to men (*puisqu'il s'agit des monuments et non pas des hommes*).[44] Making that statement, Thomas separated two distinct categories of knowledge, allowing UNESCO to declare that its resources should be prioritized away from the promotion of ethnographic work. Yet how could this separation between ancient monument and contemporary humanity so easily be made at an organization whose own, 1945 constitution stated that "it is in the minds of men that the defences of peace must be constructed"?[45] What, too, did that separation mean for the pathways that Nubians now took?

Lynn Meskell has noted that UNESCO's work during the 1950s and 60s shifted "from the utopian [post-war] ideology of scientific humanism to one of technocracy and functionalism."[46] In the case of Nubia, however, the long-term epistemological separation of Nubians from the remains among which they lived clearly made this process easier. Moreover, it was the coupling of this process with knowledge dependent on documentary practices that really gave it impetus, determining that the Nubians' own mobility should be far removed from that of the monuments with which UNESCO expressed its concern. Among official circles, Thomas was not necessarily expressing a controversial opinion, despite the callousness with which, in hindsight, it can

---

43. Most recently in Meskell, *A Future*, 56.
44. J. K. Van der Haagen to René Maheu, August 1, 1959. Folder 069 (62) NUBIE (Part III): "Museums-Egypt-Nubia (Part III)," UNESCO Archives. This and other parts of this section follow Carruthers, "Records."
45. UNESCO, *UNESCO Constitution* (1945), accessed September 7, 2020, http://portal.unesco.org/en/ev.php-URL_ID=15244&URL_DO=DO_TOPIC&URL_SECTION=201.html.
46. Meskell, *A Future*, 56.

be characterized. The Nubians would be "saved" through other documentary conventions and the forms of knowledge tied to them—ones, moreover, that other organizations specialized in such work might arrange. This process, meanwhile, allowed Nubian mobility to be hastened in a way comparable to that of the remains being removed from the region, even as it helped to create a physical and epistemological separation from them. UNESCO gave the Nubians to forms of documented knowledge whose potential to help create local *social* acceleration seemed beyond doubt.

Art and Ethnography

The future, tempered by the right documentary tools, promised speedy progress, sometimes seductively so. But it only ever did so at a local or national level. UNESCO officials, ever trying to lessen the organization's commitments in Nubia (and to maintain good relationships with Egypt and Sudan), would not stand in the future's way. And why would they? Events might well have seemed like they were effectively—and speedily—in hand. The Fine Arts Administration (Idarat al-Funun al-Jamila) of Egypt's Ministry of Culture and National Guidance would sponsor twenty-five Egyptian artists to document life in Egyptian Nubia (and the construction of the High Dam) before the forced migration of the Nubians took place.[47] The project produced a work—Abdel Hadi al-Gazzar's (1964) *The High Dam*, a surrealist amalgam of man and construction—that became "the icon of Egypt of the moment," even as it expressed "complex feelings on the eve of the nation's entry into its new, progressive technological era."[48] Concurrently, the artists' campaign generated pieces celebrating the Nubians. Those creations were decorated with state prizes, even as, years later, the implicit racism of that work has been questioned by critics like Ismail and Sarah Fayed: noting, for instance, that Adham Wanly's (1959) *Reciting Quran in the Region of Nubia* "portrays Nubians in a caricature that resembles a typically racist representation (blackface) of African people everywhere."[49]

In 1961, meanwhile, a Ford Foundation–funded Nubian Ethnological Survey began its work on the Egyptian side of the Nubian border, continuing until

---

47. Hussein Bicar, "Infi'al wa-Ifti'al" ["Reacting and inventing"], *Akhir Sa'a* 1546, June 10, 1964, 42.
48. Avinoam Shalem, "Man's Conquest of Nature: Al-Gazzar, Sartre, and Nasser's Great Aswan Dam," *Nka: Journal of Contemporary African Art* 32 (2013): 22, 28.
49. Ismail Fayed and Sarah Fayed, "Avant-Garde Art between Egypt and the Soviet Union: Visual Comparisons," *Mada Masr*, October 15, 2015, https://www.madamasr.com/en/2015/10/15/feature/culture/avant-garde-art-between-egypt-and-the-soviet-union-visual-comparisons/.

1964 and the completion of the first phase of the High Dam. As a retrospective volume discussing the survey emphasizes, it was inevitably "conceived and conducted within a framework of the anthropology of the late 1950s and 1960s . . . with an emphasis on the bounded community . . . [and] strongly influenced by British structural-functionalism."[50] The project also had a strong applied element, influenced by development thinking and by contemporary attempts to remake Egyptian society more generally. "The [American-Egyptian] team [whose institutional base was the American University in Cairo] argued that the Nubian experience should not be allowed to disappear and that the lessons of that variant for social theory should be recorded." Simultaneously, the survey "was intended to facilitate the process of resettlement as administrators and others were apprised" of its work.[51] The ethnographic documentation of Egyptian Nubians promised social mobility, even if bounded within local borders. In effect, Egypt's Nubians had become a population problem, subject to survey funded by an organization that, through its largesse toward New York's Population Council, already held a significant stake in the formulation of the demographic (and neo-Malthusian) research within which that population—and Egypt's more generally—had become embedded.[52]

In Sudan too, Nubians found themselves embroiled within a similar set of practices. In January 1960, "a ministerial decision was taken directing the Department of Statistics to carry out a series of social and economic surveys in the affected area."[53] The District Commissioner of Wadi Halfa, Hassan Dafalla, took charge of the population's migration, and noted that "the object was to collect information which would be useful for the emigration and the resettlement of the displaced inhabitants." Thus, surveys collected statistical information about "population, dwelling houses, furniture, household equipment and baggage in Halfa town; livestock in the town; furniture and livestock in the area (a sample), and sample surveys of income and expenditure and diet."[54] Dafalla himself simultaneously "appointed seven committees for the enumeration of date and fruit trees in the area, presided over by administrative officers experienced in fieldwork."[55] Articulating with the wider statistical concerns of the Sudanese government, such documentation sought to aid

---

50. Hopkins and Mehanna, "The Nubian Ethnological Survey," 12–13.
51. Hopkins and Mehanna, "The Nubian Ethnological Survey," 4.
52. Matthew Connelly, *Fatal Misconception: The Struggle to Control World Population* (Cambridge, MA: Harvard University Press, 2008), 180–81, 188–89. On Malthusianism and Egyptian development, see Mitchell, *Rule*, 209–43.
53. Hassan Dafalla, *The Nubian Exodus* (London: C. Hurst, 1975), 95.
54. Dafalla, *The Nubian Exodus*, 95.
55. Dafalla, *The Nubian Exodus*, 100.

future mobility on a local level.[56] The same was the case from 1961 until 1964, when, overlapping with Dafalla's work, the Sudan Antiquities Service employed two German anthropologists, Andreas and Waltraud Kronenberg, to document the Sudanese Nubians. The Kronenbergs followed a method making use of "the traditional ethnographic and the structural-functional approach," largely echoing Egypt's Nubian Ethnological Survey with their emphasis "on the study of dynamics in a changing society."[57] Ethnographic (and statistical) documentation of Sudan's Nubians was attuned to their local, *social* mobility, even as the archaeological documentation of Sudanese Nubia took on a different sense of movement.

Marketing Mobility

Paper performances, meanwhile, aimed to give this social mobility a positive press, at least to a selective audience. In 1963, promotional pamphlets for Khashm El Girba appeared in English, with Arabic appearing only as part of the logo of the organization in charge. As part of the process of moving Sudan's Nubian population, the Halfa Resettlement Commission (Lajnat Tawtin Ahali Halfa) produced leaflets describing not only the Khashm El Girba project, but also the facilities being developed in conjunction with that plan: a sugar factory; numerous social service amenities; and facilities in irrigation, agriculture, and electricity. The leaflets were attractively designed, featuring stylized renderings of maps charting the Khashm El Girba project's boundaries overlaid with drawings of the structures being built at the site (figure 5.1).

Coupled with the text printed on them, the brochures depicted a modern, progressive, and developed future for the Halfawi Nubian population, one that assured a form of social mobility on the local level—and even as the High Dam had occasioned upon them a stark spatial relocation. The Halfa Resettlement Commission assured readers "that an inhabitant of Khashm El Girba will enjoy many services e.g. education, transport, health which he did not have in Halfa." Moreover, "by making full use of the services it is hoped that the people of Khashm El Girba will become worthy citizens who will contribute a great deal to the development of the whole country."[58] Social mobility

---

56. On those statistical concerns, see Young, *Transforming*, 76–106.
57. Andreas Kronenberg and Waltraud Kronenberg, "Preliminary Report on Anthropological Fieldwork 1961–62 in Sudanese Nubia," *Kush: Journal of the Sudan Antiquities Service* 11 (1963): 303.
58. Lajnat Tawtin Ahali Halfa [Halfa Resettlement Commission], "Khashm El Girba Project: Social Services in Khashm El Girba" leaflet (T. Press, 1963). Sudan Archaeological Research Society Laurence P. Kirwan Archive, London.

Figure 5.1. Cover of Khashm El Girba Project introductory leaflet (T. Press, 1963). Sudan Archaeological Research Society Laurence P. Kirwan Archive KIR D129.08.

within Sudan was assured, even as the forms of international mobility attached to UNESCO's Nubian campaign were not.

Putting paper to work promoting national-scale social mobility also had a corollary in Egypt. There, the Nubian migration to New Nubia (al-Nuba al-Jadida, as the government named it) became much more of a press event than UNESCO's campaign. Promoted as one element of the edifice's construction, Egypt's Nubian migration helped journalists to constitute the High Dam "as part of a wider national project to ensure self-sufficiency and remake citizenship in Egypt's postcolonial era."[59] A special issue of *al-Ahram* distributed in May 1964 to mark the completion of the dam's first stage did not include a single article about the UNESCO campaign throughout its 135 pages. But the

---

59. Reynolds, "City," 213.

publication certainly made clear the centrality of both High Dam and migration to the Egyptian nation.[60]

How this special issue constituted that centrality is worth dwelling upon, because the publication did not take the usual form of *al-Ahram*: instead of a broadsheet newspaper, the issue was closer to the format of an illustrated magazine. Discussing such magazines in interwar Egypt, Walter Armbrust has noted that these publications "deserve to be considered a medium in their own right," not least because they "combine text and image in ways that are distinct from other media."

> Illustrated magazines are made to be perused by individuals, who take in imagery that could not possibly be read out loud. Sally Stein argues that illustrated magazines work along the same lines as American television: the viewing (or reading) experience is not of discrete elements, but of uninterrupted 'flow' of content and advertising, to the degree that the distinction between the two becomes blurred.... If slippage between categories and blurred boundaries form the raw material of social performance in books and newspapers, then the illustrated magazines put such slippages and boundary blurrings right at the center of the reading experience.[61]

In the *al-Ahram* special number, however, there was to be no slippage into the Nubian campaign, no blurring of the issue at hand with remnants of the past. Instead, reading about the High Dam meant reading Egypt's future, one in which local forms of (social) mobility related to the dam took overwhelming precedent, and to which the issue's slippages were plainly directed. UNESCO was simply absent from the special issue's pages. Instead, readers would turn from a full-page advertisement for the General Egyptian Organization for Savings—"The High Dam Means Prosperity for Your Homeland," it proclaimed—to an article on the Nubian migration.[62] That migration, as the article's title put it, represented "The Journey of History" ("Rihlat al-Tarikh").[63] But the article's surrounding contents made clear that that journey was one whose culmination constituted not simply the future, but also a

---

60. Al-Ahram, ed., *al-Sadd al-'Ali*.
61. Walter Armbrust, "The Formation of National Culture in Egypt in the Interwar Period: Cultural Trajectories," *History Compass* 7, no. 1 (2009): 165, citing Sally Stein, "The Graphic Ordering of Desire: Modernization of a Middle-Class Women's Magazine," in *The Contest of Meaning: Critical Histories of Photography*, ed. Richard Bolton (Cambridge, MA: MIT Press, 1992), 145–62.
62. "al-Sadd al-'Ali Rakha' li-Watanak" ["The High Dam means prosperity for your homeland"], in al-Ahram, ed., *al-Sadd al-'Ali*, 31.
63. Al-Ahram, ed., *al-Sadd al-'Ali*, "Rihlat al-Tarikh" ["The Journey of History"], 32–34.

future tied to social and other forms of development. Readers of this special number would discover, piecemeal but consistently, how that future was to come about.

Reading this issue of *al-Ahram* helped the past become the future: the journey of history made real. In New Nubia, the Egyptian government built a series of villages that acted as simulacra of the settlements then being flooded on the banks of the Nile. As the publication visualized in map form, the villages were given names corresponding to the former settlements, all of which—as had been requested by the Nubians themselves—were officially preceded by the word "New."[64] Thus, the village of Ballana came to exist, once again, as New Ballana (and in two distinct parts, "Ballana the First," and "Ballana the Second").[65] Consequently, rather than simply echoing the past, this simulacrum of Nubia constituted a materialization of the modern forms of expertise discussed throughout the *al-Ahram* issue. Readers of the issue, moreover, had been equipped to expect exactly that outcome.

After turning from heavily illustrated articles discussing the engineering prowess that went into tunnels used to divert the waters of the Nile onto pieces discussing the development of the city of Aswan, the construction of workers' accommodation at the High Dam, and the development of a new type of brick for future building work, this materialization seems quite logical.[66] With these precedents, it is unsurprising to turn to an article including a map of New Nubia that explains how the region came into being. New Nubia, in this logic, represented the self-evident culmination of all of these acts and all of these images, an outcome which the title of the article laboriously made clear: "Building the Villages Consumes an Amount of Stone One-and-a-Half Times that Used in the Great Pyramid, Seventy-Five Million Bricks, 150 Thousand Meters of Lime, One-and a Half Million Meters of Gravel and Sand and 250 Thousand Tons of Cement."[67] Leafing through the special issue, the ar-

---

64. Hopkins and Mehanna, "The Nubian Ethnological Survey," 8.

65. "Sura al-Intilaq al-Mi'mariyya al-Dakhma allati Khuququha Wizarat al-Askan" ["A picture of the beginning of the huge architectural project which the Ministry of Housing made happen"], in al-Ahram, ed., *al-Sadd al-'Ali*, 88.

66. The following all comprise articles in al-Ahram, ed., *al-Sadd al-'Ali*: "Al-Anfaq al-Sitta allati Satatahakam fi Miyyah al-Nil" ["The six tunnels which will control the waters of the Nile"], 26–29; "Aswan wa-l-Sadd" ["Aswan and the dam"], 53–55; "Fila min 3 Masakin wa-Mu'askar tuwwal al-Saif li-l-Mu'amalin bi-l-Sadd al-'Ali" ["Villa from 3 dwellings and a camp throughout the summer for workers at the High Dam"], 60–61; "Al-Tub al-Ahmar Sayantafi ba'da Bina' al-Sadd" ["The red brick won't exist after the building of the dam"], 74–75.

67. "Bina' al-Qura Yastahlik Ahjaran Tablughu Muhjim al-Haram al-Akbar 1 ½ Marra wa-75 Milyun Tuba wa-150 Alf Mitr Jir wa-1 ½ Milyun Mitr Zalat wa-Raml wa-250 Alf Tun Asmant" ["Building the villages consumes an amount of stone one-and-a-half times that used in the Great Pyramid, seventy-five million bricks, 150 thousand meters of lime, one-and a half million meters of gravel and sand and 250 thousand tons of cement"], in al-Ahram, ed., *al-Sadd al-'Ali*, 92–93.

ticle could be seen as one culmination of the sorts of nation-building actions discussed within it. The future appeared as readers turned pages, and even as Nubian mobility was placed within firmly national limits.

Mobility Contested

Reading, though, did not always conjure reality. The fate of the Nubians had been a constant source of tension in the period leading up to their forced migrations in a way that spilled into other forms of document. Working in Sudanese Nubia, Andreas and Waltraud Kronenberg noted their concern with "anthropological analysis . . . considered in the light of a people's past as revealed by historical and archaeological evidence."[68] Doing so, they seemed to acknowledge that the past, present, and future of Nubians could not be conveniently subdivided, even as fixing the population within national, future-oriented resettlement schemes required exactly that act to take place. The Kronenbergs' related publication on *Nubische Märchen* (Nubian fairytales) seemed to reduce Nubian life to the status of the compilation of folkloric stories, and their ethnographic work often attended to this temporal jumble using, once again, the colonial category of "survivals."[69] But the realization that Nubia's populations had complex historical experiences—and, in particular, complex historical experiences of mobility—was a consistent one, undermining the ways in which Nubians might become imbricated with forms of motion mandated by national social policies.

Nubian migration did not occur quite as simply as certain pieces of paper tried to make out. Above all, that act entailed the reassembly of former forms of mobility into new ones, often with considerable difficulty. In his account of the migration in Sudan, Hassan Dafalla wrote that

> I saw a young girl in her twenties embracing an old woman and each passionately hugging the other and weeping hot tears. Their wailing and lamentations were deeply touching, and I asked the *omda* [the mayor] the reason for it. I was told that they were mother and daughter; the girl and her husband were living in Adindan village, next to Faras East, on the Egyptian border. As they were emigrating to Kom Ombo,

---

68. Andreas Kronenberg and Waltraud Kronenberg, "Parallel Cousin Marriage in Mediaeval and Modern Nubia—Part I," *Kush: Journal of the Sudan Antiquities Service* 13 (1965): 242.
69. Andreas Kronenberg and Waltraud Kronenberg, *Nubische Märchen* (Düsseldorf: Diederichs, 1978). On their use of "survivals," see Kronenberg and Kronenberg, "Preliminary Report on Anthropological Field-Work in Nubia, 1962–63," *Kush: Journal of the Sudan Antiquities Service* 12 (1964): 285.

near Aswan, she had come to say good-bye to her father and mother, who were taking the train to Khashm el Girba.[70]

Even as participants in the Nubian campaign promoted Nubia as a region possessing a deep historical experience of mobility, so the official action that had allowed the campaign to occur curtailed and deemed unacceptable the still-recent mobility of the people living there, causing deep emotional trauma.[71] Discussing the Nubians who, for many years, had moved to Egyptian cities to earn money for their families, Mohamed Fikri Abdul Wahab noted that "if they were not present in 1960 they are not entitled to resettlement in the first stage but are to be resettled later on. . . . This decision has caused some resentment."[72] The state would justify a certain type of mobility, but other forms of the same phenomenon appeared to be outside the limits it deemed acceptable.

At times, Egypt had managed to work with its Nubian population. In 1960, the Committee for the Investigation of Nubian Demands had been formed to deal with issues that could be anticipated during the planning stages of relocation. An agreement to move settlements from Nubia to New Nubia as complete units was one result of this process, even as the design of those settlements received criticism from another quarter.[73] Hassan Fathy, known for his promotion of an "architecture for the poor," had been involved in initial plans for the resettlement.[74] Both the Egyptian government and the Nubians themselves rejected Fathy's designs for the scheme, however. Fathy apparently suggested that the Nubians had done so "in pursuit of an illusory dream of modernity" (*à la poursuite d'un illusoire rêve de modernité*).[75] Yet his (patronizing) opinions were neither here nor there. The pursuit of localized modernity could be shaped as much from below as it had been from above. More problematic, however, was that official promises did not always translate into practice: even when moved as units, it transpired that the housing patterns developed for New Nubia led to the dispersion of people from the same family who had previously lived next to each other.[76] Not every dispute

---

70. Dafalla, *The Nubian Exodus*, 241.
71. Beyond UNESCO's own actions, Adams, *Nubia*, was the most obvious manifestation of the promotion of Nubia as a "mobile" region.
72. Mohamed Fikri Abdul Wahab, "Problems of Nubian Migration," in Hopkins and Mehanna, *Nubian Encounters*, 230.
73. Hopkins and Mehanna, "The Nubian Ethnological Survey," 8.
74. Hassan Fathy, *Architecture for the Poor: An Experiment in Rural Egypt* (Chicago: University of Chicago Press, 1973). Cf. Mitchell, *Rule*, 179–205.
75. Lëila al-Wakil, "Les villages des fellahs," in *Hassan Fathy dans son temps*, ed. Lëila al-Wakil (Gollion, Switzerland: Infolio, 2013), 224, citing unpublished remarks made by Fathy at a 1978 conference.
76. Abdul Wahab, "Problems," 234.

could be resolved, and New Nubia continued to generate problems. Indeed, the Nubians themselves ultimately refused to call these settlements New Nubia, instead naming them Tahgir, or the "Place of Displacement."[77]

Events in Sudan, meanwhile, forcefully illustrate the consequences of this issue. In late 1960, demonstrations against the move to Khashm El Girba started in Wadi Halfa. Having initially been "encouraged by the authorities to make their own choice of a new home" from several possible locations, the same authorities went on to reject the decision made by the Halfawi population.[78] Guessing that this decision meant that the Sudanese government wanted to resettle them at Khashm El Girba, Halfawi suspicions were confirmed when "trunk operators [in the telephone exchange] . . . probably released the information which they overheard from conversations between the authorities in Khartoum and the Commissioner of Wadi Halfa."[79] When, in October 1960, a Sudanese ministerial delegation arrived at the town to communicate the government's decision about where Nubian resettlement should take place, "anti-Government shouts were heard." Ultimately, "demonstrations took place," and "the demonstrators cut down telegraph and telephone wires, leaving Wadi Halfa virtually isolated from the rest of the country for three days."[80]

With the right sort of physical action, accelerated mobility could be slowed in an instant. This activity came close to constituting the sort of "counter-tempo" characterized by On Barak in the case of interwar Egypt. Even as it did not quite manifest "a disdain for dehumanizing European standards of efficiency, linearity, and punctuality," the cutting of phone lines did indicate that colonial-era struggles surrounding conventions of mobility would not simply disappear in newly independent nations (or, more specifically, under the Ibrahim 'Abbud government).[81] And as Isma'il Hussein Abdalla related,

> the Halfawis, who were well represented in all walks of life in the country, decided to resist Government policy and consequently they began to make their voice heard. In Khartoum, Atbara, Port Sudan and Kosti, demonstrations spread fast and began further to reduce the Military regime's dwindling popularity. The Communist party and university students soon diverted these demonstrations to serve their own

---

77. Agha, "Nubia," 2.
78. Abdalla, "The Choice," 56.
79. Abdalla, "The Choice," 66.
80. Abdalla, "The Choice," 67. These demonstrations did not go unnoticed by archaeologists, for which see the letter from William Y. Adams to Hiroshi Daifuku, November 14, 1960. Folder 069 (62) Nubie: 930.26 (624) (Part IIa): "Mus-Egypt-Nubia-Excavations-Sudan (Part IIa, 1961)," UNESCO Archives.
81. Barak, *On Time*, 5.

political ends. Originally, the demonstrations were against Government, because of its failure to respect its word toward the Halfawis. Later the slogan was changed—demonstrators called for the complete withdrawal of the Army from power.[82]

Like the case of the Wadi es-Sebua workers, Sudanese Nubian mobility was subject to action from below. But it was also through working with Nubians that officials could reassert at least some state authority. Hassan Dafalla began to send groups from Wadi Halfa to Khashm El Girba to enable them to see the site for themselves.[83] *'Umād* (mayors; sing. *'Umda*) within Wadi Halfa district also aided these efforts. First, because "as civil servants, they could not oppose, even if they wanted, the general policy of the Administration." Additionally, "because of their high status in the community, they seemed to have influenced a good number of the Halfawis to agree to move to Khashm al-Girba" anyway.[84] Even then, though, about three thousand members of the Sudanese Nubian population refused to move, their affective tie to the region too strong.[85] After the rest of the population had relocated to Khashm El Girba, those remaining "lived in temporary dwellings built of wooden railway sleepers, which had to be dismantled each time the water approached and erected again at a reasonable distance, only to wait for another rise in the water level to be demolished again." Since the High Dam's floodwaters would ultimately extend 24 kilometers from the former course of the Nile, this process meant that the remaining population "endured years of hardship in this mobile state."[86] Contending state-regulated resettlement led to populational disenfranchisement and the wrong sort of mobility: one highlighting the callousness of the state. It was only in March 1967 that the Sudanese government decided to establish a new town next to the now-submerged Wadi Halfa.[87] And it was only in 1970 that work on the town began.[88] Nubian mobility could never entirely be controlled, and the new Wadi Halfa stands today as material evidence of the failure of officialdom to implement such regulation in the face of still-resonant affective ties to place.

---

82. Abdalla, "The Choice," 68.
83. Abdalla, "The Choice," 72.
84. Abdalla, "The Choice," 73.
85. Hussein M. Fahim, *Dams, People and Development: The Aswan High Dam Case* (New York: Pergamon Press, 1981), 96.
86. Dafalla, *The Nubian Exodus*, 297. There were problems at Khashm El Girba, too, for which see Salih A. El Arifi, "Problems in Planning Extensive Agricultural Projects: The Case of New Halfa, Sudan," *Applied Geography* 8, no. 1 (1988): 37–52.
87. Dafalla, *The Nubian Exodus*, 297.
88. Fahim, *Dams*, 97.

Settling Abu Simbel (and Other Sites)

Suffice to say, during the Nubian campaign, similar tensions around (re-) settlement became evident. As work in Egypt and Sudan gathered pace, so, too, did the mobile populations connected to that process themselves require places to live. As with Nubian resettlement, however, a gap existed between plans for, and the reality of, this process. Here, I set out some of these plans to illustrate how and why the forms of mobility promoted during the project often seemed to presage social frictions rather than the smooth sorts of movement promoted by UNESCO. However carefully planned, the results of these schemes—hierarchical, racialized, and gendered—laid bare longstanding social tensions surrounding work carried out at archaeological sites: often because those schemes were based on colonial-era norms. In a time of social upheaval, careful planning did not always demonstrate social care.

Set down on paper, the regulation of settlement connected to the Nubian campaign was often highly organized, aiming to make onsite life as straightforward as possible. Nowhere was such organization clearer than in terms of the accommodation constructed for the workers employed at Abu Simbel. An international cadre of engineers, archaeological experts, stonecutters from Carrara, Italy, and Egyptian laborers undertook the Abu Simbel work, and the project's consulting engineers (Sweden's Vattenbyggnadsbyrån, or VBB) constructed a "colony" in collaboration with Egypt's Ministry of Culture and National Guidance.[89] That development now forms part of the contemporary town located by the site, a subtle reminder that archaeology and monument preservation are never far from their colonial roots. Yet the incorporation of the colony into Abu Simbel's built fabric also works to elide the social meanings that settlement once fostered, meanings that enforced division in various complex ways.

Here was a settlement that seemed to divide rather than enfold, or at least did so once it had been built. Conforming to the Nubian campaign's purposefully internationalist outlook, work at the site was run by the "Joint Venture Abu Simbel," an engineering consortium comprising the West German company Hochtief, Italy's Impregilo, France's Grands travaux de Marseille, Sweden's Sentab and Skånska Cementgjuteriet, and Egypt's Atlas.[90] For a while, too, everyone employed at Abu Simbel found themselves in the same boat,

---

89. For colony house plans, see "United Arab Republic, Ministry of Culture and National Guidance Abu Simbel Department: Abu Simbel," brochure held in file 1A-a4, "Housing," Nubia Museum. For the use of the word "colony," see plans contained in file 1A-a3, "Kharā'it Kuntūriyya" ["Contour maps"], Nubia Museum.

90. Säve-Söderbergh, *Temples*, 102, 104.

sometimes quite literally. As Torgny Säve-Söderbergh relates, an astonishing number of people lived at the site: "approximately 1700 workmen and 200 staff members were employed" there, "and when their families had joined the growing community, approximately 3000 people" made Abu Simbel their home. Yet when work at the site started, no accommodation had been built there: "all the personnel had to live in tents, sheds or on houseboats," because the need to build a cofferdam to protect the temples from the Nile's rising waters delayed the initial plans to construct Abu Simbel's "township" (as Säve-Söderbergh calls it) by nearly a year and a half. The temporary accommodation provided was, needless to say, "unenviable, especially during the summer season when the temperature could rise to around 45° to 50° in the shade."[91] Unenviable, in this usage, seems diplomatic.

As Säve-Söderbergh has it, however, when the Abu Simbel settlement finally appeared, conditions at the site improved. "Besides houses and offices, the township had a mosque, a police station, a hotel, mess rooms, a swimming pool, tennis court, etc., and on the whole . . . the facilities matched those of any other civilized community."[92] Yet the use of "civilized" here is key. The township might well have possessed such social facilities, yet the settlement also fostered social divisions. Fondly remembered by some, plans of the town indicate a strong hierarchy: divided into a "contractor's colony" and the "government's colony," Abu Simbel was a divided settlement, reminiscent—at least on paper—of colonial notions of civilization.[93] Other social divisions were also maintained, not least in the housing drawings showing how certain types of structure were given over to different types of employees. The Ministry of Housing's "Type D" house was designed for gardeners and servants, for instance, while the much larger "Type A" (which in fact had its own servant's room) was given to the chief engineers and archaeologist on the project, and "Type B2" was built for married engineers and chiefs of staff.[94] Racialized and gendered, wider Egyptian and international domestic arrangements—and

---

91. Säve-Söderbergh, *Temples*, 111.
92. Säve-Söderbergh, *Temples*, 111.
93. For one such reminiscence, see the words of Luciano Paoli, one of the Carrara stonecutters employed at the site, in "My Days at Abu Simbel: Luciano Paoli Shares His Experience as an Expert Stonecutter in Nubia," in *Nubiana: The Great Undertaking that Saved the Temples of Abu Simbel*, ed. Cristina Scalabrini (Milan: Rizzoli, 2019), 250–51. On p. 251, Paoli explicitly notes that "in the evening, after the day's work, we used to get together in the village with the other workers. They came from around the world—Americans, Swedes, French and Germans." Egyptians are not mentioned. For the colony plans, see file 1A-a3, "Kharā'it Kuntūriyya," Nubia Museum.
94. For the housing types at Abu Simbel, see "United Arab Republic, Ministry of Culture and National Guidance Abu Simbel Department: Abu Simbel."

the growing social importance of the technocrats building the country's revolution—seemed to be imported wholesale to the site.[95]

Predictably, such structural hierarchy was familiar from settlements constructed by another venture utilizing colonies of workers in Egypt: the Suez Canal Company. The town of Ismaʿiliyya, situated roughly at the canal's halfway point, was composed of several square modules, each of which was designated as belonging to a particular ethnic community: Arab, Greek, or French. The town represented *"la segregation spatiale caractéristique des villes coloniales,"* as Claudine Piaton states.[96] But that spatial segregation continued despite the official end of colonial intervention in Egypt, and the settlement at Abu Simbel constituted part of this process, alongside housing built for the wider High Dam project. That housing was promoted as part of a modern future for the city of Aswan.[97] So, too, was it supposedly connected to the strengthening of Egyptian-Russian relations, even as "Russians were renowned in official circles for their disinterest in socializing with the Egyptians."[98] As Alia Mossallam notes,

> the egalitarian [inter/national] community that the Dam was meant to promote was hampered by the very structures associated with the Dam. Labourers who came to work [there] . . . from its inception lived in shacks, sometimes without shelter, under conditions that did not allow for families or spouses to join them until the end of the first phase in 1964. Meanwhile, technicians and engineers lived in well-built compounds with sophisticated facilities and services, such as sports clubs, which more than 50 years later remain in good condition. A hierarchal or class structure was thus embedded into the very living conditions this 'community' shared.[99]

At both High Dam and Abu Simbel, settlement constituted segregation. Such social division, however, simply echoed the history and practice of archaeology in Egypt and Sudan. Living arrangements on Egyptian and Sudanese

---

95. On domesticity and Egypt's revolution, see, e.g., Bier, *Revolutionary Womanhood*.
96. Claudine Piaton, "Villes et architectures dans l'isthme de Suez," in *L'épopée du canal de Suez*, eds. Gilles Gauthier, Nala Aloudat, and Agnès Carayon (Marseille and Paris: Musée d'Histoire de Marseille, Gallimard, and Institut du monde arabe, 2018), 107.
97. Reynolds, "City," 221–22.
98. Reynolds, "City," 222, citing Tom Little, *High Dam at Aswan: The Subjugation of the Nile* (London: Methuen, 1965), 120. An article like "Ikhwat al-Sadd baina al-Sufiyyit wa-l-Misriyyin" ["Brothers of the dam between the Soviets and the Egyptians"], *al-Musawwar* 2414, 15 January 1971, 32–33, attempted to claim otherwise.
99. Mossallam, "'We Are the Ones,'" 313.

archaeological sites had long been hierarchical, and the "dig houses" and official rest houses in which members of archaeological missions and government archaeological inspectors lived continued to be symptomatic of such order as the two countries gained independence.[100] Consequently, during the Nubian campaign, living arrangements in the field reflected—and were sometimes literally built on—colonial foundations. At the site of Buhen in Sudanese Nubia (where, as I discuss later, ongoing excavation work was enfolded into the campaign when it began), the use of a dig house by Britain's EES rested on reconditioning a structure which had once accommodated the team excavating the site on behalf of the University of Pennsylvania's 1909–10 Eckley B. Coxe Junior Expedition to Nubia. As the society—promoting its archival material—now has it, this process of reconditioning can be summed up with the phrase "a dig house becomes a home."[101] Perhaps this image of domesticity rang true for certain of the excavation team's members. But it also conceals how the (fairly basic) living conditions at the house were themselves a cut above the circumstances endured by others employed at the site.

The EES was not a spendthrift organization. It would, however, stoop to certain expenses. Realizing that the house was in "a poorer state of preservation than I had expected," and that "if we do any work here on a large scale we will have to make extra rooms in the numerous and useless courtyards," the institution's Field Director Bryan Emery replanned the structure (figure 5.2), making arrangements with a local contractor to carry out "brickwork reconstruction" and for a local carpenter "to make tables shelving [sic] and general furniture."[102] He also concluded that "the kitchen and servants [sic] quarters have to be almost entirely rebuilt. Also a lavatory."[103] Yet basic as this situation was (even despite the employment of domestic staff), it still trumped that of the workers employed on the dig. For them, Emery had rented two ruined buildings located nearby, for which he only seemed willing to provide roofing and new doors.[104] Meanwhile, his wife, Mollie (as she did on all his excavations), "supervised the commissariat and all domestic arrangements," and was certainly not the only archaeological spouse forced into that position.[105]

---

100. William Carruthers, "Credibility, Civility, and the Archaeological Dig-House in Mid-1950s Egypt," *Journal of Social Archaeology* 19, no. 2 (2019): 255–76.

101. "Buhen: A Dig House Becomes a Home . . . ," The Egypt Exploration Society website, accessed September 10, 2020, https://www.ees.ac.uk/buhen-a-dig-house-becomes-a-home.

102. "E.E.S. Day Book: Sudan, 1957–58," November 12, 13, and 14, 1957, EES Archives (folder BUH.001).

103. "E.E.S. Day Book: Sudan, 1957–58," November 15, 1957.

104. "E.E.S. Day Book: Sudan, 1957–58," December 23, 1957.

105. EES, *Report of the Seventy-Fourth Ordinary General Meeting (Seventy-Eighth Annual General Meeting) 1960: Subscription List and Balance Sheets* (London: EES, 1960), 5.

Nov. 12th Visit to Buhen with Gamel of the Antiquities Dept. Arrangements made for the reconstruction of the house which now cleared of sand shows a poorer state of preservation than I had expected.
I have written to Zaki Saad regarding the Guftis.

Nov. 13th Visit to Buhen. Measurements taken for doors and windows and arrangements made with a carpenter at Halfa to make them by Nov 21st.
The house is very badly designed and although covering a large area is in fact very small indeed. If we do any work here on a large scale we will have to make extra rooms in the numerous and useless courtyards.
Hussein arrived and is now installed in a small hotel in Halfa.

Nov. 14th Visit to the house with the contractor who has undertaken to complete the brickwork reconstruction by the end of the month. He will also install the doors and windows when they are finished by the carpenter.
I have also contracted another carpenter to make tables shelving and general furniture.

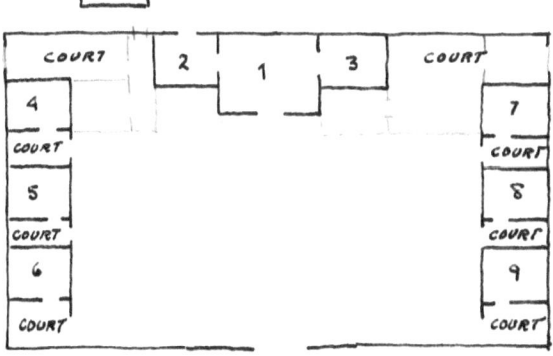

Nov. 15th Have employed Beshir Koko as a cook from today's date. At the house the kitchen and servants' quarters have to be almost entirely rebuilt. Also a lavatory

FIGURE 5.2. Emery's plan for the Buhen dig house. Entry for November 14, 1957 in "E.E.S. Day Book: Sudan, 1957–58," courtesy of the Egypt Exploration Society (Egypt Exploration Society Archives BUH.001).

Colonial hierarchy—and the hierarchical division of living space on archaeological sites—did not simply disappear as countries gained independence. Instead, the Nubian campaign constituted a reflorescence of this process, and not even one with which all the (Euro-American) participants in the work seemed to be comfortable. Reflecting on his years working in Sudan, Bill Adams claimed that, for he and his wife Nettie, "there were . . . a good many things that we couldn't do for ourselves because our status [sponsored by UNESCO] wouldn't allow it." Of course,

> Nettie had always done all our cooking and housekeeping, and she took charge of the Wadi Halfa household as a matter of course. But this no longer meant cooking and housekeeping; it meant telling the cook what to buy, what to cook, and how to cook it, giving the *saffragi* [servant] instructions about cleaning and other chores, and keeping the household accounts.[106]

Comfortable or not, the Adams' partook in a form of archaeological domesticity that persisted, victims—or recipients of the fruits of—their mobility. Moreover, they were dependent on the relative immobility of the groups of people who helped to buttress Bill Adams's status as technical expert. As ever, bureaucracy regulated that situation.

Channeling Quftis

The work in Nubia was dependent not only on longstanding labor practices in archaeological survey and excavation, but also on the ability of administrative systems to ensure that such practices continued. As excavation and survey took place on both sides of the Nubian border, laborers and foremen seemed to stream up and down the Nile Valley, a mirror image of the laborers who traveled to Aswan to build the High Dam. This movement, however, was tied to historical judgments about whose mobility officials and archaeologists considered worthwhile. As Valeska Huber would term it, the systems that determined who could now be "channeled" up and down the Nile related to longstanding genealogies of mobility in archaeological work.

At the heart of this process were the immigration formalities necessary to travel between Egypt and Sudan. While certain archaeologists experienced little to no problem attempting this journey, it was clear that only certain workers they employed enjoyed the same freedom. At the start of the EES ar-

---

106. Adams, *The Road*, 155–56.

chaeological survey of Egyptian Nubia in January 1961, Harry Smith, the archaeologist in charge of the work, arrived at Wadi Halfa, just south of the Egyptian border, accompanied by two members of the EES staff, who hailed from Australia and Britain respectively. There, the three men were joined by Ali Hassan, an inspector of the Egyptian Department of Antiquities from Mallawi in Middle Egypt, who had crossed into Sudan on official business. The next morning, after police and customs checks, the group traveled down the Nile into Egypt on the Abu Nawas, a departmental pontoon.[107] Not everyone, though, could float across the border so easily. The chance to take "the view from the boat" was not one given to everybody who might desire it.

Making such a trip involved having permission to do so. That permission relied on a certain conception of skill, in addition to the existence of individuals who had been determined by (authoritative) others as possessing it. Five days after Harry Smith, Ali Hassan, and their colleagues had arrived in Egypt, the survey's "Day Book" noted that "15 Quftis arrived by the Post Boat at 10.00 a.m. Camp was pitched by the ʿAwameh [sic]."[108] Arriving from further north in the country, these "Quftis" (as they have become known to archaeologists) represented the generally agreed pinnacle of Egyptian archaeological skill among those who employed them, Egyptian or otherwise. Consequently, the Quftis also represented a group whose mobility, whether local or international, had been invested in by institutions like the EES for quite some time.

Hailing from the village of Qift (or Quft) in Upper Egypt (hence their name), Quftis—as is now well-related—had initially worked for British-sponsored archaeological digs taking place in Egypt during the 1890s, most famously for the archaeologist Flinders Petrie.[109] The demand for their well-honed excavation skills in a region where Euro-American archaeologists often seemed to roam at will meant that Quftis were widely employed. Prior to World War I,

---

107. "Egypt Exploration Society Sondage Survey, Season 1961: Day Book," January 4 and 5, 1961. Folder NUB.001, EES Archives.

108. "Egypt Exploration Society Sondage Survey, Season 1961: Day Book," January 10, 1961.

109. On this history (and on the history of labor in Egyptian archaeology), see Wendy Doyon, "On Archaeological Labor in Modern Egypt," in *Histories of Egyptology: Interdisciplinary Measures*, ed. William Carruthers (New York: Routledge, 2015), 141–56, and Doyon, "The History of Archaeology through the Eyes of Egyptians," in *Unmasking Ideology in Imperial and Colonial Archaeology: Vocabulary, Symbols, and Legacy*, eds. Bonnie Effros and Guolong Lai (Los Angeles: The Cotsen Institute of Archaeology Press, 2018), 173–200. Cf. Stephen Quirke, *Hidden Hands: Egyptian Workforces in Petrie Excavation Archives, 1880–1924* (London: Duckworth, 2010), and Christina Riggs, "Shouldering the Past: Photography, Archaeology, and Collective Effort at the Tomb of Tutankhamun," *History of Science* 55, no. 3 (2017): 336–63. On labor in the history of archaeology more broadly, see, e.g., Allison Mickel, *Why Those Who Shovel Are Silent: A History of Local Archaeological Knowledge and Labor* (Louisville: University Press of Colorado, 2021); Nick Shepherd, "'When the Hand that Holds the Trowel is Black . . .': Disciplinary Practices of Self-Representation and the Issue of 'Native' Labor in Archaeology," *Journal of Social Archaeology* 3, no. 3 (2003): 334–52.

various excavations in the Levant and Sudan made use of this skilled group of Egyptian "go-betweens."[110] At the Sudanese site of Jebel Moya, where excavations were funded by the pharmaceutical entrepreneur Henry Wellcome, the Quftis even held enough clout to go on strike, demanding (among other things) the provision of their own, private water supply. The expedition's leaders obliged, providing the Egyptians with a supply of water from the Nile: a journey of twenty miles by train and a further two miles from the railway station to the expedition's camp via camel.[111] Such effort expended on their behalf, the Quftis constituted a group whose value to archaeological expeditions both inside and outside Egypt had become of immense (and obvious) importance.

By employing them on its survey of Egyptian Nubia, the EES ensured that this colonial-era judgment about the value of the Quftis remained consistent, as did the regional mobility that this valuation allowed. However, the institution was not alone. During the Nubian project, the movement of local archaeological expertise in Egyptian Nubia became an avowedly one-way process—one that the Quftis dominated. As the Nubian campaign got under way in Sudan, meanwhile, and international archaeological missions started to mull over the idea of working in the country, Bill Adams wrote a guide discussing "Living and Working Conditions for Archaeologists in Sudanese Nubia." In it, he noted that

> there are no trained diggers, comparable to the Quftis of Egypt, in the Sudan. It will therefore be necessary for field parties either to import Quftis from Egypt or else act as their own foremen, exercising extremely close control over every phase of excavation until local men can be trained to positions of authority.[112]

Channels of mobility up the Nile and into Sudanese Nubia—and the immigration facilities necessary to create them—could be carved out for international archaeological missions and (if they wished to employ them) Quftis, too. The historical attribution of archaeological skill to this group of Egyptians meant that their value to the Nubian campaign became too great to ignore. Adams, despite (or perhaps because of) his training in North America, saw no reason to counter precedent, even as he had no great enthusiasm for this way of doing things. Years later, he wrote that "I had to adapt myself, willy-nilly, to the excavation methods that had been traditional in this region for a century, employing masses of mostly unskilled laborers."[113] Adams was not,

---

110. Doyon, "The History," 180. On "go-betweens," see Schaffer *et al.*, *The Brokered World*.
111. Doyon, "The History," 187.
112. Adams, "Living and Working Conditions," 11.
113. Adams, *The Road*, 150.

of course, referring to the Quftis. Their place in this system, however, now seemed as fixed as that of the laborers themselves.

Excavation diaries emphasized this fixity—and obvious concern that it could change.[114] Pointing to the ways in which this anxiety overlapped with much older genealogies of archaeological work, the possibility that Qufti expertise might be unavailable was greeted with apprehension even before the Nubian campaign began, slowly filtering into the campaign itself through a fog of disquiet connected to the end of colonial control over Egypt. Bryan Emery had earlier dismissed the field skills of Nubian workers during the second Archaeological Survey of Nubia. Now, however, he found himself expressing concern about the prospect of having to employ them. Working for the EES since 1952 (and employed as Edwards Professor of Egyptology at London's University College since 1951), Emery's anxieties represented the dying days of empire come home to roost. Post-Suez, those concerns only heightened.

Visiting Sudan in 1957, Emery looked for an archaeological site for the EES that would help to continue the society's—and British—archaeological influence.[115] If not in Egypt, where the possibility of British archaeological work now seemed vanishingly small, then that site could at least be in the country's neighbor, whose Antiquities Service was still under the direction of a European, Jean Vercoutter. Buhen was that site: an ancient fortress just north of the Second Cataract of the Nile. Ideally for the EES, the locale had long been identified as an Egyptian colonial outpost, and Emery cannily compared its fortifications to those of Beaumaris Castle on Anglesey in Wales.[116] Given that Emery's own Nubian expertise meant that he was rapidly drafted into plans for the Nubian campaign itself, meanwhile, almost by default the work at Buhen became part of the British contribution to UNESCO's project.[117] Yet

---

114. In an examination of excavation diaries at the Turkish site of Çatalhöyük, Allison Mickel, "Reasons for Redundancy in Reflexivity: The Role of Diaries in Archaeological Epistemology," *Journal of Field Archaeology* 40, no. 3 (2015): 8, noted that the use of diaries in the "reflexive" form of archaeology practiced at the site helped to "make one's assertions less vulnerable to challenge, even by other authoritative records produced by the project." In Nubia, years earlier, excavation diaries implied similar anxiety, although they did not necessarily act as a device countering that concern. In this sense, the diaries were closer to the colonial archives discussed in Stoler, *Along*.

115. Minutes of the Executive Committee of the EES, March 27, 1957, *Egypt Exploration Society Committee Minutes, 1956–1963*, EES Archives.

116. "Editorial Foreword," *The Journal of Egyptian Archaeology* 45 (1959): 1–2. Minutes of the Executive Committee of the EES, March 27, 1958, *Egypt Exploration Society Committee Minutes, 1956–1963*, EES Archives, notes that Buhen was "probably the most valuable Pharaonic site in the Sudan," emphasizing the Egypto-centric way the society conceptualized its work there. For a wider discussion of this move to Sudan, see William Carruthers, "Egyptology, Archaeology and the Making of Revolutionary Egypt, c. 1925–1958." PhD diss., University of Cambridge, 2014.

117. For instance, Buhen is featured heavily in Jean Vercoutter's *UNESCO Courier* article, "Sudanese Nubia: 'Terra Incognita' of Archaeologists."

Emery's concern at the prospect of having to employ Nubian workers at the site gradually seemed to filter into the wider campaign, not least in Bill Adams's comments about "local men."

Imperial norms begat postimperial anxieties. Writing in the Day Book of the excavation's 1957–58 season, the racial formulas by which Emery had lived his Egyptian life sprung clearly from the page. Emery described a local *raʾis*, or (excavation) foreman, one "Sheik Waladallah," as showing "very little promise as a leader being far too familiar with his men."[118] This sort of wording is familiar from the British archaeologist Flinders Petrie's now-infamous 1904 excavation manual, *Methods and Aims in Archaeology*, and Emery happily followed such judgments because, as Petrie stated, "there is a danger in letting control [of workers] slip away."[119] Indeed, fretting about the lack of Quftis available to him, almost immediately upon arrival at Buhen Emery wrote to his former excavating colleague—and Director of Inspectorates at the Egyptian Department of Antiquities—Zaki Y. Saad, asking about the possibility of arranging for Quftis to work at the site.[120] Saad did not reply for some time and, after almost a fortnight, Emery became increasingly desperate: first sending a telegram, and then relying on an officer of the Sudan Antiquities Service, Ahmad Hassan Ibrahim, to travel to Cairo to "arrange for the employment of our Gufties [sic] and their transfer to Sudan."[121]

Presaging the ease with which he traversed Egypt and Sudan during the Nubian campaign (a function of sitting on the expert committees connected to both countries), Emery expected quick communication regarding labor almost as a right; a function of a colonial system within which he had once enjoyed considerable power and comfort, despite the precarity that had sometimes afflicted his archaeological employment.[122] And if communication was slow, Emery at least expected that someone else would carry a message for him. As On Barak's description of Egypt's colonial "countertempo" notes, however, not every attempt at speedy communication went unhindered.[123] Emery eventually received a reply from Zaki Saad in December 1957, over a month after writing to him. Saad let him know "that Reis Ahmed and my Guft-

---

118. "E.E.S. Day Book: Sudan, 1957–58," December 22, 1957.

119. William Matthew Flinders Petrie, *Methods and Aims in Archaeology* (London: Macmillan, 1904), 22.

120. "E.E.S. Day Book: Sudan, 1957–58," November 12, 1957. Saad and Emery worked together at Saqqara in the 1930s, for which see Bierbrier, *Who*.

121. "E.E.S. Day Book: Sudan, 1957–58," November 25 and December 7, 1957.

122. On Emery, see Clare Lewis, "Inaugural Lectures in Egyptology: T. E. Peet and His Pupil W. B. Emery," *Bulletin of the History of Archaeology* 26, no. 1, article 9 (2016): 1–15.

123. Barak, *On Time*, 5.

ies [sic] are all employed at Tura," just south of Cairo.[124] A few days later, meanwhile, Ahmad Hassan Ibrahim sent a telegram to Emery informing him of "delays regarding the departure of the Gufties [sic] because of new Egyptian regulations."[125] Despite the occasional countertempo, communication could still be quick. It might not, though, provide the anticipated answer. Bureaucratic channels could close all too easily.

Ultimately, Quftis did arrive at Buhen, but only after Ahmad Hassan Ibrahim obtained a permit from the Egyptian government making it possible for them to travel to Sudan alongside him.[126] When they arrived at the site on (Western) Christmas Day, 1957, Emery "paid off the local Reis and his ten men as they were not satisfactory. Ahmed Eff," meanwhile, "has undertaken to get new locals at PT [piastres] 25 rather than P.T. 30 [sic]."[127] Reliant on a Sudanese go-between to travel to Egypt and arrange for the mobility of a particular set of Egyptians, Emery also depended on that same go-between to enforce the immobility of the local workers traditionally employed to labor on archaeological digs and follow Qufti orders.[128] When Bill Adams wrote his guide on "Living and Working Conditions," he made clear that "local laborers, both men and boys, receive 25 piastres ($0.75) a day for a six day week," even as "they are not in general very diligent workers, and they take little interest in the progress of the job."[129] The attitudes of Adams and Emery, then, seemed to merge in terms of their views on Sudanese labor. This convergence was hardly surprising, since Adams both developed cordial relations with Emery and would also come to rely upon a go-between, a clerk in the Sudan Antiquities Service named "Gamal Ahmad Hassan [Ibrahim?]," who "was a factotum to put Figaro to shame."[130] Using paperwork to permit some forms of mobility (whose realization was only ever achieved with local assistance) meant constituting the immobility of locals, too, as had long been the case in colonial archaeological work. The question now was how this situation might coalesce not only as the Nubian campaign's fieldwork progressed, but also as the availability of even local labor in Nubia started to dwindle.

---

124. "E.E.S. Day Book: Sudan, 1957–58," December 16, 1957.
125. "E.E.S. Day Book: Sudan, 1957–58," December 18, 1957.
126. "E.E.S. Day Book: Sudan, 1957–58," December 21, 1957.
127. "E.E.S. Day Book: Sudan, 1957–58," December 25, 1957.
128. Allison Mickel, "Essential Excavation Experts: Alienation and Agency in the History of Archaeological Labor," *Archaeologies: Journal of the World Archaeological Congress* 15, no. 2 (2019): 181–205, discusses such divide-and-rule tactics.
129. Adams, "Living and Working Conditions," 12.
130. Adams, *The Road*, 153.

Papering Labor

Ironically, it proved more difficult to enforce local immobility than expected. During the Nubian campaign, paperwork became entangled in attempts to make the place of laborers as precarious as possible. Given that treatment, those same laborers sometimes voted with their feet. At Buhen, for instance, Emery's attitude to staff hardly occasioned devotion to their employer. During the 1962–63 excavation season, the EES employed men from Atbara, two hundred miles or more to the southeast, attempting to bolster the number of workers at the site.[131] Soon afterward, Emery wrote comments in the excavation's day books displaying anxiety conditioned by a situation whose colonial resonances were tangible but whose postcolonial conditions were clear. In early December 1962, the British archaeologist wrote that:

> Eighteen men refused to work this morning and were promptly sacked. The Commissioner and Chief Inspector came over immediately and have promised to get me better workers. What we need is local men and not gangs from Khartoum and Atbara who are worse than useless.[132]

Certain locals seemed better than others, although never better than the Quftis, some of whom were "fortunately ... already here."[133] Yet such cursive empiricism in the description of labor—as if setting opinion down on paper had rendered it objective fact—belied the colonial origins of the obvious racial judgments behind Emery's words. So, too, did it fail to assuage the fact that those judgments were unacceptable to Sudanese officials. A few days after Emery sacked his laborers for apparent refusal to work came a "visit of Chief Inspector of Antiquities [Thabit Hassan Thabit] and a representative of the Labour Office to enquire into the complaints of the impacted workers from Atbara and Abu Hamid." The visit was unwelcome. As Emery continued: "these men have caused nothing but trouble since they came. Certain of their complaints were perhaps justified, such as water supply and crowded quarters. These have been put right but demands for Friday pay etc. were refused."[134] Despite this refusal, in what seemed like an embarrassing climbdown, the EES—and Bryan Emery in particular—discovered that the presumption that local laborers needed the institution more than the institution needed them was not always correct. Now, the subjects of empire might start to strike back.

---

131. "Day-Book: Sudan, 1962–63," November 26, 1962, EES Archives (folder BUH.001).
132. "Day-Book: Sudan, 1962–63," December 4, 1962.
133. "Day-Book: Sudan, 1962–63," November 13, 1962.
134. "Day-Book: Sudan, 1962–63," December 9, 1962.

The British institution was not the only one to find itself in this situation. As part of its work in Nubia, for two seasons during 1962–63 and 1963–64 the OI of the University of Chicago excavated in Egypt in the region between Abu Simbel and, to its south, the Sudanese border. The mission recorded the names, wages, and days worked of its various casual laborers inside a "Standard Roll Book No. 1470" that had been adapted for the job: produced by Standard B & P, the book indicated that the OI was ready to enforce the system of labor time practiced in Egyptian excavation work for many decades.[135] More accurately, however, one of the mission's local staff in fact performed this job, indicating once again the extent to which such excavations—and such tasks, apparently unbecoming of an American worker—were reliant on the cooperation of local go-betweens: as a tiny, handwritten inscription under the book's title indicates, the task of actually compiling this record fell on Mourad Abdel Razek, "interpreter and assistant to the director."[136] Mourad Abdel Razek, meanwhile, made certain to attend to his task with no small amount of diligence, providing a record that indicates not only the precarity of the local laborers employed by the OI, but also the way in which they responded to that situation. Leafing through the pages of the roll book, what is most notable is the page-by-page calculation of wages owed, coupled with the signatures or fingerprints of the workers—apparently from the local villages of Ballana and Qustul—made as they collected those wages each week. Days working at the site are ticked lightly in pencil, while days away from the site are often (although not always) highlighted with red pen. Gradations in rates of pay are also given, with child labor clearly worth less than that of men (figure 5.3; 25 piastres as opposed to 30).[137] The petty violence of the record is hard to miss, its shaded variation indicating the use and abuse of those with little choice other than to work on the excavation.

In this record, though, also lies an indication that such violence might be countered. Crosses marked absence, but they also marked potential decisions not to attend. Excavations, of course, did not always require laborers, and sustained rows of crosses indicate that situation. The occasional cross within the same worker's record (figure 5.4), however, would seem to mark something else: perhaps an absence due to illness, but perhaps also the sort of decision to forsake the indignities of such work familiar from Buhen.

---

135. On this system, see Quirke, *Hidden*.

136. Mourad Abdel Razek was also acknowledged in the eventual publication of the work, for which see Bruce Beyer Williams, *Excavations Between Abu Simbel and the Sudan Frontier*, Part 1, *The A-Group Royal Cemetery at Qustul: Cemetery L*, The University of Chicago Oriental Institute Nubian Expedition 3 (Chicago: The Oriental Institute of the University of Chicago, 1986), xxxiv.

137. Ibid., xxxiv, details the origin of the OI's workers. For further discussion of pay rates for Egyptian laborers, see Doyon, "On Archaeological Labor," and Quirke, *Hidden*.

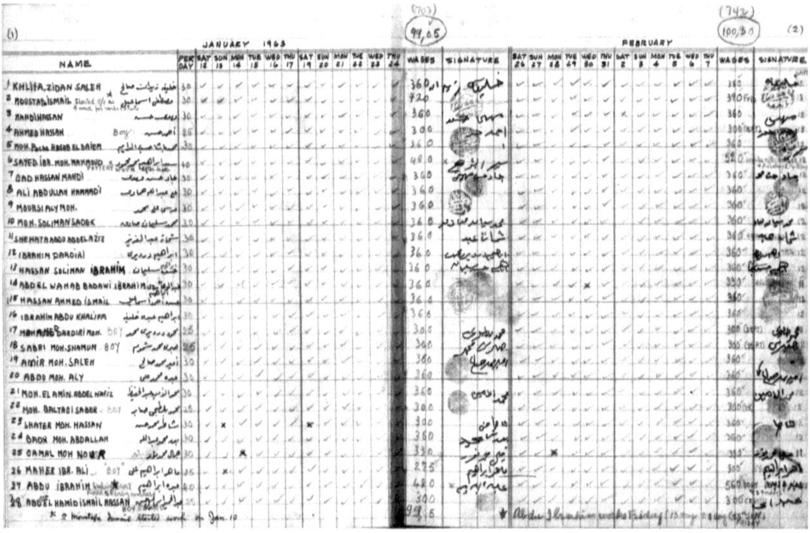

FIGURE 5.3. First part of the University of Chicago Oriental Institute's Nubian payroll for January and February 1963, various instances of workers being a "boy" clearly labeled. "Oriental Institute Nubian Expedition: Field Labor Attendance and Pay Record; 1962–1963 Season; 1963–1964 Season." Nubian Expedition. Records. [Box 029], The Museum Archives at the Oriental Institute of the University of Chicago.

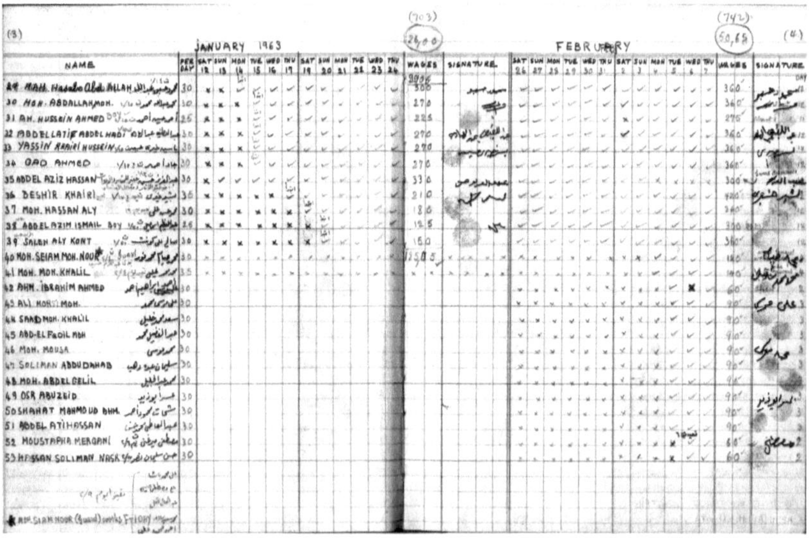

FIGURE 5.4. Second part of the University of Chicago Oriental Institute's Nubian payroll for January and February 1963, with crosses indicating either sustained or isolated absences. "Oriental Institute Nubian Expedition: Field Labor Attendance and Pay Record; 1962–1963 Season; 1963–1964 Season." Nubian Expedition. Records. [Box 029], The Museum Archives at the Oriental Institute of the University of Chicago.

Precarity could be rejected.[138] This reading fits, moreover, with a discussion of Polish archaeological work in Nubia by Patrycja and Arkadiusz Klimowicz. In their discussion, the pair discuss how Kazimierz Michałowski, who directed that work, developed a protocol adopting "rules of behaviour [between the Poles and their Egyptian workers that] differed from those of other archaeological missions at that time." As they continue:

> the custom of shaking hands with the Egyptian supervisor . . . and workers . . . assumed harmonious relations between the staff members and the local communities. The request that archaeologists refrain from being seated during working hours within the excavation area followed from a similar logic, as an expression of respect for the *fellaheen*'s [sic] labour.[139]

This argument is potentially self-serving, somewhat patrician, and certainly anachronistic in its concerns: discussing "the custom of a courtesy visit to the [community] Elders' homes" instituted by Michałowski, the authors indicate that "the elders were informed about the archaeological objectives, actual events and contingent discoveries" made on the relevant excavation, an objective not far from those employed on community archaeological excavations within the last couple of decades.[140] Perhaps, though, the authors have a point, at least in identifying that relationships with workers on excavations in Nubia were not a priority for the majority of archaeological missions there. Or, put another way, that the priority was often to regulate those relationships at arm's length rather than to cultivate them meaningfully. Precarity, indignity, and bureaucracy were the watchwords, even as changing geopolitical currents emphasized that indignity in newly independent countries should be a thing of the past. The rearrangement of labor relations by an archaeological team from a Warsaw Pact country—although not specifically the result of a Warsaw Pact policy—constituted one way in which archaeology in Nubia reflected that change.[141] The Nubian campaign also reflected these circumstances in other ways.

---

138. On examples of resistance among Egyptian archaeological laborers and Quftis, see Carruthers, "Visualizing," 289; Doyon, "On Archaeological Labor," 152; Quirke, *Hidden*, 47.

139. Patrycja Klimowicz and Arkadiusz Klimowicz, "Polish Archaeology in Egypt and Sudan: An Historical Overview," in *European Archaeology Abroad: Global Settings, Comparative Perspectives*, eds. Sjoerd J. Van der Linde, Monique Henriëtte Van den Dries, Nathan Schlanger, and Corijanne G. Slappendel (Leiden: Sidestone, 2012), 118.

140. Klimowicz and Klimowicz "Polish Archaeology," 119. On "community archaeology" (and its many possible definitions), see Gabriel Moshenska and Sarah Dhanjal, eds., *Community Archaeology: Themes, Methods and Practices* (Oxford: Oxbow, 2012).

141. Klimowicz and Klimowicz "Polish Archaeology," 115, emphasizes how Kazimierz Michałowski deliberately took an "ostensibly neutral attitude" in Egypt and Sudan.

Chapter 6

Nubia in the (Non-Aligned) World

UNESCO's Nubian campaign is easily placed within Cold War binaries, not least the vision of Euro-American-led archaeological missions excavating as the Soviet-backed Aswan High Dam rose.[1] Beyond, however, this interpretation's erasure of the Egyptian and Sudanese experts and officials—and the thousands of Egyptian and Sudanese laborers—involved in both projects, as the High Dam itself had a more complex reality, so this bipolar frame is inadequate to understand what happened in Nubia. Due in no small part to the geopolitical contention surrounding the funding of the scheme, many Western commentators have long considered the High Dam as not only *the* emblematic project of an autocratic revolution led by Nasser, but also an event fundamentally tied to Soviet technical assistance. As Ahmad Shokr has demonstrated, this characterization ignores the High Dam's place within contemporary global thinking about river development.[2] Similarly, despite the central involvement of US government money in the project, UNESCO's campaign in Nubia was entangled with forms of postwar politics beyond the bipolar and cannot be reduced to being symptomatic of Cold War political contention, despite appearances otherwise.

---

1. Allais, "The Design," 184, describes the Nubian campaign as "largely a Western affair," which was itself "a response to an Eastern project," i.e., the High Dam.
2. Shokr, "Hydropolitics."

Like all multilateral institutions, UNESCO's position as reliant on, and constitutive of, a particular form of territorial nation-state is well enough noted.[3] Such nation-states spoke not only a particular language of "self-determination" in the era of global "decolonization," but also became embedded within political "institutions of [community] representation" like the UN, whose "idea of 'community' had an active life in the colonial era."[4] That colonial genealogy points to the ease, too, with which these institutions now became connected to US attempts to reshape the world in the country's image. As John D. Kelly and Martha Kaplan argue, "all came to embody . . . the doctrine that the Americans were already calling 'multilateralism.'" New international organizations like the UN "were products of literal dialogue among official representatives of the powerful nations of the globe. But the locations of the most significant negotiations and inaugurations . . . [for example] signing the charter for a UN to be built in New York" indicate "the degree to which the United States dominated the planning of the postwar world."[5]

At the UN in particular, the extent of this US influence is arguable, at least after the immediate postwar years.[6] In UNESCO's case, too, the early sway of Britain is clear, as are the organization's genealogies in the League of Nations' International Committee on Intellectual Cooperation.[7] But the wider Cold War overtones remain, as do the connections to the growing system of nation-states that multilateralism depended on. As Kelly and Kaplan argue, "it is no paradox to say that the United States, while a minor overseas colonizer, was the world's leader at decolonizing," the country expressing global power through the use of new institutions like the UN and the system of "self-determined" nation-states that such institutions relied on to function.[8] As they worked with

---

3. For the UN system and the postwar nation-state, see Eva-Maria Muschik, "Managing the World: The United Nations, Decolonization, and the Strange Triumph of State Sovereignty in the 1950s and 1960s," *Journal of Global History* 13 (2018): 121–44.
4. John D. Kelly and Martha Kaplan, *Represented Communities: Fiji and World Decolonization* (Chicago: University of Chicago Press, 2001), ix, 4.
5. Kelly and Kaplan, *Represented*, 15.
6. Due to the rapid pace at which new nations came into being after World War II, by the early 1960s, "the Afro-Asian bloc dominated the [UN] General Assembly," as Mark Mazower, *Governing the World: The History of an Idea* (New York: The Penguin Press, 2012), 259, states. For the way in which Nasser's Cairo itself welcomed the Afro-Asian bloc, see Reem Abou-El-Fadl, "Building Egypt's Afro-Asian Hub: Infrastructures of Solidarity and the 1957 Cairo Conference," *Journal of World History* 30, nos. 1–2 (2019): 157–92.
7. For which see Meskell, *A Future*, 1–27. Cf. Daniel Laqua, "Transnational Intellectual Cooperation, the League of Nations, and the Problem of Order," *Journal of Global History* 6, no. 2 (2011): 223–47; Sluga, "UNESCO."
8. Kelly and Kaplan, *Represented*, 16. For another perspective on US imperialism, see Daniel Immerwahr, *How to Hide an Empire: A Short History of the Greater United States* (London: The Bodley Head, 2019).

organizations like UNESCO, so newly independent countries like Egypt and Sudan found themselves caught within that project.

Frederick Cooper has noted, however, that "if the last fifty years have made it seem as if the territorial nation-state is both 'modern' and inevitable, in 1958 [two years before the Nubian campaign started] it did not appear to some to be either."[9] Thinking through this conundrum, Cooper suggests that "what gets lost in narrating history as the triumph of [anti-colonial] freedom followed by failure to use that freedom is a sense of process."[10] Here, I turn to that sense of process, outlining the emergent political possibilities that the Nubian campaign helped both to open and to close. In particular, I examine the Nubian campaign's links with the nascent—and institutionalized—Non-Aligned Movement (NAM), whose members (Egypt, India, and Yugoslavia among them) sought to distance themselves from outright membership of the Cold War power blocs.

The NAM, as Robert Vitalis notes, was far less cohesive—and, in its organizational existence, far less attached to Afro-Asianism and events like the 1955 Asian-African Conference held in Bandung, Indonesia—than many scholars have presumed.[11] Yet little consideration seems to have been paid to the Nubian campaign, the NAM, and that institution's shifting relationship with other political organizations and sodalities, despite the prominent role of Egypt—and Nasser in particular—within the group. Indeed, the Conference of Heads of State or Government of Non-Aligned Countries, the movement's founding event, took place in Belgrade in September 1961, just as UNESCO's project was gaining strength (the Brioni Agreement of 1956, signed by Nasser, Indian Prime Minister Jawaharlal Nehru, and Yugoslavian President Josip Broz Tito, had earlier affirmed the relationship between those three leaders and the prosecution of a "non-aligned" foreign policy).[12] Moreover, the campaign's links to the NAM go beyond the centrality of Nasser and Egypt to the project's existence, or, likewise, the centrality of Sudan, itself a non-aligned country.

As they had done at the UN more generally, members of the NAM proved able to influence UNESCO's campaign. Participants in the incipient organ-

---

9. Cooper, "Possibility," 168. Cf. Getachew, *Worldmaking*, and Wilder, *Freedom*.
10. Cooper, "Possibility," 169.
11. Scholars have often lent the NAM a genealogy that, however inaccurately, takes in Bandung and often elides disagreement between the states and figures involved in the organization (not least Nasser and Jawaharlal Nehru of India), for which see Robert Vitalis, "The Midnight Ride of Kwame Nkrumah and Other Fables of Bandung (Ban-doong)," *Humanity: An International Journal of Human Rights, Humanitarianism, and Development* 4, no. 2 (2013): 261–88.
12. On Belgrade, see Vitalis, "The Midnight Ride," 261–62. On Brioni, see Cindy Ewing, "The Colombo Powers: Crafting Diplomacy in the Third World and Launching Afro-Asia at Bandung," *Cold War History* 19, no. 1 (2019): 16.

ization developed considerable leverage at the UN during the Congo crisis of the early 1960s. In that period, Congo's independence from Belgium led to multiple civil wars and, notoriously, the assassination of Patrice Lumumba, the new Republic's prime minister. During the Nubian campaign, this upheaval manifested itself when "strained relations over the Congo [reportedly] put an end to" a Belgian expedition to Egypt's Temple of Dendur.[13] Given such outcomes, this chapter considers the Nubian campaign's relationship with NAM and the various other solidarity organizations and movements circulating around—but not necessarily directly linked to—it. It was at the intersection of these entanglements that non-aligned countries, however fleetingly (and whatever their connections with other geopolitical groupings), found their footing. The "global Cold War" coursed through work in Nubia, but it never governed it entirely.[14]

The Nubian Campaign, the Cold War, and "the New Nations"

The Nubian campaign became embedded within Cold War strategizing, but it was not a project in which participants from Western Europe and the United States believed that they were working toward a common, anti-Soviet goal. As highlighted in chapter 1, Cold War tensions simmered prior to the project, particularly regarding the presence of a Polish archaeological mission in Egypt. The idea, however, that the campaign constituted a coherent counter to an (unspecified) threat posed by the Soviet Union is one whose analytic heft needs to be considered, not least because the national interest always seemed to take precedence—regardless of which nation.[15]

For instance, consider the bid to ensure that US funding to aid the work at Abu Simbel—initially promised by President John F. Kennedy in April 1961—could be secured. Appearing at the Senate Appropriations Subcommittee for the fiscal year 1964, Assistant Secretary of State for Educational and Cultural Affairs Lucius D. Battle stated that

> no member of the Soviet Bloc is making a contribution [in Nubia] and . . . only Yugoslavia of the Communist-dominated countries, is doing so. This

---

13. Leslie Greener, *High Dam Over Nubia* (London: Cassell, 1962), 179. For context, see Alana O'Malley, "Ghana, India, and the Transnational Dynamics of the Congo Crisis at the United Nations, 1960–61," *The International History Review* 37, no. 5 (2015): 970–90.
14. Westad, *The Global*. Cf. Meskell, *A Future*, 48, for similar thoughts.
15. Cf. Meskell, *A Future*, 32.

difference in attitude towards the protection of these monuments marks a fundamental difference in our regard for the validity of history and for the common cultural heritage of Western Man.[16]

Battle's words made it seem as if a Soviet threat hovered over Nubia, despite a lack of physical presence. Yet he was also being somewhat disingenuous. Under Tito, Yugoslavia had split with the Soviet Union in 1948 and, despite reconfirming its relationship with global socialism after the death of Stalin in 1953, the country had since taken an independent course: manifested most obviously in Tito's prominent position in the NAM.[17] Representing Nubia as an anti-Soviet project thus proved to be an unsuccessful means of persuading US senators to back the now-deceased Kennedy's Abu Simbel promise: "JFK Pledge to Egypt Blocked," as *The Washington Post* noted of one contentious meeting of the House Appropriations Committee.[18] Indeed, it was only when nonconvertible Egyptian currency derived from the sale of American wheat to the country became usable as foreign aid under US Public Law 480—the 1954 Agricultural Trade Development and Assistance Act instituting the Office of Food for Peace—that US lawmakers found a solution to this issue.[19] Incapable of providing the hard currency payment necessary to purchase the equipment needed to salvage the temples through lifting, the United States could spend Public Law 480 money on wages for the local laborers used to perform cutting work at the site.[20] In Nubia, what mattered most was a—very contingent—national interest. As internal US negotiations surrounding the Abu Simbel funding dragged on, one expert stated that "when it came time to re-negotiate our excavation and exploration concessions [in Egypt], I believe they might well go to other nations."[21]

---

16. "Statement of Lucius D. Battle, Secretary of State for Educational and Cultural Affairs, before the Senate Appropriations Subcommittee, on the Fiscal Year 1964 Supplemental Appropriation Request for the Preservation of Ancient Nubian Monuments (the Temples of Abu Simbel)," transcript held in "Abu Simbel-Washington Council of Am. Com. (2)," Smithsonian Institution Archives, Record Unit 91, Smithsonian Institution, Office of International Activities, Records, 1963–1969 (hereafter Smithsonian 1963–1969). For Battle and Abu Simbel, see Luke, *A Pearl*, 113–40.

17. For the Yugoslav-Soviet split, see Jeronim Perović, "The Tito-Stalin Split: A Reassessment in Light of New Evidence," *Journal of Cold War Studies* 9, no. 2 (2007): 32–63.

18. Drew Pearson, "JFK Pledge to Egypt Blocked," *The Washington Post*, June 3, 1964.

19. On "Food for Peace," see, e.g., Kristin L. Ahlberg, *Transplanting the Great Society: Lyndon Johnson and Food for Peace* (Columbia, MO, and London: University of Missouri Press, 2008).

20. Allais, "Integrities," 21–22. For more on the relationship between Public Law 480 and archaeology, see Luke, *A Pearl*. When applied to archaeological projects, the funds were administered by the Smithsonian Institution, for which see "Fellowships and Grants: Smithsonian Institution Foreign Currency Program in Archeology and Related Disciplines," American Anthropological Association *Fellow Newsletter* 8 (1965): 4–5.

21. Transcript of unidentified expert giving evidence to (presumably) the Senate Appropriations Subcommittee, held in "Abu Simbel-Washington Council of Am. Com. (3)," Smithsonian 1963–1969.

The Cold War undoubtedly enabled American archaeology and its methods to move around the globe, grounding the US interest in a very material form of soft power.[22] Yet it was the US interest in the Eastern Mediterranean and Middle East that was paramount, not the Cold War one in general. Emphasizing this point, Secretary of the Smithsonian Institution S. Dillon Ripley told members of the Senate Appropriations Subcommittee that

> in recent weeks we have received a number of communications from the American universities and museums for whom we act as spokesman expressing the gravest concern about what our failure to participate in the rescue of the Nubian monuments might mean to the future of American archaeology in the classical and Bible lands. They point out that when President Kennedy first publicly announced our intention to join the Nubian salvage campaign, important new exploration concessions, research opportunities and agreements for the equal sharing of findings opened up to us in Egypt and the Middle East in general. These universities and museums believe that if the United States is not in the forefront of the campaign to save the monuments from the rising Nile waters, these new avenues of cooperation will be closed to us and passed on to other nations.[23]

US "research opportunities" were said to include investigation into "the beginnings of Western man's agriculture ... historical verification of the Biblical narrative ... [and] understanding of the birth of Western civilization," indicating the ways in which some in the country hoped that the United States might take on the leadership of—or at least play a newly emboldened role in—archaeological research in a region that the country's geopolitical interest now helped to shape. These research themes were, moreover, long-running ones, and that leadership would not brook resistance.[24] Ripley's reference to "other nations" might have pointed to the USSR or its allies. Yet the innuendo could just as easily have referred to Western countries. Actual common cause in making the Nubian

---

22. On which see Christina Luke and Morag M. Kersel, *U.S. Cultural Diplomacy and Archaeology: Soft Power and Hard Heritage* (New York and London: Routledge, 2013). For the vagaries of this situation see Carruthers, "Visualizing"; Luke, *A Pearl*; and Maurizio Peleggi, "Excavating Prehistory in the Cold War: American Archaeology in Neocolonial Thailand," *Journal of Social Archaeology* 16, no. 1 (2016): 94–111.

23. Ripley to Spessard L. Holland, June 15, 1964, held in "Abu Simbel (1963, 4, 5)," Smithsonian 1963–1969.

24. Ripley to Spessard L. Holland, June 15, 1964. The work of James Henry Breasted indicates US interest in (some of) these areas well before World War II, for which see Abt, *American Egyptologist*. In Egypt, meanwhile, "verification of the Biblical narrative" had been a particular interest of Victorian Britain, for which see Gange, *Dialogues*. Elsewhere, in Palestine, as Thomas W. Davis, *Shifting Sands: The Rise and Fall of Biblical Archaeology* (Oxford: Oxford University Press, 2004), vii, states, "before the 1970s, biblical archaeology was the dominant research paradigm."

campaign a project directed against the Soviet bloc was, then, far from the norm, as Battle had earlier implied when he noted that "the Federal Republic of Germany has done a magnificent job of dismantling and reconstructing the great temple of Kalabsha."[25] International rivalries, strengthened by long-existing tensions at play between—and sometimes within—US-allied nations, ruled.[26]

"Western'" unity in relation to the Nubian campaign thus only ever coalesced in terms of negative action. The goals that Western countries would collectively *not* work toward were far clearer than the goals they displayed a common interest in. Even then, that process seemed to involve the participation of the Soviet Union. By late 1962, the need to take decisive action regarding Abu Simbel was becoming ever more urgent "due to the time-limit imposed by the scheduled rise in the level of the Nile." At UNESCO's twelfth General Conference in Paris that November and December, the institution's Secretariat proposed the raising of a long-term loan from member-states of thirty-and-a-half million US dollars in order to meet the costs of the preservation project then proposed. The loan was predicated on "the fact that the voluntary contributions on which the original plan was premised had proved inadequate."[27] If enough of UNESCO's member-states voted in agreement, all member states would thus be forced to fund a substantial cash advance.

Given the growing unease with which some nation-states viewed international organizations and the voice they gave to newly independent countries, the proposal was predictably unpopular with certain parties, fueling a surge in diplomatic wrangling aimed at stopping the loan agreement in its tracks.[28] Among British officials, for instance, the merest suggestion of the payment caused outrage. One Treasury civil servant suggested that "we should declare openly that . . . the UK will decline to pay its assessed share," not least because "this may be the only finally effective way of bringing these international organisations to reason."[29] A confidential telegram sent from the UK's UNESCO delegation both to the Foreign Office and to Permanent Secretary in the Ministry of Education Mary Smieton noted that "we shall be discussing . . . tactics with the United States and other delegations with similar views (France, Aus-

---

25. "Statement of Lucius D. Battle."
26. Although, as Meskell, *A Future*, 41, notes, "national interests routinely trumped international efforts . . . [and] American archaeologists were the most egregious here."
27. UNESCO, "Records of the General Conference: Twelfth Session, Paris, 1962; Resolutions," (Paris: UNESCO, 1963), 199.
28. For that unease, see Mazower, *Governing*, 257–72.
29. Illegible (Ronald?) to (Stuart?) Milner-Barry, December 4, 1962. Records of HM Treasury file T 317/45, The National Archives of the UK.

tralia, Canada, New Zealand, Japan)."[30] A later Foreign Office telegram even noted that "this resolution is similarly objectionable ... to the Soviet Union." If UNESCO's member states passed the loan resolution, "it will be a misuse of the voting strength of [the implicitly newly independent] countries whose assessments to the Regular Budget are small." The loan would "create a division between the large and the small contributors which can only harm UNESCO."[31] Needless to say, the resolution regarding the loan failed to pass.[32]

Rather than a coherent effort to counter Soviet influence in Egypt, Western "solidarity" regarding Nubia was, if anything, a means to counter the growing agency of newly independent and non-aligned countries like Egypt and Sudan. For some countries, the Nubian campaign was as much an attempt to stop the growing number of new nations cultivating multilateral influence as it was an attempt to influence them. UNESCO's involvement in Nubia thus helped to develop paranoia surrounding the growing strength of former colonies over whom both the USSR and Western nations wanted to assert control. Part and parcel of the Cold War, the Cold War, however, was not that paranoia's only referent, especially as the world's new nations grew in influence. In July 1962, several months before UNESCO's General Conference, a large group of these new nations—including Sudan, Yugoslavia, and India—met in Cairo at an event titled the Conference on the Problems of Economic Development. That September, they released the "Cairo Declaration of Developing Countries," affirming future economic collaboration between themselves and criticizing the perpetuation of past power structures hindering their growth.[33] Two years later, the United Nations Conference on Trade and Development (UNCTAD) was born, aiming to foster precisely this collaboration.[34] Seemingly outgunned, Western countries sought to counter this growing shift in global political and economic power.[35] Their solidarity regarding Nubia was a symptom of that concern.

---

30. Telegram from UK delegation, UNESCO General Conference, to UK Foreign Office and Mary Smieton, December 4, 1962. Records of HM Treasury file T 317/45.

31. Telegram from UK Foreign Office to "Vienna," December 5, 1962. Records of HM Treasury file T 317/45.

32. UNESCO, "Records of the General Conference: Twelfth Session," 199–200.

33. United Nations Economic and Social Council, "Economic Commission for Africa, Standing Committee on Trade, First Session, Addis Ababa, 12–22 September 1962; Cairo Declaration of Developing Countries (Document Submitted by the Delegation of the UAR)," document E/CN.14/STC/16, September 14, 1962.

34. Mazower, *Governing*, 299–300.

35. Mazower, *Governing*, 308–14. On UNCTAD, cf. Vijay Prashad, *The Darker Nations: A People's History of the Third World* (New York and London: The New Press, 2007).

The geopolitics of the Nubian campaign created an environment in which newly independent countries could attempt to gain global influence: equals, almost, alongside other countries with the same aim, and consequently causing a certain amount of anxiety. During the project, not only the Soviet Union, but also Warsaw Pact countries sent missions to Nubia: Czechoslovakia, Hungary, and the USSR to Egypt, and East Germany and Poland to Sudan.[36] At no point did these teams seem to represent a threat. But missions from the new nations were present in Nubia, too, and attempt to become equals they did. For example, Ghana worked in Sudan (with a team led by former Commissioner for Archaeology Peter Shinnie), and Yugoslavia and India in Egypt. Financially, too, the campaign represented contributions from across the globe, albeit of decidedly unequal amounts.[37] One of those contributions illustrates how, despite an environment in which large nations worked together to stifle the influence of "small contributors," the space offered by UNESCO's involvement in Nubia meant that the countries at whom this British innuendo was aimed could still find means through which to advance their interests. Ironically, too, in some spaces, the contributions of those countries seemed to be welcomed.

"Dinar Diplomacy"

During the Nubian campaign, the United States ultimately spent far more money than any other nation. But other countries also made significant financial contributions, using the project to prosecute their own interests. Kuwait—which gained independence from Britain in 1961, was present at the Cairo conference in 1962, and which ultimately joined the NAM in 1964—was one such participant. The country's "dinar diplomacy" was indicative of the ways UNESCO's involvement in Nubia helped both the rhetoric and the practice of non-alignment—not to mention pan-Arabism—to circulate, even as it also reveals why such processes were unstable.[38]

As Abdul-Reda Assiri notes, after Iraq had threatened to invade the new nation in 1961, "it became obvious that most Arab countries would more readily support Kuwait if it agreed to share its [oil] wealth with its less fortunate

---

36. On the Czech mission, see Hana Navrátilová, "Layered Agendas: Jaroslav Černý, Stateless Egyptologist between Decolonization and the Cold War," *Práce z dějin Akademie věd* 10, no. 1 (2018): 53–98.

37. For an illustration see Allais, "The Design."

38. Abdul-Reda Assiri, "Kuwait's Dinar Diplomacy: The Role of Donor-Mediator," *Journal of South Asian and Middle Eastern Studies* 14, no. 3 (1991): 25, citing Martha Dukas, *Azmat al-Kuwait: Al-ʿAlaqat al-Kuwaitiyya al-ʿIraqiyya 1961–1963* [The crisis of Kuwait: Kuwaiti-Iraqi Relations 1961–1963] (Beirut: Dar al-Nahar li-l-Nashr, 1973), 69 (although Dukas does not actually seem to use the phrase).

brethren."³⁹ Among those brethren, Egypt—which had been vital in enabling Arab recognition of Kuwaiti independence—was one willing recipient.⁴⁰ In May 1963, the Kuwaiti Prime Minister (and later Emir), Shaykh Sabah al-Salim al-Sabah, announced upon his country's accession to the UN that it would practice the "positive neutrality" championed by Nasser. That rhetoric not only helped to navigate a difficult regional political environment, but also allowed Kuwait to follow the non-aligned example set by Egypt and pay heed to Nasser's endeavors to lead a pan-Arab fold.⁴¹ Later that year, the country finalized a financial proposal with Egypt that would safeguard the then endangered plans for the temples at Abu Simbel from complete collapse. Kuwait had seen a chance to act.

Late the previous year, on November 20, 1962—just as British officials were about to express their outrage at UNESCO's loan proposal—Egypt's ambassador to Kuwait pressed the country's Foreign Minister (and another later Emir), Shaykh Jaber al-Ahmad al-Sabah, about a suggestion that the country could guarantee a loan for the Abu Simbel work that UNESCO would take out at a British bank.⁴² UNESCO had unsuccessfully asked multiple financial institutions for a loan to help finance the Abu Simbel operation: Crédit Suisse and the International Bank for Reconstruction and Development (IBRD), for instance, had both proven skeptical.⁴³ The good news now, though, was that the Kuwaiti government and the country's ruler, Shaykh Abdullah III, had agreed to the plan, communicating with Egypt "asking to know" (*talab mʿarifa*) the name of the British bank that would be involved.⁴⁴ UNESCO had played a

---

39. Assiri, "Kuwait's Dinar Diplomacy," 25.

40. Walid E. Moubarak, "The Kuwait Fund in the Context of Arab and Third World Politics," *Middle East Journal* 41, no. 4 (1987): 548. As Moubarak notes on p. 542, "before [the signing of the] Camp David [Accords of 1978 between Egypt and Israel, when Kuwait stopped making loans to the country for several years], Egypt was the largest recipient of Kuwaiti aid and has always been important in Kuwait's policy calculations."

41. Neil Partrick, "Kuwait's Foreign Policy (1961–1977): Non-Alignment, Ideology and the Pursuit of Security" (PhD diss., London School of Economics and Political Science, 2006), 58, http://etheses.lse.ac.uk/3164/1/Partrick_Kuwait%27s_Foreign_Policy.pdf.

42. Set out in a letter from the Under-Secretary of the Egyptian Ministry of Foreign Affairs to the Under-Secretary, Nubia Office, December 2, 1962. File 2A-a5, "Qarḍ al-Kuwait li-Āthār al-Nūba" ["Loan of Kuwait for the Nubian Antiquities"], Nubia Museum. The original proposal seems to have been made in September 1962, judging by Jessim Qatami to Director-General, UNESCO, December 11, 1962. Folder 069 (62) N/A 116: "Nubia-Crédits bancaires," UNESCO Archives.

43. For these rejections, see F. W. Schulthess to Ali Vrioni, July 23, 1962, and Eugene R. Black to René Maheu, October 4, 1962, in "Nubia-Crédits bancaires," UNESCO Archives. The IBRD had also been involved in the failed attempts of Britain and the US to finance the High Dam, for which see Peter L. Hahn, *The United States, Great Britain, and Egypt, 1945–1956: Strategy and Diplomacy in the Early Cold War* (Chapel Hill: University of North Carolina Press, 1991), 194.

44. Under-Secretary of the Egyptian Ministry of Foreign Affairs to the Under-Secretary of Egypt's Nubia Office, December 2, 1962, in "Qarḍ al-Kuwait li-Āthār al-Nūba," Nubia Museum.

role in instituting this agreement, but it took back-channel negotiations between Egypt and Kuwait to confirm its possibility. The Nubian campaign allowed discrete political alliances to prosper.

Given UNESCO's issues with loan agreements, the organization had to create such political spaces. UNESCO's comptroller was concerned about the long-term financial and legal implications of any loan taken out by the institution.[45] Coupled with events at the Paris General Conference of 1962, this concern led to the need "to envisage only procedures which would not involve the direct contracting of debt by the Organization [UNESCO's capitalization]."[46] Consequently, the comptroller had advanced the suggestion that a bilateral "loan from Kuwait to the UAR would seem to be a better solution."[47] Working out the details of this new plan, however, would delay work at Abu Simbel further. Egyptian officials were frustrated, to say the least, laying bare the extent to which the whole Nubian project—promoted by UNESCO as representative of global cooperation—rested not only on rather more national interests, but also the way in which those interests were best met through a strategy of "positive neutrality." ʿAbd al-Munʿim al-Sawi, who was under-secretary at Egypt's Ministry of Culture and National Guidance (and did a significant amount of the day-to-day work on the Nubian campaign), wrote an "urgent and important" (ʿājila wa-hāmiyya) memo stating that, "firstly and lastly" (awwalan wa-akhīran), Abu Simbel constituted "our national heritage" (turāthunā al-qawmī). Consequently, he proposed to travel to Kuwait to finalize the agreement himself.[48] Egypt, it seemed, would have to sort out UNESCO's problem, because UNESCO was incapable of doing so itself.

When Kuwait wrote to UNESCO in September 1963 to inform the organization that the country would be unable to agree to its new plan, ʿAbd al-Munʿim al-Sawi could wait no longer.[49] He traveled to the Gulf that October.[50] By November, he was writing to Kuwait's ambassador in Cairo thanking him for the country's contribution to the work and praising the "high spirit" (rūḥ

---

45. Reginald Harper-Smith to Malcolm Adiseshiah, July 11, 1963, in "Nubia-Crédits bancaires," UNESCO Archives.

46. Adiseshiah to Shaykh Sabah al-Ahmad al-Sabah, July 22, 1963, in "Nubia-Crédits bancaires," UNESCO Archives.

47. Harper-Smith to Adiseshiah, July 11, 1963, in "Nubia-Crédits bancaires," UNESCO Archives.

48. "Mudhakkira ʿAjīla wa-Hāmiyya li-l-ʿArd ʿala al-Sayyid Wazīr al-Thaqāfa wa-l-Irshād al-Qawmī" ["Urgent and important memo to be shown to the minister of culture and national guidance"], written by ʿAbd al-Munʿim al-Sawi, August 15, 1963, in "Qarḍ al-Kuwait li-Āthār al-Nūba," Nubia Museum.

49. Abdul Rahman Salem al-Ateeqi to Director-General, UNESCO, September 14, 1963, in "Nubia-Crédits bancaires," UNESCO Archives.

50. Al-Sawi to Egyptian ambassador to Kuwait, September 30, 1963, in "Qarḍ al-Kuwait li-Āthār al-Nūba," Nubia Museum.

'āliyya) among Arab States that that contribution had helped to constitute.[51] Meanwhile, Egypt's then Minister of Culture and National Guidance, ʿAbd al-Qadir Hatem, had a speech prepared for broadcast stating that, while the UAR was undoubtedly "proud" (fakhūra) of the work at Abu Simbel, that work was nonetheless being conducted "to save the heritage of humanity" (inqādh turāth al-insāniyya).[52] The register of the work in Nubia could now shift from the non-aligned and pan-Arab to the universal that UNESCO desired. For its part, Kuwait had made similar suggestions, stressing that its loan would help to carry out "the Arab plan" (al-mashrūʿ al-ʿarabī) at Abu Simbel. Simultaneously, though, the country emphasized that the temples at the site constituted part of "the civilization of the world" (ḥaḍārat al-ʿālim).[53] US finance later buttressed the Abu Simbel preservation project. But arriving at that conclusion, it took a Kuwaiti loan, negotiated at Egyptian behest, to enable Egypt to undertake the "immediate payment operations" allowing initial work at Abu Simbel to happen.[54] "Dinar diplomacy" created the conditions in which US strategy at the site might be made operational.

India, Egypt, and Non-Alignment

Such international solidarity was always contingent upon circumstances. The involvement of the Archaeological Survey of India (ASI) in the Nubian campaign emphasizes why: the work of this institution of the British Raj (founded 1861) illustrates how UNESCO's project could both help and hinder contemporary geopolitical alliances.[55] Discussing Indian cultural diplomacy in the second half of the twentieth century, Claire Wintle notes how that diplomacy "require[d] human interaction beyond the nation," its transnational aspects

---

51. Al-Sawi to Kuwaiti ambassador to Egypt, November 11, 1963, in "Qarḍ al-Kuwait li-Āthār al-Nūba," Nubia Museum.
52. Undated transcript of broadcast by ʿAbd al-Qadir Hatem, c. November 1963, in "Qarḍ al-Kuwait li-Āthār al-Nūba," Nubia Museum.
53. "Naṣ Taṣrīḥ Hakūmat al-Kuwayt fī Ijtimaʿ al-Duwwal al-Musāhima fī Inqādh Maʿbadayy Abu Simbal" ["Press release of the government of Kuwait at the meeting of donor states for the preservation of the two temples at Abu Simbel"], presumably October 1963, in "Qarḍ al-Kuwait li-Āthār al-Nūba," Nubia Museum.
54. UNESCO, "International Campaign to Save the Monuments of Nubia; Executive Committee, Sixth Session, Cairo, 5–9 November 1963," UNESCO/Nubia/CE/VI/3, November 27, 1963, 8. Interestingly, the loan was not registered by UNESCO in its accounting of contributions to the campaign, for which see Säve-Söderbergh, Temples, 232–33.
55. Much of the rest of this chapter reproduces William Carruthers, "Archaeological (Non?) Alignments: Egypt, India, and Global Geographies of the Post-War Past," South Asian Studies 36, no. 1 (2020): 45–60.

invariably complicating an analysis taking in the nation-state alone.[56] The ASI's excavations at Afyeh in Egyptian Nubia fit within this frame: the Indian national interest coupled to the transnational alliances within which the country became entangled as it sought to stay out of bipolar "bloc" politics.[57] Unlike other "nonaligned" excavations in Nubia, the ASI's work in the region constituted a project indubitably borne of the new nation-state's citizens. By contrast, Ghana's Nubian excavation was—at least as Peter Shinnie claimed—entirely his proposal, even if "well received in Ghana at the highest level of government."[58] Yet although the work at Afyeh was an all-Indian initiative, it was also one that enabled the country to put its (trans-) national money where its mouth was.

For India, working in Nubia constituted a win-win situation: involvement in the Nubian campaign let the country advance several of its interests at once. In his preliminary field report, published some years after the excavation, the archaeologist B. B. Lal, the ASI's field director at Afyeh, noted that "for any developing country, self-sufficiency is the basic key-note; and . . . the United Arab Republic is doing all it can to achieve the objective."[59] Likewise, he stated that "the construction of the High Dam will no doubt be beneficial," even though "it has its repercussions too." Thus, "ever willing to co-operate in all international schemes of merit, the Government of India . . . decided to send out an Archaeological Expedition to Lower Nubia."[60] Lal's explanation reflected India's contemporary geopolitical self-fashioning, emphasizing his country's support for modernization and particular transnational alliances at the same time as embedding that support within the national interest. In 1958, three years before the two nations had become founder members of the NAM (and indicating how that organization and other forms of solidarity were not necessarily mutually exclusive), Egypt and India had signed the Indo-UAR Cultural Agreement in order "to bring into effect the principles of the Joint Communique[sic] issued on the occasion of the [1955] Afro-Asian Conference

---

56. Claire Wintle, "India on Display: Nationalism, Transnationalism and Collaboration, 1964–1986," *Third Text* 31, nos. 2–3 (2017): 303.

57. According to Itty Abraham, "From Bandung to NAM: Non-Alignment and Indian Foreign Policy, 1947–1965," *Commonwealth and Comparative Politics* 46, no. 2 (2008): 211, the NAM allowed "the non-aligned states . . . to define a more active engagement with the international system in the joint pursuit of their individual and collective interests" at the same time as "remaining outside superpower blocs."

58. Shinnie, "A Personal Memoir," 229.

59. B. B. Lal, "Indian Archaeological Expedition to Nubia, 1962: A Preliminary Report," in *Campagne internationale de l'Unesco pour la sauvegarde des monuments de la Nubie: fouilles en Nubie (1961–1963)*, ed. République Arabe Unie, Ministere du tourisme et des antiquités, Service des antiquités de l'Egypte (Cairo: Organisme general des imprimeries gouvernementales, 1967), 97.

60. Lal, "Indian Archaeological Expedition," 98.

at Bandung."[61] Additionally, the Indian government saw UNESCO itself as strategically important, as it increasingly did also UN multilateralism.[62] In 1954, Humayun Kabir, India's minister of education, wrote to Luther Evans, UNESCO's then director-general, to request that India be permitted to host the organization's ninth General Conference in New Delhi. Kabir, who had also contributed to UNESCO's first (1950) "Statement on Race," stressed that no session of the event had previously been held east of the Mediterranean.[63] And when, in 1956, that conference came to India, it opened with a speech by Nehru requesting that "the meeting of this organisation, in this ancient city of Delhi, will turn your minds more to the needs of these underdeveloped countries of the world."[64] India's work at Afyeh fit such sentiments.

However, such rhetoric provides an imprecise explanation as to why the ASI went to Egypt. Files relating to the Indo-UAR Cultural Agreement, for example, reveal some inactivity regarding its implementation. The Indian Council for Cultural Relations might well have published an Arabic-language journal called *Thaqafat al-Hind* (Indian culture) summarizing news of India's international cultural projects.[65] Yet a March 1962 memo relates that the Indian government had been waiting a year for word from Cairo on a final program of events.[66] In a climate where agreements said one thing and practice suggested another, what made it worthwhile to send an Indian archaeological team to Nubia? Emphasizing just how contingent this apparent act of transnational solidarity was, as ever in relation to the Nubian campaign, the translation and mobilization of colonial practices made for postcolonial possibilities. For India, excavating in Nubia offered not only the potential of turning the hierarchy of colonial archaeology on its head, but also the possibility of asserting its own place as regional archaeological leader.

---

61. Memo entitled "Suggestions for the Implementation of the Indo-U.A.R. Cultural Agreement," August 3, 1960. Ministry of External Affairs file 37 (4) WANA/60, National Archives of India, New Delhi (NAI). On India's approach to Bandung, NAM, and their entangled histories, see Abraham, "From Bandung."

62. For the way in which this view of the UN overlapped with India's acceptance of the NAM, see Abraham, "From Bandung," 211.

63. Kabir to Evans, September 4, 1954. Ministry of Education A5 section; file 7–2/54A5 (Part II), NAI. For the 1950 race statement, see UNESCO, *Four Statements on the Race Question* (Paris: UNESCO, 1969), 30–35.

64. Jawaharlal Nehru, "Address to the UNESCO Delegates in New Delhi, 1956," in *Paths to Peace: India's Voices in UNESCO*, ed. UNESCO New Delhi (New Delhi: UNESCO, 2009), 18.

65. Similar to the conclusions apparently raised by the Afyeh excavation, in October 1962 the journal published an article on the long cultural links between India and Egypt: Pran Nath Chopra, "al-'Alaqat al-Thaqafiyya baina al-Hind wa-l-Jumhuriyya al-'Arabiyya al-Muttahida" ["The cultural links between India and the UAR"], *Thaqafat al-Hind* 13, no. 4 (1962): 102–108.

66. Note by N. V. Rao, March 23, 1962. Ministry of External Affairs file 37 (4) WANA/60, NAI.

Reimagining Colonial Archaeology for India

It is difficult to extricate the ASI's work at Afyeh from the dying days of British India. B. B. Lal was a product of the field training school held by his institution at the site of Taxila (now in Pakistan) in 1944.[67] The school took place under the charge of the ASI's last British director, the archaeologist Mortimer Wheeler, who had been employed to reform the institution's practices. At Taxila, Wheeler aimed to inculcate a very particular, highly regimented form of excavation practice: a former soldier, he was obsessed with discipline and order in the field.[68] Despite his high-flung rhetoric and obsessive promotion of particular forms of archaeological visualization, there was often little difference between the work that Wheeler undertook and that of his directorial predecessors, as Sudeshna Guha and Robin Boast have noted.[69] Yet the ASI's school at Taxila took on significance in the lives of those Indian archaeologists who attended it, and who, after the partition of 1947, took over control of archaeology in the country. In his autobiography, B. B. Lal notes that for several years "very little was done after the departure of Wheeler in terms of training." A connection with Wheeler, though, continued to produce dividends: Lal explaining that "in 1959 a School of Archaeology was founded under the auspices of the Survey and I was given the privilege of being its first Director."[70]

Drawing on Taxila's precedent, the new School of Archaeology's program was modeled after training conducted by the University of London's Institute of Archaeology, which Wheeler and his former wife Tessa Verney Wheeler had worked together to found.[71] Reworked for the era of Indian independence, however, the use of "British" archaeological pedagogy now took on a new sense of national and regional urgency. In 1957, at a meeting of the country's Central Advisory Board for Archaeology, India's Minister of Education, Maulana Azad, had stated that "in 1947 there was an Englishman as Director [of the ASI]. I talked to him. The first point was whether we have got the necessary material if our Department were to open a school to give practical

---

67. B. B. Lal, *Piecing Together: Memoirs of an Archaeologist* (New Delhi: Aryan Books International, 2011), 100.
68. For Wheeler's archaeological militarism, see Christopher J. Evans, "Soldiering Archaeology: Pitt Rivers and 'Militarism,'" *Bulletin of the History of Archaeology* 24, no. 4 (2014): 1–20.
69. Robin Boast, "Mortimer Wheeler's Science of Order: The Tradition of Accuracy at Arikamedu," *Antiquity* 76 (2002): 165–70; Sudeshna Guha, "Mortimer Wheeler's Archaeology in South Asia and its Photographic Representation," *South Asian Studies* 19, no. 1 (2003): 43–55.
70. Lal, *Piecing*, 100.
71. "Institute of Archaeology," *Hindustan Times*, February 2, 1958. For the Wheelers, see Lydia C. Carr, *Tessa Verney Wheeler: Women and Archaeology Before World War Two* (Oxford: Oxford University Press, 2012).

training." Azad ruefully noted that "ten years have elapsed since then."[72] Meanwhile, the (now-renamed) Ministry of Education and Scientific Research also indicated the urgency of the proposed school, which ultimately employed Wheeler as external examiner of its diploma.[73] The ministry published a memo noting that, since independence, India had in fact run a limited scheme for training "outsiders" in excavation practices. Those outsiders included Indians with no affiliation to the ASI, but also included "persons from abroad," including Burma, Cambodia, and China. The memo went on to suggest that the ability to attract such people "signifies that our Department of Archaeology has the best organised service at least in this part of the world."[74]

Founding a School of Archaeology in India would indicate that the country constituted a regional center of expertise in archaeological knowledge production. India could put this position to good use, establishing archaeology as a credible tool in strengthening the country's chosen geopolitical role as a (trans-) national force among its Asian neighbors (a position that some neighboring countries were far from enamored by).[75] Before the trip to Nubia, the ASI had already sent delegations to Indonesia, Afghanistan, and Nepal, all three founder members of the NAM.[76] Working through UNESCO's multilateral auspices, the Indian government now sensed that it had a chance to strengthen this regional prominence. That Wheeler himself had been co-opted on to certain of the Nubian campaign's committees can only have bolstered this position.[77]

In March 1960, just after the Nubian campaign's launch, Humayun Kabir wrote to Vittorino Veronese (UNESCO's director-general since 1958), confidently stating that the Indian government had "a number of really first rate experts" ready to work in Nubia. Those experts, Kabir noted, had "worked on an identical problem at [the site of] Nagarjunakonda which will be submerged by the [Nagarjuna Sagar] dam being built across the river Krishna."[78] Embedded within a discourse of national technological development, the dam constituted one of Nehru's so-called industrial temples of modern India, and

---

72. Extract of Maulana Azad's address to Central Advisory Board of Archaeology, September 14, 1957, in memo entitled "Opening of a Training School in the Department of Archaeology," presumably late 1957. Ministry of Education C-1 Section; file (1957) 1–40/57–C1, NAI.

73. Memo entitled "Opening of a Training School." For Wheeler's position, see Sudeshna Guha, *Artefacts of History: Archaeology, Historiography and Indian Pasts* (New Delhi: Sage, 2015), 195.

74. Memo entitled "Opening of a Training School."

75. For which see Abraham, "From Bandung," 209–11. Cf. Ewing, "The Colombo Powers," 18.

76. B. B. Lal, *Indian Archaeology Since Independence* (Delhi, Varanasi, and Patna: Motilal Banarsidass, 1964), 60–61.

77. For Wheeler and Nubia, see Jacquetta Hawkes, *Mortimer Wheeler: Adventurer in Archaeology* (London: Weidenfeld and Nicolson, 1982), 334–37.

78. Kabir to Veronese, March 6, 1960. Folder CA 120/56, 069 (62) N/A 114/113 (540): "Museums-Nubia-World-Wide Appeal-Offer of Participation-India," UNESCO Archives.

at the same time had submerged the ancient remains located in its vicinity; B. B. Lal later termed the whole scheme "the Indian Nubia."[79] And the force of this precedent, not least the similarity of its rhetorical and material assemblage of past, present, and future to the Nubian work, allowed Kabir to attempt to put Indian archaeological expertise into further regional circulation. Nagarjunakonda suggested that this expertise had the strength to become an immutable mobile: a freely circulating fact no longer dependent for credibility on the context in which it developed.[80] The question was whether that circulation might credibly take place. Prior to the ASI working in Nubia, the institution had to take obtaining a site in the region into its own hands. Postcolonial possibilities had to be made.

Circulation Troubles

Before India could send anyone to Nubia, the ASI needed a site to excavate. Obtaining this site, however, was easier said than done. Despite UNESCO's soaring internationalist rhetoric, India's arrival in Egypt again calls into question the extent to which the organization controlled patterns of Nubian archaeological circulation.[81] At best, the process of organizing excavation work was *ad hoc*, resembling more a process of *bricolage* than the order that UNESCO promoted. In India's case, this *bricolage* also became entangled with specific forms of archaeological knowledge. All archaeologists were equal, but the disarray and equivocation of the Nubian campaign ultimately helped the ASI's archaeologists become more equal than others.

India's initial communication with UNESCO took place at cross purposes. When Humayun Kabir wrote to Vittorino Veronese, he cautiously stated that India might provide

> technical assistance to the Egyptian government or UNESCO by loaning the services of some of our officers, if necessary at our own cost, or we might send a small survey party which could help the Egyptian government or UNESCO in exploration as well as excavation.[82]

---

79. Lal, *Indian Archaeology*, 49. For Nehru's "temples," see, e.g., David Arnold, "Nehruvian Science and Postcolonial India," *Isis* 104, no. 2 (2013): 360–70; Sunil Purushotham, "World History in the Atomic Age: Past, Present and Future in the Political Thought of Jawaharlal Nehru," *Modern Intellectual History* 14, no. 3 (2016): 837–67.

80. Bruno Latour, *Science in Action* (Cambridge, MA: Harvard University Press, 1987).

81. For similar thoughts on UNESCO's lack of control in Nubia, see Meskell, *A Future*, 32.

82. Kabir to Veronese, March 6, 1960, "Museums-Nubia-World-Wide Appeal-Offer of Participation-India," UNESCO Archives.

As Veronese explained, this caution was unnecessary because he was unable to provide Kabir with information about whether such terms were acceptable. "UNESCO's task," he wrote, "is to be an intermediary between the two governments who have asked for help."[83] Lucia Allais has noted how UNESCO utilized the Nubian campaign to set itself up as "a mediating agency that enforces international standards."[84] Disavowing its own agency, however, it is unclear whether UNESCO wanted—or was able—to enforce much of anything. The organization forwarded Indian correspondence to Egypt, but also encouraged bilateral communication between the two countries, asking India to give further information to Egypt about the work it would carry out.[85] Reinforcing the system of nation-states upon which multilateralism depended, UNESCO's mediating role could often be extremely—and purposefully—limited.

Even attempting to mediate, UNESCO was not a convincing enforcer. Toward the end of 1960, Jean Thomas, the organization's assistant director-general, wrote to Humayun Kabir informing him that Egypt's Department of Antiquities wanted India to conduct prehistoric work "when the general survey of the prehistoric sites of [Egyptian] Nubia is completed." The problem was that the survey (discussed in chapter 3) had not yet been organized.[86] Much of UNESCO's work during the Nubian campaign existed as representation, the smoke and mirrors of the project's spectacle making it appear as if the organization was in total control.[87] Yet UNESCO officials often complained that they were out of the loop, and either had to or wanted to let countries like India negotiate the specifics of the campaign's archaeological work themselves.

This situation played into India's hands, enabling officials to promote the country's archaeological interests. In December 1960, Humayun Kabir, B. B. Lal, and Amalananda Ghosh, the director-general of the ASI, visited Egypt as guests of the country's Ministry of Education.[88] Relationships blossomed and, by February 1961, Ghosh was communicating directly with Anwar Shoukry, director-general of the Egyptian Department of Antiquities. When he did so, he inquired after the Nubian archaeological survey and requested "a list of about half-a-dozen sites which you would suggest for our excavations," pointedly

---

83. Veronese to Kabir, March 30, 1960, "Museums-Nubia-World-Wide Appeal-Offer of Participation-India," UNESCO Archives.
84. Allais, "The Design," 194.
85. Giorgio Rosi to A. Ghosh, October 10, 1960, "Museums-Nubia-World-Wide Appeal-Offer of Participation-India," UNESCO Archives.
86. Thomas to Kabir, November 19, 1960. "Museums-Nubia-World-Wide Appeal-Offer of Participation-India," UNESCO Archives.
87. Allais, "Integrities."
88. Shehata Adam to J. K. Van der Haagen, December 21, 1960, "Museums-Nubia-World-Wide Appeal-Offer of Participation-India," UNESCO Archives.

stating that, "as I told you, we would like . . . a pre-Dynastic [pre-pharaonic] site with an associated cemetery."[89] This request considered, correspondence between UNESCO officials ended up summarizing the process by which the ASI accepted Egypt's offer of a concession at Afyeh.[90] The only control UNESCO retained over the situation was financial, converting Indian rupees into Egyptian pounds to assist the ASI's work.[91] Despite even this power, however, to some extent the organization faced a *fait accompli*. If UNESCO wanted countries like India to take part in the Nubian campaign, these were the conditions under which that participation would happen. Constituting an international campaign under multilateralism involved submitting to national wishes even as the nations involved were embedded in this new form of political "community." And in this instance, it seemed that Egyptian-Indian cultural collaboration could be mobilized in the form of an archaeological project geared toward Indian interests.

The ASI In the Field

At work in Nubia, the ASI team did all it could to strengthen its plausibility as one among many excavating equals: a non-aligned mobile freely at work and a performance calculated to bring later gain. Key to this outcome was routine and the representation of a job well done. True to Mortimer Wheeler's (and archaeology's) own form, this representation was strongly visual. Records from Afyeh adhere not only to longstanding canons of archaeological illustration, but also to styles of illustration promoted by Wheeler himself. UNESCO promoted the Nubian campaign by associating it with technological innovation in recording technique. But much of the actual fieldwork in the region relied on a combination of photographic and drawing methods that had existed for some time, often had colonial precedents, and of which Lal and others were well aware.

Compare Amir Singh's drawing of a grave at Afyeh's neighboring site of Tumas (figure 6.1, more below) with the way in which Wheeler suggested that sections—the vertical sides of an archaeological trench—might be depicted. Singh's schematized illustration, layers delineated through numbering and different types of shading, related to a distinct style of drawing put into practice

---

89. A. Ghosh to Shoukry, February 9, 1961, "Museums-Nubia-World-Wide Appeal-Offer of Participation-India," UNESCO Archives.

90. Louis Christophe to J. K. Van der Haagen, October 2, 1961. "Museums-Nubia-World-Wide Appeal-Offer of Participation-India," UNESCO Archives.

91. Ali Vrioni to Malcolm Adiseshiah, January 23, 1962. "Museums-Nubia-World-Wide Appeal-Offer of Participation-India," UNESCO Archives.

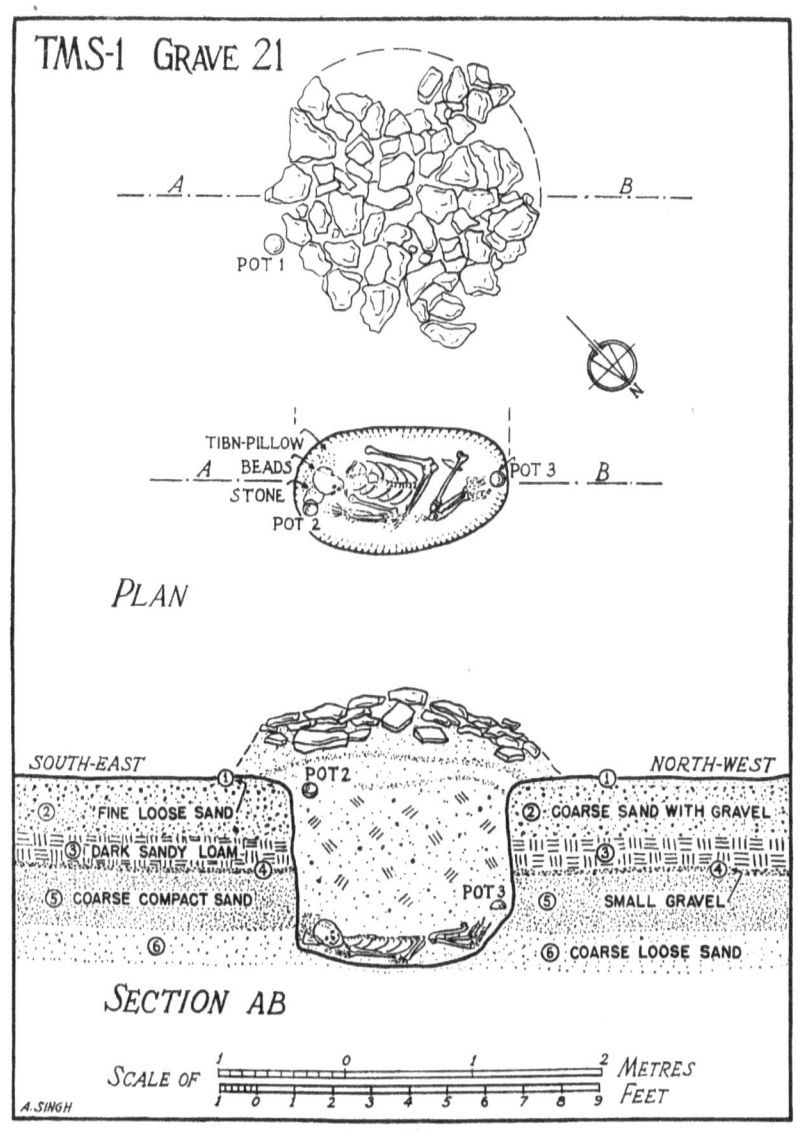

Figure 6.1. Amir Singh's plan and section drawing of a grave at the site of Tumas in Egyptian Nubia, published in *Indian Archaeology 1961–62: A Review*, ed. A. Ghosh (New Delhi: Archaeological Survey of India, 1964), 68.

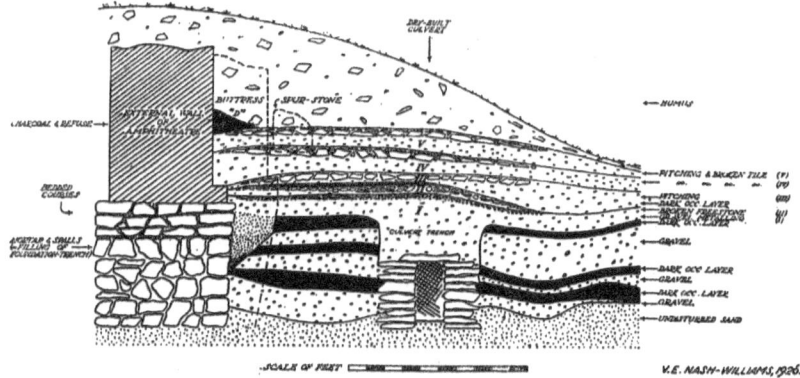

FIGURE 6.2. Wheeler-style stratigraphy, as drawn by Victor Nash-Williams and published in Mortimer Wheeler's *Archaeology from the Earth* (Oxford: Clarendon Press, 1954), fig. 17 ("Stratification in relation to the external wall of the Roman amphitheatre at Caerleon, Monmouthshire, 1926"). Image reproduced by permission of Oxford University Press and Cambridge University Library.

on interwar digs run by Tessa and Mortimer Wheeler and publicized by him in his 1954 book *Archaeology from the Earth* (figure 6.2).[92] Other images drew on wider canons, not least the Orientalist tropes associated with archaeological work in Egypt and the Middle East. Albums held by the ASI in Delhi consciously preserve photographs that often depict "locals" as lending interest and scale.[93] For instance, one photograph (figure 6.3) illustrates a trench whose excavation is apparently complete. A measuring rod stands at the front of the photo, but at the rear is a crouching, unnamed laborer, perhaps with brush or trowel in hand, but more than likely not. Labor in the archaeological field was as much racial as physical, giving the lie to the global impact of UNESCO's race statements.[94]

Gender, intertwined with the politics and practices of modernization projects like the Nubian campaign, played a similar role. Following normative archaeological routine supposedly meant following the heroic, masculine roles set forward by (often former military) men like Wheeler.[95] Decades after the dig at Afyeh finished, Lal took care to note in his autobiography that "my wife [Kusum Lal] volunteered to register the antiquities, prepare cards for them and

---

92. Mortimer Wheeler, *Archaeology from the Earth* (Oxford: Clarendon Press, 1954). For competing methods of archaeological illustration, see Christopher J. Evans, "Archaeology and Modern Times: Bersu's Woodbury 1938 and 1939," *Antiquity* 63 (1989): 436–50.

93. For the relationship of archaeological photography and labor in Egyptian archaeology, see Riggs, "Shouldering."

94. On controversies surrounding those statements, see Selcer, "Beyond the Cephalic Index."

95. For which see Evans, "Soldiering."

FIGURE 6.3. Trench and unnamed laborer at Afyeh. Image reproduced courtesy of the Archaeological Survey of India Photo Archives, New Delhi.

sort out and mark the pottery."[96] True to archaeological convention, however, in his official report on the excavation, Lal only mentions male colleagues as participants: Senior Exploration Assistant K. M. Srivastava; Photographer-Instructor R. Chatterjee; Surveyor-Instructor S. P. Jain; and Draftsman Amir Singh. Kusum Lal is thanked, but because she "had accompanied her husband, the author, on the expedition."[97] Gender frames meant that work in archaeology did not always count as work, and—as elsewhere during the Nubian campaign—the dig at Afyeh did not question this reality.

Conversely, at certain times norms related to field personnel threatened to disrupt the smooth running of field work. This disruption hampered the ASI's ability to act as one among archaeological equals, emphasizing the extent to which creating that impression mattered. Sometimes, this disruption seems minor: at the start of the excavation, Lal complained that the Indian Embassy in Cairo had not recruited a "Stenographer-cum-Accountant" for the project, as

---

96. Lal, *Piecing*, 110.
97. Lal, "Indian Archaeological Expedition," 98. The lack of recognition given to Kusum Lal surprised Amalananda Ghosh, who noted in a memo dated September 29, 1962 and held in ASI; Monuments; file 9/5/5/62–M/1962/Monuments, NAI (ASI Sudan file), that she had "not been mentioned . . . in the report at all!"

had been planned.⁹⁸ At other times, disruption seemed more serious. Throughout the ASI's time in Nubia, a running issue was related to the labor force under the institution's control. Field labor represented a long-term source of anxiety for archaeologists working in Egypt. Yet now those anxieties reached Delhi.

As soon as he arrived in Cairo, Lal wrote to Amalananda Ghosh about "the great discontentment among the members of the staff regarding the very low rates of the daily allowances in Nubia." Describing his ASI charges as "almost-starving," Lal explained that this situation threatened to undermine Egyptian archaeological norms: the Department of Antiquities had told him that excavation staff should be paid double the normal daily allowance when working in Nubia.⁹⁹ But worse than that, a few days later, Lal revealed a further reason for his concern.

> I am enclosing herewith a copy of the correspondence which has passed between me and Dr. Shoukry [sic] regarding the employment of labour and a foreman in Nubia. It will be seen that even a foreman has to be paid at the rate of L.E. 1.50 per day. According to the rates now in force for Nubia . . . I will be getting [sic] at the rate of L.E. 1.75 per day and the other members of the delegation at the rate of L.E. 1.31 per day. Does the Government of India want us to live at the same standard as would the head labourer at the site?¹⁰⁰

Paid less than their laborers, the ASI team's position in a normative racial hierarchy was threatened. Yet try as he might (including sending multiple telegrams from Nubia itself), Lal could not fix the issue.¹⁰¹ The Indian Ministry of Scientific Research and Cultural Affairs (MSRCA), now responsible for the ASI, denied his request to raise his team's field allowances.¹⁰²

Worse still, the ASI had been granted a site concession that, at least given established norms of Egyptian excavation, appeared to give them little chance to display their credibility as archaeologists. That situation further undermined personnel who were by now "greatly upset," making clear their exact place in archaeology's racial hierarchy.¹⁰³ As originally agreed, the concession constituted a small settlement site and some grave tumuli, which the ASI spent about a month excavating.¹⁰⁴ This situation made the secondary importance

---

98. Lal to A. Ghosh, January 26, 1962, ASI Sudan file.
99. Lal to A. Ghosh, January 21, 1962. ASI; Monuments; file 9/5/1/62–M/1962/Monuments, NAI (ASI Afyeh file).
100. Lal to A. Ghosh, January 26, 1962, ASI Afyeh file.
101. Telegrams from Lal to A. Ghosh, February 9 and 26, 1962, ASI Afyeh file.
102. A. K. Ghosh to B. Ch. Chhabra, March 20, 1962, ASI Afyeh file.
103. Lal to A. Ghosh, February 26, 1962, ASI Afyeh file.
104. Lal, "Indian Archaeological Expedition," 99.

of prehistory in Egypt clear and was a cause of some embarrassment. Realizing how quickly the ASI's work might finish, Lal sent a telegram to Ghosh (due to visit Egypt), asking him to: "please plan your visit earliest stop."[105] Again undermining UNESCO's committee structure, Lal also lobbied the Egyptian Department of Antiquities to provide further areas to excavate, apparently "not without great difficulty."[106]

Consequently, Egypt granted the ASI permission to excavate a cemetery site located next to the nearby village of Tumas, which was itself located alongside the Nile terraces in their concession.[107] Notwithstanding that some of this work provided "a great addition to our knowledge of the area," a report from the field indicated the disappointment that the new site was "again a rather small one."[108] Ghosh, in addition to the Indian Ambassador to Egypt, visited the ASI's work, "which gave much encouragement and pleasure to the team."[109] But this valedictory act of witnessing was at best a minor fillip. The ASI now had to labor hard to prove the value of the work they had done to the government that had funded it.

Mobile Pasts, Mobile Futures

The malleability of colonial-era field routine helped to create this proof. As discussed in chapter 3, during their archaeological survey of Egyptian Nubia, Harry Smith and the EES made sites like Afyeh "archaeological" by placing them within a sequential numbering pattern developed during colonial surveys of the region—past work constituted future pasts. Once again asserting the primacy of the nation-state, the interwar survey of Egyptian Nubia had finished at Cemetery 227, and the new, UNESCO-era survey started with Cemetery 228.[110] An additional organizational scheme was developed for the settlements now increasingly of interest to prehistorians, meanwhile. Such sites were registered sequentially, in addition to being given an indicator relating to their periodization: Afyeh was thus recorded as Settlement A5, indicating that the site constituted the fifth settlement surveyed and that the pottery found there indicated an "A-Group" date. Likewise, sequential coding systems

---

105. Lal to A. Ghosh, February 9, 1962, ASI Afyeh file.
106. Report by Lal dated March 28, 1962, ASI Afyeh file.
107. Lal, "Indian Archaeological Expedition," 99.
108. Report by Lal dated March 28, 1962, ASI Afyeh file.
109. Report by Lal dated March 28, 1962.
110. Emery and Kirwan, *The Excavations*, vol. 1. For the UNESCO-era survey, see "Egypt Exploration Society Sondage Survey, Season 1961: Day Book," January 11, 1961.

FIGURE 6.4. Excavated objects from Afyeh marked with site codes. Image reproduced courtesy of the Archaeological Survey of India Photo Archives, New Delhi.

were developed for other facets of Egyptian Nubia: "IT," for instance, meant "Isolated Tumulus."[111] Archaeological routine meant that the survey always already understood Egyptian Nubia as a coherent and bounded whole. The region's past constituted a tangible product of an already existing recording system tied to national and colonial imperatives.[112]

However, as the Nubian campaign's cross-border work began to undermine this perspective, the concentration on routine also played into other national realities. Excavating Afyeh, the ASI's team in fact began to enfold the site within their own organizational schema. Settlement A5 thus became AFH–1, and the ASI renamed other excavated areas, too. As Lal noted, "IT 34 and IT 35, forming more or less a homogeneous lot have been dealt with under a single title, AFH–2."[113] Meanwhile, photos indicate that the team recorded and marked excavated objects with numbers connected to these new site codes (figure 6.4).

---

111. For these systems in action, see Smith, *Preliminary Reports.* Cf. "Site List and Numeration Jan–Mar 1961," EES Archives (folder NUB.005).

112. Even as Smith, *Preliminary Reports,* 3, noted an intention to do so, the maps upon which the EES marked these registration sequences were never published. Instead, they were lodged in Cairo under the authority of the director-general of the Department of Antiquities, further instantiating the Nubian campaign's relationship to Egyptian state power.

113. Lal, "Indian Archaeological Expedition," 99.

The mutability of archaeological sites and excavated things meant that they could be enfolded within organizational frameworks other than those intended, translating them into other jurisdictional schemes. Despite UNESCO's announcement that items considered unnecessary for the "completion" of Egypt's national collections might be exported to other nation-states, the interaction of the ASI's routinized field practices with Egyptian Nubian precedent suggests that other processes were at play in the way that excavated objects—and the pasts that could be connected to them—became mobile. From the moment of excavation, the mutability of the objects dug and recorded by the ASI meant that these things became part of a scheme promoted by the Indian team, one that was at once national and transnational. When the ASI managed to export most of these things from the country, routinization meant that they had long been ready to be part of this "Indian" transnational imaginary.

Given the ASI's regional ambitions, that imaginary unsurprisingly related to Dravidians. The Dravidians had long been a topic of interest in India and elsewhere. Emphasizing the extent to which the specter of racial politics suffused the Nubian campaign, a "Dravidian people" had been assumed since the early twentieth century to have comprised one race with the ancient Sumerians of Mesopotamia, and to have dwelt in both Sumer and the Indus Valley, now part of Pakistan.[114] Post-partition, however, when enquiry into a "Greater India" held particular appeal (as did nods to past civilizational greatness), mobilizing the Dravidians constituted a particularly useful way of justifying the Afyeh work.[115] Just before the ASI team left Egypt, *The Times of India* reported that:

> A fascinating light on the unsolved mystery of the origin of the Dravidians may be thrown by the finds of an Indian archaeological mission which is due to sail home from Alexandria on May 4 with eight crate-loads of rare Egyptian antiquities.
>
> It is known that Dravidians were not the original inhabitants of India—but where did they come from?
>
> Mr. B. Lal, director of the Indian School of Archaeology and leader of the five-man team, believes that his discoveries in Upper Egypt will help establish a significant link between the ancient Nubians of Africa and the early Dravidians of south India.

---

114. Guha, *Artefacts*, 154.
115. For "Greater India" in this context, see Guha, *Artefacts*, 236. On the continued valence of notions of "civilization" at the time, see Abraham, "From Bandung," 199–202.

As the paper related, Lal's belief was based on "several megalithic sites of ancient Nubians which bear an uncanny resemblance to cemeteries of early Dravidians which are found all over western India." While the report cautioned that further research would be necessary to investigate this resemblance, some time had been spent making sure that this research was possible.[116] At the end of March 1962, Lal wrote that "one of the skeletons [from Tumas] has been lifted up in its original form, with a view to transporting it to India, if it is included in the Indian share."[117] A month later, after "a lot of manoeuvring," Egypt permitted that division.[118] The objects from the ASI's Egyptian dig were mutable, made by routine but also by choice. The parameters of the Nubian campaign had offered the chance to make research connected to them possible.

The routine transport of the items from Afyeh back to India made this reality irreversible. Leaving Egypt, the objects constituted excavated items. But by the time they entered India, they constituted displayable, transnational things. On behalf of the ASI, India's MSRCA began a lengthy correspondence working out how to avoid paying customs duty on the objects. The question of what value the items held was central to this conversation. The ASI had already indicated to the ministry that this value should not be financial, solidifying the items' status as fragments of the (transnational) nation. In a memo that avoided denoting any clear identity to the objects and instead listed "antiquities from Nubia brought by the archaeological expedition, govt. of India," the organization assigned each of its eight crates of antiquities with a value of 100 rupees each "for customs purpose only."[119] Yet in order to avoid paying duty even on this nominal amount—to avoid any value being connected to them other than the one the ASI wished to impose—a Ministry of Finance directive insisted that the "antiquities [had to be] intended for exhibition for the public benefit in a museum managed by the Archaeological Survey of India or by a State Government."[120] Although it is unclear if this exhibition ever happened, affirming this purpose was ultimately how the ASI cleared the objects from Egyptian Nubia for import into India. The objects represented the spectacle of the past nation's presumed transnational mobility. But that spectacle also mattered to a contemporary India eager to assert its future mobility in the world.

---

116. K. C. Khanna, "New Light on the Origin of Dravidians," *The Times of India*, April 29, 1962.
117. Report by Lal dated March 28, 1962, ASI Afyeh file.
118. Lal to A. Ghosh, April 22, 1962, ASI Afyeh file.
119. A. Ghosh to the Secretary (i.e., Humayun Kabir), MSRCA, June 6, 1962, ASI Sudan file.
120. Memo from Deputy Secretary, Ministry of Finance, August 2, 1962, ASI Sudan file.

(Inter-)Governmental Reckonings

The spectacle of the past—and the report in *The Times of India*—did their work. On May 14, 1962, even as the dig's objects were in transit, the work at Afyeh was responsible for a minor sensation. Members of the Lok Sabha, the lower house of the Indian parliament, had tabled questions about the dig. Many of those queries were procedural, relating to the costs of the work. But M. K. Kumaran, a member from Kerala, asked Deputy Minister M. M. Das of the MSRCA "whether the report of the Mission throws any light on the probable relationship between the ancient Nubians and the Dravidians of India?" Das told Kumaran that his question was "premature." Not to be deterred, however, Hem Barua, the member for Gauhati in Assam, asked Humayun Kabir whether the work at Afyeh had confirmed either a geophysical or an archaeological "affinity" between India and Egypt. Pressing the matter, Kumaran next asked "whether the Government have got any proposal before them to conduct excavations in south Arabia and southern Iran?" Doing so, he thought, might determine the relationship between ancient Nubians and Dravidians.[121]

A transnational past encouraged a transnational future. Despite the caution expressed in May, parliamentary questioning about the links of the Afyeh objects to Dravidians continued in June. Now, though, the MSRCA and the ASI used this interest to their advantage. Humayun Kabir noted that "unless a great deal of further exploration is undertaken, especially in the intermediate areas [between India and Nubia], we cannot make any firm statements."[122] Further questions—and similar answers—occurred throughout the rest of the year.[123] Away from the Lok Sabha, meanwhile, comments made at the Central Advisory Board for Archaeology in December 1962 emphasized the continued importance of Indian archaeological work abroad. In the presence of Egypt's Cultural Attaché in India, Dr. Riad Eletr, the archaeologist and historian G. R. Sharma of the University of Allahabad "hoped that more foreign expeditions would be organized." Likewise, the historian Niharranjan Ray of the University of Calcutta noted that "the School of Archaeology was a venture in the right direction and should soon develop into an Institute of Archaeology, by and on behalf of which foreign expeditions should be sent out."[124]

---

121. "Starred Question No. 715," May 14, 1962. ASI; Monuments; 21/3/62–M/1962/Monuments, NAI.
122. "Starred Question No. 96," June 19, 1962. ASI; Monuments; 21/3/62–M/1962/Monuments, NAI.
123. For which see records throughout ASI; Monuments; 21/3/62–M/1962/Monuments, NAI.
124. "Minutes of the Eighteenth Meeting of the Central Advisory Board of Archaeology Held on the 23rd December, 1962." ASI; Monuments; 13/6/1/61–M/1961/Monuments, NAI.

CHAPTER 6

The Dravidians had worked their magic. By late 1963, at another Central Advisory Board meeting, a survey of the coastline between Egypt and India was proposed as an ASI project during India's next Five-Year Plan.[125]

As these moves occurred, the relationship between India's national, regional, and global ambitions met its match. The ASI attempted to use India's regional interests to its advantage, but simultaneously found itself undermined by the multilateral structures that had previously allowed it to do so. Alongside the proposed coastline survey, the ASI had started to press its case to return to Nubia. UNESCO, meanwhile, had tried to promote further Indian work in Egypt, but Amalananda Ghosh turned down that possibility on the basis that the "sites [offered] were not even recommended for excavation by the party which had undertaken the preliminary survey work."[126] The Parisian institution's authority continued to be lacking. Yet of far more interest was the excavation of a site on the Sudanese side of the Nubian border. Lal had spent time in Britain after the Afyeh work had ended and, egged on by Mortimer Wheeler, had suggested to Ghosh that work in Sudan was a real possibility.[127] Wheeler was concerned that "in 1964 the waters will begin to rise and it will be too late thereafter to do important work."[128] Ghosh now used Wheeler to make his case to his ministerial overlords, continuing the reassembly of the colonial networks of expertise that Wheeler represented.

Ghosh asked Wheeler to write to Humayun Kabir so that the ASI's proposal might "receive weight" with the minister.[129] Agreeing to Ghosh's request, Wheeler rehashed the sort of expertise-related argument that Kabir himself had made when writing to Vittorino Veronese to discuss the possibility of Egyptian excavation. Wheeler noted that the ASI had "made a splendid impression in Egyptian Nubia," suggesting that the institution might now be considered an archaeological equal to its Euro-American counterparts. He also noted that, because of "a number of very striking Middle Kingdom fortresses" near Wadi Halfa, the ASI should work in Sudanese Nubia. Wheeler claimed that "no archaeological mission could deal with [such sites] more brilliantly . . . in view of . . . [the ASI's] special experience of equivalent structures in India."[130] The ASI's expertise had become a marketable—and mobile—asset, or so Wheeler suggested. The claim persuaded Kabir to send a mission to Sudan provided that certain conditions were met: wanting to know precisely "what

---

125. Note dated October 26, 1963. ASI; Monuments; 9/2/25/63–M/Monuments, NAI.
126. A. Ghosh to Secretary, MSRCA, October 15, 1962, ASI Sudan file.
127. A. Ghosh to Wheeler, June 21, 1962, ASI Sudan file.
128. Wheeler to A. Ghosh, July 9, 1962, ASI Sudan file.
129. A. Ghosh to Wheeler, June 21, 1962, ASI Sudan file.
130. Wheeler to Kabir, July 31, 1962, ASI Sudan file.

the last expedition cost, and what it achieved."[131] Even now, the Nubian campaign's financial equations were difficult to avoid.

Undeterred, the ASI again emphasized the importance of understanding the regional nature of India's past, placing the new project within a well-rehearsed frame. Finance, Ghosh argued, was not an issue: the Afyeh expedition had spent under half the budget available to it, which could now be used to work in Sudan. Moreover, sending an expedition to Sudan would "indeed be in the fitness of things" in terms of playing an equable role in the Nubian campaign. But beyond this claim, what really mattered was not only creating "closer contacts between the Archaeological Survey of Sudan and our Survey," but also determining if there existed "a possible correlation between the C-Group material recently unearthed by our team in Egyptian Nubia and that from the megaliths of south India."[132] A regional past mattered, as did a regional archaeological future. Mobilizing the Dravidians helped to buttress that possibility.

Other issues, however, now made this regional deployment impossible. The short Sino-Indian War of October and November 1962 meant that the Indian government put the ASI mission to Sudan on hold.[133] In the summer of 1963, meanwhile, when the MSRCA revived its proposal to work in the country, the multilateral vagaries of UNESCO's project caught up with India. At first, matters seemed like they would progress easily. That April, Lal had penned an article about Afyeh for *The Illustrated London News*, a leading venue for the publication of archaeological work and a key indicator that the discipline's scientific claims were firmly connected to rather more popular—and deeply visual—means of communication.[134] Wheeler (with, presumably, Ghosh underlining his words) wrote to comment that the article "makes a good show and . . . is a credit to you and to the Indian Government!" Meanwhile, George F. Dales, the curator of the University of Pennsylvania Museum's South Asian Section, wrote that the photos in the article "should prove to be a model for grave excavations for the other expeditions in Nubia."[135] For some, the ASI now stood in a strong position as a regional, if not global, leader in archaeological technique.

---

131. A. K. Ghosh to S. Ramanathan (?), August 7, 1962, ASI Sudan file.
132. Memo written by A. Ghosh, September 29, 1962, ASI Sudan file.
133. Alluded to in Kabir to Wheeler, November 12, 1962, and confirmed in Wheeler to A. Ghosh, November 16, 1962, both in ASI Sudan file.
134. B. B. Lal, "The Only Asian Expedition in Threatened Nubia: Work by an Indian Mission at Afyeh and Tumas," *The Illustrated London News* 242, no. 6455 (April 20, 1963): 579–81. For archaeology and *The Illustrated London News*, see, e.g., Amara Thornton, *Archaeologists in Print: Publishing for the People* (London: UCL Press, 2018).
135. Letters quoted in memo written by A. Ghosh, August 1, 1963. ASI; Monuments; 9/5/2/63–M/1963/Monuments, NAI.

In order, though, that the ASI might work in Sudan, the ministry expected that UNESCO would again provide a foreign exchange facility for India; the country had not made use of the entirety of that amenity during its work in Egypt.[136] Yet by the time in 1964 that India had actually found a site to excavate, no way had been found to put that facility into place. Ali Vrioni of UNESCO sent a hurried telegram apologizing that the organization's comptroller had been unable, so far, to find a way to carry the exchange out, but it is unclear how urgently the organization had treated the request.[137] As negotiations for the funding of the Abu Simbel work show, UNESCO spent a significant amount of time ensuring what has been termed the "calculability" of work in Nubia: in this case "the potential of an architectural project to be incorporated into a project of economic development."[138] But there were times, too, when the organization was unable to make the Nubian campaign calculable. Amalananda Ghosh now had to ask India's Ministry of Education whether they could find a way of providing an exchange facility, even as the sites available in Sudan were "not very good ones."[139] In February 1965, however (with that year's Indo-Pakistan War just around the corner), a ministerial functionary wrote to Ghosh to tell him that "the proposal to send an archaeological delegation this year . . . to Sudanese Nubia is dropped."[140] Even as the UN soon had to mandate a ceasefire between Pakistan and India, multilateralism intervened in the country in yet another way. The game was up.

---

136. Memo written by A. Ghosh, August 1, 1963.
137. Vrioni to Lal, November 25, 1964. ASI; Monuments; 9/5/2/63–M/1963/Monuments, NAI.
138. Allais, "Integrities," 21.
139. A. Ghosh to the Secretary, Ministry of Education, December 3, 1964. ASI; Monuments; 9/5/2/63–M/1963/Monuments, NAI.
140. S. J. Narsian to A. Ghosh, February 3, 1965. ASI; Monuments; 9/5/2/63–M/1963/Monuments, NAI.

CHAPTER 7

Traces of Nubia

Traces of the Nubian campaign are still resonant. UNESCO and the Egyptian and Sudanese governments often worked to give the project a straightforward narrative: the Aswan High Dam flooded Nubia, and by 1980 the salvage and preservation of the region's ancient remains was complete; heritage saved. Yet the temporality of the campaign was never that straightforward. As I have shown, this story elided the complex colonial genealogies of the Nubian work. It also obscured how the project fostered disagreement and controversy. Despite the flood, traces of Nubia remained, revealing the unevenness of the task that took place there.

As the campaign's field teams left Nubia to submerge, so that unevenness became apparent. An early and obvious indication of this situation came in the different names given to the reservoir forming behind the High Dam. Lake Nasser in Egypt and Lake Nubia in Sudan denoted the same place, a body of water divided by an appellation. This disjuncture in naming, however, also echoed how the Nubian campaign's recording practices helped to create a border between the two countries—and the two, newly formed parts of Nubia—that sat at the project's center. Nubia's flooding could not conceal the incoherence of that recording work, nor its populational and cultural violence. As Reinhart Koselleck noted, "whoever seeks to form an impression of historical time in everyday life may notice the ... scars in which a former fate is preserved."[1] By that reckoning, Nubia—even flooded Nubia—was scarred beyond belief, as were the numerous records and objects that constituted the Nubian campaign's legacies.

Archivally or otherwise, these unwanted and unexpected scars constitute the legacies and afterlives of the Nubian campaign: its traces, in other words.[2] Likewise, those traces constitute the notion of heritage that the project has actually helped to produce—and with which Nubians, disaggregated from the campaign itself, have been forced to live. In this context, the double meaning of the Arabic word *āthar* as either "trace" or (as it came to develop in the mid-nineteenth century) "antiquity" and "monument" is meaningful and worthy of emphasis: the excavation and (re-) constitution of antiquities and monuments during the campaign has left scars and traces in ways that Nubians and others continue to deal with.[3]

Coupled with images of the High Dam's floodwaters, the Nubian campaign's spectacle ultimately helped to constitute UNESCO's notion of heritage as one related to threat: to a certain type of ancient monument above all else. But the traces of those two projects also constituted other, unexpected heritages, not least in the form of later interventions related to that earlier work. Such traces started to become visible throughout the 1970s not only as the High Dam's reservoir reached capacity, but also as the campaign entered its later stages with the movement and reassembly of the Egyptian temple complex of Philae. And all of this took place as Egypt and Sudan adapted to national, regional, and global political change. In Sudan, the presidency of Jaʿfar Numayri, which began in 1969, saw shifting political imperatives across the decade. Egyptians, meanwhile, dealt not only with the 1967 *naksa* ("setback") of the Arab-Israeli war, but also grappled with the death of Nasser in September 1970 and the ensuing presidency of Anwar al-Sadat. Sadat's presidency saw both changing economic policy and a shift in national geopolitical alignment toward the United States. Debates about heritage played into these changes in more ways than one. They also did so in forms far beyond those that UNESCO imagined, particularly as both countries attended to what became known as the Islamic revival: a turn to Islam that began as a reaction to 1967 and the failures of post-independence states and gained further traction

---

1. Reinhart Koselleck, *Futures Past: On the Semantics of Historical Time*, trans. and with an introduction by Keith Tribe (1985; repr., New York and Chichester: Columbia University Press, 2004), 1.

2. As Nassar, "Where the Dust," notes in reflecting upon her archival work in Cairo, Carolyn Steedman is correct "about history never going away," for which see Steedman, *Dust* (Manchester: Manchester University Press, 2001).

3. For this semantic change, see Colla, *Conflicted*, 128.

after the 1979 Iranian revolution.[4] Understanding the florescence of such consequences sits at the heart of this chapter, in addition to understanding how those outcomes enabled continued interventions in—and re-definitions of—heritage itself, whether from above or below. Traces left their marks, whether intended or not.

World Heritage?

Nubia's unwanted traces became tangible even in the most overt manifestation of UNESCO's success, further cleaving the gap that had opened between Egypt and Sudan with the flooding of the region. In 1979, the year before the Nubian campaign finished, UNESCO added the second set of citations to its new World Heritage List.[5] Among the entries was the "Nubian Monuments from Abu Simbel to Philae," alongside citations for other sites and monumental landscapes in Egypt: the town and monastery complex at Abu Mena, near Alexandria, "Ancient Thebes with its Necropolis," "Historic Cairo," and "Memphis and its Necropolis—the Pyramid Fields from Giza to Dahshur."[6] Sadat's Egypt was riding the wave of Euro-American (but certainly not Arab) praise that had arrived with the signing of the Camp David Accords in 1978 and the joint award of the Nobel Peace Prize to the Egyptian president and Menachem Begin of Israel. Consequently, Egypt now leveraged its role in the development of World Heritage into a substantive position in the project's early pantheon, ensuring that an enticing and legislatively representative cross-section of its patrimony entered UNESCO's nascent program. The cited sites chimed with the various categorizations of the past enshrined in Egypt's antiquities law, and to which tourist itineraries were directed: pharaonic, Coptic, and Islamic monuments representing the nation.[7]

Put differently, in 1979, Egypt was home to just under one-twelfth of the planet's fifty-seven World Heritage sites.[8] The country's government also emphasized what sort of sphere it saw such heritage as connected with. Under

---

4. For a longer *durée* introduction to the notion of *iḥyā* ("revival"), see As'ad Abou Khalil and Mahmoud Haddad, "Revival and Renewal," in *The Oxford Encyclopedia of the Islamic World*, accessed October 15, 2020, http://www.oxfordislamicstudies.com/article/opr/t236/e0682#bibHead1.
5. The first listings had arrived in 1978; the 1972 World Heritage Convention itself only came into force in 1975. On ratification, see Meskell, *A Future*, 68. For the list itself, see UNESCO, "World Heritage List."
6. UNESCO, "World Heritage List."
7. Categorizations described in Reid, *Whose* and *Contesting*.
8. UNESCO, "World Heritage List."

Sadat, Egypt had realigned from the Soviet Union toward the United States. After the October 1973 Arab-Israeli War, which saw the country establish a foothold east of the Suez Canal, Egypt had also started to undergo a process termed *infitāḥ* (literally "opening," but more commonly the "open door"): a move toward private investment from both Gulf and Western sources and away from the socialist policies and import substitution put into place under Nasser.[9] This process, starting in 1974, meant that culture could be used to make Egypt emblematic of the secularized, liberal-universalist ideals that UNESCO's World Heritage concept ultimately promoted (which ideals, by the late 1970s, were becoming embroiled in the global move to neoliberalism).[10] When, in 1980, the Philae complex was inaugurated at its new home on the island of Agilkia, the ceremony took place in the presence of the Cairo Symphony Orchestra, who played music by Beethoven and Grieg alongside Dvořák's ninth symphony ("From the New World"). The Egyptian soprano (and Dean of the Higher Institute of Arabic Music in Cairo) Ratiba al-Hifni performed songs by Mozart. And these engagements took place in the presence of "Egypt's first lady" (*sayiddat Miṣr al-ūlā*), Jihan al-Sadat.[11]

"The world" may have been present at the ceremony, as one report put it.[12] Egypt's changing geopolitical alignment, however, meant its officials now attempted to prosecute a particular representation of that planet, even as Anwar al-Sadat was dead—assassinated—the following year ("I have killed pharaoh," declared his assassin, the Islamist army officer Khalid al-Islambuli).[13] Ironically, UNESCO's own changing leadership at the time saw an organization that had helped to spread such liberal universalism begin to clash with the Western countries who often promoted themselves as that form of thinking's

---

9. For one account of the *infitāḥ* and its genealogies, see Malak Zaalouk, *Power, Class, and Foreign Capital in Egypt: The Rise of the New Bourgeoisie* (London: Zed, 1989).

10. As Jessica Winegar, *Creative Reckonings: The Politics of Art and Culture in Contemporary Egypt* (Stanford, CA: Stanford University Press, 2006), 148, notes, under Sadat the scale of the Nasser-era Ministry of Culture's activities was downsized "as part of a larger attempt to create a new kind of neoliberal citizen subjectivity—one that did not depend on the government but was accountable to it, and one that was flexible and mobile but also allegiant to the nation." As she discusses on p. 150, Sadat at one point called for the ministry's dissolution. Under Nasser, the Ministry of Culture was no less geared toward UNESCO-style universalisms, as the Nubian campaign evidences. Nor did the institution disavow European high culture. The Philae inauguration, however, took place in a changing ministerial context.

11. Ahmad Abu Kaf, "Izis Tatajala 'ala Ibna'iha" ["Isis presents herself to her children"], *al-Musawwar* 2892, March 14, 1980.

12. Ahmad Abu Kaf, "Al-'Alim . . . Yazifu Izis ila 'Arsh al-Jadid" ["The world conducts Isis to her new throne"], *al-Musawwar* 2893, March 21, 1980.

13. As Arthur Goldschmidt, *Biographical Dictionary of Modern Egypt* (Boulder, CO, and London: Lynne Rienner, 2000), 90, notes, Khalid al-Islambuli, one of whose motivations for the assassination was opposition to Camp David, was a member of one of the groups that became al-Jihad al-Islamiyya al-Misriyya (Egyptian Islamic Jihad). Under Sadat, neoliberal state culture coupled with the pharaonic in a way that pitted it against the wider Islamic revival.

FIGURE 7.1. Sudan National Museum, Khartoum. Photograph courtesy of Julie Anderson.

vanguard. The 1974 appointment of Senegal's Amadou-Mahtar M'Bow as UNESCO's director-general, coupled with fear of the increasing influence of Global South countries within the organization, ultimately led to the Reagan administration's withdrawal of US funding to UNESCO in 1984.[14] Egypt, though, continued to preach the UNESCO cultural mission.

Forgetting Sudan?

Heritage did not always leave such obvious traces. In Sudan, official interest in the concept seemed to dwindle even as the country's northern neighbor courted UNESCO with some zeal. A promising start, perhaps, the (UNESCO-supported) National Museum in Khartoum finally opened on May 25, 1971 (figure 7.1). In its garden stood temples from the Nubian sites of Aksha, Buhen, and Semna East and West, along with various other monumental objects recovered during UNESCO's campaign. Yet this collection of monuments did not receive any sort of World Heritage citation. Possibly this lack of recognition occurred because the temples had been moved far from their original locations. Yet given that UNESCO had encouraged the movement of Egyptian Nubian temples abroad—and also ignored how the remaining temples in Egypt had been clustered away from their original sites—a rather questionable

---

14. Meskell, *A Future*, 197.

double-standard would have been at play.[15] Indeed, the International Council on Monuments and Sites (ICOMOS) advisory document for the "Nubian Monuments from Abu Simbel to Philae" explicitly counters the argument that the Egyptian sites were spaced too broadly apart for inclusion on the World Heritage List.[16]

The more likely cause of this disparity, as Cornelia Kleinitz emphasizes, is that the nomination of World Heritage sites constituted a state-led process.[17] Sudan, however, constituted a state in some degree of turmoil. Political conditions in the country were such that the UNESCO notion of heritage did not necessarily constitute a national priority. In October 1964, the government of Ibrahim ʿAbbud had fallen. A period of civilian rule followed, during which fieldwork in Nubia continued: when Bill and Nettie Adams left the country in 1966, UNESCO continued to fund the work of Anthony Mills, who had been conducting archaeological survey in the southern part of Sudanese Nubia since the pair had returned to Khartoum to work on finds. Mills continued in the field until 1969.[18] That year—after four years of fractious parliamentary governance under the presidency of the returned Ismaʿil al-Azhari—a second Sudanese military coup (which became known as the May Revolution) saw the rise to power of Colonel Jaʿfar Numayri.

Numayri's ascension to the presidency would see, at least during his first few years, the implementation of socialist and pan-Arab policies. Administrative autonomy would also be granted to southern Sudan through the Addis Ababa Agreement of 1972.[19] Heritage played its part in this shift. The May 1971 opening of Khartoum's National Museum came on the second anniversary of Numayri's rise to power and became attached to the same revolutionary rhetoric: the institution's inauguration constituted one of a number of celebratory events that day, among them the opening of the Second Festival of Youth and the opening of the Exhibition of the Economic Revolution.[20] The same year, Negm El-Din Mohammed Sherif, now director of the Sudan Antiquities Service, authored a book, in Arabic, about *The Salvage of Nubia's Antiquities*; the frontispiece was a picture of Numayri in uniform that captioned

---

15. See Allais, "The Design," 204–205.
16. ICOMOS, "The Nubian Monuments from Abu Simbel to Philae," (Paris: ICOMOS, 1979), 4–5, https://whc.unesco.org/document/154507.
17. Kleinitz, "Between Valorisation," 437–38.
18. David Edwards, "The Archaeological Survey of Sudanese Nubia (ASSN) 1963–1969," n.d., accessed October 16, 2020, https://www2.le.ac.uk/departments/archaeology/research/projects/archaeological-survey-of-sudanese-nubia-assn-1963-1969.
19. For one overview of Sudanese political history in this period, see Collins, *A History*, 69–156.
20. "Al-Ihtifal bi-l-ʿAid al-Awwal li-l-Thawra al-Iqtisadiyya" ["Celebrations for the first anniversary of the economic revolution"], *al-Ayyam*, May 25, 1971.

him as "patron of the Sudanese heritage" (rāʿī al-turāth al-Sūdānī).²¹ Despite constant political transition, UNESCO's work in Sudan and official enthusiasm for it had, falteringly, managed to continue: traces of the Nubian campaign clearly visible as it became enfolded within the new revolutionary imaginary. Yet from 1976 onwards, Numayri's rule and the country that it created "would relentlessly disintegrate without the slightest token of remorse from his subjects," ultimately leading to another coup and the removal of the president in 1985.²² The initial nomination of World Heritage sites elsewhere would take place as this process of disintegration occurred.

Nubia and World Heritage went by the wayside as Numayri's regime grappled with Sudan's south and the rise of political Islam in the country, not to mention other, more general, dissent. Consequently, Sudan did not exploit the forms of heritage constituted by the Nubian campaign. The country ratified the World Heritage Convention in 1974.²³ Yet Sudan's first successful nomination to the World Heritage List, "Gebel Barkal and the Sites of the Napatan Region," would arrive only in 2003, and the imperatives of heritage practice have since faced considerable resistance from parts of the Sudanese population threatened by renewed dam construction in the country.²⁴

To be clear, UNESCO did not do Sudan any favors. As discussed previously, archaeologists have long derided the organization for its lack of focus on the country during the Nubian campaign (not to mention archaeology itself), and an organizational inability to cope with the demands of archaeological fieldwork manifested itself in relation to Sudan quite clearly. In 1970, Ali Vrioni, director of UNESCO's Division for the Preservation and Development of Cultural Heritage (and formerly director of the organization's Monuments of Nubia Service), wrote to Alexander Dunbar of the Calouste Gulbenkian Foundation. Dunbar had written requesting more details about an application from Anthony Mills for funding to work on the publication of the material collected during his survey: why, Dunbar wondered, couldn't UNESCO cover the costs?²⁵ Vrioni wrote that "it is true that the considerable and various

---

21. Negm El-Din Mohammed Sherif, *Inqadh Athar al-Nuba* [The salvage of Nubia's antiquities] (Khartoum: Matbaʿat al-Tamaddun, 1971).
22. Collins, *A History*, 123–24.
23. UNESCO, "States Parties Ratification Status," n.d., accessed October 19, 2020, https://whc.unesco.org/en/statesparties/.
24. For that resistance, see, e.g., Kleinitz, "Between Valorisation." For Gebel Barkal, see UNESCO, "Gebel Barkal and the Sites of the Napatan Region," n.d., accessed October 19, 2020, https://whc.unesco.org/en/list/1073/.
25. Dunbar to Vrioni, October 14, 1970. Folder 069 (62) N: 930.26 (624) (Part 7): "Museums-Egypt-Nubia-Excavations-Sudan," UNESCO Archives. On Gulbenkian, whose oil wealth powered his foundation and who had some taste for Egyptian antiquities, see Jonathan Conlin, *Mr Five Per Cent: The Many Lives of Calouste Gulbenkian, the World's Richest Man* (London: Profile, 2019).

244   CHAPTER 7

material collected during so many years in Sudanese Nubia is not ready for publication but Unesco [sic] has no means for appointing somebody for this task." Adhering to the notion that UNESCO was only ever providing funding for experts like Mills in what were officially Sudanese government posts, Vrioni claimed that "as for the publication, Unesco can not [sic] have plans for it: it will be done by the Sudanese government itself."[26] The state needed to do more.

Anthony Mills did in fact remain in Sudan after 1969, first on a brief contract extension funded by UNESCO, and then on a fixed-term contract funded by the Sudan Antiquities Service itself.[27] Attempting—and failing—to find more funding for Mills from the UN Development Program, however, UNESCO struggled to continue paying for his position even as it did manage to finance a Polish conservator, Stanisław Jasiewicz, to work on the frescoes excavated at Faras in preparation for the opening of Khartoum's National Museum. In a post that had always been paid for from an under-financed UNESCO budget (and not from Nubian campaign funds more generally), there was not enough cash—and not enough interest from the campaign's Executive Committee, then dealing with the start of work at Philae—to pay for what seemed to be two separate projects.[28] Discussing those projects in an October 1970 letter to UNESCO Director-General René Maheu, Sudan's Minister of Public and Higher Education Dr. Mohi al-Din Saber had in fact noted "the shortage of funds in the [organization's] Cultural Department."[29] Yet UNESCO, beholden to a funding and committee structure established for what it had initially envisaged as a monumental preservation campaign in Egypt, simply could not find a way to deal with the issue. Archaeology in Sudan lost, even as Khartoum's new museum—the sort of project of far more interest to UNESCO in this era—gained.[30] Meanwhile, the Mills survey remains partially unpublished.[31] The Nubian campaign's scars remain valent.

---

26. Vrioni to Dunbar, October 20, 1970. Folder 069 (62) N: 930.26 (624) (Part 7), UNESCO Archives.

27. Jaime Renart to Manuel Jimenez, March 15, 1971; Louis Christophe to Jaime Renart dated May 21, 1979 (but presumably written May 21, 1971). Folder 069 (62) N: 930.26 (624) (Part 7), UNESCO Archives.

28. Emphasized by UNESCO, "International Campaign to Save the Monuments of Nubia: Executive Committee; Eighteenth Session, Paris, 3–4 December, 1970," UNESCO/NUBIA/18, March 22, 1971, resolution III.

29. Saber to Maheu, October 30, 1970. Folder 069 (62) N: 930.26 (624) (Part 7), UNESCO Archives.

30. Allais, *Designs*, 173–217.

31. A first volume about the survey has recently appeared, for which see David Edwards, ed., *The Archaeological Survey of Sudanese Nubia, 1963–69: The Pharaonic Sites* (Oxford: Archaeopress, 2020).

Publishing Time

Publishing the traces of the Nubian campaign took time. The archival work meant to enable that act itself constituted a temporally complex and far from straightforward set of processes. Yet publication of excavations in Nubia had been fraught since the campaign began. In chapter 2, I discussed how, in 1963, Louis Christophe expressed his concern about the lack of up-to-date reports he had received on the fieldwork taking place in Egypt. That problem, though, was not easily resolved. Archaeologists had long placed an emphasis on speedy publication as a means of highlighting not only their professionalism, but also the empirical credibility of the knowledge that they created. In the case of Nubia, that prodigious self-image dissipated in the face both of UNESCO's lack of support for such work and due to a collision between representation and reality. Traces of the campaign lingered, despite statements that they should not.

The British archaeologist Flinders Petrie, whose excavation reports on work in Egypt often appeared swiftly (aided by, among others, the archaeologist, anthropologist, and folklorist Margaret Murray), once claimed that it was "imperative not only to record, but also to publish, the facts observed."[32] Doing so, Petrie used the phrase "at the moment that a fact is before the eye," as if archaeological facticity was a primordial quality.[33] This emphasis on the retrieval of empirical—inherently observable and *real*—data enjoyed a clear florescence in Nubia, not least at CEDAE and in the Sudanese archaeological archive. But the haste of the campaign, coupled with the reality that archaeologists—George Reisner, for example—had never entirely practiced what some of them preached, meant that dissemination of the work often took considerable time.[34] Perhaps more than other instances given the sheer amount of fieldwork that had taken place, the past that the Nubian campaign was meant to recover and preserve was constituted *post hoc* as archaeologists slowly set to work on the publications meant to report it.

This temporal disjunction has had consequences. Lynn Meskell has adroitly described the dislocation of archaeological work from UNESCO after the Nubian field surveys and the lack of an obvious place for archaeology within

---

32. Petrie, *Methods*, 49. On Murray, see Kathleen L. Sheppard, "Margaret Alice Murray and Archaeological Training in the Classroom: Preparing 'Petrie's Pups,'" in Carruthers, *Histories of Egyptology*, 113–28.

33. Petrie, *Methods*, 49.

34. Crawford, "People," 8, discusses Reisner's "records, now being prepared for publication" six years after his death in 1942. Much of the unpublished archival material from Reisner's work is now available via Harvard University's *Digital Giza* website, n.d., accessed March 22, 2021, http://giza.fas.harvard.edu/.

UNESCO's departmental structure.³⁵ Yet in the context of this uneasy temporality, that rupture—and the often-polemical relationship that emerged between the discipline and the organization—might seem just as much due to the cost of preparing publications than the result of the bureaucratic issues that Meskell notes. Attempting to turn the halting, if consistent, release of printed material related to the Nubian campaign to its advantage, in 1977 UNESCO published a bibliography of the more than seven hundred books and articles related to the project that Louis Christophe knew to be in existence. As Amadou-Mahtar M'Bow noted in his preface, the publication "placed the magnitude of the campaign in a new light."³⁶ Emphasizing that magnitude, though, did not dispel the fact that, as UNESCO's commitment to Sudan wavered, no new issue of *Kush* saw press between 1968 (volume XV) and 1993 (volume XVI).³⁷ Nor did it dispel the fact that some publications only saw the light of day long after the campaign ended in 1980—if they ever appeared at all. Anthony Mills is not the only person whose work in Nubia remains unpublished: publication of the work of the Chicago OI, as the institution itself states, is "near completion," but ongoing.³⁸ Traces can linger, especially without financial support (and also when people die: Keith Seele, who directed Chicago's Nubian effort, passed away in 1971).³⁹

In contrast, the temporal vagaries of publication have also constituted an opportunity for archaeologists involved in the Nubian campaign. Beyond the obvious contrasts between CEDAE and Adams's Sudan archive, field notes often reveal that practices employed by archaeologists on the ground in Nubia were not all that dissimilar. It was only during the process of publication that such differences started to become manifest, the lingering traces of archaeological work mobilizing strategic practice. Archaeological publication has always been a form of artifice, as Christina Riggs has shown in relation to the manipulation of photos of Egypt's Valley of the Kings.⁴⁰ It should be little surprise that the Nubian campaign was not immune to such craftiness: photographs of the project in Yale's Peabody Museum archive, for example, are covered in marks used to crop

---

35. Meskell, *A Future*, 46.
36. Amadou-Mahtar M'Bow, "Préface," in *Campagne internationale de l'Unesco pour la sauvegarde des sites et monuments de Nubie: bibliographie*, prepared by Louis-A. Christophe (Paris: UNESCO, 1977), 6–7.
37. Egypt's long-running *Annales du Service des antiquités de l'Égypte*, started in 1900, did not do much better. Published annually until 1952, its appearance became much more irregular: from 1952 until 1979, only twelve volumes appeared.
38. "The Nubia Salvage Project," n.d., accessed October 19, 2020, https://oi.uchicago.edu/research/projects/nubia-salvage-project.
39. "The Nubia Salvage Project."
40. Riggs, "Photography."

FIGURE 7.2. Crop marks on a photo from the Yale-Penn expedition to Arminna West. Archive of the Yale Peabody Museum of Natural History, Division of Anthropology, ANTAR.035578, Arminna West Archive.

the images for publication (figure 7.2). Yet the delayed appearance of reports on the campaign is interesting because it allows rumination on how prosaic much of the project's fieldwork was in relation to the rhetorical claims made by its progenitors. Beyond CEDAE's documentary fetish and workaday interactions with index cards, the campaign's participants utilized other material of archaeological recording: field diaries, notebooks, plans, and other paperwork helped to make the project a documentary phenomenon. That documentation enabled the production of a particular vision of "authentic" Nubia and the physical and bibliographic reassembly of the region in Egypt, Sudan, and elsewhere, even as that documentation was itself largely banal.

Archaeologists might have asserted methodological novelty, but the difference between their field notes could be slight at best. For example, the archive from the site of Kulubnarti in Sudan, at which Bill Adams (now employed by the University of Kentucky) directed excavations in 1969, is strikingly similar to archival material from the EES's dig at Buhen. That similarity persists, moreover, despite Adams's professed interest in the sort of questions about cultural difference—and differences between archaeology in Egypt and Sudan—that he thought had eluded Egypt-focused archaeologists such as Bryan Emery, the Buhen work's director.[41] The dig at Kulubnarti represented a failed attempt to trace an archaeological transition between Christianity and Islam by looking at multiple phases of the same, apparently promising, settlement site.[42] That Kulubnarti had been a settlement, meanwhile, indeed distinguished it from many of the other sites dug by archaeologists in Nubia over the years: the concentration on cemeteries in the region had been overwhelming, as Adams and others often pointed out.[43] Yet the mundanity and process of daily work recorded in diaries from both these—and most other—sites excavated in Nubia is categorically similar, whether in terms of the vehicle in which such information was recorded or in the sorts of comments within it. Adams's team "continued clearing surface level" on January 13, 1969.[44] Emery's laborers at Buhen, though, were "still clearing Square J10" on November 22, 1962.[45] Perhaps the two men harbored different thoughts about the purpose of their work. But it is hard to discern such differences in the paper mechanics of excavation. Bearing in mind that such paperwork is always already manufactured, traces of the past had to be manufactured again (and later) or else run the risk of seeming uncannily familiar.

Indeed, the on-the-ground priorities of both excavations often seem strikingly alike. Adams's notes from Kulubnarti site 21–S–2 (a "late Christian and possibly post-Christian village, citadel and church") constitute a master-class in the sort of architectural planning that Emery was involved in at Buhen (a practice that itself followed the work of the many architecturally inclined archaeologists who had excavated in Egypt over the years).[46] Architectural descriptions and reconstructions, not to mention sections and plans of various architectural layers, littered the notebooks from Kulubnarti in much the same way as they did at Emery's site (compare figures 7.3 and 7.4). Fieldwork in Nubia, then, constituted as much a shared practice of architectural empiricism

---

41. Adams, *Nubia*, 6. Cf. Adams, *The Road*, 148.
42. On this failure, see Adams, *The Road*, 201–08.
43. Adams, *The Road*, 147.
44. "W. Y. Adams Kulubnarti Excavation Diary 1969," January 13, 1969. Kulubnarti Archives, Department of Egypt and Sudan, British Museum.
45. "Day-Book: Sudan, 1962–63," November 22, 1962, EES Archives.
46. William Y. Adams, "21–S–2, Kulubnarti, Adams–I," 2. Kulubnarti Archives. On the architectural perspective in Egyptian archaeology, see Carruthers, "Visualizing."

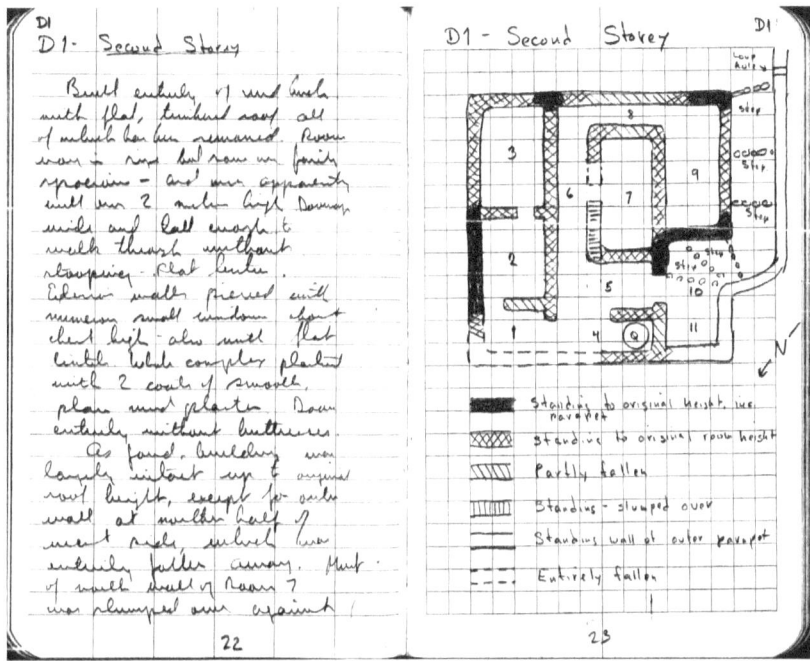

FIGURE 7.3. A page showing the intertwined relationship between text and architectural image in William Y. Adams's notebook "21–S–2, Kulubnarti, Adams–I," 22–23. Kulubnarti Archives, Department of Egypt and Sudan, British Museum. Photo courtesy of the Trustees of the British Museum.

as it did a practice of asking certain types of questions about what was uncovered. If there was a difference in such practice, it came in the writing up of notes, a process that happened sometimes long after participants had left "the field" and entered their offices, often thousands of miles away.[47] Moreover, even that process did not always promote the differences that it claimed, sometimes leaving traces in other, more disturbing, ways.

Traces of Race

The Nubian campaign took place not only after Egypt and Sudan had gained independence, but also as new nation-states came into being across the rest of Africa and the world. In the early 1960s, as much of the campaign's fieldwork happened, this process not only became much more rapid, but also solidified into one with a clear name and identity as "an all but inevitable stage

---

47. On which cf. Clifford, "Notes."

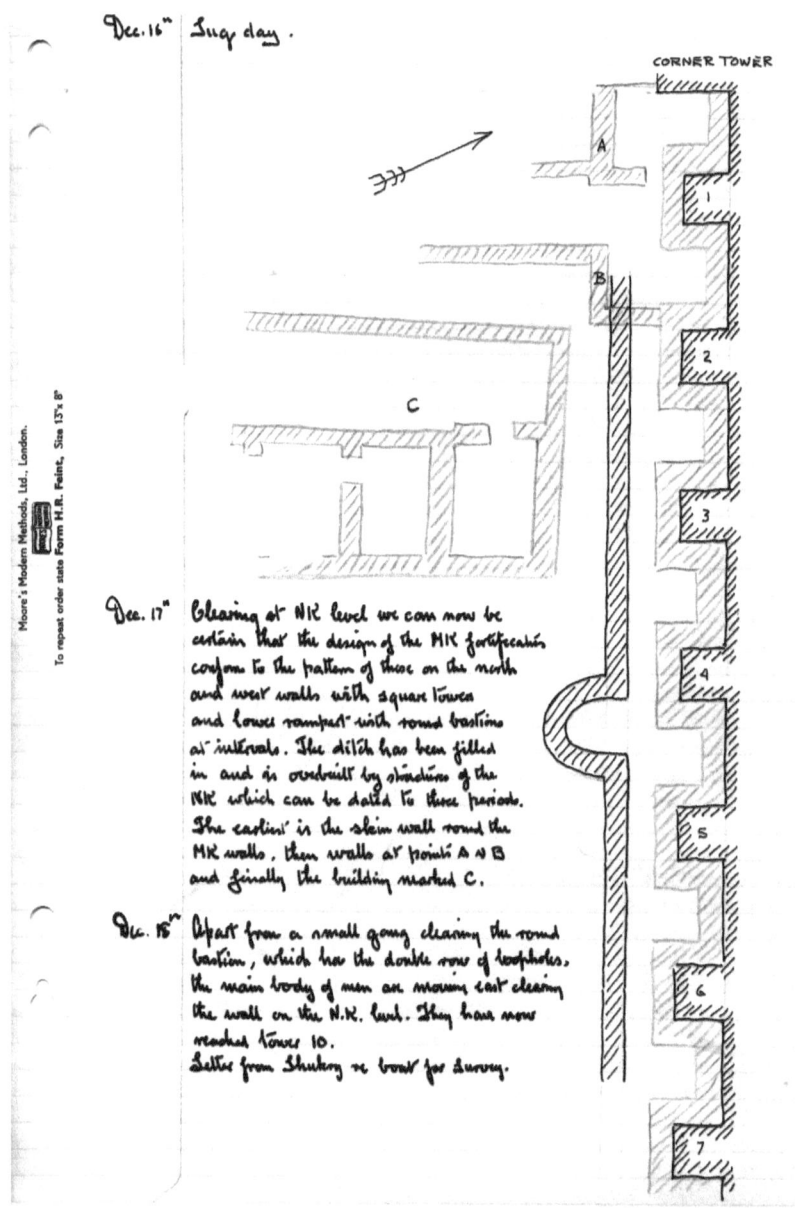

FIGURE 7.4. A page showing the intertwined relationship between text and architectural image in Bryan Emery's "E.E.S. Day-Book: Sudan, 1960–61." Courtesy of the Egypt Exploration Society (Egypt Exploration Society Archives BUH.001).

in the tide of History."⁴⁸ As Todd Shepard has argued, around this time—and particularly during French discussions about how to end the Algerian War of Independence—the term "decolonization" gained a *telos* "wholly consistent with a narrative of progress . . . [and] the ongoing extension of national self-determination."⁴⁹ This process emphasized the nation-state as the basic unit of global governance, impacting the Nubian campaign through the manner in which Egypt and Sudan were treated separately during the work. It also baked traces of that form of political organization deep into the project's field practices through the involvement, for instance, of the excavating teams from newly independent Ghana and India. Conversely, decolonization took place at the same time as geographies beyond the nation-state took shape: non-aligned, pan-African, and Afro-Asian among them. Ironically, it was at the intersection of such processes that interpretation of records made during the Nubian campaign coupled with traces of a colonial genealogy that had long been entangled with Nubia.

In 1964, UNESCO's General Conference authorized the organization's Director-General René Maheu "to take the necessary measures for the preparation and publication of a *General History of Africa*."⁵⁰ Given the Nubian campaign's geographical focus, it was clear that the project and its results could contribute to this new action, which itself chimed with UNESCO's numerous statements decrying racism (published in 1950, 1951, 1964, and 1967).⁵¹ Yet the intertwining of the Nubian campaign with UNESCO's universalist, antiracist rhetoric can hardly be taken at face value. Notably, arguments raged around the extent to which (ancient) Egypt might be considered African, even as multiple authorities argued that Nubia itself could at least partially be attached to that identity. For some, the possibility that Egypt was African was empirically impossible. For others, an entire concept of civilization was under attack.

During the campaign, some participants continued to propagate the racial understanding of Nubia familiar from earlier archaeological efforts in the region, despite UNESCO's work on race. Perhaps the most prominent proponent of such understanding was Bryan Emery. In 1965, the year after fieldwork in Egyptian Nubia ended, London's Hutchinson and Company published Emery's *Egypt in Nubia*.⁵² Emery's adherence to racial (and racist) narratives about Nubia was far

---

48. Shepard, *The Invention*, 6.
49. Shepard, *The Invention*, 6.
50. UNESCO, "Foreword: Preparation of a *General History of Africa*." In *The Peopling of Ancient Egypt and the Deciphering of the Meroitic Script: Proceedings of the Symposium Held in Cairo from 28 January to 3 February 1974*, ed. UNESCO (Paris: UNESCO, 1978), 5.
51. Noted by Nicole Blanc, "The Peopling of the Nile Valley South of the Twenty-Third Parallel," in UNESCO, *The Peopling*, 38–39. For UNESCO's race statements, see UNESCO, *Four Statements*.
52. Walter Bryan Emery, *Egypt in Nubia* (London: Hutchinson, 1965), republished in the United States as *Lost Land Emerging* (New York: Charles Scribner's Sons, 1967).

from subtle, and this new publication did little to alter his position. In the book, Emery described ancient Nubia explicitly in terms of a contest for racial primacy. The region, he said, was the location of "the struggle between the black and white peoples for the supremacy of North Africa."[53] Emery framed this struggle as one that took place between Egypt and northern Sudan, never entirely defining them as such but implying that the Egyptians were white and the northern Sudanese black. "The Egyptians, representing the highest civilization at that time," he argued, "were pushing south to exploit the gold mines and to trade in ivory, precious woods and the other products of Kush, which was the ancient name of the northern Sudan." In the meantime, "the people of the south, whose culture we are beginning to realize through recent excavations and research was by no means negligible, were pushing north."[54] This conflict seemed to suggest that Nubia, ancient and modern, was not quite as white as Egypt, because "in a land which suffered so much foreign invasion considerable racial admixture is inevitable." To that day, meanwhile, it was possible that "the modern Nubian is in large part descended from the people who lived in this part of the Nile valley in the days of the Middle Kingdom pharaohs."[55] Emery's understanding of Nubia revolved around arguments about populational and racial invasions that had a long genealogy and that placed race—and racial hierarchy—as central to the region and its relationship with Egypt.

Other participants in the Nubian campaign started to occlude this racial theorizing, promoting Nubia's "history as a highway" and the relationship with Egypt that such a geography suggested. Perhaps most notably, Bill Adams's *Nubia: Corridor to Africa*, published in 1977, not only asserted this position in its title, but also turned to (material) culture as a means of understanding how Nubia's population had remained relatively stable. Adams stated that earlier racial thinking was "supported by a web of historical fantasy which has been woven around it, [meaning that] the theory survives long after the demolition of its empirical underpinnings."[56] He was not alone in making such statements: in 1965, Bruce Trigger had noted in his *History and Settlement in Lower Nubia* that the region "stood astride the main line of communication between Egypt and the Near East and Africa south of the Sahara."[57] Both Trigger and Adams, meanwhile, came to the respective conclusions that "the resulting population is one that can only be described as Nubian,"[58] and that "Nubia

---

53. Emery, *Egypt in Nubia*, 15.
54. Emery, *Egypt in Nubia*, 15.
55. Emery, *Egypt in Nubia*, 17.
56. Adams, *Nubia*, 93.
57. Trigger, *History*, iii.
58. Trigger, *History*, 17.

has always had an African or part-African population different from that of Egypt."[59]

Yet this double move—and its accompanying turn to cultural markers and their embodiment in material culture, not race or physical anthropology—was not universally followed, helping to create the conditions for controversies that now occurred. For one, racialized language continued to appear in relation to Nubia, even as scholars attempted to move beyond race as an analytical category. As Perrin Selcer has discussed, "the well-noted irony is that the process of drafting the [UNESCO race] statements left a rich historical record demonstrating the persistence of the supposedly defeated racist science."[60] Well noted as that irony might be, however, it is worth repeating here, because UNESCO's project in Nubia was no different, even among the anthropologically trained archaeologists whose self-representation was antiracist. Trigger, for one, used the language of anthropometry to describe contemporary Nubians as being "slender and of medium stature, dolicocephalic, and medium to dark brown in complexion. They have oval faces, short but straight noses, dark eyes, thick lips, and curly hair." That same population, he continued, "is the product of a long and fairly continuous interbreeding of the existing population with increments from a surprising variety of places." Citing a 1921 study by the German archaeologist Hermann Junker, meanwhile, he noted that "the ancient population of Nubia was dark-skinned though not negroid in features."[61] Even as racial science was disavowed by the Nubian campaign's participants, race remained an operative category.

Traces of racial thought remained, meaning that Nubia was ripe for enfolding within developing arguments about race and its relationship to the African continent. For example, physical anthropologists, whose work had been sidelined during the drafting of the UNESCO race statements, continued their studies in Nubia.[62] Doing so, they rejected older analyses while simultaneously deploying racialized language. In 1965 and 1967, Eugen Strouhal of the Czechoslovak Institute of Egyptology took anthropometric measurements of the resettled Egyptian Nubian population to investigate their correlation with "breeding pattern" (or, more precisely, inbreeding).[63] Collapsing the difference between research focused on the past and the anthropological

---

59. Adams, *Nubia*, 95.
60. Selcer, "Beyond the Cephalic Index," 174.
61. Trigger, *History*, 16. The cited article is Hermann Junker, "The First Appearance of the Negroes in History," *The Journal of Egyptian Archaeology* 7, nos. 3/4 (1921): 121–32.
62. See Selcer, "Beyond the Cephalic Index," for UNESCO and physical anthropology.
63. Eugen Strouhal, "Anthropometric and Functional Evidence of Heterosis from Egyptian Nubia," *Human Biology* 43, no. 2 (1971): 272.

present, Strouhal's work recalled the practices of colonial ethnology, helping to keep the race question central to Nubia's relationship with Egypt. Ole Vagn Nielsen of the Scandinavian Joint Expedition, meanwhile, conducted a study of Nubian skeletons across four thousand years.[64] Physical anthropologists, however, were not the only ones fostering this continued interest in (a timeless sense of) race.

The Peopling of Ancient Egypt

Under Sadat, as Reem Abou-El-Fadl has noted, "the reversal . . . of much of Nasser's foreign policy led to the defunding of Cairo's infrastructures of solidarity, and the shriveling of opportunities for Afro-Asian connections" in particular.[65] Now, though, Afrocentrist imaginaries seemed to be encouraged by events in the city. In January 1974, and with some fanfare ("Thirty Scholars Research the Origin of the Egyptians," reported *al-Ahram*), UNESCO organized a meeting in Cairo on *The Peopling of Ancient Egypt* as part of the preparatory work for the *General History of Africa*.[66] The meeting was convened by the Egyptologist Gamal Mokhtar, who was not only a member of the project's International Scientific Committee and editor of the proposed second volume of the work, but also a former (1967–77) chairman of the Department of Antiquities and the EAO, not to mention a previous (1958–67) scientific director of CEDAE. In a sense, the Nubian campaign—and Egypt's place within it—helped to provide the impetus for the event, and many of its participants were among the attendees. Aaron Kamugisha has noted, however, that the conference's delegates repaid this trust in their expertise by adhering in their deliberations "to a concept of 'race' that was both shifting and problematic."[67] The event, as its own publication ultimately acknowledged, revealed that this concept had never entirely vanished, despite UNESCO's campaigning.[68] That concept's traces, moreover, would now provoke serious argument in relation to Egypt's place in Africa.

---

64. Ole Vagn Nielsen, *The Nubian Skeleton Through 4000 Years: Metrical and Non-Metrical Anatomical Variations*, trans. Nouchiravan Dianaty (Copenhagen: Andelsbogtrykkeriet i Odense, 1970).

65. Abou-El-Fadl, "Building Egypt's Afro-Asian Hub," 191.

66. UNESCO, *The Peopling*. The article is Mahmud Kamal, "30 'Aliman Yabhathuna Asl al-Misriyyin" ["Thirty scholars research the origin of the Egyptians"], *al-Ahram*, January 29, 1974.

67. Aaaron Kamugisha, "Finally in Africa? Egypt, from Diop to Celenko," *Race and Class* 45, no. 1 (2003): 37.

68. UNESCO, "Symposium on the Peopling of Ancient Egypt: A Report on the Discussions," in UNESCO, *The Peopling*, 73–103, is particularly revealing.

To provide a set of talking points for the conference, its International Scientific Committee had commissioned a paper from Jean Vercoutter on "the knowledge at present available about the ethnic origins and anthropological relationships of populations and about the cultural ties between Egypt and the rest of Africa."[69] While summarizing that knowledge, Vercoutter in response also stated "how much of the problem of the population of ancient Egypt has been distorted, how wrongly it has been approached and how, in the last analysis, it is a false problem." Noting Egypt's position as a "melting-pot," he argued that "it would be a vain and useless task to look here for a pure, primitive 'race' or homogenous population." At the same time, however, Vercoutter continued to utilize race as a viable descriptive category. Discussing the "Hamitic hypothesis" (the theory that a white race known as Hamites brought civilization to Africa), he noted that, although he thought the actual existence of the Hamites needed to be substantively investigated, if it were the case that they were real then it was necessary "to cover the connections linking this race . . . with the Negroes on the one hand, and, on the other, with the fossil African races discovered in Africa in the last few decades." Even if a "primitive 'race'" had not existed in Egypt, Vercoutter still seemed to make use of the category and its forms of description.[70]

The Cairo meeting made race a viable category, and others at the symposium thought through that classification in ways that fomented controversy about (ancient) Egypt's place in Africa that has never ended.[71] Most famously, the presence of Cheikh Anta Diop of the Institut Fondamental de l'Afrique Noir at the University of Dakar in Senegal meant that this argument filtered through the forms of thought about African continuities that his work set forward.[72] In Cairo, Diop argued that, because human beings derived from the area of the sources of the Nile, not only had that population spread northward down the river, but "the population of Egypt in the predynastic period

---

69. UNESCO, "Introduction," in UNESCO, *The Peopling*, 11.
70. Jean Vercoutter, "The Peopling of Ancient Egypt," in UNESCO, *The Peopling*, 24.
71. That argument flared with the publication of Martin Bernal, *Black Athena: The Afroasiatic Roots of Classical Civilisation*, vol. 1, *The Fabrication of Ancient Greece, 1785–1985* (London: Vintage, 1991). Recent archaeological/Egyptological attempts to address the issues at stake include: Solange Ashby, *Calling Out to Isis: The Enduring Nubian Presence at Philae*, Gorgias Studies in the Ancient Near East 13 (Piscataway, NJ: Gorgias, 2020); Karen Exell, ed., *Egypt in its African Context: Proceedings of the Conference Held at the Manchester Museum, University of Manchester, 2–4 October 2009* (Oxford: Archaeopress, 2011); David O'Connor and Andrew Reid, eds., *Ancient Egypt in Africa* (London: UCL Press, 2003); Ann Macy Roth, "Building Bridges to Afrocentrism: A Letter to my Egyptological Colleagues," *Newsletter of the American Research Center in Egypt* 167 (September 1995): 14–17, and 168 (December 1995): 15–21; David Wengrow, *The Archaeology of Early Egypt: Social Transformations in North-East Africa, 10,000 to 2650 B.C.* (Cambridge: Cambridge University Press, 2006).
72. For instance, in Cheikh Anta Diop, *The African Origin of Civilization: Myth or Reality?*, trans. Mercer Cook (Westport, CT: Lawrence Hill, 1974).

was entirely Negro, with the sole exception of a small admixture of white nomadic elements."[73] Diop countered racism and Eurocentrism by redeploying race and the racialized language that other participants at the meeting continued to use: Egypt, he argued, was African, at the same time as criticizing the use of the word "negroid" by other participants.[74] His argument drew criticism and—in at least one instance—outright rejection.[75] He was not the only person present to make such points, however. The Congolese linguist Théophile Obenga also attended the conference and gave a paper stressing the common identity of ancient Egyptian and "Negro-African" languages.[76] Obenga, though, was not taken much more seriously than his Senegalese colleague, and he and Diop found themselves sidelined during conversations about how the issues discussed might be resolved.

A vague sense that discussion of Egypt in terms of race was no longer tenable, however, did not lead to significant action on any of the discussants' parts on finding a solution to the issue, even as controversy grew. Peter Shinnie, for instance, "greatly regretted the fact that no physical anthropology specialist was present at the meeting who was qualified to state what were the latest methods of work and how they should be used by archaeologists and historians."[77] Torgny Säve-Söderbergh, meanwhile, stated that race was "a concept which was now increasingly being abandoned by anthropologists," even as he did not present an alternative.[78] Worse still, Professor G. Ghallab of the Institute of African Research and Studies at the University of Cairo went so far as to state that "the inhabitants of Egypt in palaeolithic times were caucasoids," drawing both Diop and Obenga's ire.[79] The best that the meeting's final recommendations could suggest was "that an international inquiry be organized . . . with a view to establishing very precise standards on the strictest possible scientific principles for defining races." The participants likewise recommended that Egypt set up a department of physical anthropology.[80]

UNESCO's race statements had sidelined physical anthropologists.[81] In 1974 in Cairo, their time seemed to come again, even as the group of people

---

73. Cheikh Anta Diop, quoted in UNESCO, "Symposium," 77.
74. Cheikh Anta Diop, quoted in UNESCO, "Symposium," 86.
75. UNESCO, "Symposium," 86, notes that "Professor Diop's theory was rejected in its entirety by one participant."
76. Théophile Obenga, "The Genetic Linguistic Relationship between Egyptian (Ancient Egyptian and Coptic) and Modern Negro-African Languages," in UNESCO, *The Peopling*, 65–71.
77. Peter Shinnie, quoted in UNESCO, "Symposium," 78.
78. Torgny Säve-Söderbergh, quoted in UNESCO, "Symposium," 89.
79. G. Ghallab, quoted in UNESCO, "Symposium," 87.
80. UNESCO, "Symposium," 102.
81. Selcer, "Beyond the Cephalic Index," 173–74.

recommending them seemed to suggest that physical anthropological work could be used to define the very category that the field's earlier projects had led to questioning of. All this discussion, meanwhile, caused Maurice Glélé of UNESCO's Division of Cultural Studies to make a statement more in keeping with the tenor of his organization's antiracist commitments. Present in Cairo to represent UNESCO's director-general, Glélé, later a president of Benin's Constituent Assembly, stated that "if the concepts which had been discussed were so ill-defined and perhaps so subjective or inseparable from habitual patterns of thought . . . a revision should be made of the entire terminology of world history."[82] Stoking the controversy at hand, however, that revision did not take place instantly. In 1977, Bill Adams angrily dismissed "efforts to place [Nubians] . . . in another historical pigeonhole as 'Africans,'" arguing that it was not "my place or my intention to make propaganda for nationalist or racist movements."[83] And as publication of *The General History of Africa* began in the early 1980s, the controversy further exploded into print. In the 1981 volume edited by Mokhtar on *Ancient Civilizations of Africa*, Diop's contribution (on the "Origin of the Ancient Egyptians") was published with an editorial note recording that "the arguments put forward in this chapter have not been accepted by all the experts interested in the problem."[84]

Discussions about race—and Egypt's place in Africa—seemed set to continue. In the same volume, Shehata Adam, now director of CEDAE (and soon to become head of the EAO), distanced his chapter (written with the collaboration of Vercoutter) from arguments about racial origins even as he implied that those arguments constituted a form of proper anthropological knowledge. In "The Importance of Nubia: A Link Between Central Africa and the Mediterranean," he stated that "even if we were able to do so, we should not wish to join in the purely anthropological debate as to whether the Nubians are of 'negro' or 'hamitic' origin."[85] In his introduction, meanwhile, Mokhtar (again with the collaboration of Vercoutter) noted that "the traditional criteria" of physical anthropology were no longer accepted. In a somewhat curious turn of phrase, however, he also suggested that "we run a serious risk of soon having to abandon the notion of 'white' or 'black' races" (and in a volume whose

---

82. Maurice Glélé, quoted in UNESCO, "Symposium," 97.

83. Adams, *Nubia*, 8.

84. Editorial note by Gamal Mokhtar in Cheikh Anta Diop, "Origin of the Ancient Egyptians," in *General History of Africa*, vol. 2, *Ancient Civilizations of Africa*, ed. Gamal Mokhtar (Paris and London: UNESCO and Heinemann, 1981), 51.

85. Shehata Adam, with the collaboration of Jean Vercoutter, "The Importance of Nubia: A Link Between Central Africa and the Mediterranean," in *General History of Africa*, vol. 2, *Ancient Civilizations of Africa*, ed. Gamal Mokhtar (Paris and London: UNESCO and Heinemann, 1981), 231.

804 pages were full of racial theorizing).[86] The Nubian campaign, rather than questioning ideas about race, had in fact propelled their traces forward.

The Never-Ending Campaign

As UNESCO's campaign had an official end, so in many ways it never actually ended. Nubia and its neighboring areas continued to be spaces of material intervention stemming from the project's work, particularly in Egypt. Most obviously, Qasr Ibrim in Egyptian Nubia, a site that had been occupied from approximately the eighth century BC until 1813, never entirely flooded despite the High Dam's deluge. Under the patronage of Britain's EES, excavation there started during the Nubian campaign and continued until 2006; further study seasons followed.[87] Other examples of continued intervention had been preordained by the campaign's initial *quid pro quo*. As promised by the Egyptian government, missions working in Egyptian Nubia did go on to excavate sites in the north of the country, although not always the ones they had lobbied for. The EES obtained permission to excavate at Saqqara, where Bryan Emery had worked at various points since the 1930s.[88] Yet the attempts of the Yale-Penn team to continue their collaboration at the site of Dahshur (located at the southernmost edge of the pyramid field stretching southward from Cairo) met resistance.[89] The two institutions ultimately began excavations at the site of Abydos in Middle Egypt in 1967, continuing into the twenty-first century.[90] Traces of Nubia could be redirected in unanticipated directions.

---

86. Gamal Mokhtar, with the collaboration of Jean Vercoutter, "Introduction," in *General History of Africa*, vol. 2, *Ancient Civilizations of Africa*, ed. Gamal Mokhtar (Paris and London: UNESCO and Heinemann, 1981), 14.

87. Pamela J. Rose, "Qasr Ibrim: The Last 3000 Years," *Sudan and Nubia* 15 (2011): 1–9.

88. For which see Walter Bryan Emery, "Preliminary Reports on the Excavations at North Saqqara, 1964–5," *The Journal of Egyptian Archaeology* 51 (1965): 3–8. Emery had by this point detailed his earlier work at the site in, among other publications, *Archaic Egypt* (Harmondsworth: Penguin, 1961), which, racial—and racist—narrative of civilizational development intact, was translated into Arabic by Rashid Muhammad Nawir and Muhammad ʿAli Kamal al-Din, revised by Abdel Moneim Abu Bakr, and published as *Misr fi ʿAsr al-ʿAtiq (al-Usratan al-Ula wa-l-Thaniyya)* [Egypt in the ancient period: The first and second dynasties] (Cairo: Dar Nahdat Misr, 1967).

89. The minutes of the April 6, 1965, meeting of the Board of Managers of the University Museum, University Museum Archives, note that "on his recent trip to Egypt Dr. Rainey saw the permit to dig at Dahshur through all the Egyptian committees including the army. The site borders a missile base. The only remaining step is the Minister's signature, which should be forthcoming." That signature never appeared.

90. For which see "Abydos Archaeology," n.d., accessed October 27, 2020, https://abydos.org/about.

Notable here is how heritage practices shaped by the Nubian campaign could now be repurposed in ways suiting the constellation of interests surrounding them. Given the country's strong engagement with UNESCO's heritage work (and the gradual move of Sudan away from it), this action was particularly visible in Egypt. Following the official end of the campaign in 1980, the country made sure to remove the other material incentives that had been built into the project. Following the precedent of UNESCO's own 1970 Convention on the Means of Prohibiting and Preventing the Illicit Import, Export and Transfer of Ownership of Cultural Property, Egyptian Law 117 of 1983 sought to stop the export of antiquities from the country once and for all.[91] Meanwhile, Egyptian officials made it increasingly clear that a concentration on the excavation of sites in the Nile Delta and other irrigable areas would again be welcomed. In December 1963, the Egyptian government emphasized that any request for new excavation permits north of the High Dam would go directly through the Department of Antiquities in the case of the Delta, Egypt's Faiyum Oasis, and irrigated land, but would have to be considered in the first instance by the government itself if related to the Nile Valley.[92] Over twenty years later, during a 1986 conference at the Netherlands Institute of Archaeology and Arabic Studies in Cairo, archaeologists heard Ahmed Khadry, president of the EAO, state that "the Delta is considered as a priority area by our Organization, not only for our own excavations but also for excavations carried out by the foreign missions."[93] Increased archaeological concentration on Egypt allowed officials to create new geographies of knowledge in the country, traces of Nubia redirected to more useful purpose.

Those repurposed traces told, however. Through actions like the Nubian campaign, UNESCO had sought "to create a new spatial paradigm" around the globe, one "regimented by the presumed neutrality of culture."[94] Yet if the organization's bureaucracy did manage to channel the spread of this paradigm into formerly colonized spaces like Egypt and Sudan, it only ever did so fleetingly. The postcolonial nation-state could—and did—strike back, especially in a

---

91. Until 2010, extremely limited cases of excavated objects being exported for study or exhibition purposes sometimes occurred, for which—and for Law 117 itself—see Stevenson, *Scattered*, 221–23.

92. Egyptian Ministry of Culture recommendations on future excavations cited in Louis Christophe to William Kelly Simpson, May 3, 1964. "Other Field Work, Dahshur, Planning for Concession," file (ANTAR.037110), Yale Peabody Museum of Natural History Archives.

93. Ahmed Khadry, "Inaugural Speech," in *The Archaeology of the Nile Delta: Problems and Priorities*, ed. Edwin C. M. van den Brink (Amsterdam: Netherlands Foundation for Archaeological Research in Egypt, 1988), 1.

94. Allais, "The Design," 208.

field where it had the resources to do so. Like many other indebted countries in the Global South, Egypt in the 1980s was on its way to negotiating a painful program of economic structural adjustment with the International Monetary Fund (IMF), a process enforced after attempts in the 1970s to found a "New International Economic Order" failed and the so-called Washington consensus, privileging the free market, flourished (Egypt ultimately reached agreements with the IMF in 1987 and 1991).[95] Yet while Egypt was unable to control the way it paid back debt, the country's government could to some extent control the way Egyptian cultural material was defined and manipulated. Even as UNESCO found itself increasingly marginalized by countries in the Global North, formerly colonized countries like Egypt continued to use the organization to assert their own priorities.

Simultaneously, as tourist revenue became increasingly useful to Egypt—in the period after the *infitāḥ*, tourist numbers in the country gradually rose after having remained relatively flat since the 1950s—those priorities became increasingly pressing.[96] With the onset of total perennial irrigation in Egypt made possible by the High Dam, groundwater levels in the country had remained high (previously, they had fluctuated with the changing level of the Nile). The increased soil salinity connected with this process now impacted monuments, promoting salt encrustation on stone and painted surfaces. This encrustation prompted concern. A February 1980 article in *al-Musawwar* written by the journalist Sakina al-Sadat (the then Egyptian president's half-sister) and published just before the Nubian campaign officially ended made clear the consequences of this situation: not only did groundwater "threaten [*tahaddud*] Egypt's antiquities," it also threatened the economy, because "our antiquities are our capital" (*fa-āthārnā hiya ra'smālnā*). Copiously illustrated with pictures of domestic and international tourists, the article illustrated the potential economic hit the country might take if Egypt's antiquities sustained damage.[97]

In response to this threat, al-Sadat called for local and international action. Citing, among others, the Director of Antiquities for Upper Egypt Muhammad al-Saghir, al-Sadat asked for particular help for the city of Luxor (UNESCO's "Ancient Thebes with its Necropolis"). She suggested the creation of an interna-

---

95. For the New International Economic Order and the Washington Consensus, see Mazower, *Governing*, 305–77. For Egypt's "stand-by arrangements" with the IMF, see Bessma Momani, "IMF-Egyptian Debt Negotiations," *Cairo Papers in Social Science* 26, no. 3 (2005): 1–101.

96. On tourist numbers and post-1952 tourism in Egypt, see Thomas Richter and Christian Steiner, "Politics, Economics and Tourism Development in Egypt: Insights into the Sectoral Transformations of a Neo-Patrimonial Rentier State," *Third World Quarterly* 29, no. 5 (2008): 949–50.

97. Sakina al-Sadat, "Inana Nadiqqu Naqus al-Khatar: al-Miyah al-Jufiyya Tahaddud Atharna!" ["We are ringing the warning bell: Groundwater threatens our antiquities!"], *al-Musawwar* 2890, February 29, 1980.

tional committee to be formed of "experts and professors of Egyptology and UNESCO," because the remains in Luxor constituted "the most beautiful and most important antiquities in the world."[98] Having been placed on the nascent World Heritage List partially as a result of the Nubian campaign's success, Luxor now needed protection from the consequences of the dam that constituted the campaign, and from the same organization and set of actors who thought they had successfully drawn that action to a close.

This action seemed to be of the utmost importance. Within the same issue's pages was an article highlighting the recent report of a parliamentary committee discussing both the protection of Luxor's pharaonic antiquities and the possibility of strengthening tourist infrastructure in the city. Noting that the report dealt with Luxor's "archaeological zones" (al-manāṭiq al-āthariyya), the article emphasized through semantics how the incorporation of parts of Egypt within the nascent World Heritage framework necessitated the absorption of that framework's technocratic management style. It also, though, enabled the renewal of discussions about banning the building of houses above Luxor's tombs, emphasizing once again the accusations that had helped to institute CEDAE: that the inhabitants of those houses were responsible for stealing antiquities.[99] Heritage management and touristic development was never far from colonial anxiety.

Luxor was not the only source of such anxiety. Nubia's reassembled temples also began to constitute a source of concern, albeit one in relation to which Egyptian expertise could be displayed. Removed from the path of the High Dam's floodwaters and no longer subject to the Nile's annual inundation, the temples had become renewed objects of touristic interest at the same time as becoming reliant on work that would maintain their reconstructed form: reassembled authenticity required preservation, too. In a series of articles in the mid-1980s, the EAO made this point clear in its glossy, bilingual (Arabic-English) magazine 'Alam al-Athar, which was given the English title *Archaeological Review*. This print intervention hinted at the way in which Nubian authenticity constituted not only an object of perpetual transformation, but also became an object that could be attuned to the Egyptian (and Arab) issues of the day.

---

98. Al-Sadat, "Inana Nadiqqu." By the mid-1980s, this problem constituted international discussions: the Field Director of the OI's Epigraphic Survey, Lanny Bell, used it to justify the urgency of the project's work in "The Epigraphic Survey: The Philosophy of Egyptian Epigraphy after Sixty Years' Practical Experience," in *Problems and Priorities in Egyptian Archaeology* eds. Jan Assmann, Günter Burkard, and Vivian Davies (London: KPI, 1987), 43.

99. Faruq Abaza, "Min Ajila Inqadh Athar al-Uqsur: Madha fi Taqrir Lajnat al-Tahqiq al-Barlimaniyya?" ["For the sake of the preservation of Luxor's antiquities: What's in the report of the Parliamentary Investigation Committee?"], *al-Musawwar* 2890, February 29, 1980.

The EAO produced ʿ*Alam al-Athar* in collaboration with the country's Centre of Planning and Architectural Studies (Markaz al-Dirasat al-Takhtitiyya wa-l-Miʿmariyya, or CPAS). CPAS had been founded in 1980 by ʿAbdelbaki Ibrahim, who was both head of the Department of Architecture at Cairo's ʿAin Shams University and sat on ʿ*Alam al-Athar*'s editorial board. This organizational collaboration tied the journal—and the EAO—to the forms of architectural authenticity that Ibrahim promoted. Educated in Cairo, Liverpool, and Newcastle (PhD, 1959), ʿAbdelbaki Ibrahim was employed at ʿAin Shams from 1964 onward and had not only worked as a planning expert in Cairo, but also in urban planning roles for the UN in Kuwait (1968–70) and Saudi Arabia (1973–79). Closely associated with Hassan Fathy, ʿAbdelbaki Ibrahim's work placed him not only within a particular community in Egyptian architecture, but also within post-1967 Arab circles and their connection to anxieties about "the Islamic heritage" (*al-turāth al-Islāmī*), a major topic of discussion in the wider Islamic revival. Invested in notions of Arab-Islamic urban heritage and the renaissance of this tradition in an architecture appropriate to contemporary Egyptian society, Ibrahim drew upon relevant scientific and technological approaches at the same time as promoting his ideas through the journal ʿ*Alam al-Benaʾa* (World of construction), which he cofounded the same year as his organization, and of which he was editor-in-chief.[100]

ʿAbdelbaki Ibrahim's collaboration with the EAO was therefore an intriguing one. Within ʿ*Alam al-Athar*, the issues of, and technological approaches taken to, the process of restoration (*tarmīm*) were made far more explicit in Arabic articles than they were in their English-language summaries. Reporting on the temple of Wadi es-Sebua (which had been taken apart and reassembled by the then Department of Antiquities), Wafaa El Saddik and Fathi Abu Zaid not only discussed its post-reconstruction change and "disfiguring" (*tashwīn*) due to continual changes in temperature and humidity, but also discussed the "exacerbation of ruination" (*tafāqum al-talaf*) that had been caused by multiple movements of its disassembled blocks and the presence of "iron oxides" (*akāsīd al-ḥadīd*) within them.[101] Elsewhere in the same issue, Kamal Imbabula and Muhammad Salah

---

100. Marwa M. S. El-Ashmouni, "The Rationale of Architectural Discourses in Post-Independence Egypt: A Contrapuntal Reading of ʿ*Alam al-Benaʾa* (1980–2000)," PhD diss, University of Adelaide, 2013, 201–04. Cf. ʿAbdelbaki Ibrahim, *Al-Turath al-Hidari fi-l-Madina al-ʿArabiyya al-Muʿasira* [Urban heritage in the contemporary Arab city] (Kuwait City: Baladiyyat Kuwait, 1968). The adjective *ḥiḍārī* ("urban") carries the notable double-meaning of "civilizational."

101. Wafaa El Saddik and Fathi Abu Zaid, "Mashruʿ Tarmim Maʿabid al-Nuba al-Sakhriyya" ["Restoration plan for the stone temples of Nubia"], ʿ*Alam al-Athar* 32 (October 1986): 7. Wafaa El Saddik would become director of Cairo's Egyptian Museum; for her autobiography, with contributions by Rüdiger Heimlich and trans. Russell Stockman, see *Protecting Pharaoh's Treasures: My Life in Egyptology* (Cairo: American University in Cairo Press, 2017).

Isma'il discussed the cleaning processes used to treat these issues in detail, even disclosing the ratio of, say, "phenylemulsion" (*mustaḥalib al-fināfīl*) to water used in certain cleaning compounds.[102] If anything, then, these articles constituted a performance of authentically Egyptian expertise in what were fast becoming globalized techniques of preservation: traces of global heritage mobilized to establish Egyptian competence as equal to the task at hand. Embroiled in "the modern cult of monuments," Egypt again found its monumental geography shaped partially according to the cult's precepts.[103] The country nevertheless reshaped that cult and its traces to suit official—and unofficial, but culturally pressing—ends.

Nubia in the Museum

As the 1980s progressed, museums offered a similar opportunity. As early as 1967, plans had been set forward for some form of display of the remains recovered during the Nubian campaign. That year, the engineer Albert Gawi proposed that a museum and research institute be located on the island of Biga. Biga was located just west of Philae in what had become a subsidiary reservoir formed between the Aswan Dam and the High Dam (map 2). The island constituted an ideal location for the proposed institution, not least because the formation of this new reservoir had cut Biga off from its northeastern extremity: Agilkia, the islet that the Philae complex would ultimately be moved to, and of which the museum would enjoy an unparalleled view. The new foundation, meanwhile, would be located near the island's still extant Nubian village, preserved from submersion due to its location to the north of the High Dam.[104]

Ultimately, the proposed institution never saw the light of day. Yet its story bears repeating because the traces of the museum's failure—coupled with the Nubian campaign's lack of focus on the Nubians themselves—clearly provided the impetus for later developments. The plans for the proposed institute recall not only CEDAE and Breasted's proposed research institute in Cairo (discussed in

---

102. That ratio being 1:6. Kamal Imbabula and Muhammad Salah Isma'il, "A'mal al-Tarmim bi-Ma'bid Wadi al-Sebu'a" ["Restoration Work at the Temple of Wadi es-Sebua"], *'Alam al-Athar* 32 (October 1986): 12. Compare anon., "Synopsis: Restoration Project of the Nubian Rocky Temples (Wadi el-Sebu'a Temple)," *'Alam al-Athar* 32 (October 1986): 14–15.

103. Riegl, "The Modern Cult."

104. Memo entitled "Mashrū' Iqāmat Markaz li-l-Buḥūth wa-l-Dirāsāt al-Khāsa bi-l-Ḥafā'ir al-Āthariyya bi-Jiwār al-Mawāqi' al-Jadīda al-Āthār al-Nūba" ["Plan for the foundation of a special research and study institute for archaeological excavations in the vicinity of the new archaeological sites of Nubia"], April 26, 1967, 1–2. File 3A-d2 (with same title as memo), Nubia Museum.

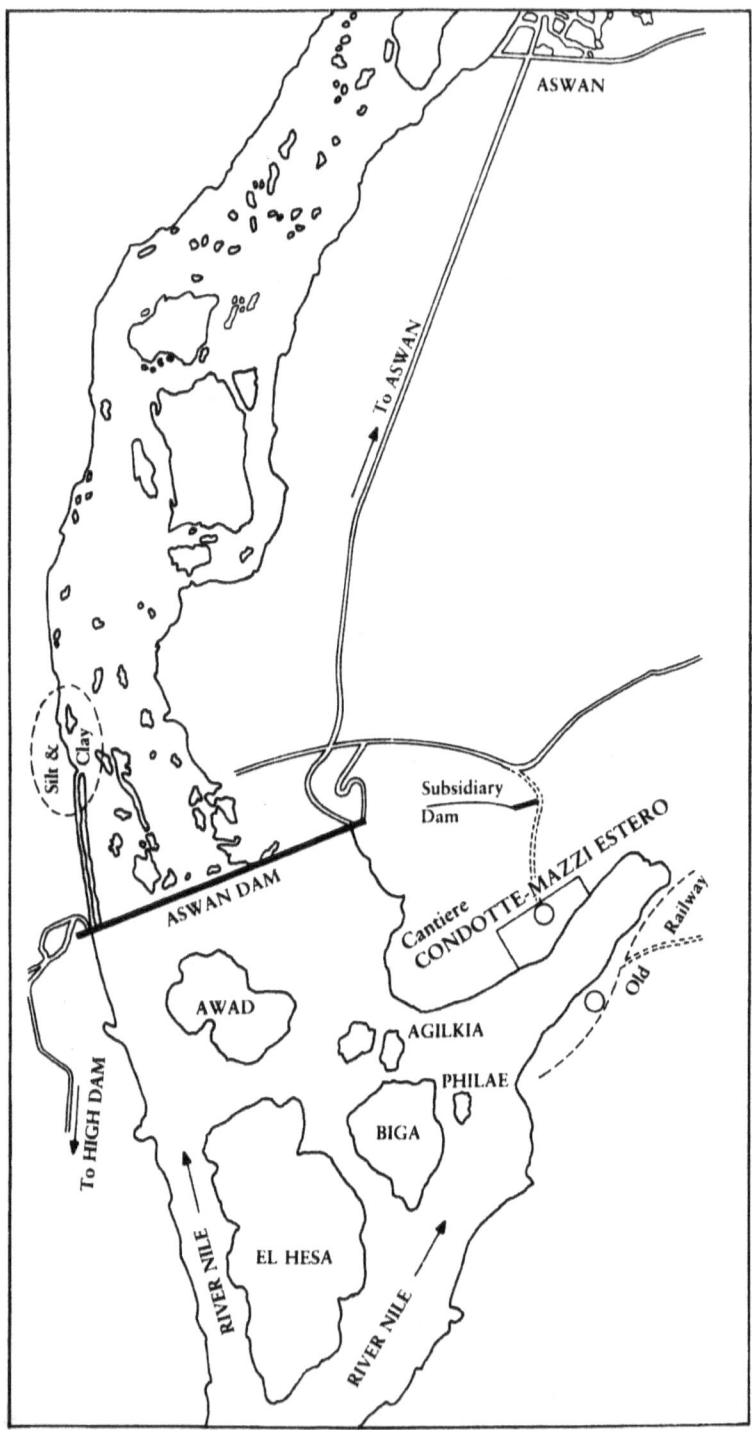

MAP 2. The relative locations of Philae, Biga, and the new islet of Agilkia. Torgny Säve-Söderbergh, *Temples and Tombs of Ancient Nubia: The International Rescue Campaign at Abu Simbel, Philae and Other Sites* (London and Paris: Thames and Hudson and UNESCO, 1987), 173.

chapter 2), but also, more directly, the Aswan museum proposed by the Egyptian Department of Antiquities in 1955 discussed in chapter 1. The archival impetus died hard. Yet—especially given the success of CEDAE—the failure of that precedent in this instance was notable. Placed under the direction of archaeologists, the institutional complex was to include a museum building containing objects recovered during the recent campaign and models of the Nubian temples. It was also to include a library, a photo library, and an archive, in addition to a reading room, a lecture theater, a cinema, restaurants, gardens, and residential accommodation for students involved in research.[105] Due to the heat of Aswan's summer, the institute would only work for six months each year.[106] Yet even that number appeared to be six months too many given that the plan seems to have been filed away and forgotten about. Importantly, too, it seems unlikely that the proposal enjoyed the support of Biga's villagers: the institute's proposed location appears to have been at least as due to a conveniently sized piece of "flat land" (*misāḥa musaṭṭaḥa*) and nearby transport links than the villagers' presence (the village would anyway begin to be abandoned in the mid-1980s).[107]

It would not take that long, however, for the idea of some sort of Nubian museum to be recast in a way that made the link between ancient past and contemporary population explicit. In 1981, the year after the Nubian campaign ended, UNESCO organized a meeting in Paris aimed at discussing ways to follow up on the project's work. At the time, Egypt was experiencing seismic change. Anwar al-Sadat's popularity in the country had plummeted to new lows after the signing of the Camp David Accords, not to mention the January 1977 "bread intifada" (*intifāḍat al-khubz*) caused by an attempt to end basic food subsidies in the country. And in October 1981, Sadat was assassinated, replaced by his Vice President Husni Mubarak.[108] Yet despite—or perhaps because of—this turmoil, Egypt proved an enthusiastic attendee in Paris. Conversely, as one UNESCO employee later glossed it, "the Sudanese authorities did not attend for internal political reasons and this marked the end of the activities related to Sudan."[109] Once again, then, Egypt—and an eager Mubarak regime—reaped the result of this surplus of organizational attention: the

---

105. Memo entitled "Mashrūʿ Iqāmat," 1–4.
106. Memo entitled "Mashrūʿ Iqāmat," 5.
107. Memo entitled "Mashrūʿ Iqāmat," 2. On the village, see Bernadeta Schäfer, "The Nubian Villages on Biga Island," *Archaeology in Egypt: Magazine of the German Archaeological Institute Cairo* 4 (2016): 20–27.
108. On the "bread intifada," see David Seddon, "The Politics of Adjustment: Egypt and the IMF, 1987–1990," *Review of African Political Economy* 47 (1990): 95.
109. Costanza de Simone, "Wadi Halfa Museum: A Rescue Mechanism for the Nubian Intangible Heritage," in "Pratiques du patrimoine en Égypte et au Soudan," eds. Omnia Aboukorah and Jean-Gabriel Leturcq, special edition of *Égypte/Monde arabe*, nos. 5–6 (2009): 410.

launch, in 1982, of the International Campaign for Egyptian Museums. This project had two aims: first, to build a National Museum of Egyptian Civilization (NMEC) in Cairo, and secondly, to construct what came to be called the Nubia Museum (Mathaf al-Nuba) in Aswan.[110] Continuing the Nubian campaign's switch from bounded event to ongoing—and apparently never-ending—saga, this new campaign has seen varied success.

NMEC, for instance, endured slow progress. Aiming to showcase Egypt's "tangible and intangible heritage" across time, the museum's foundation stone was laid only in 2004 in the presence of then first lady Suzanne Mubarak and the Minister of Culture, Faruq Hosni.[111] Opening in 2017 with a temporary exhibit on "Egyptian Crafts through the Ages," Egypt finally opened the museum's central hall—and a room dedicated to the mummies of pharaonic rulers—in early 2021 with an extravagant event dubbed the Mawkib al-Mumiyyat al-Malikiyya or, in (more spectacular) English, the Pharaohs' Golden Parade.[112] NMEC thus constitutes one of the clearest relics of Mubarak-era policies related to the Egypt-wide expansion of museums. The institution forms an apparent attempt to cross neoliberal economic development with state interest in the dissemination of certain forms of (secularized) culture unthreatening to the international tourist market (shaken by the shooting of tourists by Islamist terrorists at the temple of Deir el-Bahari in Luxor in 1997). In that sense, NMEC is similar to the—itself still to be opened—Grand Egyptian Museum in Giza, located by the pyramids and next to Cairo's ring road.[113] Until the Pharaohs' Golden Parade, NMEC has attracted—and been used to attract—far less global attention. At the time of writing, meanwhile, parts of the institution remain shuttered. Some traces of Nubia remain forever nascent.

The Nubia Museum itself, however, is a different story. Opened in 1997, the institution won the Aga Khan Award for Architecture in 2001. Pointing to the museum's adjudication as a place that "successfully address[es] the needs and aspirations of societies across the world, in which Muslims have a significant

---

110. Säve-Söderbergh, *Temples*, 217.

111. "The National Museum of Egyptian Civilization," n.d., accessed October 28, 2020, http://www.unesco.org/new/en/culture/themes/museums/museum-projects/the-national-museum-of-egyptian-civilization/.

112. The "golden" not being present in Arabic, whose literal translation is "Parade of the Royal Mummies." For the parade, see William Carruthers, "Spectacles of the Past," *Jadaliyya*, May 12, 2021, https://www.jadaliyya.com/Details/42719. For the temporary exhibit, see National Museum of Egyptian Civilization, *Egyptian Crafts through the Ages: Exhibition Catalogue* (Cairo: Ministry of Antiquities, 2017).

113. On the Grand Egyptian Museum, see Mohammed Elshahed, "The Old and New Egyptian Museums: Between Imperialists, Nationalists, and Tourists," in Carruthers, *Histories of Egyptology*, 255–69. On the spate of museum building in Egypt prior to the country's 2011 revolution, see, e.g., the article written by Secretary-General of the Supreme Council of Antiquities Zahi Hawass, "A New Era for Museums in Egypt," *Museum International* 57, nos. 1–2 (2005): 7–23.

presence," the award's description not uncoincidentally emphasizes the institution's place within the same discourse as the work of CPAS and seems to suggest another way in which Egypt has sought to cater to the concerns at hand.[114] Yet even this success story has not been immune from criticism, especially because the museum's plan adhered to the combination of interiority and exteriority entwined in the sort of "museum complex" whose growing valence across postcolonial Africa had been outlined by Senegalese cultural official Abdoulaye Diop at a UNESCO-sponsored seminar in 1972. As Lucia Allais argues, "if the colonial museum had been static . . . its postcolonial successor would be dynamic, which meant thinking in terms of the 'open-air.'"[115] Unlike the proposed Biga institution, which failed to incorporate the nearby Nubian village into its design, the Nubia Museum embodied this open-air—and self-consciously postcolonial—principle to maximum effect. Yet it did so as that same principle was becoming increasingly obsolete.

Designed by the Egyptian Mahmoud el-Hakim and with exhibition planning by the Mexican Ramirez Vazques, the new institution was integrated into a rocky hill near the Nile's First Cataract in Aswan. Incorporating both an indoor exhibition hall and a heavily landscaped outdoor display, the museum adhered to the way in which exhibitionary artifice had helped to produce a distinction between tangible and intangible heritage over the decades since formal decolonization. Displaying not only objects excavated during the Nubian campaign, but also folkloric dioramas of Nubian life, the opening of the Nubia Museum constituted one step on the road to the reification of these two categories in international law in the early part of the twenty-first century.[116] By doing so, the institution also materialized the way in which international experts started to authorize the intangible as African and/or non-European and the tangible—in this case objects gathered during a process of mostly Euro-American archaeological intervention—as the rightful object of European classificatory practice.[117] As the Nubia Museum attempted to compensate for Nubian loss through its production of a particular form of postcolonial future, that feat meant that the institution came to be haunted by its own design, continuing the accumulation of scars that the undertaking of the Nubian campaign had started.

---

114. "Aga Khan Award for Architecture," n.d., accessed October 28, 2020, https://www.akdn.org/architecture.

115. Allais, *Designs*, 192.

116. On which process see Aurélie Elisa Gfeller, "Anthropologizing and Indigenizing Heritage: The Origins of the UNESCO Global Strategy for a Representative, Balanced and Credible World Heritage List," *Journal of Social Archaeology* 15, no. 3 (2015): 366–86.

117. On such authorization, see Allais, *Designs*, 193–95.

268   CHAPTER 7

The institution's plans possess clear similarities to the museological "architecture of continuity" first set forward in the late 1940s by Georges-Henri Rivière.[118] Rivière, a one-time curator at Paris' Musée de l'Homme and associate director of the International Council of Museums from 1948 until 1965, was a prominent figure in UNESCO's museum work, which had itself started to find a foothold in former colonies as decolonization took shape; the colonial metropole once again constituting what it meant to be newly independent.[119] His exhibitionary model had developed as a means of displaying the transition of cultures across time, providing a clear organizational schema for illustrating the continuity of Nubian life that the more recent literature on the region like Bill Adams's *Nubia: Corridor to Africa* had promoted. Tracing "the history and geology of Nubia from the first traces of human presence in the region to the construction of the High Dam," initial plans—which mostly found form in the final display—proposed the visitor moving from a display on "Nubian Environment" to others on "Christian" and "Islamic Nubia," ending with displays about Nubian life before the High Dam.[120] Adapted for a changing era, however, the institution abandoned Rivière's insistence on modernism as providing the ideal architectural form for such displays, even as its plans followed his approach in adapting the museum to its local geography.[121] Based on designs chosen in 1984, the Nubia Museum's exteriors (figure 7.5) melded functional mass with the sort of imitation traditional architecture that Rivière had forbidden: a form not entirely postmodern, but certainly far from modernist.[122]

In doing so, the plans adhered to the ideals set forward through organizations like CPAS and the Aga Khan Foundation, constituting a sort of revivalist structure whose nod to now-flooded Nubian architectural heritage was overt. It was due to this and the other contradictions outlined in this chapter, however, that the Nubia Museum never entirely managed to grapple with the forms of loss that it made material. The traces of former fates remained tangible in a building whose culturally sensitive form seemed to contradict its interior's

---

118. For the "architecture of continuity," see Allais, *Designs*, 200.
119. On Rivière, see Allais, *Designs*, 189. Cf. Alice L. Conklin, *In the Museum of Man: Race, Anthropology, and Empire in France, 1850–1950* (Ithaca, NY: Cornell University Press, 2013). On UNESCO's museum work and decolonization, see Allais, *Designs*, 173–217.
120. Ibrahim al-Nawawi, Joseph Zaki, and Wafaa El Saddik, "The Nubia Museum," '*Alam al-Athar* 24 (February 1986): 13–14.
121. On these aspects of Rivière's work, see Allais, *Designs*, 200.
122. As Mohamed Elshahed, *Cairo Since 1900: An Architectural Guide* (Cairo: American University in Cairo Press, 2020), 41, notes, in the late 1980s and early 1990s, "there was not a vibrant local critical assessment of Modernism in Egypt that could produce an architecture that was consciously postmodern."

FIGURE 7.5. The Nubia Museum, Aswan. Photograph via Wikimedia, taken by Gérard Ducher.

modernist, postcolonial didacticism. State-sponsored—and internationally sanctioned—heritage practice could not achieve approval from all.

Heritage, *Turāth*, and the Nubians

What good was heritage, anyway? Not least in UNESCO's own eyes, the Nubian campaign has become closely connected to the global development of both the category and, more particularly, the 1972 World Heritage Convention.[123] On the ground, however, "heritage" was used at best inconsistently and, more commonly, not at all by project participants engaged in what they perceived to be careful technical work related to their respective disciplines. In the years leading up to—and during—the Nubian campaign, moreover, the Arabic usage of the term (*turāth*) became particularly vexed. Throughout that time, *turāth* appeared in documents, reports, and articles discussing the project. Yet what did the use of this word signify?

---

123. See, e.g., UNESCO, "40th Anniversary of Nubia Campaign Celebrated in Egypt," March 16, 2020, https://whc.unesco.org/en/news/2091.

As early as 1951, a government memo discussing that year's Law 215 for the Protection of Antiquities stressed the notion of *"al-turāth al-qawmī"* or "national heritage," a quality whose meaning had for many years been the source of some debate, and one that was entangled with discussions about national culture more generally.[124] In January 1961, meanwhile, having recently attended UNESCO's 11th General Conference in Paris, Tharwat Okasha sent a report to his fellow Free Officer Kamal al-Din Hussein, now president of Egypt's Council of Ministers. Discussing the meeting, Okasha used the word *turāth* several times. Doing so, he gave the term meaning beyond the national, reflecting the universalist leanings (and European genealogy) of the organization whose conference he had just attended. Reporting on the event's discussions on Nubia, Okasha discussed both "human cultural heritage" (*al-turāth al-thaqāfī li-l-insān*) and "human heritage" (*al-turāth al-insānī*). He deployed the phrase "African heritage" (*al-turāth al-Afrīqī*), too, skillfully referencing both Egypt's African interests and UNESCO's attention to the continent, and further broadening the category's use.[125]

Turāth had become a bureaucratic category, but one whose mutability meant that the state had little means of regimenting its use, even as, for some, that regimentation was the state's proper object. In an interview titled "How Do We Protect the Heritage of Our Civilization?" published alongside *al-Musawwar*'s coverage of the Philae inauguration, the historian of Mamluk art and architecture Laila ʿAli Ibrahim noted that "Egypt was not only a pharaonic civilization, but rather all the periods of Egyptian independence were periods of florescence [*āzdihār*]." Consequently, she also called for the unification of the country's antiquities and heritage apparatus.[126] Yet it is not clear that this was a universally popular stance, not least because *turāth* was a mutable term in contexts wider than the Egyptian.

As Nathalie Peutz has discussed, "Arab intellectuals and nationalists sought in popular folklore (*al-turāth al-shaʿabī*) a bulwark against the impacts of urbanization and (Western) modernization," not least "in the 'nativist ethnog-

---

124. "Mudhakkirat Īḍāḥiyya ʿan Mashrūʿ Qānūn Himāyyat al-Āthār" ["Explanatory memo about the plan for the protection of antiquities"], June 7, 1951, file 0081–003923, Egyptian National Archives. On Egyptian national culture, see, e.g., Armbrust, "The Formation"; Gershoni and Jankowski, *Redefining*; Winegar, *Creative*, 96–100. In 1966, Egypt's Ministry of Culture had launched a series of conferences on the future of national culture, for which see, e.g., Wizarat al-Thaqafa, *4 Muʾtamarat* [4 Conferences], vol. 1, *al-Sinima, al-Masrah, al-Kitab, al-Fann al-Tashkili* [The cinema, the theater, the book, the fine arts] (Cairo: Wizarat al-Thaqafa, al-Muʾassasa al-Misriyya al-ʿAmma li-l-Taʾlif wa-l-Nashr, and Dar al-Katib al-ʿArabi, 1967).

125. Okasha to Hussein, January 21, 1961, file 0081–003929, Egyptian National Archives.

126. Laila al-Qisi, "Kaifa Nuhafizu ʿala Turathna al-Hidari?" ["How do we protect the heritage of our civilization?"], *al-Musawwar*, March 7, 1980. For Laila ʿAli Ibrahim, see Nasser Rabbat, "Laila ʿAli Ibrahim, 1917–2002," *Mamluk Studies Review* 7, no. 1 (2003): 235–36.

raphy' of Palestinian intellectuals and folklorists in the 1920s and 1930s." As Peutz cautions, however, "what constituted the nation's essential heritage remained contested."[127] Likewise, as part of the turn to thinking about the Islamic heritage after 1967, "many Arab intellectuals questioned whether their Arab-Islamic heritage was the source of, or solution to, the perceived Arab-Muslim cultural stagnation." Consequently, those same intellectuals began to reconceptualize "*turāth* in dynamic, progressive terms—as opposed to mere passive, imitative traditions (*taqālīd*)." Opposing "'traditionalists' who advocated a return to what they considered a sacred and incontrovertible Islamic *turāth*, 'progressive' intellectuals (both religious and secular) called for a reevaluation of inherited values and traditions so as to better adapt their Arab-Islamic *turāth* to the needs of the present."[128]

Given that discourse—and even as their own definitions do not cleave to the Arab-Islamic discussion—it is hardly surprising that the forms of heritage set out at the Nubia Museum did not always meet with approval from Nubians themselves. Other understandings of Nubian heritage exist and, unsurprisingly, Nubians themselves have made efforts to promote them. As early as 1980—building on the Nubian associations that had been present in the city since the turn of the twentieth century—a Society for Nubian Heritage (Jam'iyat al-Turath al-Nubi) was founded in Cairo. As Mahir Ahmad Zaki (also known as Sayyid Duki), the author of the *Mawsu'a Nubiyya* (or Nubian encyclopedia), notes, this move came about particularly due to "fear" (*takhawwuf*) surrounding the possible "extinction" (*indithār*) of the Nubian language.[129] Members of that same society, meanwhile, sat on a committee formed to consult on the Nubia Museum's ethnographic displays. Yet "government officials, said one committee member in a 2001 . . . meeting, 'didn't listen to a thing we said,' expressing his frustration and disgust with the state and UNESCO."[130] This critical response is not uniform: as Elizabeth Smith noted, while Nubian women living in West Aswan criticized the museum displays in discussion with her, "a group of young Cairene Nubian women visiting the museum appreciated the high-civilization connotations of the archaeological artifacts."[131] It is noteworthy, though, that even as UNESCO has attempted to

---

127. Nathalie Peutz, "Heritage in (the) Ruins," *International Journal of Middle East Studies* 49, no. 4 (2017): 722.
128. Peutz, "Heritage," 723.
129. Mahir Ahmad Zaki (Sayyid Duki), *Hakadha Tukalamu al-Nubiyyun: Mawsu'a Nubiyya* [So speak the Nubians: The Nubian encyclopedia] (Cairo: Mahir Zaki al-Muhami, 2001), 173.
130. Elizabeth Smith, "Place, Class, and Race in the Barabra Café: Nubians in Egyptian Media," in *Cairo Cosmopolitan: Politics, Culture, and Urban Space in the New Globalized Middle East*, eds. Diane Singerman and Paul Amar (Cairo: American University in Cairo Press, 2006), 411.
131. Smith, "Place, Class, and Race."

address this issue (and as the museum itself has stated the importance of its community role), other responses to such criticisms have arisen, particularly as calls for a Nubian "right to return" have become louder on both sides of the Egyptian-Sudanese border.[132]

Ironically, changes in UNESCO's own definition of heritage have themselves given impetus to this shift. As Aurélie Elisa Gfeller has noted, one outcome of the Global Strategy for a Representative, Balanced and Credible World Heritage, launched as globalization gathered pace in 1994, has been an "anthropological turn," heavily promoted by the French anthropologist Isac Chiva and shaped by concern surrounding representation of the heritage of Australia's Indigenous minorities.[133] One outcome of that turn was the 2003 Convention for the Safeguarding of the Intangible Cultural Heritage, which entered into force in 2006 and sought to protect "the practices, representations, expressions, knowledge, skills—as well as the instruments, objects, artefacts and cultural spaces associated therewith—that communities, groups and, in some cases, individuals recognize as part of their cultural heritage."[134] And in 2004, the UNESCO committee concerned with the Nubia Museum and NMEC backed an Egyptian-Sudanese mission to Nubia which concluded "with the signature of a Memorandum of Understanding between Egypt and Sudan which recommends the creation of the Wadi Halfa Museum."[135] As Costanza de Simone has discussed, the institution, whose foundation stone was laid in 2008, "aims not only to be a place to display objects but a *rescue mechanism* [her italics] for intangible heritage of the Nubians living in the area and their reconnection, through the objects, with their past from which they were divorced by the construction of the High Dam."[136]

On one level, such initiatives—although to some extent top-down—appear to enjoy some success (even as the new museum has not yet opened and its projected completion date is unclear). In cooperation with UNESCO's Cairo office, the Nubian Language Society of Khartoum has been conducting an ethnographic survey of the Nubian inhabitants of (new) Wadi Halfa.[137] In late

---

132. On which calls see Maja Janmyr, "Nubians in Contemporary Egypt: Mobilizing Return to Ancestral Lands," *Middle East Critique* 23, no. 2 (2016): 127–46, and Janmyr, "Human Rights." On the Nubia Museum's own definition of its role, see Ossama Abdel Meguid, "Museums, Culture and Sustainable Development," in *From Imperial Museum to Communication Centre? On the New Role of Museums as Mediators between Science and Non-Western Societies*, eds. Lidia Guzy, Rainer Hatoum, and Susan Kamel (Würzburg: Königshausen and Neumann, 2010), 17–26.

133. Gfeller, "Anthropologizing," 367.

134. UNESCO, "Text of the Convention for the Safeguarding of the Intangible Cultural Heritage," article 2, 2003, accessed October 29, 2020, https://ich.unesco.org/en/convention.

135. De Simone, "Wadi Halfa," 411.

136. De Simone, "Wadi Halfa," 403.

137. De Simone, "Wadi Halfa," 409 (footnote 12).

2019, meanwhile, Cairo's Society for Nubian Heritage became a consultative organization to the International Governmental Committee for UNESCO's Intangible Cultural Heritage program.[138] Elsewhere, other—independent—actions have taken place. The Nubia Initiative bills itself as "a transboundary international non-profit organisation dedicated to safeguarding all things Nubia."[139] Connected to the Nubia Initiative is Nubi, a language app built by the software developer and activist Momen Talosh that provides lessons in Nubian dialects.[140] Likewise, the Koma Waidi ("Tales of the Past") initiative has used volunteers to collect Nubian words and print a small booklet providing translations into Arabic and other languages.[141] In a heritage landscape dominated by established state and institutional actors, the question is to what extent such actions might now gather force. "Nubia," as this book has revealed, has never simply been a Nubian creation.

---

138. Hussam al-Damarani, "Indimam Jam'iyyat 'al-Turath al-Nubi' li-l-Yunescu ka-Hai'at Istishariyya" ["The society for 'Nubian heritage' affiliates with UNESCO as a consultative organization"], al-Dustur, December 16, 2019, https://www.dostor.org/2941973?utm_content=bufferf5eaa&utm_medium =social&utm_source=twitter.com&utm_campaign=buffer.

139. "The Nubia Initiative: About Us," n.d., accessed October 29, 2020, http://thenubiainitiative.org/about/.

140. "What Is Nubi?" n.d., accessed October 29, 2020, http://www.nubi-app.com/about.

141. Ahmed Megahid, "First Nubian Language Dictionary Published by Volunteers," The Arab Weekly, January 19, 2020, https://thearabweekly.com/first-nubian-language-dictionary-published-volunteers.

Conclusion

Repeopling Nubia

The temple of Dendur, built on behalf of the Roman emperor Augustus around 15 BC and originally located on the Nile about fifty miles south of Aswan, today stands in New York's Metropolitan Museum of Art (figure C.1). Perhaps the most famous of the structures gifted abroad by Egypt during UNESCO's Nubian campaign, the temple sits, surrounded by an artificial lake, in the section of the institution that made the structure's reassembly there possible. Opened in 1978, the annex was known as the Sackler Wing until late 2021, when the museum removed the name as the fallout from the Sackler family's involvement in the US opioid epidemic continued.[1] In the annex, a room for the temple includes climate control technologies whose planned appearance had earlier helped the museum and Thomas Hoving, its charismatic director, to convince the administration of President Lyndon B. Johnson that the institution represented the best—and safest—place to display the structure in the United States.

As David Gissen has argued, with its windows overlooking Central Park, the planned Dendur Room seemed to incorporate the temple within the city's outside while having managed to create a space "that bridged the park with an

---

1. In a statement, members of the Sackler family agreed to the removal of their name. For the change, see Robin Pogrebin, "Met Museum Removes Sackler Name From Wing Over Opioid Ties," *New York Times*, December 9, 2021.

REPEOPLING NUBIA 275

FIGURE C.1. The temple of Dendur at the Metropolitan Museum of Art, New York. Photograph courtesy of the Metropolitan Museum of Art, New York (image in the public domain).

idealized image of the Nubian plain," and whose controlled climate would enable the preservation of the structure's fragile stone.[2] Inside while outside, the temple of Dendur consequently seems to exist in a vacuum-sealed bubble: Nubia in New York, "the view from the boat" on a pedestal on Fifth Avenue.

---

2. David Gissen, "The Architectural Production of Nature, Dendur/New York," *Grey Room* 34 (2009): 73. For Hoving, see Thomas Hoving, *Making the Mummies Dance: Inside the Metropolitan Museum of Art* (New York: Simon and Schuster, 1993).

CONCLUSION

The Met's finely tuned "Nubian" environment exists, then, within a metaphorical gilded cage. Promoted—and used, at upward of forty thousand dollars per function—as a premier event space within Manhattan, the impression of an authentic ancient Egyptian (and implicitly pharaonic) temple is one that benefit guests and museum visitors alike enjoy.[3] It is also an impression that people need to work to dispel: information panels about the structure are placed on the side of the room away from the temple itself. Even then, those panels state that "the sanctuary does not follow a Roman style; its architecture and decoration are both of Egyptian design."[4] "Egyptian," though, is a tellingly vague term. Dendur has become an archetype, a bubble of an ancient Egyptian Nubia removed from the people who lived there. Its production as such rests on the archaeological and preservation work—and colonial genealogies—discussed throughout this book.

What might it look like to think beyond the recolonized futures that the Aswan High Dam and UNESCO's Nubian campaign produced? What, more pressingly, *should* it look like, and who gets to decide? The construction of the High Dam engendered a moment in which two connected futures came into view, both of which were entangled within—and helped to constitute—the wider political environment within which they sat, and both of whose colonial genealogies were frequently clear. The first of these futures related to the forced displacement of Egyptian and Sudanese Nubian populations. The second represented the future constituted by UNESCO's Nubian campaign: one in which monument preservation and archaeological work became tied, to varying degrees, to the making of national, regional, and global pasts in the period of formal decolonization and the Cold War. This second future would have been impossible without the first. And that the first happened at all was conditioned by earlier events: when the British occupation of Egypt was still a reality, when both Britain and Egypt asserted their colonial interests in Sudan, and when the development of Nile irrigation became a pressing concern. How might such colonial genealogies and their effects on Nubia and its population be addressed?

In Nubia, the slow dispossession and disaggregation of the region's population from the ancient—and not so ancient—remains among which they lived not only served to create that population as a tangible entity. It also aided modernization policies in Egyptian and Sudanese society related to irrigation, archaeology, tourism, and what became World Heritage. Flooding "the Nubian

---

3. "Eventup: The Temple of Dendur at the Met," accessed November 13, 2020, https://eventup.com/venue/the-temple-of-dendur-at-the-met/.

4. "The Temple of Dendur" information panel, Metropolitan Museum of Art, New York, visited January 6, 2020.

past" over the course of the twentieth century—in countries and a region subject to various forms of colonial rule—enabled the constitution of that past and its people as objects of Egyptian and Sudanese modernity. At the same time, however, that process created the seeds for Nubians to contest their place within those countries in various ways.

Given, though, that the veneer of simple disagreement implied by the word "contestation" has often been used to paper over asymmetries of power, the notion of remaking might prove more useful to think with here, not least in the way it allows a potential transfer of agency. The possibility of Nubia being remade has always been apparent, even as the apparatus of empire, the nation-state, international organizations, and scholarship would have the region be a closed book (sometimes quite literally). The focus of this volume has been UNESCO's Nubian campaign, an event whose 1960 to 1980 chronology sits fixed and memorialized in numerous places. Commemorative volumes, museums, UNESCO's online presences, and the "final" publications related to archaeological and preservation work in the region all offer this chronology to their audiences. Yet as I have shown, the Nubian campaign was never conclusive. Nubia's past, the campaign claimed, would be flooded. That flood, however, elided the ways in which the campaign's colonial genealogies themselves submerged the project. Likewise, the fixity of that flood's—and the Nubian campaign's—memorialization has continued to elide the ways in which that event left traces that continue to authorize the flooding of the project and Nubia itself with new attachments.

These attachments are obvious and tangible. As Zeina Elcheikh has noted, despite Nubian concerns with the Nubia Museum, the growth in Aswan's visitor numbers fostered by the institution has simultaneously aided efforts to develop cultural tourism in Egyptian Nubian villages.[5] This process, meanwhile, has allowed Nubians to promote a culture that is "more alive and more real than the statues in the museums," a reference to the static ethnographic dioramas of pre–High Dam Nubian life on display in Aswan.[6] So successful has this movement been, moreover, that Nubians "started to use imported Chinese- and Egyptian-made products instead of their traditional handmade crafts in a response to the increasing demand accompanied by the flow of tourists." Likewise, "crafts are continually being produced for both use by locals

---

5. Zeina Elcheikh, "Tales from Two Villages: Nubian Women and Cultural Tourism in Gharb Soheil and Ballana," *Dotawo: A Journal of Nubian Studies* 5 (2018): 241–60. Nubian women have been particularly central to these touristic efforts, for which see Anne M. Jennings, *Nubian Women of West Aswan: Negotiating Tradition and Change*, 2nd ed. (Cairo: American University in Cairo Press, 2009).

6. Zeina Elcheikh, "Outside the Walls of the Nubian Museum," *e-dialogos: Annual Digital Journal on Research in Conservation and Cultural Heritage* 4 (2014): 34.

and sale to visitors." As Elcheikh states, "perhaps one could argue that cultural tourism has helped keep them [those crafts] alive."[7] Authenticity, as she hints, is always in the eye of the beholder, as the archaeological, Egyptological, and other practices discussed throughout this book emphasize, and despite the efforts of UNESCO and others to make an authentic and picturesque "Nubia" continue to cohere.[8] Consequently, this creative process of Nubian remaking is as much—if not more—authentic as any other vision of the region, its resistance to official representations of Nubian life a central part of understanding why those visions need not have the last word.

One way to think beyond the recolonized futures of Nubia that UNESCO's campaign produced is to take this process of remaking seriously. More pointedly, there is an ethical obligation on behalf of the institutions and individuals who were involved in—and who continue to hold the records of—the Nubian campaign to think carefully about the Nubian agency sitting at the heart of that process: not just remaking, but repeopling, too. If the project, at heart, was predicated on the production of documentation about Nubia and "the Nubian past," then that was not documentation constructed with any reference to the population living among that past's remains. Nubia is, of course, not an isolated case: as Rachel King and Luíseach Nic Eoin emphasize when discussing the recently built Metolong Dam in Lesotho, such "inventorying" practices remain problematic despite archaeological and anthropological efforts to achieve outcomes more meaningful for impacted communities.[9] The difference in the case of Nubia is that there was little effort to think about the implications of a connection between contemporary Nubians and the past under construction seriously—or to work with Nubians themselves. Today, however—and despite the occasional reluctance of development authorities—more (global) impetus in this direction exists. For example, during recent work in Ghana related to the Bui Dam on the Black Volta River, archaeologists overcame the resistance of the Bui Power Authority (the managers of the dam project) to enable work with impacted local communities on documenting and preserving forms of heritage identified by those communities themselves. That work also, ultimately, helped to enable resettlement.[10] Given this concentration on practices of documentation, such work might

---

7. Elcheikh, "'Tales," 256.
8. Elcheikh, "Outside," 35.
9. Rachel King and Luíseach Nic Eoin, "Before the Flood: Loss of Place, Mnemonics, and 'Resources' ahead of the Metolong Dam, Lesotho," *Journal of Social Archaeology* 14, no. 2 (2014): 213.
10. Wazi Apoh and Kodzo Gavua, "'We Will Not Relocate Until Our Ancestors and Shrines Come with Us': Heritage and Conflict Management in the Bui Dam Project Area, Ghana," in *Community Archaeology and Heritage in Africa: Decolonizing Practice*, eds. Peter R. Schmidt and Innocent Pikirayi (London: Routledge, 2016), 204–23.

seem to differ little from wider practices of inventorying and dam-related salvage. There is also a question as to what extent such initiatives can ever hope to move beyond disciplinary self-interest. Yet the successful involvement of impacted groups points to future possibilities, especially if thinking through the Nubian campaign's own archival practices.

UNESCO's project produced a disconnect between past and present constituted to a great extent by the colonial genealogy of much of the fieldwork that took place in Nubia. That disconnect, moreover, came about not least because the imperative of archaeological documentation was tied to particular ideas about what exactly that documentation should record. Pots, not people, constituted archaeology's proper object in Nubia, even as practitioners working in the region linked those same pots to published racial narratives that made this human disconnect possible. What might it look like, then, to remake UNESCO's campaign in a way that places Nubian agency front and center and that uses the project's documentation to work toward that aim? I am not self-absorbed enough to think that I have the answer to this question (or that I should have). Above all, the issue is one that relates to power and how, over time, that quality has accrued both to people like me (white, male, British) and to the academic institutions and foundations that have supported my writing this book. There are means of redistributing power, however, that might provide a way to start repeopling the knowledge created during the Nubian campaign, and which, used carefully, the documentation and archives constituted during the project can help to enable—even as the colonial genealogies of that knowledge gave that documentation form. Recently, Ariella Aïsha Azoulay has proposed a notion of "potential history" that "does not mend worlds after violence but rewinds to the moment before the violence occurred and sets off from there."[11] Given the *longue durée* histories at hand in the Nubian case, I am not certain exactly how far it is possible to rewind. What I am certain about, however, is that it is possible, as she suggests, to "overcome the disassociation between people and objects in which the experts [like archaeologists] specialize."[12] Dendur does not have to appear in its current form. The vision of Nubia of which the temple and its landscaping is both the signifier and signified need not take precedence, or even be reproduced at all. Other associations can be made.

To make other associations, as Rita Felski has suggested, it is necessary to move beyond critique and what Paul Ricoeur once called "the hermeneutics

---

11. Ariella Aïsha Azoulay, *Potential History: Unlearning Imperialism* (London and New York: Verso, 2019), 10.

12. Azoulay, *Potential History*, 7.

of suspicion."[13] This shift will involve participating in a practice "of making rather than unmaking," as opposed to the "unravelling of manifest meaning" that, in recent decades, much critical academic work has centered around (and which, to a great extent, this book itself partakes in). By making that shift, I argue that it is possible to approach the Nubian campaign's archive in ways that do not reproduce the forms of social alienation and disaggregation that are connected to, and reside within, its records.[14] That approach, of course, has to be one that is useful to, and driven by, Nubians themselves. Yet the "less hemmed-in and less rigidly constructed model of meaning" that Felski proposes is one that has potential, not least because it provides a way to foreground the experiences and emotions that UNESCO's campaign and the work that informed it so clearly ignored.[15] This move is not, as Felski emphasizes, about "a heavy-handed application of" Latourian Actor-Network Theory, the major theoretical influence over her work.[16] Rather, it is about finding a way to let the Nubian archive tell other, different stories: ones otherwise denied by that documentation's imbrication within colonial forms of knowledge.

I will therefore conclude with an example that points to the ways in which, as the Nubian scholar Menna Agha puts it, "Nubia still exists" through, among other practices, "a nostalgic initiation": the ways that Nubia might yet become "a paradise-like old land that is ours, unlike the state-built settlement that is not."[17] On the first floor of the Deutsches Archäologisches Institut Kairo (DAIK) sits a filing cabinet holding the photographic archive of the institution's work. In one of its drawers are records related to the dismantling and reconstruction of the Egyptian Nubian temple at Kalabsha, in which process DAIK was involved.[18] As an institution invested in the sort of "science of the archive" that Lorraine Daston has identified (and upon which set of practices much of the Nubian campaign sat), DAIK saw fit to keep at least some of the records of the work at Kalabsha for future reference.[19] Future reference, though, enables future remaking.

This possibility has not been a given, not least because the physical act of viewing these records embeds them further within the archive's conceptual space. Pulling the filing cabinet drawer outwards, one flicks through photo after photo of the Kalabsha temple's evolution from cohesive structure to

---

13. Rita Felski, *The Limits of Critique* (Chicago: University of Chicago Press, 2015), 9.
14. This concluding argument draws from Carruthers, "Records."
15. Felski, *The Limits*, 161 (quote), 179.
16. Felski, *The Limits*, 184.
17. Agha, "Nubia," 9.
18. G. R. H. Wright, *Kalabsha: The Preserving of the Temple* (Berlin: Gebr. Mann, 1972), 23.
19. Daston, "The Sciences."

piecemeal collection of blocks, and then views the edifice reassembled in "complete" form again. The sense is of a puzzle being finished in front of one's eyes: an objective record of how a group of people (as Daston might have it) collected, collated, and preserved the structure, making sure that others within this self-defining collective of scientists could later see how they had done so.[20] Coupled with a publication that provides a warts-and-all (but nevertheless teleological) account of work at the site, the photos present a way of checking how that group triumphed over considerable practical adversity. G. R. H. Wright's *Kalabsha: The Preserving of the Temple* indicates that it is "a detailed recital of the technical difficulties [at the site] and the measures adopted to deal with them," emphasizing that "it is hoped to render the lessons learned [...] widely accessible for reference."[21] The archived photos only further this reference model: the construction of the past preserved for similar endeavors in the future, especially when viewed in relation to Wright's book.

DAIK's photos also possess other meanings—they reveal that the Nubian campaign never took place away from the region's social life, despite UNESCO's best efforts. Never foregrounded, but always present, Nubian life flows through the photos of the work at Kalabsha. In particular, the contemporary settlement next to the site—which lent the temple its name and which was left, after the building's removal, to be submerged by the High Dam's floodwaters—stands as a fixed point of reference regarding the process of structural disassembly. The science of the archive comes undone as life itself courses through its boundaries. In one photo (figure 1.2), a group of (unnamed) men are pictured at work taking the temple apart, waiting for a crane to lift the next block from the structure. The focus is on them and their technical action. Yet to the rear, uncentered and assumed to be of secondary importance, stands part of the settlement of Kalabsha itself, its presence a reminder that the temple was never removed from its context as successfully as publications describing the work suggest. That settlement's presence, moreover, had been clear before the Nubian campaign officially started: the village was also visible in the rear of index card for Kalabsha that CEDAE had produced in 1957 (figure 2.3). Nubia would not disappear all that easily. In fact, the region's pre-flood form lives on in the archival material that this book relies on.

Such temporal fluidity prompts questions. Representations of UNESCO's Nubian campaign urged a concentration on monument preservation, archaeological survey, and excavation. However, as I have discussed (and as these archival photos emphasize), those "technical" practices were social, too, and

---

20. Paraphrasing Daston, "The Sciences," 162.
21. Wright, *Kalabsha*, 9.

indelibly linked to the social life of Nubians. This sociality prompts queries about how Nubian life related to structures like the temple at Kalabsha, in addition to how the people living such lives remember the campaign, its processes, and its wider associations. More importantly, though, the appearance of the village at Kalabsha suggests a way in which pasts other than the one that UNESCO's project constituted might still gain visibility through the Nubian campaign's own records. This suggestion is given extra force because, within the photos of Kalabsha, the local labor required to take the temple apart is clearly present. Who of this labor force survives, and what do they remember of the village? Can asking such questions constitute an act that ameliorates the dispossession that the Nubian campaign's archival impetus created? True to the tropes of such images, this human presence—whether Nubian or more broadly Egyptian is not entirely clear—remains nameless, as figure 1.2 emphasizes. Nevertheless, that labor force is present, active, and presumably sometimes young enough to be both alive and able to remember the event. The social nature of the archive provides one way to jog the memory and—subject, of course, to anyone wanting to give answers—might be asked to do so. Laborers on the High Dam have discussed their own memories of work on the structure.[22] What, though, can the archives of the Nubian campaign offer Nubians? Using pictures like the ones discussed here, is it possible (or even desired) to return "to the moment before the violence occurred" and create a new set of associations between people and the campaign's (visual) object?[23]

These are clearly open questions. They also remain difficult to answer, not least because it is unclear who speaks—or should or could speak—for Nubians as a whole. Indeed, the possibility of any Nubian speaking with reference to such measures has become more and more difficult. In Egypt, for example, allegations of Nubian separatism and the need for the multiple Nubian associations located in the country's cities to appear nonpolitical have worsened this situation.[24] Meanwhile, developments that perhaps seemed favorable to a change in this attitude turned out not to be. Egypt's January 2014 Constitution (which also heralded the election of ʿAbd al-Fattah al-Sisi to the country's presidency) declared that the country's Nubians would be allowed to return to their original lands within ten years. Subsequent developments, however, have quashed that possibility. Presidential Decree 444, also of 2014, declared the land connected to certain of Nubia's former border villages to be a military zone. Similarly, Law 157 of 2018, which established an Upper Egypt

---

22. Mossallam, "'We Are the Ones.'" Cf. Fakhuri, *Al-Tarikh al-Insani*.
23. Azoulay, *Potential History*, 10.
24. Janmyr, "Nubians," 133.

Development Authority, further raised Egyptian Nubian concerns because it did not mention any sort of right to return on their behalf. Consequently, the Egyptian government is currently attempting to offer (limited) compensation to Nubians instead of resettlement.[25] Sudan, meanwhile (whose south seceded in 2011), remains in a transitional state. In April 2019, revolution led to the overthrow of the country's president, Omar al-Bashir, who is currently due to be sent to the International Criminal Court on charges of genocide. And at the time of writing, the Sudanese political environment is in flux following a military coup in late 2021. Discussing Nubian futures in this context is fraught, to say the least.

That discussion, though, is imperative. Some of the developments discussed here may seem strikingly—and ironically—familiar from the histories discussed throughout this book. Just as the population and the past of Egyptian Nubia has long been the target of (internationally and state-sanctioned) development initiatives, so the population and the past of the Sudanese part of the region has long found itself entangled within modernization and nation-building projects whose legitimacy has been called into question by the population subject to them. The time has come, however, for the institutions that created and hold the documentation generated during this work both to reckon with these histories and to acknowledge that the making of "the Nubian past" can only continue if and when it involves Nubians themselves. Those institutions need to make that move, too, on the basis that perhaps there really will be no continuation of their work. What benefits, after all, has the constitution of such knowledge had for the Nubians impacted by that process? After more than a century of archaeological, Egyptological, and preservation work helping to constitute Nubian dispossession, these disciplines and their representatives have little other choice. Ethics matter, and so does a society that acknowledges populations like the Nubians. The view from the boat is over (or should be).

---

25. For these developments, see "Border Center for Support and Consulting (BSC)," accessed November 12, 2020, https://www.ohchr.org/Documents/Issues/Housing/IndigenousPeoples/CSO/Border%20Center%20for%20Support%20and%20Consulting%20BSC%20-%20Nubian%20indigenous%20people%20Egypt.pdf.

Bibliography

Archival and Reference Collections

Archaeological Survey of India Photo Archives, New Delhi
Christiane Desroches Noblecourt Archives, National Archives of France, Pierrefitte-sur-Seine
Deutsches Archäologisches Institut Kairo Photo Archives
Digital Giza, online
Egypt Exploration Society Archives, London
Egyptian National Archives (Dar al-Watha'iq al-Qawmiyya), Cairo
Journal d'Entrée, 1947–1970, Egyptian Museum, Cairo
Kulubnarti Archives, Department of Egypt and Sudan, British Museum, London
Museum Archives at the Oriental Institute of the University of Chicago
National Archives of India, New Delhi
Nubia Museum Documentation Center, Aswan
Oxford Dictionary of National Biography, online
Smithsonian Institution Archives, Washington, DC
Sudan Archaeological Research Society Laurence P. Kirwan Archive, London
Sudan Archaeological Research Society William Y. Adams Archive, London
The National Archives of the UK, Kew
UNESCO Archives, Paris
UNESCO Digital Archives, online
University of Pennsylvania Museum of Archaeology and Anthropology Archives, Philadelphia
Wikimedia, online
Yale Peabody Museum of Natural History Archives, New Haven

Museum Displays

"The Temple of Dendur" information panel. Metropolitan Museum of Art, New York. Visited January 6, 2020.

Newspapers and Magazines

Akhbar al-Yawm
Akhir Sa'a
Al-Ahram
Al-Ahram Weekly

'Alam al-Athar / Archaeological Review
Al-Ayyam
Aljazeera.com
Cairo Scene
Al-Dustur
Egypt Travel Magazine
Al-Hilal
Hindustan Times
Al-Jumhuriyya
La bourse égyptienne
La Stampa
Mada Masr
Al-Musawwar
Al-Ra'i al-'Amm
The Arab Weekly
The Egyptian Gazette
The Illustrated London News
The New York Times
The Times of India
The UNESCO Courier
The Washington Post

Official Publications and Reports and Archaeological and Anthropological Reports on Nubia

Adams, William Y. "Living and Working Conditions for Archaeologists in Sudanese Nubia." Document CUL(60)13, UNESCO, 1960.

———. "Archaeological Survey of Sudanese Nubia: Introduction." *Kush: Journal of the Sudan Antiquities Service* 9 (1961): 7–10.

———. "The Christian Potteries at Faras." *Kush: Journal of the Sudan Antiquities Service* 9 (1961): 30–43.

———. "An Introductory Classification of Christian Nubian Pottery." *Kush: Journal of the Sudan Antiquities Service* 10 (1962): 245–88.

Adams, William Y., and P. E. T. Allen. "The Aerial Survey of Sudanese Nubia." *Kush: The Journal of the Sudan Antiquities Service* 9 (1961): 11–14.

El Batrawi, Ahmed M. *Report on the Human Remains*. Mission archéologique de Nubie, 1929–1934. Bulaq: Government Press, 1935.

———. "The Racial History of Egypt and Nubia, Part II: The Racial Relationships of the Ancient and Modern Populations of Egypt and Nubia." *The Journal of the Royal Anthropological Institute of Great Britain and Ireland* 76, no. 2 (1946): 131–56.

CEDAE. *Publications du Centre d'Études et de Documentation sur l'Ancienne Égypte*. Cairo: CEDAE, 1981.

Dafalla, Hassan. *The Nubian Exodus*. London: C. Hurst, 1975.

Dixey, Frank, and Georges Aubert. "Report on Arid Zone Research in the Sudan." Unesco/NS/AZ/657, February 23, 1962.

Edwards, David, ed. *The Archaeological Survey of Sudanese Nubia, 1963–69: The Pharaonic Sites*. Oxford: Archaeopress, 2020.

———. "The Archaeological Survey of Sudanese Nubia (ASSN) 1963–1969." Accessed October 16, 2020. https://www2.le.ac.uk/departments/archaeology/research/projects/archaeological-survey-of-sudanese-nubia-assn-1963-1969.

EES. *Report of the Seventy-Fourth Ordinary General Meeting (Seventy-Eighth Annual General Meeting) 1960: Subscription List and Balance Sheets.* London: EES, 1960.

Egyptian Department of Antiquities. *Report on The Monuments of Nubia Likely to be Submerged by Sudd-el-ʿĀli Water.* Cairo: Government Press, 1955.

Egyptian State Tourist Administration and the Tourist Development Association of Egypt. *Egypt Tourist Guide: General Information on Travelling.* Cairo: E. and R. Schindler, ca. 1940s.

Emery, Walter Bryan. *The Royal Tombs of Ballana and Qustul*, vol. 1, *Text*. Mission archéologique de Nubie, 1929–1934. Bulaq: Government Press, 1938.

Emery, Walter Bryan, and Laurence P. Kirwan. *The Excavations and Survey between Wadi es-Sebua and Adindan, 1929–1931*, vol. 1, *Text*. Mission archéologique de Nubie, 1929–1934. Bulaq: Government Press, 1935.

———. *The Excavations and Survey between Wadi es-Sebua and Adindan, 1929–1931*, vol. 2, *Plates*. Mission archéologique de Nubie, 1929–1934. Bulaq: Government Press, 1935.

Fahim, Hussein M. *Dams, People and Development: The Aswan High Dam Case.* New York: Pergamon Press, 1981.

Firth, Cecil Mallaby. *The Archaeological Survey of Nubia: Bulletin No. 7; Dealing with the Work from November 1, 1910 to February 28, 1911.* Cairo: National Printing Department, 1911.

Garstin, William. "Introductory Note." In *A Report on the Island and Temples of Philae*, by Henry George Lyons, 5–7. London: Waterlow and Sons, 1896.

Griffith, Francis Llewellyn. "Oxford Excavations in Nubia—Continued." *University of Liverpool Annals of Archaeology and Anthropology* 13 (1926): 63–5.

Hopkins, Nicholas S., and Sohair R. Mehanna, eds. *Nubian Encounters: The Story of the Nubian Ethnological Survey, 1961–1964.* Cairo: American University in Cairo Press, 2010.

———. "The Nubian Ethnological Survey: History and Methods." In *Nubian Encounters: The Story of the Nubian Ethnological Survey, 1961–1964*, edited by Nicholas S. Hopkins and Sohair R. Mehanna, 1–78. Cairo: American University in Cairo Press, 2010.

Hughes, George R. "The Epigraphic Record." In *The Beit el-Wali Temple of Ramesses II*, by Herbert Ricke, George R. Hughes, and Edward Wente, 6–9. The University of Chicago Oriental Institute Nubian Expedition 1. Chicago: University of Chicago Press, 1967.

ICOMOS. "The Nubian Monuments from Abu Simbel to Philae." Paris: ICOMOS, 1979. https://whc.unesco.org/document/154507.

International Museums Office. *Manual on the Technique of Archaeological Excavations.* Paris: International Institute of Intellectual Cooperation, 1940.

Kronenberg, Andreas, and Waltraud Kronenberg. "Preliminary Report on Anthropological Fieldwork 1961–62 in Sudanese Nubia." *Kush: Journal of the Sudan Antiquities Service* 11 (1963): 302–11.

———. "Preliminary Report on Anthropological Field-Work in Nubia, 1962–63." *Kush: Journal of the Sudan Antiquities Service* 12 (1964): 282–90.

———. "Parallel Cousin Marriage in Mediaeval and Modern Nubia—Part I." *Kush: Journal of the Sudan Antiquities Service* 13 (1965): 241–60.
———. *Nubische Märchen*. Düsseldorf: Diederichs, 1978.
Lajnat Tawtin Ahali Halfa [Halfa Resettlement Commission]. "Khashm El Girba Project: Social Services in Khashm El Girba" leaflet. T. Press, 1963.
Lal, B. B. "Indian Archaeological Expedition to Nubia, 1962: A Preliminary Report." In *Campagne internationale de l'Unesco pour la sauvegarde des monuments de la Nubie: fouilles en Nubie (1961–1963)*, edited by République Arabe Unie, Ministere du tourisme et des antiquités, Service des antiquités de l'Egypte, 97–118. Cairo: Organisme général des imprimeries gouvernementales, 1967.
Lyons, Henry George. *A Report on the Island and Temples of Philae*. London: Waterlow and Sons, 1896.
Markaz Tasjil al-Athar al-Misriyya [Centre for registering Egyptian antiquities]. Cairo: Wizarat al-Thaqafa wa-l-Irshad al-Qawmi, Markaz Tasjil al-Athar al-Misriyya, n.d.
Maspero, Gaston. *Les temples immergés de la Nubie: rapports relatifs à la consolidation des temples*. Vol. 1. Cairo: Service des antiquités de l'Égypte, 1911.
M'Bow, Amadou-Mahtar. "Préface." In *Campagne internationale de l'Unesco pour la sauvegarde des sites et monuments de Nubie: bibliographie*, prepared by Louis-A. Christophe, 6–7. Paris: UNESCO, 1977.
Monneret de Villard, Ugo. *La Nubia Medioevale*, vol. 1, *Inventario dei Monumenti*. Mission archéologique de Nubie, 1929–1934. Cairo: Institut français d'archéologie orientale, 1935.
National Council for Production and Economic Affairs. *Al-Sadd al-ʿAli wa-Atharihi / The High Dam and Its Effects*. Cairo: Al-Ahram, 1976.
National Museum of Egyptian Civilization. *Egyptian Crafts through the Ages: Exhibition Catalogue*. Cairo: Ministry of Antiquities, 2017.
Nielsen, Ole Vagn. *The Nubian Skeleton Through 4000 Years: Metrical and Non-Metrical Anatomical Variations*. Translated by Nouchiravan Dianaty. Copenhagen: Andelsbogtrykkeriet i Odense, 1970.
Noblecourt, Christiane Desroches, Gamal Moukhtar, Sergio Donadoni, Michel Dewachter, Hassan el-Achiery, and M. Aly. *Le Speos d'El-Lessiya*, 2 vols. Cairo: Centre de documentation et d'études sur l'Ancienne Égypte, 1968.
Progress: 2nd Anniversary Sudan Revolution, 17th November, 1960. Khartoum: The Central Office of Information, 1960.
Reisner, George Andrew. "The Archaeological Survey of Nubia." In *The Archaeological Survey of Nubia: Bulletin No. 1, Dealing with the Work up to November 30, 1907*, edited by the Survey Department, Ministry of Finance, Egypt, 9–24. Cairo: National Printing Department, 1908.
———. "The Archaeological Survey of Nubia: Progress of Survey." In *The Archaeological Survey of Nubia: Bulletin No. 2, Dealing with the Work from December 1, 1907, to March 31, 1908*, edited by the Survey Department, Ministry of Finance, Egypt, 3–27. Cairo: National Printing Department, 1908.
République Arabe Unie: Centre de documentation sur l'Égypte ancienne. Paris: Délégation Permanente de la R.A.U. auprès de l'U.N.E.S.C.O., 1959.
Ricke, Herbert. "The Architecture and Construction of the Temple." In *The Beit el-Wali Temple of Ramesses II*, by Herbert Ricke, George R. Hughes, and

Edward Wente, 1–5. The University of Chicago Oriental Institute Nubian Expedition 1. Chicago: University of Chicago Press, 1967.

Roeder, Günther. *Der Felsentempel von Bet el-Wali*. Cairo: Institut français d'archéologie orientale, 1938.

Rose, Pamela J. "Qasr Ibrim: The Last 3000 Years." *Sudan and Nubia* 15 (2011): 1–9.

Säve-Söderbergh, Torgny. "The Scandinavian Joint Expedition to Sudanese Nubia." *Historisk-filosofiske Meddelelser udgivet af Det Kongelige Danske Videnskabernes Selskab* 49 (1979): 1–53.

———. *Temples and Tombs of Ancient Nubia: The International Rescue Campaign at Abu Simbel, Philae and Other Sites*. London and Paris: Thames and Hudson and UNESCO, 1987.

Sherif, Negm El-Din Mohammed. *Inqadh Athar al-Nuba* [The salvage of Nubia's antiquities]. Khartoum: Matba'at al-Tamaddun, 1971.

Smith, Grafton Elliot. "The Anatomical Report." In *The Archaeological Survey of Nubia: Bulletin No. 1, Dealing with the Work up to November 30, 1907*, edited by the Survey Department, Ministry of Finance, Egypt, 25–35. Cairo: National Printing Department, 1908.

Smith, Harry S. *Preliminary Reports of the Egypt Exploration Society's Nubian Survey*. United Arab Republic, Ministry of Culture and National Guidance, Antiquities Department of Egypt: UNESCO's International Campaign to Save the Monuments of Nubia. Cairo: General Organisation for Government Printing Offices, 1962.

———. "The Nubian B-Group." *Kush: Journal of the Sudan Antiquities Service* 14 (1966): 69–124.

Strouhal, Eugen. "Anthropometric and Functional Evidence of Heterosis from Egyptian Nubia." *Human Biology* 43, no. 2 (1971): 271–87.

The Geographer, Department of State. *International Boundary Study No. 18—July 27, 1962: Sudan-Egypt (United Arab Republic) Boundary (Country Codes: SU-EG)*. Washington, DC: United States of America Department of State, Office of the Geographer, Bureau of Intelligence and Research, 1962.

Trigger, Bruce G. *History and Settlement in Lower Nubia*. Yale University Publications in Anthropology 69. New Haven, CT: Department of Anthropology, Yale University, 1965.

UNESCO. *UNESCO Constitution* (1945). http://portal.unesco.org/en/ev.php-URL _ID=15244&URL_DO=DO_TOPIC&URL_SECTION=201.html.

———. "International Principles Governing Archaeological Excavations: Preliminary Report Compiled in Accordance with the Provisions of Article 10.1 of the Rules of Procedure Concerning Recommendations to Member States and International Conventions Covered by the Terms of Article IV, Paragraph 4, of the Constitution." UNESCO/CUA/68, August 9, 1955.

———. "Records of the General Conference, Ninth Session, New Delhi, 1956: Resolutions." Paris: UNESCO, 1957.

———. "International Campaign to Save the Monuments of Nubia; Executive Committee, Sixth Session, Cairo, 5–9 November 1963." UNESCO/Nubia/CE/VI/3, November 27, 1963.

———. "Records of the General Conference: Twelfth Session, Paris, 1962; Resolutions." Paris: UNESCO, 1963.

———. *Four Statements on the Race Question.* Paris: UNESCO, 1969.
———. "International Campaign to Save the Monuments of Nubia: Executive Committee; Eighteenth Session, Paris, 3–4 December, 1970." UNESCO/NUBIA/18, March 22, 1971.
———. *Philae Resurrected.* Paris: UNESCO, 1980.
———. "Text of the Convention for the Safeguarding of the Intangible Cultural Heritage." Article 2, 2003. Accessed October 29, 2020. https://ich.unesco.org/en/convention.
———. "40th Anniversary of Nubia Campaign Celebrated in Egypt." March 16, 2020. https://whc.unesco.org/en/news/2091.
———. "Abu Simbel: The Campaign That Revolutionized the International Approach to Safeguarding Heritage." Accessed January 18, 2021. https://en.unesco.org/70years/abusimbelsafeguardingheritage.
———. "Gebel Barkal and the Sites of the Napatan Region." Accessed October 19, 2020. https://whc.unesco.org/en/list/1073/.
———. "States Parties Ratification Status." Accessed October 19, 2020. https://whc.unesco.org/en/statesparties/.
———. "The National Museum of Egyptian Civilization." Accessed October 28, 2020. http://www.unesco.org/new/en/culture/themes/museums/museum-projects/the-national-museum-of-egyptian-civilization/.
———. "World Heritage List." Accessed October 15, 2020. http://whc.unesco.org/en/list/&order=year.
United Nations Economic and Social Council. "Economic Commission for Africa, Standing Committee on Trade, First Session, Addis Ababa, 12–22 September 1962; Cairo Declaration of Developing Countries (Document Submitted by the Delegation of the UAR)." Document E/CN.14/STC/16, September 14, 1962.
United Nations Statistics Division. "Country Profile of Egypt." Accessed July 27, 2020. https://unstats.un.org/unsd/dnss/docViewer.aspx?docID=506#start.
Vercoutter, Jean. "Archaeological Survey in the Sudan, 1955–57." *Sudan Notes and Records* 38 (1957): 111–17.
Vercoutter, Jean, and William Y. Adams. *Why Excavate in Sudanese Nubia? An Appeal of the Sudan Antiquities Service.* Gloucester: John Bellows, 1960.
Wahab, Mohamed Fikri Abdul. "Problems of Nubian Migration." In *Nubian Encounters: The Story of the Nubian Ethnological Survey 1961–1964,* edited by Nicholas S. Hopkins and Sohair R. Mehanna, 227–36. Cairo: American University in Cairo Press, 2010.
Weeks, Kent R. *The Classic Christian Townsite at Arminna West.* Publications of the Pennsylvania-Yale Expedition to Egypt 3. New Haven, CT, and Philadelphia: The Peabody Museum of Natural History of Yale University and the University Museum of the University of Pennsylvania, 1967.
Weigall, Arthur. *A Report on the Antiquities of Lower Nubia (the First Cataract to the Sudan Frontier) and Their Condition in 1906–7.* Oxford: Oxford University Press, 1907.
Wendorf, Fred. "Introduction." In *The Prehistory of Nubia,* vol. 1, ed. Fred Wendorf, 3–18. Taos, NM: Fort Burgwin Research Center and Southern Methodist University Press, 1968.

———. "Preface." In *The Prehistory of Nubia*, vol. 1, edited by Fred Wendorf, vii–x. Taos, NM: Fort Burgwin Research Center and Southern Methodist University Press, 1968.

Williams, Bruce Beyer. *Excavations Between Abu Simbel and the Sudan Frontier*, Part 1, *The A-Group Royal Cemetery at Qustul: Cemetery L*. The University of Chicago Oriental Institute Nubian Expedition 3. Chicago: The Oriental Institute of the University of Chicago, 1986.

Wizarat al-Thaqafa. *4 Mu'tamarat* [4 Conferences], vol. 1, *al-Sinima, al-Masrah, al-Kitab, al-Fann al-Tashkili* [The cinema, the theater, the book, the fine arts]. Cairo: Wizarat al-Thaqafa, al-Mu'assasa al-Misriyya al-'Amma li-l-Ta'lif wa-l-Nashr, and Dar al-Katib al-'Arabi, 1967.

Wright, G. R. H. *Kalabsha: The Preserving of the Temple*. Berlin: Gebr. Mann, 1972.

Radio and Television Broadcasts and Films

Al-Nas wa-l-Nil [The People and the Nile], directed by Youssef Chahine, 1968.

UNESCO Radio. "World Heritage: A Conversation between Dr. Brew, Dr. Amer and Rex Keating on the Purpose of the Committee on Monuments, Artistic and Historical Sites and Archaeological Investigations." Produced by Rex Keating, Paris, 1961.

Books and Articles

Abdalla, Isma'il Hussein. "The Choice of Khashm al-Girba Area for the Resettlement of the Halfawis." *Sudan Notes and Records* 51 (1970): 56–74.

Abdeen, Mamdouh M. "Biography of Professor M. El-Bahay Issawi." *Journal of African Earth Sciences* 136 (2017): 5–9.

Abou-El-Fadl, Reem. "Building Egypt's Afro-Asian Hub: Infrastructures of Solidarity and the 1957 Cairo Conference." *Journal of World History* 30, nos. 1–2 (2019): 157–92.

Abraham, Itty. "From Bandung to NAM: Non-Alignment and Indian Foreign Policy, 1947–1965." *Commonwealth and Comparative Politics* 46, no. 2 (2008): 195–219.

Abt, Jeffrey. "Toward a Historian's Laboratory: The Breasted-Rockefeller Museum Projects in Egypt, Palestine, and America." *Journal of the American Research Center in Egypt* 33 (1996): 173–94.

———. *American Egyptologist: The Life of James Henry Breasted and the Creation of His Oriental Institute*. Chicago: University of Chicago Press, 2011.

Abu el-Haj, Nadia. *Facts on the Ground: Archaeological Practice and Territorial Self-Fashioning in Israeli Society*. Chicago: University of Chicago Press, 2001.

Abul-Magd, Zeinab. *Imagined Empires: A History of Revolt in Egypt*. Berkeley: University of California Press, 2013.

"Abydos Archaeology." Accessed October 27, 2020. https://abydos.org/about.

Adam, Shehata. "The Importance of Nubia: A Link Between Central Africa and the Mediterranean." With the collaboration of Jean Vercoutter. In *General History of Africa*, vol. 2, *Ancient Civilizations of Africa*, edited by Gamal Mokhtar, 226–44. Paris and London: UNESCO and Heinemann, 1981.

Adams, William Y. "Organizational Problems in International Salvage Archaeology." *Anthropological Quarterly* 41 (1968): 110–21.
———. *Nubia: Corridor to Africa*. London: Allen Lane, 1977.
———. *The Road from Frijoles Canyon: Anthropological Adventures on Four Continents*. Albuquerque: University of New Mexico Press, 2009.
"Aga Khan Award for Architecture." Accessed October 28, 2020. https://www.akdn.org/architecture.
Agha, Menna. "Nubia Still Exists: On the Utility of the Nostalgic Space." *Humanities* 8, no. 1 (2019): 1–12.
Ahlberg, Kristin L. *Transplanting the Great Society: Lyndon Johnson and Food for Peace*. Columbia and London: University of Missouri Press, 2008.
Al-Ahram, ed. *Al-Sadd al-ʿAli: ʿAdad Khas Yasduruh al-Ahram* [The High Dam: Special number issued by Al-Ahram]. Cairo: Al-Ahram, May 15, 1964.
Allais, Lucia. "The Design of the Nubian Desert: Monuments, Mobility, and the Space of Global Culture." In *Governing by Design: Architecture, Economy, and Politics in the Twentieth Century*, edited by the Aggregate Architectural History Collaborative, 179–215. Pittsburgh: University of Pittsburgh Press, 2012.
———. "Integrities: The Salvage of Abu Simbel." *Grey Room* 50 (2013): 6–45.
———. *Designs of Destruction: The Making of Monuments in the Twentieth Century*. Chicago: University of Chicago Press, 2018.
Alterman, Jon B. *Egypt and American Foreign Assistance, 1952–1956*. Basingstoke and New York: Palgrave, 2002.
Amrith, Sunil, and Glenda Sluga. "New Histories of the United Nations." *Journal of World History* 19, no. 2 (2008): 251–74.
Anon. Untitled, *American Research Center in Egypt, Incorporated: Newsletter* 27 (1958): 1–3.
Ansari, Hamied. *Egypt: The Stalled Society*. Albany: State University of New York Press, 1986.
Apoh, Wazi, and Kodzo Gavua. "'We Will Not Relocate Until Our Ancestors and Shrines Come with Us': Heritage and Conflict Management in the Bui Dam Project Area, Ghana." In *Community Archaeology and Heritage in Africa: Decolonizing Practice*, edited by Peter R. Schmidt and Innocent Pikirayi, 204–23. London: Routledge, 2016.
Araoz, Gustavo. "In Memoriam: Hiroshi Daifuku." July 23, 2012. https://www.icomos.org/en/9-uncategorised/494-in-memoriam-hiroshi-daifuku.
El Arifi, Salih A. "Problems in Planning Extensive Agricultural Projects: The Case of New Halfa, Sudan." *Applied Geography* 8, no. 1 (1988): 37–52.
Armando, Silvia. "Ugo Monneret de Villard (1881–1954) and the Establishment of Islamic Art Studies in Italy." *Muqarnas* 30 (2013): 35–71.
Armbrust, Walter. "The Formation of National Culture in Egypt in the Interwar Period: Cultural Trajectories." *History Compass* 7, no. 1 (2009): 155–80.
———. *Martyrs and Tricksters: An Ethnography of the Egyptian Revolution*. Princeton, NJ: Princeton University Press, 2019.
Arnold, David. *Everyday Technology: Machines and the Making of India's Modernity*. Chicago: University of Chicago Press, 2013.
———. "Nehruvian Science and Postcolonial India." *Isis* 104, no. 2 (2013): 360–70.
Aronova, Elena, Christine von Oertzen, and David Sepkoski. "Introduction: Historicizing Big Data." *Osiris* 32 (2017): 1–17.

Ashby, Solange. *Calling Out to Isis: The Enduring Nubian Presence at Philae*. Gorgias Studies in the Ancient Near East 13. Piscataway, NJ: Gorgias, 2020.
Al-'Ashmawi, Ashraf. *Sariqat Mashru'a* [Legal robberies]. Cairo: Al-Dar al-Misriyya al-Lubnaniyya, 2012.
El-Ashmouni, Marwa M. S. "The Rationale of Architectural Discourses in Post-Independence Egypt: A Contrapuntal Reading of '*Alam al-Bena'a* (1980–2000)." PhD diss., University of Adelaide, 2013.
Assiri, Abdul-Reda. "Kuwait's Dinar Diplomacy: The Role of Donor-Mediator." *Journal of South Asian and Middle Eastern Studies* 14, no. 3 (1991): 24–32.
Aswan li-l-Ma'rid al-Zira'i al-Sina'i al-Sadis 'Ashar [Aswan on the occasion of the sixteenth agricultural and manufacturing exhibit]. Cairo: Matba'at al-Ittihad, 1949.
'Awad, Muhammad. "Nomadism in the Arab Lands of the Middle East." *Arid Zone Research* 18 (1962): 325–40.
Azoulay, Ariella Aïsha. *Potential History: Unlearning Imperialism*. London and New York: Verso, 2019.
Baedeker, Karl, ed. *Egypt: Handbook for Travellers*, vol. 2, *Upper Egypt with Nubia as Far as the Second Cataract and the Western Oases*. Leipzig: Karl Baedeker, 1892.
———. *Egypt and the Sûdân: Handbook for Travellers*, 8th rev. ed. Newton Abbot: David & Charles, 1974 (reprint of 1929 edition).
Barak, On. *On Time: Technology and Temporality in Modern Egypt*. Berkeley: University of California Press, 2013.
Basu, Paul, and Vinita Damodaran. "Colonial Histories of Heritage: Legislative Migrations and the Politics of Preservation." *Past and Present* Supplement 10 (2015): 240–71.
Bednarski, Andrew. *Holding Egypt: Tracing the Reception of the 'Description de l'Égypte' in Nineteenth-Century Great Britain*. London: Golden House, 2005.
Behm, Amanda, Christienna Fryar, Emma Hunter, Elisabeth Leake, Su Lin Lewis, and Sarah Miller-Davenport. "Decolonizing History: Enquiry and Practice." *History Workshop Journal* 89 (2020): 169–91.
Beinin, Joel. *The Dispersion of Egyptian Jewry: Culture, Politics, and the Formation of a Modern Diaspora*. Cairo: American University in Cairo Press, 2005 (reprint of Berkeley: University of California Press, 1998 edition).
Bell, Lanny. "The Epigraphic Survey: The Philosophy of Egyptian Epigraphy after Sixty Years' Practical Experience." In *Problems and Priorities in Egyptian Archaeology*, edited by Jan Assmann, Günter Burkard, and Vivian Davies, 43–55. London: KPI, 1987.
Bernal, Martin. *Black Athena: The Afroasiatic Roots of Classical Civilisation*, vol. 1, *The Fabrication of Ancient Greece, 1785–1985*. London: Vintage, 1991.
Bier, Laura. *Revolutionary Womanhood: Feminisms, Modernity, and the State in Nasser's Egypt*. Cairo: American University in Cairo Press, 2011.
Bierbrier, Morris L., ed. *Who Was Who in Egyptology?* 4th ed. London: Egypt Exploration Society, 2012.
Bishop, Elizabeth. "Control Room: Visible and Concealed Spaces of the Aswan High Dam." In *Landscapes of Development: The Impact of Modernization Discourses on the Physical Environment of the Eastern Mediterranean*, edited by Panayiota Pyla, 72–87. Cambridge, MA: Harvard University Press, 2013.

Blanc, Nicole. "The Peopling of the Nile Valley South of the Twenty-Third Parallel." In *The Peopling of Ancient Egypt and the Deciphering of the Meroitic Script: Proceedings of the Symposium Held in Cairo from 28 January to 3 February 1974*, edited by UNESCO, 37–63. Paris: UNESCO, 1978.

Bloembergen, Marieke, and Martijn Eickhoff. *The Politics of Heritage in Indonesia: A Cultural History*. Cambridge: Cambridge University Press, 2020.

Boast, Robin. "Mortimer Wheeler's Science of Order: The Tradition of Accuracy at Arikamedu." *Antiquity* 76 (2002): 165–70.

"Border Center for Support and Consulting (BSC)." Accessed November 12, 2020. https://www.ohchr.org/Documents/Issues/Housing/IndigenousPeoples/CSO/Border%20Center%20for%20Support%20and%20Consulting%20BSC%20-%20Nubian%20indigenous%20people%20Egypt.pdf.

Bothmer, Bernard V. *Egypt 1950: My First Visit*. Edited by Emma Swan Hall. Oxford: Oxbow, 2003.

Brew, John Otis. "Emergency Archaeology: Salvage in Advance of Technological Progress." *Proceedings of the American Philosophical Society* 105, no. 1 (1961): 1–10.

Brusius, Mirjam. "Towards a History of Preservation Practices: Archaeology, Heritage, and the History of Science." *International Journal of Middle East Studies* 47, no. 3 (2015): 574–79.

———. "Introduction—What Is Preservation?" *Review of Middle East Studies* 51, no. 2 (2017): 177–82.

———. "The Field in the Museum: Puzzling Out Babylon in Berlin." *Osiris* 32 (2017): 264–85.

Brusius, Mirjam, and Kavita Singh, eds. *Museum Storage and Meaning: Tales from the Crypt*. London and New York: Routledge, 2018.

"Buhen: A Dig House Becomes a Home . . ." *The Egypt Exploration Society* website. Accessed September 10, 2020. https://www.ees.ac.uk/buhen-a-dig-house-becomes-a-home.

Butler, Beverley. *Return to Alexandria: An Ethnography of Cultural Heritage, Revivalism, and Museum Memory*. Walnut Creek, CA: Left Coast Press, 2007.

Carr, Lydia C. *Tessa Verney Wheeler: Women and Archaeology Before World War Two*. Oxford: Oxford University Press, 2012.

Carruthers, William. "Egyptology, Archaeology and the Making of Revolutionary Egypt, c. 1925–1958." PhD diss., University of Cambridge, 2014.

———. "The Planned Past: Policy and (Ancient) Egypt." *Egyptian and Egyptological Documents, Archives, Libraries* 4 (2015): 229–40.

———. "Multilateral Possibilities: Decolonization, Preservation, and the Case of Egypt." *Future Anterior: Journal of Historic Preservation History, Theory, and Criticism* 13, no. 1 (2016): 36–48.

———. "Rule of Objects: On the De-Peopling of Safe Havens." *Review of Middle East Studies* 51, no. 2 (2017): 228–33.

———. "Visualizing a Monumental Past: Archeology, Nasser's Egypt, and the Early Cold War." *History of Science* 55, no. 3 (2017): 273–301.

———. "Credibility, Civility, and the Archaeological Dig-House in Mid-1950s Egypt." *Journal of Social Archaeology* 19, no. 2 (2019): 255–76.

——. "Heritage, Preservation, and Decolonization: Entanglements, Consequences, Action?" *Future Anterior: Journal of Historic Preservation History, Theory, and Criticism* 16, no. 2 (2019): ii–xxiv.
——. "Archaeological (Non?) Alignments: Egypt, India, and Global Geographies of the Post-War Past." *South Asian Studies* 36, no. 1 (2020): 45–60.
——. "Records of Dispossession: Archival Thinking and UNESCO's Nubian Campaign in Egypt and Sudan." *International Journal of Islamic Architecture* 9, no. 2 (2020): 287–314.
——. "Spectacles of the Past." *Jadaliyya* May 12, 2021. https://www.jadaliyya.com/Details/42719.
Cheta, Omar Youssef. "A Prehistory of the Modern Legal Profession in Egypt, 1840s–1870s." *International Journal of Middle East Studies* 50 (2018): 649–68.
"Chicago House Projects." Accessed July 9, 2020. https://oi.uchicago.edu/research/projects/epi/chicago-house-projects.
Chopra, Pran Nath. "Al-Alaqat al-Thaqafiyya baina al-Hind wa-l-Jumhuriyya al-ʻArabiyya al-Muttahida" ["The cultural links between India and the UAR"]. *Thaqafat al-Hind* 13, no. 4 (1962): 102–108.
Clifford, James. "Notes on (Field)notes." In *Fieldnotes: The Makings of Anthropology*, edited by Roger Sanjek, 47–70. Ithaca: Cornell University Press, 1990.
Colla, Elliott. *Conflicted Antiquities: Egyptology, Egyptomania, Egyptian Modernity*. Durham, NC: Duke University Press, 2007.
Collins, Robert O. *A History of Modern Sudan*. Cambridge: Cambridge University Press, 2008.
Condopoulo, P. *An Illustrated Guide Book on Egypt and Nubia*. Cairo: E. Menikidis, 1930.
Conklin, Alice L. *In the Museum of Man: Race, Anthropology, and Empire in France, 1850–1950*. Ithaca, NY: Cornell University Press, 2013.
Conlin, Jonathan. *Mr Five Per Cent: The Many Lives of Calouste Gulbenkian, the World's Richest Man*. London: Profile, 2019.
Connelly, Matthew. *Fatal Misconception: The Struggle to Control World Population*. Cambridge, MA: Harvard University Press, 2008.
Cooper, Artemis. *Cairo in the War, 1939–1945*. London: Penguin, 1989.
Cooper, Frederick. "Possibility and Constraint: African Independence in Historical Perspective." *Journal of African History* 49, no. 2 (2008): 167–96.
Crawford, O. G. S. "People Without a History." *Antiquity* 22 (1948): 8–12.
——. "Field Archaeology of the Middle Nile Region." *Kush: Journal of the Sudan Antiquities Service* 1 (1954): 2–29.
Daston, Lorraine. "The Sciences of the Archive." *Osiris* 27 (2012): 156–87.
Davis, Thomas W. *Shifting Sands: The Rise and Fall of Biblical Archaeology*. Oxford: Oxford University Press, 2004.
Derr, Jennifer L. "Drafting a Map of Colonial Egypt: The 1902 Aswan Dam, Historical Imagination, and the Production of Agricultural Geography." In *Environmental Imaginaries of the Middle East and North Africa*, edited by Diana K. Davis and Edmund Burke III, 136–57. Athens: Ohio University Press, 2011.
——. "Labor-Time: Ecological Bodies and Agricultural Labor in 19th and Early 20th-Century Egypt." *International Journal of Middle East Studies* 50, no. 2 (2018): 195–212.

———. *The Lived Nile: Environment, Disease, and Material Colonial Economy in Egypt.* Stanford: Stanford University Press, 2019.

De Simone, Costanza. "Wadi Halfa Museum: A Rescue Mechanism for the Nubian Intangible Heritage." In "Pratiques du patrimoine en Égypte et au Soudan," edited by Omnia Aboukorah and Jean-Gabriel Leturcq, special edition of *Égypte/Monde arabe,* nos. 5–6 (2009): 403–16.

Deutsche Börse Photography Foundation. "Paul Almasy." Accessed May 27, 2020. https://www.deutscheboersephotographyfoundation.org/en/collect/artists/paul-almasy.php.

Di-Capua, Yoav. *Gatekeepers of the Arab Past: Historians and History-Writing in Twentieth-Century Egypt.* Berkeley: University of California Press, 2009.

DiMeo, David F. *Committed to Disillusion: Activist Writers in Egypt from the 1950s to the 1980s.* Cairo: American University in Cairo Press, 2016.

Diop, Cheikh Anta. *The African Origin of Civilization: Myth or Reality?* Translated by Mercer Cook. Westport, CT: Lawrence Hill, 1974.

———. "Origin of the Ancient Egyptians." In *General History of Africa,* vol. 2, *Ancient Civilizations of Africa,* edited by Gamal Mokhtar, 27–57. Paris and London: UNESCO and Heinemann, 1981.

Dissard, Laurent. "Learning by Doing: Archaeological Excavations as 'Communities of Practice.'" *Bulletin of the History of Archaeology* 29, no. 1, article 5 (2019): 1–8.

Doyon, Wendy. "On Archaeological Labor in Modern Egypt." In *Histories of Egyptology: Interdisciplinary Measures,* edited by William Carruthers, 141–56. New York: Routledge, 2015.

———. "The History of Archaeology through the Eyes of Egyptians." In *Unmasking Ideology in Imperial and Colonial Archaeology: Vocabulary, Symbols, and Legacy,* edited by Bonnie Effros and Guolong Lai, 173–200. Los Angeles: The Cotsen Institute of Archaeology Press, 2018.

"Dr. Kent R. Weeks, Director." Theban Mapping Project website. Accessed August 25, 2020. https://web.archive.org/web/20161111093307/http://www.thebanmappingproject.com/about/staff_1.html.

Dukas, Martha. *Azmat al-Kuwait: al-ʿAlaqat al-Kuwaitiyya al-ʿIraqiyya 1961–1963* [The crisis of Kuwait: Kuwaiti-Iraqi relations, 1961–1963]. Beirut: Dar al-Nahar li-l-Nashr, 1973.

Dunham, Kingsley. "Frank Dixey: 7 April 1892–1 November 1982." *Biographical Memoirs of Fellows of the Royal Society* 29 (1983): 158–76.

Edgerton, David. *The Shock of the Old: Technology and Global History since 1900.* New York: Oxford University Press, 2007.

"Editorial Foreword." *The Journal of Egyptian Archaeology* 45 (1959): 1–2.

Edwards, David. *The Nubian Past: An Archaeology of the Sudan.* London and New York: Routledge, 2004.

Ekbladh, David. *The Great American Mission: Modernization and the Construction of an American World Order.* Princeton, NJ: Princeton University Press, 2010.

Elcheikh, Zeina. "Outside the Walls of the Nubian Museum." *e-dialogos: Annual Digital Journal on Research in Conservation and Cultural Heritage* 4 (2014): 31–37.

———. "Tales from Two Villages: Nubian Women and Cultural Tourism in Gharb Soheil and Ballana." *Dotawo: A Journal of Nubian Studies* 5 (2018): 241–60.

Elshahed, Mohammed. "The Old and New Egyptian Museums: Between Imperialists, Nationalists, and Tourists." In *Histories of Egyptology: Interdisciplinary Measures*, edited by William Carruthers, 255–69. New York and Abingdon: Routledge, 2015.
———. *Cairo Since 1900: An Architectural Guide*. Cairo: American University in Cairo Press, 2020.
Emery, Walter Bryan. *Nubian Treasure*. London: Methuen, 1948.
———. *Archaic Egypt*. Harmondsworth: Penguin, 1961.
———. *Egypt in Nubia*. London: Hutchinson, 1965.
———. "Preliminary Reports on the Excavations at North Saqqara, 1964–5." *The Journal of Egyptian Archaeology* 51 (1965): 3–8.
———. *Lost Land Emerging*. New York: Charles Scribner's Sons, 1967.
———. *Misr fi ʿAsr al-ʿAtiq (Al-Usratan al-Ula wa-l-Thaniyya)* [Egypt in the ancient period: The first and second dynasties]. Revised by Abdel Moneim Abu Bakr. Translated by Rashid Muhammad Nawir and Muhammad ʿAli Kamal al-Din. Cairo: Dar Nahdat Misr, 1967.
Escobar, Arturo. *Encountering Development: The Making and Unmaking of the Third World*. Princeton, NJ: Princeton University Press, 1995.
"Espionage Charges Against Members of French Assets Mission." *Middle East Record* 2 (1961): 643–44.
Evans, Christopher J. "Archaeology and Modern Times: Bersu's Woodbury 1938 and 1939." *Antiquity* 63 (1989): 436–50.
———. "Soldiering Archaeology: Pitt Rivers and 'Militarism.'" *Bulletin of the History of Archaeology* 24, no. 4 (2014): 1–20.
"Eventup: The Temple of Dendur at the Met." Accessed November 13, 2020. https://eventup.com/venue/the-temple-of-dendur-at-the-met/.
Ewing, Cindy. "The Colombo Powers: Crafting Diplomacy in the Third World and Launching Afro-Asia at Bandung." *Cold War History* 19, no. 1 (2019): 1–19.
Exell, Karen, ed. *Egypt in its African Context: Proceedings of the Conference Held at the Manchester Museum, University of Manchester, 2–4 October 2009*. Oxford: Archaeopress, 2011.
Fahmy, Khaled. *All the Pasha's Men: Mehmed Ali, His Army and the Making of Modern Egypt*. Cambridge: Cambridge University Press, 1997.
———. "National Security and Canned Sardines." February 9, 2013. https://khaledfahmy.org/en/2013/02/09/national-security-and-canned-sardines/.
Al-Fakahani, Hassan. *Al-Mawsuʿa al-Tashriʿiyya al-Haditha* [The contemporary legislative encyclopaedia]. Cairo: Al-Dar al-ʿArabiyya li-l-Mawsuʿat, 1964.
Fakhuri, Yussef. *Al-Tarikh al-Insani li-l-Sadd al-ʿAli* [The human history of the High Dam]. Cairo: Al-Haiʾa al-ʿAma li-Qusur al-Thaqafa, 2016.
Falser, Michael. *Angkor Wat: A Transcultural History of Heritage*. 2 vols. Berlin: De Gruyter, 2020.
Fathy, Hassan. *Architecture for the Poor: An Experiment in Rural Egypt*. Chicago: University of Chicago Press, 1973.
Feldman, Ilana. *Governing Gaza: Bureaucracy, Authority, and the Work of Rule (1917–1967)*. Durham, NC: Duke University Press, 2008.
"Fellowships and Grants: Smithsonian Institution Foreign Currency Program in Archeology and Related Disciplines." *American Anthropological Association Fellow Newsletter* 8 (1965): 4–5.

Felski, Rita. *The Limits of Critique*. Chicago: University of Chicago Press, 2015.
Foster, Dawn. *Lean Out*. London: Repeater, 2016.
Fuller, Steven. *Social Epistemology*. Bloomington: Indiana University Press, 2002.
Gange, David. *Dialogues with the Dead: Egyptology in British Culture and Religion, 1822–1922*. Oxford: Oxford University Press, 2013.
———. "Unholy Water: Archaeology, the Bible, and the First Aswan Dam." In *From Plunder to Preservation: Britain and the Heritage of Empire c. 1800–1940*, edited by Astrid Swenson and Peter Mandler, 93–114. Proceedings of the British Academy 187. Oxford: Oxford University Press, 2013.
Gauthier, Gilles, Nala Aloudat, and Agnès Carayon, eds. *L'épopée du canal de Suez*. Marseille and Paris: Musée d'Histoire de Marseille, Gallimard, and Institut du monde arabe, 2018.
Gershoni, Israel, and James P. Jankowski. *Redefining the Egyptian Nation, 1930–1945*. Cambridge: Cambridge University Press, 1995.
Gertzen, Thomas L. *École de Berlin und "Goldenes Zeitalter" (1882–1914) der Ägyptologie als Wissenschaft: Das Lehrer-Schüler-Verhältnis von Ebers, Erman und Sethe*. Berlin: De Gruyter, 2013.
Getachew, Adom. *Worldmaking after Empire: The Rise and Fall of Self-Determination*. Princeton, NJ: Princeton University Press, 2019.
Gfeller, Aurélie Elisa. "Anthropologizing and Indigenizing Heritage: The Origins of the UNESCO Global Strategy for a Representative, Balanced and Credible World Heritage List." *Journal of Social Archaeology* 15, no. 3 (2015): 366–86.
Ghosh, A., ed. *Indian Archaeology 1961–62: A Review*. New Delhi: Archaeological Survey of India, 1964.
Gilmore, Christine. "'A Minor Literature in a Major Voice': Narrating Nubian Identity in Contemporary Egypt." *Alif: Journal of Comparative Poetics* 35 (2015): 52–74.
———. "Speaking through the Silence." In *Development-Induced Displacement and Resettlement: New Perspectives on Persisting Problems*, edited by Irge Satiroglu and Narae Choi, 199–211. Abingdon: Routledge, 2015.
Gissen, David. "The Architectural Production of Nature, Dendur/New York." *Grey Room* 34 (2009): 58–79.
Godlewska, Anne. "Map, Text and Image: The Mentality of Enlightened Conquerors; A New Look at the *Description de l'Egypte*." *Transactions of the Institute of British Geographers* 20, no. 1 (1995): 5–28.
Goedicke, Hans. "The Beit el-Wali Temple of Ramesses II by Herbert Ricke, George R. Hughes, Edward G. Wente." *Journal of the American Research Center in Egypt* 7 (1968): 138.
Goldschmidt, Arthur. *Biographical Dictionary of Modern Egypt*. Boulder, CO, and London: Lynne Rienner, 2000.
Goldschmidt, Arthur, Amy J. Johnson, and Barak A. Salmoni, eds. *Re-Envisioning Egypt, 1919–1952*. Cairo: American University in Cairo Press, 2005.
Gordon, Joel. *Nasser's Blessed Movement: Egypt's Free Officers and the July Revolution*. New York: Oxford University Press, 1992.
Greener, Leslie. *High Dam Over Nubia*. London: Cassell, 1962.
Gregory, Derek. "Colonial Nostalgia and Cultures of Travel: Spaces of Constructed Visibility in Egypt." In *Consuming Tradition, Manufacturing Heritage: Global*

Norms and Urban Forms in the Age of Tourism, edited by Nezar AlSayyad, 111–51. London: E. and F. Spon and Routledge, 2001.
Griswold, Sarah. "High-Tech Heritage: Planes, Photography, and the Ancient Past in the French Mandate for Syria and Lebanon." *Future Anterior: Journal of Historic Preservation, History, Theory, and Criticism* 16, no. 2 (2019): 1–15.
Guerville, Amédée Baillot de. *New Egypt*. New York: E. P. Dutton and Company, 1906.
Guha, Sudeshna. "Mortimer Wheeler's Archaeology in South Asia and its Photographic Representation." *South Asian Studies* 19, no. 1 (2003): 43–55.
———. *Artefacts of History: Archaeology, Historiography and Indian Pasts*. New Delhi: Sage, 2015.
Hagen, Fredrik, and Kim Ryholt. *The Antiquities Trade in Egypt 1880–1930*. Copenhagen: The Royal Danish Academy of Sciences and Letters, 2016.
Hahn, Peter L. *The United States, Great Britain, and Egypt, 1945–1956: Strategy and Diplomacy in the Early Cold War*. Chapel Hill: University of North Carolina Press, 1991.
Hamad, Bushra. "*Sudan Notes and Records* and Sudanese Nationalism, 1918–1956." *History in Africa* 22 (1995): 239–70.
Hamza, Muhammad Shahin. *Rihla ila al-Sudan* [Journey to Sudan]. [Cairo?], 1954.
Hankey, Julie. *A Passion for Egypt: A Biography of Arthur Weigall*. London and New York: I. B. Tauris, 2001.
Hauser, Kitty. *Shadow Sites: Photography, Archaeology, and the British Landscape, 1927–1955*. Oxford: Oxford University Press, 2007.
Hawass, Zahi A. "A New Era for Museums in Egypt." *Museum International* 57, nos. 1–2 (2005): 7–23.
Hawkes, Jacquetta. *Mortimer Wheeler: Adventurer in Archaeology*. London: Weidenfeld and Nicolson, 1982.
Hoving, Thomas. *Making the Mummies Dance: Inside the Metropolitan Museum of Art*. New York: Simon and Schuster, 1993.
Huber, Marie. *Developing Heritage—Developing Countries: Ethiopian Nation-Building and the Origins of UNESCO World Heritage, 1960–1980*. Berlin and Boston: De Gruyter, 2021.
Huber, Valeska. *Channelling Mobilities: Migration and Globalisation in the Suez Canal Region and Beyond, 1869–1914*. Cambridge: Cambridge University Press, 2013.
Hudson, Corey M. "Walter Taylor and the History of American Archaeology." *Journal of Anthropological Archaeology* 27, no. 2 (2008): 192–200.
Ibrahim, ʿAbdelbaki. *Al-Turath al-Hidari fi-l-Madina al-ʿArabiyya al-Muʿasira* [Urban heritage in the contemporary Arab city]. Kuwait City: Baladiyyat Kuwait, 1968.
Ibrahim, Sonallah. *Najmat Aghustus* [August star]. Damascus: Ittihad al-Kitab al-ʿArab Dimashq, 1974.
Ibrahim, Sonallah, Kamal al-Qilsh, and Raʾuf Musʿad. *Insan al-Sadd al-ʿAli* [The man of the High Dam]. Cairo: Dar al-Kitab al-ʿArabi li-l-Tibaʿa wa-l-Nashr, 1967.
Immerwahr, Daniel. *How to Hide an Empire: A Short History of the Greater United States*. London: The Bodley Head, 2019.
"Important Archaeological Discoveries in Northern Sudan." *Republic of the Sudan News* 2 (February 1962): 4.

Jacob, Wilson Chacko. *Working Out Egypt: Effendi Masculinity and Subject Formation in Colonial Modernity, 1870–1940*. Durham, NC: Duke University Press, 2011.

Jakes, Aaron. *Egypt's Occupation: Colonial Economism and the Crises of Capitalism*. Stanford: Stanford University Press, 2020.

Jankowski, James. *Nasser's Egypt, Arab Nationalism, and the United Arab Republic*. Boulder, CO, and London: Lynne Rienner, 2002.

Janmyr, Maja. "Nubians in Contemporary Egypt: Mobilizing Return to Ancestral Lands." *Middle East Critique* 23, no. 2 (2016): 127–46.

———. "Human Rights and Nubian Mobilisation in Egypt: Towards Recognition of Indigeneity." *Third World Quarterly* 38, no. 3 (2017): 717–33.

Jennings, Anne M. *Nubian Women of West Aswan: Negotiating Tradition and Change*, 2nd ed. Cairo: American University in Cairo Press, 2009.

"John Spencer Purvis Bradford (1918–1975)." *Monuments Men Foundation for the Preservation of Art* website. Accessed August 13, 2020. https://www.monumentsmenfoundation.org/the-heroes/the-monuments-men/bradford-capt.-john-s.p.

Juret, Michèle. *Étienne Drioton: l'Égypte, une passion*. Haroué: Gérard Louis, 2013.

Kamil, Jill. *Labib Habachi: The Life and Legacy of an Egyptologist*. Cairo: American University in Cairo Press, 2007.

Kamugisha, Aaaron. "Finally in Africa? Egypt, from Diop to Celenko." *Race and Class* 45, no. 1 (2003): 31–60.

Kassem-Draz, Céza. "Opaque and Transparent Discourse: A Contrastive Analysis of the "Star of August" and "The Man of the High Dam" by Son'Allah Ibrahim." *Alif: Journal of Comparative Poetics* 2 (1982): 32–50.

Keating, Rex. *Nubian Twilight*. London: Rupert Hart-Davis, 1962.

———. *Nubian Rescue*. London, Robert Hale, 1975.

Kelly, John D., and Martha Kaplan. *Represented Communities: Fiji and World Decolonization*. Chicago: University of Chicago Press, 2001.

Khadry, Ahmed. "Inaugural Speech." In *The Archaeology of the Nile Delta: Problems and Priorities*, edited by Edwin C. M. van den Brink, 1–2. Amsterdam: Netherlands Foundation for Archaeological Research in Egypt, 1988.

Khalil, Asʿad Abou, and Mahmoud Haddad. "Revival and Renewal." In *The Oxford Encyclopedia of the Islamic World*. Accessed October 15, 2020. http://www.oxfordislamicstudies.com/article/opr/t236/e0682#bibHead1.

Khater, Antoine. *Le régime juridique des fouilles et des antiquités en Égypte*. Cairo: Institut français d'archéologie orientale, 1960.

King, Rachel, and Luíseach Nic Eoin. "Before the Flood: Loss of Place, Mnemonics, and 'Resources' ahead of the Metolong Dam, Lesotho." *Journal of Social Archaeology* 14, no. 2 (2014): 196–223.

Kleinitz, Cornelia. "Between Valorisation and Devaluation: Making and Unmaking (World) Heritage in Sudan." *Archaeologies: Journal of the World Archaeological Congress* 9, no. 3 (2013): 427–69.

Klimowicz, Patrycja, and Arkadiusz Klimowicz. "Polish Archaeology in Egypt and Sudan: An Historical Overview." In *European Archaeology Abroad: Global Settings, Comparative Perspectives*, edited by Sjoerd J. Van der Linde, Monique Henriëtte Van den Dries, Nathan Schlanger, and Corijanne G. Slappendel, 105–24. Leiden: Sidestone, 2012.

Kohler, Robert. *Landscapes and Labscapes: Exploring the Lab-Field Border in Biology.* Chicago: University of Chicago Press, 2002.
Koning, Anouk de. *Global Dreams: Class, Gender, and Public Space in Cosmopolitan Cairo.* Cairo: American University in Cairo Press, 2009.
Koselleck, Reinhart. *Futures Past: On the Semantics of Historical Time.* Translated and with an introduction by Keith Tribe. New York and Chichester: Columbia University Press, 2004. Reprint of 1985 MIT Press edition.
Kuklick, Henrika. *The Savage Within: The Social History of British Anthropology, 1885–1945.* Cambridge: Cambridge University Press, 1991.
Junker, Hermann. "The First Appearance of the Negroes in History." *The Journal of Egyptian Archaeology* 7, nos. 3/4 (1921): 121–32.
Lal, B. B. *Indian Archaeology Since Independence.* Delhi, Varanasi, and Patna: Motilal Banarsidass, 1964.
———. *Piecing Together: Memoirs of an Archaeologist.* New Delhi: Aryan Books International, 2011.
Langer, Christian. "Informal Colonialism of Egyptology: The French Expedition to the Security State." *E-International Relations*, June 16, 2017. https://www.e-ir.info/2017/06/16/informal-colonialism-of-egyptology-the-french-expedition-to-the-security-state/.
Laqua, Daniel. "Transnational Intellectual Cooperation, the League of Nations, and the Problem of Order." *Journal of Global History* 6, no. 2 (2011): 223–47.
Latour, Bruno. *Science in Action.* Cambridge, MA: Harvard University Press, 1987.
Lebovics, Herman. *Mona Lisa's Escort: André Malraux and the Reinvention of French Culture.* Ithaca, NY: Cornell University Press, 1999.
Lewis, Clare. "Inaugural Lectures in Egyptology: T. E. Peet and His Pupil W. B. Emery." *Bulletin of the History of Archaeology* 26, no. 1, article 9 (2016): 1–15.
Little, Tom. *High Dam at Aswan: The Subjugation of the Nile.* London: Methuen, 1965.
Luke, Christina. *A Pearl in Peril: Heritage and Diplomacy in Turkey.* New York: Oxford University Press, 2019.
Luke, Christina, and Morag M. Kersel. *U.S. Cultural Diplomacy and Archaeology: Soft Power and Hard Heritage.* New York and London: Routledge, 2013.
Luke, Christina, and Lynn Meskell. "New Deals for the Past: The Cold War, American Archaeology, and UNESCO in Egypt and Syria," *History and Anthropology* online pre-publication (2020). https://doi.org/10.1080/02757206.2020.1830769.
Macková, Adéla Jůnová. "Journey of Czechoslovak Cultural Delegation to Egypt in 1956: 'Cultural Agreement' between Egypt and the Czechoslovak Republic." *Acta Fakulty filozofické Západočeské univerzity v Pizni* 3 (2011): 101–110.
Malek, Amy. "Clickbait Orientalism and Vintage Iranian Snapshots." *International Journal of Cultural Studies* 24, no. 2 (2021): 266–89.
Al-Maqrizi, Taqi al-Din Ahmad ibn ʿAli ibn ʿAbd al-Qadir ibn Muhammad. *Kitab al-Mawaʿiz wa-l-Iʿtibar bi-Dhikr al-Khitat wa-l-Athar* [Book of lessons and reflections recalling plans and monuments], 2 vols. Bulaq: 1853.
Martin, Geoffrey Thorndike. "The Early Dynastic Necropolis at North Saqqara: The Unpublished Excavations of W. B. Emery and C. M. Firth." In *The Archaeology and Art of Ancient Egypt: Essays in Honour of David B. O'Connor*, Supplément aux Annales du Service des antiquités de l'Égypte 36, vol. 1, edited by Zahi A.

Hawass and Janet Richards, 121–26. Cairo: Supreme Council of Antiquities, 2007.

Maurel, Chloé. "Le sauvetage des monuments de Nubie par l'Unesco (1955–1968)." *Égypte/Monde arabe* 10 (2013): 1–22.

Mazower, Mark. *Governing the World: The History of an Idea*. New York: The Penguin Press, 2012.

Means, Bernard K. "Introduction: 'Alphabet Soup' and American Archaeology." In *Shovel Ready: Archaeology and Roosevelt's New Deal for America*, edited by Bernard K. Means, 1–18. Tuscaloosa: University of Alabama Press, 2013.

Meguid, Ossama Abdel. "Museums, Culture and Sustainable Development." In *From Imperial Museum to Communication Centre? On the New Role of Museums as Mediators between Science and Non-Western Societies*, edited by Lidia Guzy, Rainer Hatoum, and Susan Kamel, 17–26. Würzburg: Königshausen and Neumann, 2010.

Meijer, Roel. *The Quest for Modernity: Secular Liberal and Left-Wing Political Thought in Egypt, 1945–1958*. London: Routledge Curzon, 2002.

Meskell, Lynn. *A Future in Ruins: UNESCO, World Heritage, and the Dream of Peace*. New York: Oxford University Press, 2018.

——. "Imperialism, Internationalism, and Archaeology in the Un/Making of the Middle East." *American Anthropologist* 122, no. 3 (2020): 554–67.

El-Messiri, Sawsan. *Ibn al-Balad: A Concept of Egyptian Identity*. Leiden: E. J. Brill, 1978.

Mickel, Allison. "Reasons for Redundancy in Reflexivity: The Role of Diaries in Archaeological Epistemology." *Journal of Field Archaeology* 40, no. 3 (2015): 300–309.

——. "Essential Excavation Experts: Alienation and Agency in the History of Archaeological Labor." *Archaeologies: Journal of the World Archaeological Congress* 15, no. 2 (2019): 181–205.

——. *Why Those Who Shovel Are Silent: A History of Local Archaeological Knowledge and Labor*. Louisville: University Press of Colorado, 2021.

Mierzejewska, Bożena, Aleksandra Sulikowska, and Tomasz Górecki. *Faras Gallery: Guidebook*. Warsaw: The National Museum in Warsaw, 2014.

Mignolo, Walter, and Rolando Vazquez. "Decolonial Aesthesis: Colonial Wounds/Decolonial Healings." *Social Text Online* July 15, 2013. https://socialtextjournal.org/periscope_article/decolonial-aesthesis-colonial-woundsdecolonial-healings/.

Mikhail, Alan. "From the Bottom Up: The Nile, Silt, and Humans in Ottoman Egypt." In *Environmental Imaginaries of the Middle East and North Africa*, edited by Diana K. Davis and Edmund Burke III, 113–35. Athens: Ohio University Press, 2011.

Mitchell, Timothy. *Colonising Egypt*. Berkeley: University of California Press, 1988.

——. "Making the Nation: The Politics of Heritage in Egypt." In *Consuming Tradition, Manufacturing Heritage: Global Norms and Urban Forms in the Age of Tourism*, edited by Nezar Al Sayyad, 212–39. London: E. and F. Spon and Routledge, 2001.

——. *Rule of Experts: Egypt, Techno-Politics, Modernity*. Berkeley: University of California Press, 2002.

——. *Carbon Democracy: Political Power in the Age of Oil*. London and New York: Verso, 2013.

Mokhtar, Gamal. "Introduction." With the collaboration of Jean Vercoutter. In *General History of Africa*, vol. 2, *Ancient Civilizations of Africa*, edited by Gamal Mokhtar, 1–26. Paris and London: UNESCO and Heinemann, 1981.

Momani, Bessma. "IMF-Egyptian Debt Negotiations." *Cairo Papers in Social Science* 26, no. 3 (2005): 1–101.

Moshenska, Gabriel, and Sarah Dhanjal, eds. *Community Archaeology: Themes, Methods and Practices*. Oxford: Oxbow, 2012.

Mossallam, Alia. "'We Are the Ones Who Made This Dam "High"!' A Builders' History of the Aswan High Dam." *Water History* 6, no. 4 (2014): 297–314.

Moubarak, Walid E. "The Kuwait Fund in the Context of Arab and Third World Politics." *Middle East Journal* 41, no. 4 (1987): 538–52.

Mubarak, ʿAli. *Al-Khitat al-Tawfiqiyya al-Jadida li-Misr wa-l-Qahira wa-Muduniha wa-Biladiha al-Qadima wa-l-Shahira* [Plans of the new Tawfiqiyya for Egypt, Cairo, and its old and famous cities and lands], 3rd ed. Cairo: Matbaʿat Dar al-Wathaʾiq wa-l-Kutub al-Qawmiyya bi-l-Qahira, 2005.

Muehlhaeusler, Mark, ed. *The Story of Anas al-Wujūd: Nineteenth-Century Verse Recensions of an "Arabian Nights" Tale in Egyptian Colloquial Arabic*. Oxford, OH: Faenum, 2015.

Muschik, Eva-Maria. "Managing the World: The United Nations, Decolonization, and the Strange Triumph of State Sovereignty in the 1950s and 1960s." *Journal of Global History* 13 (2018): 121–44.

Myers, Oliver H. "Review of 'Kush: Journal of the Sudan Antiquities Service, Annual, 1953.'" *Sudan Notes and Records* 36, no. 2 (1955): 196–97.

Naaman, Mara. *Urban Space in Contemporary Egyptian Literature: Portraits of Cairo*. New York: Palgrave Macmillan, 2011.

Nassar, Aya. "Where the Dust Settles: Fieldwork, Subjectivity and Materiality in Cairo." *Contemporary Social Science: Journal of the Academy of Social Sciences* 13, nos. 3–4 (2018): 412–28.

Navrátilová, Hana. "Layered Agendas: Jaroslav Černý, Stateless Egyptologist between Decolonization and the Cold War." *Práce z dějin Akademie věd* 10, no. 1 (2018): 53–98.

Nehru, Jawaharlal. "Address to the UNESCO Delegates in New Delhi, 1956." In *Paths to Peace: India's Voices in UNESCO*, edited by UNESCO New Delhi, 13–18. New Delhi: UNESCO, 2009.

Nichols, Catherine A. "Exchanging Anthropological Duplicates at the Smithsonian Institution." *Museum Anthropology* 29, no. 2 (2016): 130–46.

Nixon, Rob. *Slow Violence and the Environmentalism of the Poor*. Cambridge, MA: Harvard University Press, 2011.

Noblecourt, Christiane Desroches. *La grande Nubiade, ou, le parcours d'une Égyptologue*. Paris: Stock/Pernoud, 1992.

Nortcliff, Stephen. "In Memoriam—Georges Aubert (1913–2006)." Adapted from the French by Georges Pedro. *International Union of Soil Sciences* website. Accessed September 5, 2019. https://www.iuss.org/about-the-iuss/iuss-history/obituaries-to-great-soil-scientists/g-aubert-1913-2006/.

Obenga, Théophile. "The Genetic Linguistic Relationship between Egyptian (Ancient Egyptian and Coptic) and Modern Negro-African Languages." In *The Peopling of Ancient Egypt and the Deciphering of the Meroitic Script: Proceedings of the Symposium Held in Cairo from 28 January to 3 February 1974*, edited by UNESCO, 65–71. Paris: UNESCO, 1978.

"Obituary: Richard Woodbury, First Anthropology Chair." *University of Massachusetts Amherst* website. February 25, 2010. https://www.umass.edu/newsoffice/article/obituary-richard-woodbury-first-anthropology-chair.

O'Connor, David, and Andrew Reid, eds. *Ancient Egypt in Africa*. London: UCL Press, 2003.

Okasha, Tharwat. *Mudhakkirati fi al-Siyyasa wa-l-Thaqafa* [My reminiscences in politics and culture]. Cairo: Dar al-Shuruq, 2000. First published in Cairo, 1988, by Madbuli.

—— [name given as "Sarwat"]. "Ramses Recrowned: The International Campaign to Preserve the Monuments of Nubia, 1959–1968." In *Offerings to the Discerning Eye: An Egyptological Medley in Honor of Jack A. Josephson*, edited by Sue H. D'Auria, 223–44. Leiden and Boston, MA: Brill, 2010.

Olesko, Kathryn M. "Tacit Knowledge and School Formation." *Osiris* 8 (1993): 16–29.

O'Malley, Alana. "Ghana, India, and the Transnational Dynamics of the Congo Crisis at the United Nations, 1960–61." *The International History Review* 37, no. 5 (2015): 970–90.

Owen, Roger. *Lord Cromer: Victorian Imperialist, Edwardian Proconsul*. Oxford: Oxford University Press, 2004.

Paoli, Luciano. "My Days at Abu Simbel: Luciano Paoli Shares His Experience as an Expert Stonecutter in Nubia." In *Nubiana: The Great Undertaking that Saved the Temples of Abu Simbel*, edited by Cristina Scalabrini, 250–51. Milan: Rizzoli, 2019.

Partrick, Neil. "Kuwait's Foreign Policy (1961–1977): Non-Alignment, Ideology and the Pursuit of Security." PhD diss., London School of Economics and Political Science, 2006. http://etheses.lse.ac.uk/3164/1/Partrick_Kuwait%27s_Foreign_Policy.pdf.

Pedersen, Susan. *The Guardians: The League of Nations and the Crisis of Empire*. Oxford: Oxford University Press, 2015.

Peleggi, Maurizio. "Excavating Prehistory in the Cold War: American Archaeology in Neocolonial Thailand." *Journal of Social Archaeology* 16, no. 1 (2016): 94–111.

Perović, Jeronim. "The Tito-Stalin Split: A Reassessment in Light of New Evidence." *Journal of Cold War Studies* 9, no. 2 (2007): 32–63.

Petrie, William Matthew Flinders. *Methods and Aims in Archaeology*. London: Macmillan, 1904.

Peutz, Nathalie. "Heritage in (the) Ruins." *International Journal of Middle East Studies* 49, no. 4 (2017): 721–28.

Piaton, Claudine. "Villes et architectures dans l'isthme de Suez." in *L'épopée du canal de Suez*, edited by Gilles Gauthier, Nala Aloudat, and Agnès Carayon, 104–13. Marseille and Paris: Musée d'Histoire de Marseille, Gallimard, and Institut du monde arabe, 2018.

Porter, Bertha, and Rosalind L. B. Moss (with the assistance of Ethel W. Burney). *Topographical Bibliography of Ancient Egyptian Hieroglyphic Texts, Reliefs, and Paintings*, vol. 1, *The Theban Necropolis*, part 2, *Royal Tombs and Smaller Cemeteries*. 2nd ed. Oxford: Clarendon Press, 1964.

Powell, Eve Troutt. *A Different Shade of Colonialism: Egypt, Great Britain, and the Mastery of the Sudan.* Berkeley: University of California Press, 2003.

Prashad, Vijay. *The Darker Nations: A People's History of the Third World.* New York and London: The New Press, 2007.

Pritchard, Erin E. *TVA Archaeology: Seventy-Five Years of Prehistoric Site Research.* Knoxville: University of Tennessee Press, 2009.

Purushotham, Sunil. "World History in the Atomic Age: Past, Present and Future in the Political Thought of Jawaharlal Nehru." *Modern Intellectual History* 14, no. 3 (2016), 837–67.

Qasim, Muhammad Khalil. *Al-Shamandura* [The buoy], 3rd ed. Cairo: Al-Hai'a al-'Ama li-Qusur al-Thaqafa, 2011.

Quirke, Stephen. *Hidden Hands: Egyptian Workforces in Petrie Excavation Archives, 1880–1924.* London: Duckworth, 2010.

Rabbat, Nasser. "Laila 'Ali Ibrahim, 1917–2002." *Mamluk Studies Review* 7, no. 1 (2003): 235–36.

Reid, Donald Malcolm. "Indigenous Egyptology: The Decolonization of a Profession?" *Journal of the American Oriental Society* 105, no. 2 (1985): 233–46.

———. *Whose Pharaohs? Archaeology, Museums, and Egyptian National Identity from Napoleon to World War I.* Berkeley: University of California Press, 2002.

———. *Contesting Antiquity in Egypt: Archaeologies, Museums, and the Struggle for Identities from World War I to Nasser.* Cairo: American University in Cairo Press, 2015.

Reynolds, Nancy Y. *A City Consumed: Urban Commerce, the Cairo Fire, and the Politics of Decolonization in Egypt.* Stanford: Stanford University Press, 2012.

———. "Building the Past: Rockscapes and the Aswan High Dam in Egypt." In *Water on Sand: Environmental Histories of the Middle East and North Africa*, edited by Alan Mikhail, 181–205. New York: Oxford University Press, 2013.

———. "City of the High Dam: Aswan and the Promise of Postcolonialism in Egypt." *City and Society* 29, no. 1 (2017): 213–35.

Richter, Thomas, and Christian Steiner. "Politics, Economics and Tourism Development in Egypt: Insights into the Sectoral Transformations of a Neo-Patrimonial Rentier State." *Third World Quarterly* 29, no. 5 (2008): 939–59.

Riegl, Alois. "The Modern Cult of Monuments: Its Character and Its Origin." Translated by Kurt W. Forster and Diane Ghirardo. *Oppositions* 25 (1982; originally published in German in 1903): 21–51.

Riggs, Christina. "Photography and Antiquity in the Archive, or How Howard Carter Moved the Road to the Valley of the Kings." *History of Photography* 40, no. 3 (2016): 267–82.

———. "Shouldering the Past: Photography, Archaeology, and Collective Effort at the Tomb of Tutankhamun." *History of Science* 55, no. 3 (2017): 336–63.

———. *Photographing Tutankhamun: Archaeology, Ancient Egypt, and the Archive.* London: Bloomsbury, 2019.

Ronayne, Maggie. "Archaeology against Cultural Destruction: The Case of the Ilısu Dam in the Kurdish Region of Turkey." *Public Archaeology* 5, no. 4 (2006): 223–36.

Roth, Ann Macy. "Building Bridges to Afrocentrism: A Letter to my Egyptological Colleagues." *Newsletter of the American Research Center in Egypt* 167 (September 1995): 14–17, and 168 (December 1995): 15–21.

Rothschild, Emma. "The Archives of Universal History." *Journal of World History* 19, no. 3 (2008): 375–401.

Růžová, Jiřina. *The Scribe of the Place of Truth: The Life of the Egyptologist Jaroslav Černý*. Prague: Libri, 2010.

Ryzova, Lucie. "Egyptianizing Modernity through the 'New Effendiya': Social and Cultural Constructions of the Middle Class in Egypt under the Monarchy." In *Re-Envisioning Egypt, 1919–1952*, edited by Arthur Goldschmidt, Amy J. Johnson, and Barak A. Salmoni, 124–63. Cairo: American University in Cairo Press, 2005.

———. "Unstable Icons, Contested Histories: Vintage Photographs and Neoliberal Memory in Contemporary Egypt." *Middle East Journal of Culture and Communication* 8 (2015): 37–68.

———. *The Age of the Efendiyya: Passages to Modernity in National-Colonial Egypt*. Oxford: Oxford University Press, 2018.

El Saddik, Wafaa. *Protecting Pharaoh's Treasures: My Life in Egyptology*. With contributions by Rüdiger Heimlich and translated by Russell Stockman. Cairo: American University in Cairo Press, 2017.

Said, Rushdi. *The Geology of Egypt*. Amsterdam and New York: Elsevier, 1962.

———. *Science and Politics in Egypt*. Cairo: American University in Cairo Press, 2004.

Säve-Söderbergh, Torgny. "International Salvage Archaeology: Some Organizational and Technical Aspects of the Nubian Campaign." *Annales Academiae Regiae Scientiarum Upsaliensis* 15–16 (1971–72): 116–40.

Scalf, Foy. "A Kind of Paradise: The Research Archives of the OI." In *Discovering New Pasts: The OI at 100*, edited by Theo van den Hout, 134–56. Chicago: The Oriental Institute, 2019.

Schäfer, Bernadeta. "The Nubian Villages on Biga Island." *Archaeology in Egypt: Magazine of the German Archaeological Institute Cairo* 4 (2016): 20–27.

Schaffer, Simon, Lissa Roberts, Kapil Raj, and James Delbourgo, eds. *The Brokered World: Go-Betweens and Global Intelligence, 1770–1820*. Sagamore Beach, MA: Watson Publishing International.

Schumaker, Lyn. *Africanizing Anthropology: Fieldwork, Networks, and the Making of Cultural Knowledge in Central Africa*. Durham, NC: Duke University Press, 2001.

Seddon, David. "The Politics of Adjustment: Egypt and the IMF, 1987–1990." *Review of African Political Economy* 47 (1990): 95–104.

Selcer, Perrin. "Beyond the Cephalic Index: Negotiating Politics to Produce UNESCO's Scientific Statements on Race." *Current Anthropology* 53, supplement 5 (2012): 173–84.

———. *The Postwar Origins of the Global Environment: How the United Nations Built Spaceship Earth*. New York: Columbia University Press, 2018.

Shafiee, Katayoun. "Technopolitics of a Concessionary Contract: How International Law Was Transformed by Its Encounter with Anglo-Iranian Oil." *International Journal of Middle East Studies* 50 (2018): 627–48.

El Shakry, Omnia. *The Great Social Laboratory: Subjects of Knowledge in Colonial and Postcolonial Egypt*. Stanford: Stanford University Press, 2007.

———. "'History without Documents': The Vexed Archives of Decolonization in the Middle East." *American Historical Review* 120, no. 3 (2015): 920–34.

Shalem, Avinoam. "Man's Conquest of Nature: Al-Gazzar, Sartre, and Nasser's Great Aswan Dam." *Nka: Journal of Contemporary African Art* 32 (2013): 18–29.

Shapin, Steven. "The Invisible Technician." *American Scientist* 77, no. 6 (1989): 554–63.
Shapin, Steven, and Simon Schaffer. *Leviathan and the Air-Pump: Hobbes, Boyle, and the Experimental Life.* 2011 reprint with a new introduction. Princeton, NJ: Princeton University Press, 2011 (originally published 1985).
Sharkey, Heather J. "A Century in Print: Arabic Journalism and Nationalism in Sudan, 1899–1999." *International Journal of Middle East Studies* 31, no. 4 (1999): 531–49.
———. *Living with Colonialism: Nationalism and Culture in the Anglo-Egyptian Sudan.* Berkeley: University of California Press, 2003.
Shepard, Todd. *The Invention of Decolonization: The Algerian War and the Remaking of France.* Ithaca, NY: Cornell University Press, 2006.
———. "'Of Sovereignty': Disputed Archives, 'Wholly Modern' Archives, and the Post-Decolonization French and Algerian Republics, 1962–2012." *American Historical Review* 120, no. 3 (2015): 869–83.
Shepherd, Nick. "'When the Hand that Holds the Trowel is Black . . .': Disciplinary Practices of Self-Representation and the Issue of 'Native' Labor in Archaeology." *Journal of Social Archaeology* 3, no. 3 (2003): 334–52.
Sheppard, Kathleen L. "Margaret Alice Murray and Archaeological Training in the Classroom: Preparing 'Petrie's Pups.'" In *Histories of Egyptology: Interdisciplinary Measures,* edited by William Carruthers, 113–28. New York: Routledge, 2015.
Shinnie, Peter L. "Editorial Notes." *Kush: Journal of the Sudan Antiquities Service* 2 (1954): 3–4.
———. "A Personal Memoir." In *A History of African Archaeology,* edited by Peter Robertshaw, 221–35. London and Portsmouth: James Currey and Heinemann Educational, 1990.
Shokr, Ahmad. "Hydropolitics, Economy, and the Aswan High Dam in Mid-Century Egypt." *The Arab Studies Journal* 17, no. 1 (2009): 9–31.
Siegler, Karl Georg. "Der Abbruch des Tempels." In *Kalabsha: Der grösste Tempel Nubiens und das Abenteuer seiner Rettung,* by Hanns Stock and Karl Georg Siegler, 64–75. Wiesbaden: F. A. Brockhaus, 1965.
Sluga, Glenda. "UNESCO and the One World of Julian Huxley." *Journal of World History* 21, no. 3 (2010): 393–417.
Smith, Elizabeth. "Place, Class, and Race in the Barabra Café: Nubians in Egyptian Media." In *Cairo Cosmopolitan: Politics, Culture, and Urban Space in the New Globalized Middle East,* edited by Diane Singerman and Paul Amar, 399–413. Cairo: American University in Cairo Press, 2006.
Solecki, Ralph S. "Shanidar Cave, a Paleolithic Site in Northern Iraq." *Annual Report of the Board of Regents of the Smithsonian Institution 1954* (1955): 389–426.
Spaulding, Albert C. "Conference on Prehistoric Archaeology in the Aswan Dam Area, Bellagio, Italy, August 24–28, 1964." *American Antiquity* 31, no. 2, part 1 (1965): 303–4.
Spaull, Cyril H. S. "Centre de Documentation et d'Études sur l'Ancienne Égypte: Collection Scientifique." *The Journal of Egyptian Archaeology* 59 (1973): 249–51.
Spek, Kees van der. *The Modern Neighbors of Tutankhamun: History, Life, and Work in the Villages of the Theban West Bank.* New York: Oxford University Press, 2011.

Spivak, Gayatri Chakravorty. "Can the Subaltern Speak?" In *Colonial Discourse and Post-Colonial Theory: A Reader*, edited by Patrick Williams and Laura Chrisman, 66–111. Harlow: Pearson Education, 1994 (originally published 1988).
Star, Susan Leigh, and James R. Griesemer. "Institutional Ecology, 'Translations' and Boundary Objects: Amateurs and Professionals in Berkeley's Museum of Vertebrate Zoology, 1907–39." *Social Studies of Science* 19 (1989): 387–420.
Starkey, Paul. *Sonallah Ibrahim: Rebel with a Pen*. Edinburgh: Edinburgh University Press, 2016.
Steedman, Carolyn. "Something She Called a Fever: Michelet, Derrida, and Dust." *American Historical Review* 106, no. 4 (2001): 1159–80.
———. *Dust*. Manchester: Manchester University Press, 2001.
Stein, Sally. "The Graphic Ordering of Desire: Modernization of a Middle-Class Women's Magazine." In *The Contest of Meaning: Critical Histories of Photography*, edited by Richard Bolton, 145–62. Cambridge, MA: MIT Press, 1992.
Stevenson, Alice. "Artefacts of Excavation: The British Collection and Distribution of Egyptian Finds to Museums, 1880–1915." *Journal of the History of Collections* 26, no. 1 (2014): 89–102.
———. *Scattered Finds: Archaeology, Egyptology and Museums*. London: UCL Press, 2019.
Stoler, Ann Laura. *Along the Archival Grain: Epistemic Anxieties and Colonial Common Sense*. Oxford: Princeton University Press, 2009.
Strouhal, Eugen. "In Memory of Professor Ahmed Mahmoud el-Batrawi." *Anthropologie* 4, no. 3 (1966): 93–94.
Al-Tahtawi, Rifaʿa Rafiʿ. *Manahij al-Albab al-Misriyya fi Mabahij al-Adab al-ʿAsriyya* [The paths of Egyptian hearts in the joys of the contemporary arts]. Bulaq: al-Matbaʿa al-Kubra al-Amiriyya, 1869.
"The 'Chicago House Method.'" Accessed July 9, 2020. https://oi.uchicago.edu/research/projects/epi/chicago-house-method.
"The Nubia Initiative: About Us." Accessed October 29, 2020. http://thenubiainitiative.org/about/.
"The Nubia Salvage Project." Accessed August 6, 2020. https://oi.uchicago.edu/research/projects/nubia-salvage-project.
Thomas, Jean. *U.N.E.S.C.O.* Paris: Gallimard, 1962.
Thornton, Amara. *Archaeologists in Print: Publishing for the People*. London: UCL Press, 2018.
Tignor, Robert L. *Modernization and British Colonial Rule in Egypt, 1882–1914*. Princeton, NJ: Princeton University Press, 1966.
Tilley, Helen. *Africa as a Living Laboratory: Empire, Development, and the Problem of Scientific Knowledge, 1870–1950*. Chicago: University of Chicago Press, 2011.
Trigger, Bruce G. *A History of Archaeological Thought*. Cambridge: Cambridge University Press, 1989.
Tvedt, Terje. *The River Nile in the Age of the British: Political Ecology and the Quest for Economic Power*. Cairo: American University in Cairo Press, 2006. First published 2004 by Bloomsbury Academic.
UNESCO. *Egypt: Paintings from Tombs and Temples*. Greenwich, CT: New York Graphic Society, 1954.
———. "Foreword: Preparation of a *General History of Africa*." In *The Peopling of Ancient Egypt and the Deciphering of the Meroitic Script: Proceedings of the Symposium Held*

in *Cairo from 28 January to 3 February 1974*, edited by UNESCO, 5–7. Paris: UNESCO, 1978.
———. "Introduction." In *The Peopling of Ancient Egypt and the Deciphering of the Meroitic Script: Proceedings of the Symposium Held in Cairo from 28 January to 3 February 1974*, edited by UNESCO, 11. Paris: UNESCO, 1978.
———. "Symposium on the Peopling of Ancient Egypt: A Report on the Discussions." In *The Peopling of Ancient Egypt and the Deciphering of the Meroitic Script: Proceedings of the Symposium Held in Cairo from 28 January to 3 February 1974*, edited by UNESCO, 73–103. Paris: UNESCO, 1978.
———, ed. *The Peopling of Ancient Egypt and the Deciphering of the Meroitic Script: Proceedings of the Symposium Held in Cairo from 28 January to 3 February 1974*. Paris: UNESCO, 1978.
Veeser, Cyrus. "A Forgotten Instrument of Global Capitalism? International Concessions, 1870–1930." *International History Review* 35, no. 5 (2013): 1136–55.
Vercoutter, Jean. "Editorial Notes." *Kush: Journal of the Sudan Antiquities Service* 4 (1956): 3.
———. "Editorial Notes." *Kush: Journal of the Sudan Antiquities Service* 8 (1960): 5–6.
———. "The Peopling of Ancient Egypt." In *The Peopling of Ancient Egypt and the Deciphering of the Meroitic Script: Proceedings of the Symposium Held in Cairo from 28 January to 3 February 1974*, edited by UNESCO, 15–36. Paris: UNESCO, 1978.
Vitalis, Robert. "The Midnight Ride of Kwame Nkrumah and Other Fables of Bandung (Ban-doong)." *Humanity: An International Journal of Human Rights, Humanitarianism, and Development* 4, no. 2 (2013): 261–88.
Voss, Susanne. *Die Geschichte der Abteilung Kairo des DAI im Spannungsfeld deutscher politischer Interessen*, vol. 2, *1929–1966*. Rahden, Germany: Marie Leidorf, 2017.
Vrdoljak, Ana Filipa. *International Law, Museums and the Return of Cultural Objects*. Cambridge: Cambridge University Press, 2006.
Al-Wakil, Lëila. "Les villages des fellahs." In *Hassan Fathy dans son temps*, edited by Lëila al-Wakil, 220–35. Gollion, Switzerland: Infolio, 2013.
Ward, Stuart. "The European Provenance of Decolonization." *Past and Present* 230 (2016): 227–60.
Webster, David. "Development Advisers in a Time of Cold War and Decolonization: The United Nations Technical Assistance Administration, 1950–59." *Journal of Global History* 6, no. 2 (2011): 249–72.
Weeks, Kent R., ed. *Egyptology and the Social Sciences: Five Studies*. Cairo: American University in Cairo Press, 1979.
Wendorf, Fred. *Desert Days: My Life as a Field Archaeologist*. Dallas: Southern Methodist University Press, 2008.
Wendorf, Fred, and Raymond H. Thompson. "The Committee for the Recovery of Archaeological Remains: Three Decades of Service to the Archaeological Profession." *American Antiquity* 67, no. 2 (2002): 317–30.
Wengrow, David. *The Archaeology of Early Egypt: Social Transformations in North-East Africa, 10,000 to 2650 B.C.*. Cambridge: Cambridge University Press, 2006.
Wente, Edward. "Letters from Egypt." *American Research Center in Egypt, Incorporated: Newsletter* 26 (1957): 2–4.
Werrett, Simon. *Thrifty Science: Making the Most of Materials in the History of Experiment*. Chicago: University of Chicago Press, 2019.

Westad, Odd Arne. *The Global Cold War: Third World Interventions and the Making of Our Times*. Cambridge: Cambridge University Press, 2005.
"What Is Nubi?" Accessed October 29, 2020. http://www.nubi-app.com/about.
Wheeler, Mortimer. *Archaeology from the Earth*. Oxford: Clarendon Press, 1954.
Wilder, Gary. *Freedom Time: Negritude, Decolonization, and the Future of the World*. Durham, NC: Duke University Press, 2015.
Willey, Gordon. *Prehistoric Settlement Patterns in the Virú Valley, Perú*. Smithsonian Institution Bureau of American Ethnology Bulletin 155. Washington, DC: United States Government Printing Office, 1953.
Wilson, John. *Thousands of Years: An Archaeologist's Search for Ancient Egypt*. New York: Charles Scribner's Sons, 1972.
Winegar, Jessica. *Creative Reckonings: The Politics of Art and Culture in Contemporary Egypt*. Stanford: Stanford University Press, 2006.
Winter, Tim. "Heritage Diplomacy." *International Journal of Heritage Studies* 21, no. 10 (2015): 997–1015.
Wintle, Claire. "India on Display: Nationalism, Transnationalism and Collaboration, 1964–1986." *Third Text* 31, nos. 2–3 (2017): 301–20.
Woodbury, Richard B. "A Reappraisal of Hohokam Irrigation." *American Anthropologist* n.s. 63, no. 3 (1961): 550–60.
Young, Alden. *Transforming Sudan: Decolonization, Development, and State Formation*. Cambridge: Cambridge University Press, 2017.
Zaalouk, Malak. *Power, Class, and Foreign Capital in Egypt: The Rise of the New Bourgeoisie*. London: Zed, 1989.
Zaki, Mahir Ahmad (Sayyid Duki). *Hakadha Tukalamu al-Nubiyyun: Mawsuʻa Nubiyya* [So speak the Nubians: The Nubian encyclopedia]. Cairo: Mahir Zaki al-Muhami, 2001.

Index

Page references in *italics* refer to illustrative material.

'Abbud, Ibrahim (General), 22, 135, 147, 149, 189, 242
'Abbud Pasha, Muhammad, 7
Abdalla, Isma'il Hussein, 179n42, 189–90
'Abd al–Rusul, Sa'id Labib, 174
'Abduh, Ibrahim, 70
Abdullah III, Shaykh of Kuwait, 215
Abdul Wahab, Mohamed Fikri, 188
Abou–El–Fadl, Reem, 254
Abt, Jeffrey, 72
Abu Bakr, Abdel Moneim, 57
Abu el–Haj, Nadia, 16
Abu Mena, 239
Abu Simbel, 2, 5, 19, 61, 69, 99, 106, 209; documentation of, 67, 68, 84, 92–93, 99–101, 110, 176; financing for project, 23, 125, 170, 209–10, 214–17, 236; working conditions at, 191–94
Abu Zaid, Fathi, 262
Abydos, 258
Adam, Shehata, 20, 257
Adams, William Yewdale, 50–51, 140–41, 143–46, 151–62, 196, 198–201, 242, 248, *249*, 252–53, 257
Addis Ababa Agreement (1972), 242
Adindan, 111, 187
Afrocentrism, 254–56
Afyeh, 120; excavation by Archaeological Survey of India (ASI), 123–24, 218–20, 224, 226, *227*, 228–35
Aga Khan Award for Architecture, 266
Agha, Menna, 47, 178, 280
Agilkia (island), 24, 240, 163, *264*
Ahram, al–, 21, 53, 57, 88, 184–86, 254
Ahram al–Iqtisadi, al–, 17
Akhbar al–Yawm, 62, 88
Akhir Sa'a, 86
'Alam al–Athar (Archaeological Review), 261–63
'Alam al–Bena'a (World of construction), 262

Algerian War of Independence, 65, 251
'Ali, 'Abd al–Rahman, 150
'Ali, Idris, 177
Ali, Mehmed (Ottoman viceroy of Egypt, 1805–1849), 6, 28, 30, 43–44
Allais, Lucia, 15, 23, 26–27, 115, 142, 171, 223, 267
Allen, P. E. T. ("Pete"), 144–45
Almásy, Paul, 67
Amada, 23, 112
Amer, Mustafa, 18, 55, 78–81, 84, 87–88, 92–93
American Research Center in Egypt, 56, 112–13
Amin, Quranis Daud, 149
Anglo–Egyptian Condominium. *See* Sudan: Anglo–Egyptian Condominium
Anglo–Egyptian Treaty (1936), 116
Aniba, 57
Anthes, Rudolf, 55, 56, 112
anthropology, 16, 131, 133, 143–44, 153, 159, 164, 181–82, 187, 272, 278; colonial, 16, 42, 44, 117–18, 178–79; physical, 253–56
antiquities, 17, 62–63, 148–49, 260–61; export of, 85–88, 112, 123n96, 124, 231–32; legislation regarding, 54n113, 111–12, 115–18, 259, 270; *partage*, 12
Antiquity (journal), 134
Arabic language, 14, 37, 53, 59, 85, 89–90, 106, 148, 177–78, 183, 258n88, 262, 269
Arab–Israeli Wars: 1967 "Six Day War", 24, 238; 1973, "October War," "Ramadan War," "Yom Kippur War", 24, 240. *See also* Camp David Accords; Suez Canal conflict (1956)
Archaeological Survey of India (ASI), 123, 217–24, *225*, 226, *227*, 228–35; proposed work in Sudan, 234–36. *See also* Afyeh
Archaeological Survey of Nubia, first (1907–1911), 34, 36, 40, 42–45; second (1929–1934), 46–52, 199

311

312   INDEX

archaeology, 5, 6, 7, 9–10, 25, 98, 113, 159, 222–24, 259; colonial origins and characteristics of, 5–6, 10–14, 59, 115–18, 132–33, 140, 171, 196–205; documentation methods, 16–18, 66–70, 67, 68, 74–78, 89–93, 154–61, *225*–29, 245–49, *250*; politicization of, 15–16, 54–58, 211; racialization of, 14, 16, 42, 44, 49–51, 101–2, 226, 228, 251–53; surveys, 11, 20–21, 31, 66, 119, 130–31, 138, 140, 153. See also anthropology; archives; Egyptology; *and entries for specific archaeological surveys and teams*
archives, 15–17, 69–72, 74–76, 78, 80–84, 88–90, 93–95, 162, 246–47, 280–82
Arkell, Anthony, 133
Armbrust, Walter, 185
Arminna West, 66–67, 122, 162, *163*, 164, 247
Assiri, Abdul–Reda, 214–15
Aswan (city), 39, 126–27, 186, 193
Aswan Dam (Khazan Aswan, "low dam"), 3, 7, 11, 20, 32–35, 38–40, 137, 177
Aswan High Dam, 3, 6–10, 53, 58, 84, 174–75; construction of, 20, 22, 25, *26*; groundwater impact, 260–61; as political symbol, 21–22, 54, 126–27, 132, 165, 174–77, 181, 184–85, 206. See also United States: financing of Aswan High Dam
Aswan Museum, 120–21, 127
'Atabani, Isma'il al–, 149
'Awad, Muhammad, 84, 138
Azad, Maulana, 220–21
Azhari, Isma'il al–, 22, 242
Azoulay, Ariella Aïsha, 279

Baedeker, Karl, 37, 39, 40, 107n35
Ballana, 52–53, 59–60, 186, 203
Barak, On, 145, 189, 200
Barua, Hem, 233
Bashir, Omar al–, 283
Batrawi, Ahmed El, 50–53
Battle, Lucius D., 114n61, 209–12
Bayoumi, Abbas, 57
Bednarski, Andrew, 108
Begin, Menachem, 239
Beit el–Wali, 103–5, 107–8, 110, 124–25
Bier, Laura, 175
Biga, *45*, *263*, *264*
Blanco Y. Caro, Rafael, 178
Boast, Robin, 220
bourse égyptienne, La, 88
Bradford, John Spencer Purvis, 143
Breasted, James Henry, 72–73, 102–3

Brew, John Otis, 11–14, 16, 18, 140–42, 153, 165, 166
Buhen, 147, 194, *195*, 199–202, 248
Bui Dam (Ghana), 278
Burckhardt, Johann Ludwig, 37

Cairo Conference. See International Conference on Excavations, Cairo (1937)
Cairo Scene (magazine), 1–6, 10, 19
Cairo University, 73
Calouste Gulbenkian Foundation, 243
Camp David Accords, 24, 239, 240n13, 265
Carter, Howard, 70
Central Advisory Board for Archaeology (India), 220–21, 233–34
Central Office of Information (Sudan), 147
Centre d'étude et de documentation sur l'Ancienne Égypte (CEDAE), 20, 64–65, 67, 69–70, 71–72, 88–95, 99–101, 104–7, 119, 122, 140, 143, 245, 247, 265, 281; establishment of, 74–77, 80–88; publications, 107–10, *109*. See also archaeology: documentation methods
Chahine, Youssef, 66
Chatterjee, R., 227
Chevrier, Henri, 76
Chiva, Isac, 272
Christophe, Louis, 64, 104, 245–46
Cold War, 3, 21, 54–59, 206–9, 213, 276
Combined Prehistoric Expedition (CPE), 167–68
Committee for the Investigation of Nubian Demands, 188
Cooper, Frederick, 208
Corrective Revolution (*Tharwat al–Taṣḥīḥ*), 17, 176
Crawford, O. G. S. (Osbert Guy Stanhope), 134
Cromer, 1st Earl of (Evelyn Baring), 29, 31

Dafalla, Hassan, 182–83, 187–88, 190
Dahshur, 86n91, 114, 258
Daifuku, Hiroshi, 141–43
Dakka (temple), 35, 42
Dales, George F., 235
Daninos, Adrian, 58
Das, M. M., 233
Daston, Lorraine, 71–72, 280–81
Debod, 10n25, 60
decolonization, 3, 5, 12–14, 15n51, 70–71, 81–82, 207, 251, 276; of archaeology, 12–14
De Guerville, Amédée, *34*
Demhid, 43

Democratic Movement for National Liberation (al-Haraka al-Dimuqratiyya li-l-Tahrir al-Watani, HADETU), 175–76
Dendur, 10n25, 209, 274–76, *275*
Department of Statistics (Sudan), 182
Derr (village and site of temple, also referred to as "Ed Derr"), 48
Derr, Jennifer L., 38–39, 46
Description de l'Égypte, 72, 108
Dessuqi, Faruq Barakat al-, 174
DiMeo, David, 176–77
Dinka, 36
Diop, Abdoulaye, 267
Diop, Cheikh Anta, 255–56
Diradour, K. S., 76
Donadoni, Sergio, 79
Dravidians, 231–35
Drioton, Canon Étienne, 74, 92–93
Dunbar, Alexander, 243

Edgerton, David, 66
effendiyya, 50
Egypt, 43–44, 54–58, 70–73, 77, 130, 176–79, 238–41, 259–60, 265–66; as part of Africa, 251, 254–56; British occupation of (1882–1923), 3, 28–32, 38, 276; independence from Britain (1923), 7, 29; Ottoman rule over, 28–29; political alignment of, 21–22, 24, 57–58, 116–18, 208, 213, 215–19, 221–23, 228–29, 232–34, 238, 240; use of ancient sites as national symbol, 5, 85, 87, 126, 262–63; 1952 Free Officers' coup, 7, 9, 54, 73, 74. *See also* Sudan: Anglo–Egyptian Condominium
Egypt Exploration Society (Egypt Exploration Fund, 1882–1919), 32, 113–14, 147, 202, 229, *250*, 258; Nubian survey by, 119–120, 197
Egyptian Antiquities Service (1858–1952), 11, 31, 34, 38, 51, 74. *See also* Egyptian Department of Antiquities
Egyptian Department of Antiquities (1952–1971; Egyptian Antiquities Organization 1971–1994; Supreme Council of Antiquities 1994–2011; Ministry of State for Antiquities 2011–2019; Ministry of Tourism and Antiquities 2019–), 18, 54–55, 58, 63, 77–79, 84, 88, 92, 123, 166, 173, 223, 228, 229, 261–63. *See also* Egyptian Antiquities Service (1858–1952)
Egyptian Geological and Mining Organization, 165

Egyptian Geological Survey, 166–68
Egyptian Mail, The, 53
Egyptian Museum, Cairo, 36, 81
Egyptian State Tourist Administration, 39
Egypt in Nubia (1965 book), 251–52. *See also* Emery, Walter Bryan
Egyptology (field), 10, 15–16, 32–33, 55, 64, 68–69, 71–76, 89–90, 92, 102–7, 140. *See also* archaeology
Egypt Travel Magazine, 55–56
Elcheikh, Zeina, 277–78
Elephantine (island), *127*
Eletr, Riad, 233
El Shakry, Omnia, 15n51, 70–71
Emery, Mollie, 194
Emery, Walter Bryan, 46–49, 52–53, 113–14, 119–20, 147, 150, 194, *195*, 199–202, 248, *250*, 251–52, 258
Entente Cordiale (Anglo–French agreement, 1904), 74
Eoin, Luíseach Nic, 278
Erman, Adolf, 103
Evans, Luther, 63, 80–81, 84, 219

Facebook, 1, 4
Fadija language, 14
Fakhry, Ahmed, 59
Faras (Sudan), 150, 159–60, 244
Farid, Shafiq, 87
Faruq I (King of Egypt and the Sudan, 1936–52), 9, 40
Fathy, Hassan, 188, 262
Fayed, Ismail, 181
Fayed, Sarah, 181
Feldman, Ilana, 83–84, 172–73
Felski, Rita, 279–80
Firth, Cecil Mallaby, 42, 47–48
Food for Peace program (US Public Law 480), 23, 165, 210
Ford Foundation, 9, 181
Fowler, John, 32–33
Free Officers, 7, 54, 57, 58
French Geographic Society, 44
Friedmann, Gerda, 96–97
Fu'ad I (Sultan of Egypt, 1917–1922; King of Egypt, Sovereign of Bunia, Sudan, Kordofan and Darfur, 1922–1936), 73

Gange, David, 16n55, 32–33, 42n60
Garstin, William, 33, 36–37
Gawi, Albert, 263
Gaza, 172–73
Gazzar, Abdel Hadi al-, 181

… INDEX

Gazzola, Piero, 22–23
Gebel Barkal, 243
General History of Africa, The, 251, 254, 257
Gerf Hussein, 106
German Archaeological Institute in Cairo, 112
Gezira Scheme, 31, 135
Gezira Sporting Club, 38
Gfeller, Aurélie Elisa, 272
Ghallab, G., 256
Ghana, 132, 214, 218, 278
Ghosh, Amalananda, 223, 227n97, 228–29, 234–36
Gilmore, Christine, 177
Gissen, David, 274
Glélé, Maurice, 257
Godlewska, Anne, 72
Goedicke, Hans, 110
Gomaa, Farouk, 67
Gordon, Charles, 31
Grand Egyptian Museum, 266
Great Britain, 116, 207; foreign aid to Egypt, 3, 62, 212–13; rule in Egypt, 5–7, 9, 28–30, 73, 116, 276; rule in Sudan, 25–26, 31, 131–33, 276
Griffith, Francis Llewellyn, 159–60
Griffith Institute (Ashmolean Museum, Oxford), 76–77, 84, 93–95
Guha, Sudeshna, 220

Habachi, Labib, 59, 104
Hakim, Mahmoud el–, 267
Halfa Resettlement Commission (Lajnat Tawtin Ahali Halfa), 183
Hamad, Bushra, 133
Hamdi, 'Emad, 66
Harden, Donald B., 76–77
Hassan, 'Abdel Latif, 101
Hassan, Ali, 197
Hassan, Selim, 59, 92, 95
Hatem, 'Abd al-Qadir, 217
heritage (concept), 131, 217, 259, 262, 267; cultural, 136–37, 142, 209–10, 268–73; national, 149–50, 216, 242–43, 266, 270; world, 4–5, 10–11, 17–18, 62n140, 121, 131, 237–42, 261, 276. *See also* UNESCO: World Heritage Convention (1972); UNESCO: World Heritage List
Hifni, Ratiba al–, 240
High Dam, The (1964 painting), 181
Higher Council of Antiquities, 59
History and Settlement in Lower Nubia (1965 book), 252
Hopkins, Nicholas S., 32

Huber, Valeska, 171–72, 196
Hughes, George R., 79–80, 103–6, 110
Hussein, Kamal al-Din, 84–85, 88, 270
Huzayyin, Soliman, 80

IBM, 96
Ibrahim, 'Abdelbaki, 262
Ibrahim, Ahmad Hassan, 200–201
Ibrahim, Laila 'Ali, 270
Ibrahim, Sonallah, 175–77
Illustrated London News, The, 235
Imbabula, Kamal, 262–63
India, 208, 217–24, 227–28, 231–36, 251. *See also* Archaeological Survey of India (ASI); Dravidians
Indo–UAR Cultural Agreement, 218–19
infitāḥ (open door policy), 24, 240, 260
Insan al-Sadd al-'Ali (The man of the High Dam, 1967 reportage), 176
Institut géographique national (France), 69, 104
International Campaign to Save the Monuments of Nubia. *See* UNESCO: International Campaign to Save the Monuments of Nubia
International Conference on Excavations, Cairo (1937), 116–18, 121
Iran, 116
Islambuli, Khalid al–, 240
Isma'il, Khedive, 29
Isma'il, Muhammad Salah, 262–63
Isma'iliyya, 193
Israel, 24
Issawi, Mohamed El-Bahay, 167

Jacquet, Jean, 67–68, 112
Jacquet-Gordon (née Wall), Helen, 56, 68
Jain, S. P., 227
Jasiewicz, Stanisław, 244
Jebel Moya, 198
Jomard, Edme-François, 44
al-Jumhuriyya, 87
Junker, Hermann, 253

Kabir, Humayun, 219, 221–23, 233–35
Kalabsha, 27, 91, 106, 212, 280–82
Kalabsha: The Preserving of the Temple (1972 book), 281
Kamal, Moharram, 112
Kamugisha, Aaron, 254
Kaplan, Martha, 207
Kassem–Draz, Céza, 176
Keating, Rex, 178

Kelly, John D., 207
Kennedy, John F., 22, 106, 209, 211
Kenzi language, 14
Kerma, 111
Khartoum, 23, 30, 31, 241
Khashm El Girba, 8–9, 179, 183–84, 188–90
Khater, Antoine, 116
Khrushchev, Nikita, 22, 127, 176
King, Rachel, 278
Kirwan, Laurence P., 47–49
Kitchener, 1st Earl, 31
Kleinitz, Cornelia, 9, 242
Klimowicz, Arkadiusz, 205
Klimowicz, Patrycja, 205
Koma Waidi ("Tales of the Past"), 273
Koselleck, Reinhart, 237–38
Kronenberg, Andreas, 183, 187
Kronenberg, Waltraud, 183, 187
Kulubnarti (site), 159, 247–48, 249
Kumaran, M. K., 233
Kush (journal), 133, 159–61, 246
Kuwait, 214–17

Lake Nasser / Lake Nubia, 6–7, 237
Lal, B. B., 218, 220–24, 226–32, 235
Lal, Kusum, 226–27
League of Nations, 116–17, 207
Leake, Elisabeth, 13
Lok Sabha, 233
Lumumba, Patrice, 209
Luxor, 20, 39, 57, 75n40, 239, 260–61
Lyons, Henry George, 36–37, 39

Mahdi (Muhammad Ahmad ibn 'Abd Allah), 31
Mahdi, Muhammed, 92–93
Maheu, René, 244, 251
Malraux, André, 10, 139–40
Manasir, 9
Maqrizi, al—(d. 1442), 71
Maspero, Gaston, 34–35, 103
Mawsu'a Nubiyya (Nubian encyclopedia), 271
M'Bow, Amadou–Mahtar, 241, 246
Mehanna, Sohair R., 32
Meinarti (site), 159
Merowe Dam, 9
Meskell, Lynn, 180, 245–46
Metolong Dam (Lesotho), 278
Metropolitan Museum of Art, New York, 274–76, *275*
Michałowski, Kazimierz, 205
Mignolo, Walter, 12

Mills, Anthony, 242–44, 246
Ministry of Culture (Egypt), 9, 20, 126; Fine Arts Administration (Idarat al-Funun al-Jamila), 181
Ministry of Education (Egypt), 32, 77, 86
Ministry of Education and Scientific Research (India), 221
Ministry of Finance and Economics (Sudan), 136
Ministry of Public Works (Egypt), 31, 33, 34, 36, 38, 46, 59
Ministry of Scientific Research and Cultural Affairs (India), 228, 232–33, 235
Mitchell, Timothy, 39, 42
Mit Rahina (ancient Memphis), 55–57, 112
Mitry, Philip, 86
Mokhtar, Gamal, 254, 257–58
Monneret de Villard, Ugo, 51–52
Morsi, Mohamed, 4
Moss, Rosalind, 76, 79–80, 89, 93–95
Mossallam, Alia, 175, 193
Mubarak, 'Ali, 71
Mubarak, Husni, 177, 265
Mubarak, Suzanne, 266
Muhammad V, King of Morocco, 57
Mukhtar, Yahya, 177
Murray, Margaret, 245
Mus'ad, Ra'uf, 176
Musawwar, al-, 26, 65, 260
Muses, Charles, 86, 87
Myers, Oliver H., 135, 159

Nahas, Mahmoud, 79–80
Najmat Aghustus (August star, 1974 novel), 175–76
Nasser, Gamal Abdel, 2–3, 7, 20–22, 23–24, 57, 208, 238
Nas wa-l-Nil, al- (The people and the Nile, 1968 film), 66
National Museum (Khartoum), 23, 240–42, 241, 244
National Museum of Egyptian Civilization (NMEC), 266
National Science Foundation (USA), 23, 165, 168
Nehru, Jawaharlal, 208, 219
Nelson, Harold H., 102
New Deal (USA), 139
New Kalabsha, 23
Nielsen, Ole Vagn, 254
Nil, al-, 149
Nile River, 6, 25, 28–30, 36, 43–44, 53, 63, 127, 190, 198, 260, 276

INDEX

Nile Waters Agreement (1959), 6, 20, 130, 138
Nims, Charles, 89, 100–102, 103
Nixon, Rob, 177
Noblecourt, Christiane Desroches, 63, 79–85, 88–89, 92–93, 95, 96, 99n10, 100–101, 107, 140
Non–Aligned Movement, 137, 208–9, 211, 213–17, 218
Nordström, Hans–Åke, 145, 159–60
Nuba al-Jadida, al—(New Nubia), 7–8, 184, 186–89
Nubi (app), 273
Nubia, 3, 5–7, 16, 20, 30–32, 40, 48, 52, 57–58, 60–63, 84–88, 92–93, 118–21, 170–74, 178, 180–83, 217–21, 237–38, 250–53, 258–59, 276–80; Egyptian, 98, 103–4, 110–16, 126, 138; Sudanese, 111, 129–34, 136, 138–50, 152–65, 242–44. *See also* Archaeological Survey of Nubia; Nubians; racialization and racism; *and specific locations by name*
Nubia: Corridor to Africa (1977 book), 252–53, 268
Nubia Initiative, 273
Nubia Museum, 24, 62, 267–69, 271, 277
Nubian Ethnological Survey (1961–1964), 181–82
Nubian languages, 14, 106, 178. *See also* Fadija language; Kenzi language
Nubian Language Society of Khartoum, 272
Nubians, 3, 62, 106, 130, 138, 178, 180–83, 238, 271–73, 277–83; anthropological surveys of, 9, 146, 253; displacement and resettlement of, 4–5, 7–9, 20–21, 32, 147, 179, 187–90; identity formation, 179; lobbying of Egyptian government, 46; perceptions of, 9, 30–31, 44, 46–47, 53, 145, 263; protests by, 189–90; "right-to-return," 24, 282. *See also* racialization and racism
Nubian Twilight (1962 book), 178
Nubische Märchen (Nubian Fairytales, 1978 book), 187
Nuer, 36
Numayri, Ja'far, 22, 238, 242–43

Obenga, Théophile, 256
Oddoul, Haggag Hassan, 177
Okasha, Tharwat, 9, 57, 63, 114, 125–26, 180, 270
oral history, 175, 178

Organization for the Preservation of Nubian Monuments (Hay'at Sunduq Inqadh Athar al–Nuba), 20
Oriental Institute (OI). *See* University of Chicago

Panofsky, Erwin, 64, 123
Papadopoulo, Alexander, 65, 95
Parthenon (Athens), 101
Paul, Hilary N., 136–37
Peabody Museum of Archaeology and Ethnology (Harvard), 11, 67
Peabody Museum of Natural History (Yale), 67, 122, 182, 246–47
Permanent Council for the Development of National Production, 58
Pérotin, Yves, 82
Petrie, William Matthew Flinders, 197, 200, 245
Peutz, Nathalie, 270–71
Philae (temple complex; Qasr Anas al–Wujud), 5, 23–24, 33, 34, 36–39, 61, 106, 264
photogrammetry, 69–70, 101, 141
photography, 69, 100–102, 105, 119–20, 246–47; aerial, 136–38, 143–47
Piaton, Claudine, 193
Powell, Eve Troutt, 31, 43–44, 46n77
Progress (1960 almanac), 147–48
Purnell, W. E., 79

Qabbani, Isma'il al–, 78
Qapudan, Selim, 43–44
Qasim, Muhammad Khalil, 177
Qasr Ibrim, 155, 258
Qilsh, Kamal al–, 176
Qustul, 52, 53, 124–25, 203

race theory, 231
racialization and racism, 16, 106–7, 110, 181, 200, 202, 226, 251–58; scientific racism, 44, 47, 49, 50–51, 123, 164, 178. *See also* archaeology: racialization of; Nubians: perceptions of; UNESCO: "race statements" by
Ra'i al-'Amm, al–, 148–49, 150
Rainey, Froelich, 112, 114, 124–25, 258n89
Ray, Niharranjan, 233
Razek, Mourad Abdel, 203
Reciting Quran in the Region of Nubia (1959 painting), 181
Reed, Charles, 166–68
Refaat, Wafaa, 1–6, *2*, 10, 12, 19

Reisner, George Andrew, 42, 45, 56, 119–20, 245
Report on the Monuments of Nubia (1955), 111
Reynolds, Nancy Y., 21, 126–27, 165
Ricoeur, Paul, 279–80
Ricou, Léonie, 74
Riegl, Alois, 39
Riggs, Christina, 14, 16, 70, 246
Ripley, S. Dillon, 211
Rivière, Georges–Henri, 268
Rockefeller Foundation, 105, 142
Rockefeller Jr., John D., 72, 105
Roeder, Günther, 103–4
Rostom, Osman, 92–93
Rusk, Dean, 105–6
Ryzova, Lucie, 4

Saad, Zaki Y., 200
Sabah, Shaykh Jaber al–Ahmad al–, 215
Sabah, Shaykh Sabah al–Salim al–, 215
Saber, Mohi al–Din, 244
Sadat, Anwar al–, 17, 24, 176, 238–40, 265
Sadat, Jihan al–, 240
Sadat, Sakina al–, 260
Saddik, Wafaa El, 262
Saghir, Muhammad al–, 260
Sahwa al–Nubiyya, al– (The Nubian Awakening), 177
Said, Rushdi, 165–67
Sallal, Abdullah al–, 22
salvage archaeology, 11–12, 141–43
Salvage of Nubia's Antiquities, The (1971 book), 242–43
Saqqara, 114
Säve–Söderbergh, Torgny, 192, 256
Sawi, 'Abd al–Mun'im al–, 216
Scandinavian Joint Expedition to Sudanese Nubia, 152, 158, 254
Schaffer, Simon, 132
Schweizerisches Institut für Ägyptisches Bauforschung und Altertumskunde, 103
Seele, Keith, 104–6, 110, 124–25, 246
Selcer, Perrin, 138, 253
Sennar Dam, 31
Shamandura, al– (The buoy, 1968 novel), 177
Shapin, Steven, 132
Sharkey, Heather J., 148, 152
Sharma, G. R., 233
Shepard, Todd, 13, 70, 81–82, 251
Sherif, Negm El–Din Mohammed, 150, 154, 242–43
Shilluk, 36

Shinnie, Peter, 63, 132–34, 143, 150, 214, 218, 256
Shokr, Ahmad, 58, 206
Shoukry, Anwar, 166–67, 223–24, 228
Simone, Costanza de, 272
Simpson, William Kelly, 124
Singh, Amir, 224, *225*, 227
Sisi, 'Abd al–Fattah al–, 282
Slocum, John, 125
slow violence, 177
Smieton, Mary, 212
Smith, Elizabeth, 271
Smith, Grafton Elliot, 42–44, 50
Smith, Harry S, 119, 122, 197, 229, 230n112
Smith, Phillip, 166–68
Smithsonian Institution, 23, 210n20
Society for Nubian Heritage (Jam'iyat al–Turath al–Nubi), 271, 273
Society for the Preservation of the Monuments of Ancient Egypt (SPMAE), 33
Solecki, Ralph, 141–43, 166
Spaull, Cyril H. S., 109–10
Stein, Sally, 185
Stevenson, Alice, 14
Stoler, Ann Laura, 15, 70
Stoppelaëre, Alexandre, 74–77, 80
Strouhal, Eugen, 253–54
Sudan, 3, 5–6, 15, 22–23, 98, 111, 118, 131–32, 135–37, 140, 146–52, 165, 179–80, 189–90, 214, 238, 241–42, 276, 283; Anglo–Egyptian condominium (1899–1956), 6, 30–31, 129, 132; foreign relations with Egypt, 53, 129–31, 196–201; independence (1956), 9, 133; May Revolution (1969), 242; Ottoman–Egyptian period (1821–1899), 5, 6, 30, 43–44; relationship with UNESCO, 136, 208, 241–49, 259, 265, 272. *See also* Nubia: Sudanese; Nubians; *and specific locations by name*
Sudan Antiquities Service, 9, 20, 132, 146, 148, 152, 158–61, 183, 200, 242–44
Sudan Archaeological Research Society, *155*, *156*, *157*, 161
Sudan Notes and Records, 133, 159
Sudan Survey Department, 144
Suez Canal, 28–30, 171–72
Suez Canal Company, 193
Suez Canal conflict (Tripartite Aggression, 1956), 3, 6, 9, 20, 29, 55
Supreme Council of Antiquities. *See* Egyptian Department of Antiquities
Supreme Council of the Armed Forces, 135

Tahrir Province, 54
Tahtawi, Rifa'a Rafi' al–, 43
Talosh, Momen, 273
Tambal, Hamza al–Malik, 148
Tawfiq (Khedive of Egypt), 29
Taylor, John W., 75
Tell Atrib, 55–57, 113
Tennessee Valley Authority (TVA), 11, 54, 139–41, 168
Terrace, Edward, 124
Thabit, Thabit Hassan, 63, 148, 158, 161, 166, 202
Thomas, Jean, 74–75, 84–85, 180–81, 223
Thomas Cook company, 38, 40, 42, 47, 52–53
Times of India, The, 231–32
Tito, Josip Broz, 208, 210
Torres Bodet, Jaime, 74
tourism, 38–42, 147, 260n96, 277–78
Trigger, Bruce G., 164, 252–53
Tripartite Aggression. *See* Suez Canal conflict
Truman, Harry S., 55
Tumas, 224, *225*, 229, 232
Tvedt, Terje, 30, 36, 38

UNESCO (United Nations Educational, Scientific and Cultural Organization), 3, 14, 17–18, 114; Arid Zone Program, 136–37, 142–43, 168; Convention for the Safeguarding of the Intangible Cultural Heritage (2003), 272; financing of, 22–23, 77, 213, 215–16, 241; ideology of, 13, 17–18, 74, 85, 150, 207–8; International Campaign to Save the Monuments of Nubia, 1–6, 9–11, 15–21, 64, 93, 98–102, 115, 130–31, 140–41, 150, 153, 170–71, 179–81, 223–24, 258, 265; International Campaign for Egyptian Museums, 24, 266; International Committee for Monuments, Historic Sites, and Archaeological Excavations, 11, 18, 242; publicity, 121; "race statements" by, 14, 219, 226, 251, 253, 256–57; requests for assistance from, 20, 77, 136; World Heritage Convention (1972), 116, 269; World Heritage List, 10, 18–19, 24, 239, 261. *See also* Centre d'étude et de documentation sur l'Ancienne Égypte (CEDAE); Sudan: relationship with UNESCO
UNESCO Courier, The, 69, 147, 170, 171
United Arab Republic. *See* Egypt
United States, 207; financing of Aswan High Dam, 3, 62; foreign aid to Egypt, 210; support for Nubia campaign, 23, 209–11, 214
University of Chicago, Oriental Institute (OI), 72, 100, 102, 107, 110, 203–4, 246; Nubian Expedition of, 103–6, 124; publications, 107, 110
University of Pennsylvania, University Museum of the, 55, 112. *See also* Yale–University of Pennsylvania expedition
'Urabi, Ahmad, 29

Van der Haagen, J. K, 75, 78–79, 180
Vazques, Ramirez, 267
Vazquez, Rolando, 12
Vercoutter, Jean, 132–34, 148, 151, 199, 255, 257
Veronese, Vittorino, 221–23, 234
Verwers, G. Jan, 145, 160–61
Vitalis, Robert, 208
Vrioni, Ali, 170, 236, 243–44

Wadi es–Sebua, 23, 173–74, 190, 262
Wadi Halfa (town), 7, 30, 63, 146, 160, 189–90
Wadi Halfa Museum, 154, 272
Wadi Halfa Salient, 129–30, 151, 159
Wanly, Adham, 181
Ward, Stuart, 13
Weeks, Kent R., 164
Weigall, Arthur, 34
Wellcome, Henry, 198
Wendorf, Fred, 165–69
Wente, Edward G., 113–14
Westad, Odd Arne, 54
Wheeler, Mortimer, 220–21, 224–26, 234–35
Wheeler, Tessa Verney, 220, 224–26
Willey, Gordon, 164
Winter, Tim, 18
Wintle, Claire, 217
Woodbury, Richard B., 141–44
Works Progress Administration, 139, 141; Historical Records Survey of, 81
World War I, 7
Wright, G. R. H. (George Roy Haslam), 27, *127*, 281

Yale–University of Pennsylvania expedition ("Yale–Penn"), 122–24, 162, *163*, 258
Young, Alden, 131

Zaki, Hassan Effendi, 102
Zaki, Mahir Ahmad (Sayyid Duki), 271
Ziwar, Ahmad, 73

www.ingramcontent.com/pod-product-compliance
Lightning Source LLC
Chambersburg PA
CBHW030116240426
43673CB00041B/1301